Yale Historical Publications

DAVID HORNE, editor

STUDIES 21

NO TRANSFER

An American Security Principle

by JOHN A. LOGAN, Jr.

NEW HAVEN AND LONDON, YALE UNIVERSITY PRESS

First published, May 1961
Second printing, January 1962

Library of Congress catalog card number: 61–6592

Published under the direction of the
Department of History of Yale University,
with assistance from the income of the
Frederick John Kingsbury Memorial Fund

Acknowledgments

Part of this book, in substantially different form, was first written as a dissertation for the degree of doctor of philosophy at Yale. As teacher, friend, and colleague, Samuel Flagg Bemis has contributed more to the compilation of the volume than any other individual. It was he who suggested to me the need for a study of the No-Transfer principle, and his encouragement and interest in the progress of my work leave me deeply in his debt.

I am grateful to John M. Blum for reading the manuscript and making many valuable suggestions. As does every scholar in this field, I owe much to the wisdom and resourcefulness of E. Taylor Parks of the Research and Publications Division of the Department of State and to the archivists of its records. Stetson Conn of the Office of the Chief of Military History of the Department of the Army very generously allowed me to see his manuscript study on "Defense of the Hemisphere," while it was awaiting publication. This now comprises the first twelve chapters of *The Framework of Hemisphere Defense,* with Byron Fairchild as co-author.

I want to record my gratitude to Yale University for a Morse Fellowship, which freed me of teaching duties for a year to finish this book, and to Mrs. Anne Granger for her help in preparing the manuscript for publication.

J. A. L., Jr.

New Haven, Conn.
September 1960

Short Titles

ASPFR   *American State Papers. Class I. Foreign Relations,* 6 vols. Washington, 1832–39.

GW   J. C. Fitzpatrick, ed., *The Writings of George Washington,* 37 vols. Washington, 1931–44.

JCC   Ford, Hunt, Fitzpatrick, et al., eds. *Journal of the Continental Congress, 1774–1789,* 31 vols. Washington, 1904–34.

Manning, CR   W. R. Manning, ed., *Diplomatic Correspondence of the United States: Canadian Relations, 1784–1860,* 3 vols. Washington, 1940–43.

Manning, IA   W. R. Manning, *Diplomatic Correspondence of the United States: Inter-American Affairs, 1830–1860,* 12 vols. Washington, 1932–39.

Manning, LA   W. R. Manning, ed., *Diplomatic Correspondence of the United States Concerning the Independence of the Latin American Nations,* 3 vols. New York, 1925.

Wharton   Francis Wharton, ed., *The Revolutionary Diplomatic Correspondence of the United States,* 6 vols. Washington, 1889.

Contents

MAPS SHOWING APPLICATIONS OF THE
NO-TRANSFER PRINCIPLE FOLLOW
PAGES 50 AND 300.

Introduction

The United States cannot see with indifference the transfer of European colonies in the Western Hemisphere to another non-American power. This, stated in its most generalized form, is the No-Transfer principle, one of the oldest and most fundamental of American security policies, certainly the most frequently and continuously applied, and the most unanimously approved foreign policy in the history of the United States. It is undeniably power-political, based on strategic military considerations, and practiced even during the long years when the people of the United States professed abhorrence of balance-of-power politics.

Americans[1] tend to forget that much of their national experience in foreign affairs took place during the century of relative world peace following the Congress of Vienna, and that the experience was unique. Modern history affords no other example of a nation permitted to rise to great power status almost totally free of direct threats to its physical security. During these years the American people congratulated themselves on evolving a political system happily free of alliances, secret diplomacy, and large military estab-

---

1. Throughout Latin America, "American" is used to designate all the peoples and nations of the New World. In the United States, though wider meaning is certainly not unknown, the word is usually meant to apply exclusively to citizens of that country. I have used the word in both senses in this study, trusting that the context will prevent ambiguity.

lishments, and came to think of power politics as something alien and immoral, peculiar to decadent Europe.

This illusion, born of a highly special and by no means permanent set of historical circumstances, has faded in our own day in the face of the discomforting realization that the peace and well-being of the United States have in fact always depended upon an American and a world balance of power. The nation is once again learning, however reluctantly, to admit the connection between diplomacy and military force; the Pact of Rio de Janeiro, the North Atlantic Treaty Organization, and the rest of the security systems which the United States has organized against the threat of Soviet aggression represent a kind of willingness to think in terms of military strategy and to form commitments with other nations which were as impossible as they were unnecessary a few decades ago.

In the kind and importance of security problems confronting the United States, the period 1775 to 1823 most nearly resembles our own. The generation of the Founding Fathers habitually thought in terms of power. The experience of the great colonial wars of the seventeenth and eighteenth centuries which involved North America as the stakes òf European diplomacy necessarily controlled the thought of statesmen who guided the destinies of a new nation which was still surrounded on all sides by possessions of the maritime nations of Europe. It was generally assumed that Europe would continue to be torn by perpetual warfare, and the wars of the American Revolution and of the French Revolution and Empire confirmed the conclusion reached by American statesmen that only by expelling European sovereignty from North America—and eventually from the entire hemisphere—could the United States enjoy the peace and prosperity promised by its geographical position and the bounty of its land. In a letter to a friend on the eve of the War of 1812, Thomas Jefferson described the ideal toward

which American diplomacy was directed during the first
half century of independence, and illustrated how clearly he
appreciated the dependence of American security on the
maintenance of an American and European balance of
power:

> We especially ought to pray that the powers of Europe
> may be so poised and counterpoised among themselves,
> that their own safety may require the presence of all
> their force at home, leaving the other quarters of the
> globe in undisturbed tranquility. When our strength
> will permit us to give the law of our hemisphere . . .
> the meridian of the mid-Atlantic should be the line of
> demarcation between war and peace, on this side of
> which no act of hostility should be committed, and the
> lion and the lamb lie down in peace together.[2]

The present study deals with the origins and development of the No-Transfer principle, the chief instrument
devised by American diplomatists to accomplish the "Grand
Design" described here by Jefferson, in the years when the
United States was the only independent nation in a hemisphere still largely subject to European sovereignty. Historically, it has generally been applied to prevent the transfer of neighboring colonies from a weak nation like Spain
to a stronger one like Britain or France, which would alter
the balance of power unfavorably in our vicinity. It is essentially preventive diplomacy designed to preserve the territorial status quo, and even to declare an option on territory considered vital to the national interest. It was negative
in the sense that it was power politics resorted to in order
to banish power politics from the Americas.

2. Jefferson to Dr. John Crawford (Jan. 2, 1812), Andrew A. Lipscomb and Albert E. Bergh, eds., *The Writings of Thomas Jefferson*
(20 vols. Washington, 1903–04), *13*, 119.

The importance of the No-Transfer principle in the diplomacy of the United States has been too little appreciated. It is one of the major purposes of this book to bring to light the fact that its origins coincide with the very birth of the Republic, and that throughout the entire span of American history the principle has been one of the most important security policies of the United States. In its purpose it is closely related to the Non-Colonization and Non-Intervention principles of the Monroe Doctrine, which likewise supported the grand strategy of expelling European power and influence from the American hemisphere. The No-Transfer principle was the original instrument devised for this object, and Monroe's principles were derived from it after 1822, when recognition by the United States of the independence of Latin America required new formulas to deal with independent nations rather than colonies.

Considering its importance, it is remarkable that the No-Transfer principle should not already have found its historian, but in spite of the fact that it has long been recognized as a fundamental policy in American diplomacy, there is almost no detailed treatment of it anywhere. The single exception is the third volume of Dexter Perkins' history of the Monroe Doctrine, which contains a chapter on the development of the No-Transfer principle from 1870, when it was officially associated with the Doctrine by Grant and Fish, to 1893.[3] In his earlier volume on the origins of the Doctrine, Perkins barely mentions the No-Transfer principle, and suggests no earlier pronouncement than the Congressional Joint Resolution of January 15, 1811.[4] In an historical survey of the Latin American policy of the United States, Samuel Flagg Bemis mentions the No-Transfer resolution of 1808 in the Cabinet, and sketches the subsequent

3. *The Monroe Doctrine, 1867–1907* (Baltimore, 1937), chap. 1.
4. *The Monroe Doctrine, 1823–1826* (Cambridge, 1932), p. 203.

history of the policy to 1940, but necessarily in the most general terms.[5]

Few of the diplomatic episodes presented in the following pages are unfamiliar to specialists, yet the interpretation placed upon them here is, as far as I know, wholly new, even though drawn for the most part from well-known materials. What this study attempts to do is shift the emphasis, provide a unifying principle for previously disconnected events, link them with a policy already recognized to exist at a later day, and place the emerging pattern in the broader context of America's position in world affairs at the time.

Most policies have more informal beginnings than many politicians and some historians like to admit, and the No-Transfer principle is no exception here. George Washington's objections to a joint expedition with France into Canada for fear the province would be transferred to France was an intuitive reflex rather than a policy. Danger of a British conquest of Spanish Louisiana and Florida in the Nootka crisis of 1790 threatened encirclement by the greatest power of the day, and provoked the first full-dress discussion of foreign policy under the new federal government. The No-Transfer concept was here first articulated in a formal way. Probably the greatest threat to American security during the early national period was the actual retrocession of Louisiana to Napoleonic France. To prevent the vital Mississippi outlet from falling into the hands of the master of Europe, the No-Transfer policy was invoked and elaborated, and backed with threats of force. After the Louisiana Purchase it was logically extended, first to the Floridas, in the Joint Resolution of 1811, and, after their acquisition, to Cuba, in order to protect the New Orleans traffic upon which the prosperity of the West depended. Finally, with the recognition of the independence of Latin

5. *The Latin American Policy of the United States* (New York, 1943), pp. 27–28.

America, the Monroe Doctrine was created as altered forms of the No-Transfer principle, to meet a new situation.

The policy continued in a long and varied series of applications, chiefly to Cuba, Puerto Rico, and other European possessions in the Caribbean which were important to the security of the continental United States and to the transit across the Isthmus of Panama. The continuing vitality of the No-Transfer principle received dramatic illustration during the second World War by its embodiment in the Pittman-Bloom Joint No-Transfer Resolution of June 1940 in Congress, and the Declaration XX of the Second Consultative Meeting of Foreign Ministers at Havana the following month, both issued in the face of a threatened transfer to the Third Reich of the American possessions of conquered France and Holland.

The history of the No-Transfer principle is an integral and indispensable part of the history of American hemispheric isolationism, of which it has been an essential instrument from the outset. In the months before American entry into the second World War, the threat to the security of the United States created by Hitler's stunning victories and the mortal peril of Britain necessitated an extension of the No-Transfer principle far beyond the traditional boundaries of the Hemisphere, to Iceland, the Azores, Cape Verde, the Canary Islands, and even to Dakar on the west coast of Africa. This was in effect an admission that the Monroe Doctrine could be upheld only by violating its basic postulate, the doctrine of the two political spheres, European and American. The war itself and the Cold War of the aftermath completed the demolition of the Western Hemisphere idea, and with it the American policy of aloofness from world politics. In its classic form the No-Transfer principle has faded into relative insignificance, but its essence survives in the global policy of containment of Soviet aggression.

CHAPTER 1

The First Defensive Reflexes

FRANCE AND CANADA

The news late in 1760 that Canada had fallen before Amherst's victorious army was received with great rejoicing in New England. Governor Bernard of Massachusetts proclaimed a day of thanksgiving, and in Boston the occasion was celebrated with parades and music, followed at night by a great banquet at Faneuil Hall. Outside, happy throngs surged in and out of the circles of light from huge bonfires, or were caught in the glow of the festive illumination of buildings. At intervals the merrymaking was punctuated by the thud of great guns firing salutes. And of course there were sermons. From every pulpit in the province arose prayers of gratitude for victory, for deliverance forever from the French menace. Thomas Foxcroft of the Old Church in Boston voiced the general feeling when he said that "long had it been the common opinion, *Delenda est Carthago.* Canada must be conquered, or we could hope for no lasting quiet in these parts; and now, through the good hand of our God upon us, we see the happy day of its accomplishment." In the little village of Brookfield, Massachusetts, the minister exulted that "God has given us to sing this day the downfall of New France, the North American Babylon, New England's rival."[1]

1. Francis Parkman, *Montcalm and Wolfe* (2 vols. Boston, 1899), 2, 391–93.

For the British colonists in North America this was more than the celebration of a single victory in a single war; it was the culmination of a century-long duel between Britain and France, which had periodically erupted in wars that in Europe bore other names but which Americans called after their sovereigns, King William's War, Queen Anne's War, King George's War. Each of these struggles had turned the frontier into a bloody battleground, and for years none of the northern colonies had known when the French and their savage Indian allies would descend on their outlying settlements with fire and sword. Now half the continent had changed hands. Canada was won by British arms and soon the Floridas to the south would be also, while France would cede Louisiana to Spain, reducing the pressure from the west. The Treaty of Paris in 1763 effected a revolution in the strategic situation of the British colonies, giving them prospects of a peace and security they had never before enjoyed.

The train of events in North America set in motion by the Treaty of Paris, which led to a new war—this time for American independence—is a familiar one. The English colonies, less in need of protection after the removal of hostile powers to the north and south, were freer to resent the unaccustomed taxes and restrictions imposed by the British government in its fumbling attempt to reorganize a vastly enlarged and heterogeneous empire on a rational, paying basis. Americans felt secure enough to indulge their passion for liberty and for westward expansion, now that the French were gone from the Continent.

After Lexington and Concord, as the quarrel with London deepened and broadened to an extent that seemed to a growing number of Americans to preclude attempts at reconciliation, one of the most telling arguments in favor of a declaration of independence was the peace and prosperity to be enjoyed by separation from Britain and her wars.

Looking back from their new position of safety, Americans were quickly persuaded that the century of colonial wars they had fought had been unnecessary, that they had stemmed solely from the imperial connection. "Dependence on Great Britain," wrote Tom Paine in *Common Sense,*

> tends directly to involve this continent in European wars and quarrels, and set us at variance with nations who would otherwise seek our friendship, and against whom we have neither anger or complaint. . . . France and Spain never were, nor perhaps ever will be, our enemies as Americans, but as our being subjects of Great Britain. . . . Our plan is commerce, and that, well attended to, will secure us the peace and friendship of all Europe. . . . As Europe is our market for trade we ought to form no partial connection with any part of it. It is the true interest of America to steer clear of European contentions, which she can never do while, by her dependence on Britain, she is made the make-weight in the scale of British politics.[2]

These words struck a responsive chord in the hearts of most Americans. They epitomized not only the immediate hopes of the revolutionary generation, but what has been probably the most fundamental of all American foreign policy objectives—the political separation of the Old and New Worlds in the interest of peace through the reduction and, if possible, the elimination of European power and influence in the Western Hemisphere. The No-Transfer principle—the opposition to transfer of European colonies in the New World to another European power—has been from the outset of our national life perhaps the chief instrument for accomplishing this isolation.

2. W. M. Van der Weyde, ed., *The Life and Works of Thomas Paine* (10 vols. New Rochelle, New York, 1825), 2, 126, 129–30.

It was as easy as it was dangerous in 1775 for Americans to overestimate the disadvantages and underestimate the privileges of membership in the British empire, where they enjoyed at very little relative expense the protection of a system of collective security which brought troops to their defense on land and guarded their commerce at sea. After the United States had achieved independence but while it was still surrounded by European territories, it became painfully clear that Spain and France had been enemies not simply because of European rivalries but also because they were neighbors, and that Americans had been fighting for their own interests and for their own security in the endless chain of eighteenth-century wars. It had been disheartening, of course, for colonial troops who had fought alongside British soldiers to capture French citadels like Port Royal or Louisbourg, to see their prizes returned to France at Ryswick and Utrecht out of considerations that for London transcended the local interests of British North America. On the other hand, because colonial contributions to their own defense, in both money and manpower, had usually been grudging and unreliable, there had always been British regulars for garrison duty on the frontiers and for the hard fighting, while the Royal Navy commanded the lines of communication to Europe. An independent United States found it difficult to duplicate these services at any cost. Ultimately, the only way to be free of the wars, taxes, and quartering and levies of troops was to be rid of strong European neighbors entirely. This was the grand design of early American foreign policy and diplomacy, and through a remarkable combination of skillful statecraft, blind luck, and political disturbances abroad which Americans could utilize if not control, this design was substantially accomplished by 1823, though not without interludes of serious danger.

One such danger arose out of the necessity of an alliance

with France. It was clear from the beginning of the War for Independence that the American states needed outside assistance, particularly financial support, to win. The logical ally was France, Britain's traditional antagonist, which after its recent defeat was spoiling for revenge and already doling out small amounts of covert aid. But the Americans, remembering the years of the Gallic peril in North America, approached this liaison gingerly, alert to the possibility that in soliciting French help they ran the risk of exchanging one tyrant for another. Echoing Paine's injunction to steer clear of entanglements, John Adams warned the Continental Congress in March 1776 that if they were to remain free of external control, the new American states must form no military or political connection with France, receive no troops, governors, or officers from her, and restrict their relations with her to commerce.[3]

Clearly Adams' counsel of perfection would not do under the circumstances, but the original Plan for a Treaty with France, drafted for the Congress in July, still sought to keep the French at arm's length, and particularly to see that they did not again acquire territory on the continent of North America. Article IX provided that "the Most Christian King shall never invade, nor under any pretence, attempt to possess himself of Labrador, New Britain, Nova Scotia, Acadia, Canada, Florida, nor of any of the countries, cities or towns on the continent of North America, nor the islands of Newfoundland, Cape Breton, St. John's, Anacosti, nor any other island lying near to said continent."[4] Here, contemporaneous with the Declaration of Independence, is the first seed of what was to become the No-Transfer principle

3. Charles F. Adams, ed., *The Works of John Adams* (10 vols. Boston, 1850–56), 2, 488.

4. Ford, Hunt, Fitzpatrick, et al., eds., *Journals of the Continental Congress, 1774–1789* (31 vols. Washington, 1904–34), 5, 768–79 (cited as *JCC*).

in American diplomacy, expressed in this instance as an aversion to the replacement of Britain by an old and implacable enemy on the borders of the new United States. When the treaty of alliance with France was eventually concluded in February 1778, it necessarily contained a great many commitments Congress had been reluctant earlier to undertake—a promise to fight until independence was won, a mutual pledge not to make a separate peace, and a mutual guarantee of each other's territories in the New World. But the prohibition of French conquests on the continent remained adamantly intact.

This feature of the Treaty Plan of 1776 and of the Treaty of Alliance with France reflects in part, of course, American ambitions for continental expansion, but it also underscores a determination that if the United States failed to acquire Canada or the Floridas, at least the nation would not find itself in the old strategic vise, caught between the possessions of the great European antagonists as the battleground it had been before 1763. Few American leaders cherished any illusions about French policy; they understood the motives that impelled the Comte de Vergennes, foreign minister of Louis XVI, to assist in the birth of a republic, and recognized them as being wholly selfish, governed by considerations of the colonial and European balance of power. Knowing this, they practiced eternal vigilance against French attempts to establish a tutelary relationship or territorial neighborhood in order to make the United States an unwilling creature of the French crown.

Americans were particularly sensitive in this connection about any French design for the reconquest of Canada, from which France had been driven only a few years before and where the predominantly French population would certainly welcome their return. Because the French Canadians lay restlessly under the yoke of Britain, that country was less a danger than under France as sovereign, but the best solution seemed to be to join Canada to the American confederation. Most Americans firmly believed that possession of Canada was absolutely essential to their safety and well-being in the future. Canada was not the only object of attention among neighboring British possessions, but it was by far the most important. Both in private utterances and in official statements of the Continental Congress, the conviction was openly and often expressed that the security of the United States also demanded the acquisition of Nova Scotia, the Floridas, and perhaps Bermuda. John Adams, just returned from his mission to Paris, in a report to the President of Congress on the diplomatic outlook abroad warned of the danger from nearby British colonies to an independent United States:

> [England's] envy, her jealousy and resentment will never leave us, while we are what we must unavoidably be, her rivals in the fisheries, in various other branches of commerce, and even in naval power. If peace should unhappily be made, leaving Canada, Nova Scotia, or even the Floridas, or any of them, in her hands, jealousies and controversies will be perpetually arising.[5]

Boston's fiery demagogue, Samuel Adams, saw eye to eye with his Braintree kinsman on this matter, if not on all others. Writing to James Warren in November 1778, he expressed hope that the United States would secure Canada, Nova Scotia, and Florida, adding with more than a trace of the later sense of Manifest Destiny that "we shall never be on a solid footing till G.B. cedes to us what Nature designs we sh[ould] have or we wrest it from her."[6] Failure

5. Letter to John Jay, Aug. 4, 1779, in Francis Wharton, ed., *The Revolutionary Diplomatic Correspondence of the United States* (6 vols. Washington, 1889), *3*, 273 (cited as Wharton).

6. H. A. Cushing, ed., *The Writings of Samuel Adams* (4 vols. New York, 1904–08), *4*, 90.

to procure these territories would expose the new nation to "a source of corrupt British Influence which . . . might diffuse mischief and poison through the States."[7]

The expedition against Quebec in 1775–76, so confidently launched and so disastrously terminated, had taught Washington a deep lesson in cautious and thorough logistical planning. Ill-starred though it was, the operation produced positive results. In the first place, concern for Quebec caused the forces sent over by Lord Germain in 1777 to be divided, part of them going to reinforce the Canadian stronghold. This considerably lightened Washington's defensive problems, and set the stage for the decisive victory over General Burgoyne at Saratoga, which, since it induced Vergennes to conclude the Franco–American alliance of February 6, 1778, was probably of more importance to the securing of American independence than the victory at Yorktown. In the second place, the Quebec expedition brought home to Washington, if not to other commanders or to Congress, the impossibility of conducting a successful attack on Canada without preliminary stockpiling of supplies, and assuring adequate transport for them by land or sea.

The delegates to the Continental Congress soon recovered from the shock of the bad news from Quebec. When the Congress adopted the Articles of Confederation on November 15, 1777, provision was made in Article XI for the accession of Canada, and two weeks later Congress appointed a committee to draw up an Address to the inhabitants of that region, inviting them to join the Confederation.[8]

In an excess of enthusiasm over Burgoyne's surrender at Saratoga on October 17, 1777, Congress at the instigation of the victorious Gates developed a grandiose plan for an "ir-

7. Ibid., pp. 149–50.
8. *JCC*, 9, 924, 981.

ruption" into Canada, to be led by the youthful Marquis de Lafayette, recently arrived from France. Although the exact details of the arrangement are not clear, it appears that the command was to be virtually independent of the Commander in Chief. Washington considered the enterprise impracticable from a military standpoint but hesitated to intervene, because this was the first project of the new Board of War, which had not consulted him in the matter, and because of his friendship for Lafayette.[9] This was the period of the "Conway Cabal," when Washington's Fabian tactics were being unfavorably compared with the smashing victories won by Gates.[10]

The "irruption" evaporated when it became clear to Lafayette that neither men nor supplies were available for so ambitious a scheme. On March 3, 1778, Congress voted to suspend the operation on the advice of the Board of War, and Lafayette shortly returned to Washington's headquarters, bitterly chagrined at the ridiculous fiasco into which he had been innocently drawn.[11]

Meanwhile France had become the ally of the United States, an event which completely altered the complexion of military affairs in North America. With the arrival at Boston of a French squadron under the command of Admiral d'Estaing in midsummer 1778, the prospect of win-

9. J. C. Fitzpatrick, ed., *The Writings of George Washington* (37 vols. Washington, 1931–44), *10*, 432–33 (cited as GW). When at length he was consulted by the Board, Washington declined to give advice, pointing out that he knew too little about the aims of the expedition or the means by which it was to be carried out (*10*, 355–56).

10. For an illuminating study of the extent of the criticism of Washington at this time and of the circumstances surrounding the appointment of Lafayette to head the Canadian expedition, see Bernhard Knollenberg, *Washington and the Revolution: A Reappraisal* (New York, 1940), pp. 178–215.

11. *JCC, 10*, 107. On Lafayette's attitude see Louis Gottschalk, ed., *The Letters of Lafayette to Washington* (New York, 1944), p. 26.

ning naval superiority and consequently of being able to
supply a Canadian expedition by sea through the St. Lawrence River became a distinct possibility. Furthermore,
many Americans anticipated a more receptive attitude on
the part of the French Canadians to union with a United
States which was the ally of Louis XVI.[12]

When in a fresh burst of optimism Congress approved,
on October 26, 1778, another plan for an attack on Quebec,
Washington's advice was at once asked.[13] His objections on
this occasion were both military and political, based on an
apprehension that a joint Franco–American expedition to
Quebec might end by increasing the threat to the security
of the United States rather than lessening it, in case the war
should result in a transfer of Canada back to French sovereignty.

WASHINGTON'S OBJECTIONS TO THE
CANADIAN EXPEDITION

The "providential" intervention of Louis XVI in the
struggle between Great Britain and her former colonies,
together with France's renunciation of all designs against
British possessions on the continent of North America and
the adjacent islands (in Article VI of the Treaty of Alliance
of 1778), had encouraged the Continental Congress to plan

12. American outcries against the Quebec Act of 1774—which had
attached the French Canadians more firmly to England by favoring
Catholics in Canada—were not calculated to endear their cause to
their northern neighbors. It was hoped that the appointment of
Lafayette to command the abortive "irruption" of 1777–78 would win
the inhabitants over to the American cause. See the letter of Henry
Laurens to John Rutledge of Feb. 3, 1778, Edmund C. Burnett, ed.,
Letters of Members of the Continental Congress (8 vols. Washington,
1921–36), *3*, 65–66.

13. *JCC, 12*, 1042.

a joint Franco–American operation against Quebec for the campaign of 1779.[14]

General Washington, however, felt constrained to state his objections to this enterprise in a public letter to Congress and in a private letter to Henry Laurens. There can be no question of the importance attached by the Commander in Chief to the acquisition of Canada by the United States. The previous spring his friend Landon Carter had written him, hoping to get confirmation of a rumor that Canada had joined the Confederation. Washington had to disappoint him on that score, but assured Carter that "your ideas of its [Canada's] importance to our political union coincide exactly with mine. If that country is not with us, it will, from its proximity to the Eastern States, its intercourse and connexion with the numerous tribes of western Indians . . . be at least a troublesome if not a dangerous neighbor to us; and ought, at all events, to be in the same interests and politics, of the other states."[15] Washington nevertheless considered an attempt on Canada impractical for 1779, and on November 1 and 14, 1778, he sent two letters, an official one to Congress designed for the public eye, which dealt exclusively with the military situation, and a second addressed privately to Henry Laurens, President of the Congress, to be employed as the latter saw fit in guiding the deliberations of Congress.

Washington's estimate of the military situation, carefully prepared from reports he had requested from his commanders in the Northern Department, was enough to chill the enthusiasm of any sensible man for a northern expedition.[16] He began by reminding Congress of the responsibility it now bore toward France, for not embarking on ill-conceived and ruinous enterprises. Then he addressed himself to the

14. Ibid., *11*, 450; *12*, 1042.
15. *GW, 6*, 492–93.
16. The letter is printed in *GW, 13*, 223–44.

question of means. The plan drawn up by Congress envisaged a three-pronged attack to be launched June 1, 1779, one American force against Detroit and Niagara, another against Montreal and St. John, and a French force to travel by sea up the St. Lawrence to Quebec, making contact with the Montreal column after both places had been secured.[17] Washington pointed out that the plan called for virtually the whole force he then had in the field, doubted that many more men could be raised, and wondered what was to be done about defending the countryside of New York and Rhode Island against the British forces there, which showed no intention of leaving. Patiently explaining the fundamentals of military supply, the Commander in Chief recalled to Congress the distances involved, the absence of roads, the difficulty of procuring stores of any sort because of depreciation of the Continental currency. He dwelt at length on the strength and determination of the British defenses and on the superiority the enemy still enjoyed at sea, warning that even if Howe should evacuate the United States, the task would be formidable and success in doubt.

These arguments sufficed to convince the public that the project must be abandoned, but Washington had withheld what seemed to him the most pressing objection to the joint expedition. Three days after he had dispatched his letter to Congress, his anxiety compelled him to write Henry Laurens in order to "unbosom" himself "on a point of the most delicate and important Nature." Apologizing for intruding into politics, he at once showed himself to be adept in that subject:

> The question of the Canadian expedition in the form it now stands appears to me one of the most interesting that has hitherto agitated our national deliberations. I have one objection to it, untouched on in my public

17. *Secret Journals of Congress* (4 vols. Boston, 1820), 2, 111–17.

letter, which is in my estimation, insurmountable, and alarms all my feelings for the true and permanent interests of my country. This is the introduction of a large body of French troops into Canada, and putting them into possession of the capital of that Province, attached to them by all the ties of blood, habits, manners, religion and former connexions of government. I fear this would be too great a temptation, to be resisted by any power actuated by the common maxims of national policy.[18]

Washington had no doubt that such "maxims of national policy" guided the Court of France, and went on to enumerate the "striking advantages" which would come to her with the transfer of Canada, by way of an enlarged commerce, a source of supply for her West Indian possessions, and a means of securing them against attack, not to speak of "the finest nursery of seamen in the world." Finally, most important to France and dangerous to the United States would be "the facility of awing and controlling these states, the natural and most formidable rival of every maritime power in Europe."

Surely and succinctly, Washington sketched the strategic situation of the United States in the event of such a transfer of sovereignty, revealing an appreciation of the broad play of forces in European politics and of the part British dominion of the seas had played in American security. "France," Washington wrote, "acknowledged for some time past the

18. *GW, 13*, 254–57. The only other discoverable statement of a suspicion like Washington's is to be found in a letter of Gouverneur Morris to Henry Laurens written on the occasion of the Lafayette expedition of the year previous, in which Morris questioned the propriety of sending as first and second in command two subjects of "the Grande Monarque who may as probably like Canada as well as any of his predecessors." No evidence of a correspondence or meeting on this subject is to be found, however. For the letter see Burnett, *3*, 50–51.

most powerful monarchy in Europe by land, able now to dispute the empire of the sea with Great Britain, and, if joined by Spain, I may say certainly superior, possessed of New Orleans, on our Right, Canada on our left and seconded by the numerous tribes of Indians on our Rear from one extremity to the other . . . , would, it is much to be apprehended have it in her power to give law to these states."

With five thousand troops in Canada, Washington suggested, France might trump up any excuse to retain its former colony. She might, for example, claim it as security for the payment of the American debt. Any pretense would suffice, for with Canadian support and possibly control of the seas, little would be left for the United States except "resentment, reproaches, and submission."

Aware that he would be charged in many quarters with being ungracious and ungrateful to France, Washington anticipated the objection by restating his basic postulate on the nature of international politics. "I am heartily disposed to entertain the most favorable sentiments of our new ally and to cherish them in others to a reasonable degree; but it is a maxim founded on the universal experience of mankind, that no nation is to be trusted farther than it is bound by its interests; and no prudent statesman or politician will venture to depart from it."

In Washington's letter to Laurens we find another tentative approach to a statement of the principle that it should be an objective of the United States policy to prevent, if possible, transfers of North American territory from one European sovereign to another if such a transfer would be contrary to the interests of the nation. It is appropriate that the author of this statement should have been Washington—the man under whose leadership independence was achieved and form was to be given to the national government of 1789; and because strategy and diplomacy are inseparable, it is doubly appropriate that it should have been the Commander in Chief of the Continental Army who brought into sharp focus America's position in the balance of power of the time.

It is not unlikely that one of the immediate occasions for the misgivings Washington revealed in his letter was an address to the Canadian people delivered at Boston by the French admiral, Count d'Estaing, on October 28, 1778.[19] Estaing's instructions from the King had directed that a message from the French sovereign be conveyed to his former subjects in Canada, and the admiral chose as the occasion to carry out those orders a visit by a delegation of Canadians who had been sent to learn if the news of the Franco–American alliance was true.[20]

The message itself was actually an appeal to the French Canadians to join the United States in rebellion against England, but there was a great deal about France in it, and little or nothing about the United States. Estaing appealed in succession to each class of French Canadian, evoking old loyalties and memories of a better day. To the *noblesse* he recalled the pride taken by Henri IV in the title "Gentleman of France," and to the soldiers the valor of Lévis and Montcalm. The clergy he confronted with the specter of heresy and temporal control and the people at large with that of oppression by tyrants who had no sympathy for the language, customs, religion, or ancient family ties of their subjects.[21]

19. Printed in translation in Justin H. Smith, *Our Struggle for the Fourteenth Colony* (2 vols. New York, 1907), 2, 536–38.

20. Henri Doniol, *Histoire de la participation de la France à l'établissement des Etats-Unis d'Amérique* (5 vols. and supplement to Vol. 5, Paris, 1886–92), 3, 423–24.

21. Compare the distinct similarity of language between Washington's letter and Estaing's reference to "a vast Kingdom having the same religion, the same customs, the same language, where relatives, old friends, and brethren are to be found . . ."

Whatever the intention of the admiral or his king, the appeal was too predominantly French to be comforting to American ears. It was surely no coincidence that Estaing's address was read to Congress on the same day that the committee appointed to study Washington's letter reported its recommendation that plans for the expedition be suspended.[22] From the point of view of the United States it was preferable that Britain should retain Canada, with an alien population among whom American appeals might stir up discontent amounting to rebelliousness, than that France should acquire it and establish a cohesive, loyal power on the northern frontier, which would threaten a revival of the bloody incidents of the days of Louis XIV.

By way of an important and anomalous postscript to this episode of Washington's veto of the project of 1779, it is interesting to note that in 1782 Washington himself proposed a joint Franco–American expedition against Canada. Whether his suspicions of France had relaxed, or whether his conviction of the necessity of acquiring Canada for the United States had persuaded him to take the risk of a transfer to France, it is impossible to say, but in any case, he was balked by a demurrer from Rochambeau himself.[23] The truth of the matter was that the French government opposed a joint expedition against Canada, though for reasons it would have been difficult for Washington to guess and which would scarcely have allayed his uneasiness if known to him.

---

22. *JCC*, *12*, 1190.

23. For the final conference between Washington and Rochambeau at which the subject of Canada was raised, see *GW*, *24*, 433–35. Rochambeau explained his need for special authorization from his government before undertaking the operation in question; see also, among others, J. J. Meng, "The Place of Canada in French Diplomacy of the American Revolution," *Bulletin des recherches historiques*, *39* (1933), 665–87.

In his letter to Henry Laurens, Washington expressed his suspicions that the idea of a joint expedition in 1779 had been broached to Congress by Lafayette only as a cover for the designs of the "Cabinet of France."[24] Nothing could have been farther from the truth. Actually Lafayette's enthusiasms were as embarrassing to Vergennes as they were to Washington.

The conclusion of the Alliance of 1778 made Canada an active factor in Franco–American relations, as we have seen. French policy in the matter was determined as soon as a minister was sent to the United States, and remained inflexible thereafter. Vergennes' instructions of March 29, 1778, to Gérard, who was about to depart for America, contained the following explanation of France's policy:

> The delegates to Congress have proposed that the King engage to assist in the conquest of Canada, Nova Scotia and the Floridas which the Americans would undertake. . . . But the King considers that the possession of these three countries, or at least of Canada by England, would be a useful source of anxiety and vigilance for the Americans, which would make them feel in the future a need of the friendship and alliance of the King, which it is not in his interest to destroy.[25]

Washington's estimate that the purpose of France was to use the United States to suit her own political ends was correct, then, but the means to be employed were more subtle than he imagined. The keynote of French policy was repeatedly to deny any interest in acquiring Canada, to encourage American aspirations in that direction only sufficiently to allay suspicion of France, but to do absolutely nothing to forward these designs.[26]

24. *GW, 13,* 257.
25. Doniol, *3,* 156.
26. Estaing's instructions to this effect are in Doniol, *3,* 191–92.

Thus we find the French ministers gently discouraging American plans for attacks on Canada, though not so obviously as to arouse a general suspicion that France herself intended to take it, and stressing that the alliance had been concluded to secure the independence of the United States, not for aggrandizement.[27]

To distract American attention from Canada, the French representatives to Congress lost no opportunity of suggesting an expedition against the Floridas in cooperation with Spanish forces, a proposition which had the additional advantage of meshing perfectly with French commitments to Spain.[28]

It is evident that Washington might have saved himself the trouble of vetoing the joint expedition, since the French would almost certainly have done so themselves. He misjudged the means the French intended to employ in 1778, but he read their ultimate aims correctly. What is believed to be the situation is often more important in the formulation of foreign policy than the actual facts. Washington was quick to apprehend that American security was vitally involved in any shifting of the balance of power on or near this continent. France's determination to erect a client state in North America persisted, though it was not until Napoleon's day that this objective was pursued through the ac-

27. See the report of a conversation in Oct. 1778 between Gouverneur Morris and Gérard in Jared Sparks, *The Life of Gouverneur Morris* (3 vols. Boston, 1832), *1,* 188–90. See also on a meeting of La Luzerne and Washington of Sept. 16, 1779, in Wharton, *3,* 321, in which the French minister indirectly suggested the inadvisability of another Canadian expedition by telling Washington how highly French military experts had spoken of his letter to Congress of Nov. 11, 1778.

28. See, e.g., Gérard's suggestion to this effect to certain members of Congress on Feb. 15, 1779, in Burnett, *4,* 70, and the instructions given Lafayette on his return from a visit to France (March 5, 1780), Doniol, *4,* 318.

quisition of territory on the boundaries of the United States. When Louisiana passed again into French hands in 1800, the danger which had evoked the instinctive defensive reflex of Washington's letter to Laurens in 1778 reappeared in a very real way and in aggravated dimensions, and on this occasion the American government responded with more elaborate statements of concern at disturbances in the American constellation of power which might be caused by the transfer from one European sovereign to another of territories on the borders of the new republic.

THE NOOTKA SOUND CONTROVERSY

Few of Washington's countrymen would have disagreed with him about the undesirability of reconstituting the strategic situation of 1756 by encouraging a French occupation of Canada, and many were equally concerned about having Britain as a neighbor after independence was won. Both the military campaigns of the war and the diplomatic campaign at the peace conference in Paris failed, however, to secure a cession of Canada to the United States, and so to provide an ideal solution by doing away altogether with the British–American boundary in North America. British Canada was actually as much a threat to the peace of the New England states as French Canada had been. Severing the imperial tie had left the United States less secure than before. This uneasy strategic situation was dramatized during the Anglo–Spanish war scare in 1790 which arose out of the seizure of British ships by Spanish authorities at Nootka Sound in Vancouver Island.

The peace settlement at Paris in 1783 had left the United States surrounded by European possessions—British Canada, Spanish Louisiana, and the Floridas—with Britain, as always, commanding the Atlantic as well. During the period of the weak Confederation both these neighboring powers proved troublesome, to an extent that threatened the territorial integrity of the United States. Britain refused to honor the agreement on the generous river and lake boundary drawn at Paris and remained illegally in occupation of the northwest posts that controlled the fur trade and the Indians of Upper Canada. Though perhaps not directly inciting raids by their Indian allies against American settlements on the northern frontier, Canadian authorities did nothing actively to discourage them, and the border reverted to the bloody havoc of a generation before. The boundary problem, like the equally irritating lack of a commercial treaty with Britain, was difficult to resolve because no regular exchange of diplomatic representatives had taken place after the war.

Things were no better with Spain, with whom there was also a boundary dispute, an Indian problem, and an uncertain commercial relationship resting on the day-to-day caprice of Spanish officialdom. And, most acute of all, there was the Mississippi question. Since the only commercially practicable outlet for the surplus produce of the trans-Appalachian West was down the tributary streams and mighty highway of the Mississippi, the prosperity of the western frontier settlements in Kentucky and Tennessee depended heavily on securing free navigation of the Mississippi and the right to deposit cargoes for trans-shipment to ocean-going vessels at New Orleans or some similar point at the mouth of the river. For over twenty years, until the question was finally settled by the Louisiana Purchase, the United States contended for these privileges, while Spain hedged and delayed, yielding and then retracting their grants of passage and entrepôt.

The Spanish government had no interest in hastening the development of American frontier communities which would all too soon grow to be a constant threat to Spanish sovereignty in Louisiana and the Floridas. When Congress sent John Jay to Spain during the Revolution to secure agreement on the Mississippi boundary on the west and the 31° line on the south, as well as free navigation and the right of deposit, the authorities at Madrid took no official notice of his presence, partly because they feared that recognizing the independence of the United States might encourage revolts in their own American colonies, and partly out of a desire to delay facing the Mississippi question. Evasiveness is one of the last refuges in the diplomacy of a failing power, and Spanish diplomatists raised it to the level of high art in the last years of the empire of Tordesillas.

At the peace conference of Paris in 1782 the Spanish tried vainly through their French allies to persuade the American delegation to accept the Appalachian chain as a western boundary, with neutral Indian barrier states in the southwest as a buffer between American and Spanish territories, and though the British agreed to the Mississippi boundary, Spain refused to recognize it, occupied parts of the disputed territory, allied herself with the Indian nations there, and in 1784 closed the lower Mississippi to navigation by Americans. During the Jay–Gardoqui negotiations at New York in 1786, Spain was willing to concede the Mississippi line if the United States would agree to "forbear" navigation of the river for twenty-five years, but with the formation of the new government under the federal constitution, these talks were discontinued amid howls of protest from the West.

No matter how obstructionistic Spain was in these matters, scarcely anyone in the United States would have welcomed Britain or France as a substitute sovereign in Louisiana or the Floridas. John Jay was perhaps briefly an exception, for in his disillusionment and irritation over the treatment he had received at Madrid he was willing in 1782 to promise the British a slightly more favorable boundary than the 31° line in the Floridas if they retained the provinces after the war. But this view was unusual, and did not speak particularly well for Jay's sense of strategic values. More typical of American opinion was John Adams' estimate of the insignificance of having Spanish possessions on our border because "the genius and interest of [that] nation incline to repose."[29] Spanish power had waned steadily and palpably since the golden days of Philip II. None of the other large maritime powers of Europe situated on our borders would have constituted so little immediate threat to our security nor have been eventually so easy to displace. On the southern and western borders no less than on the northern, one of the earliest and most consistent aims of American foreign policy was to diminish foreign power and influence or remove it entirely.

Among the strongest arguments for adoption of the new federal constitution of 1787 with its provision for more centralized authority over military, commercial, fiscal, and diplomatic affairs was the advantages it offered for national defense. In *The Federalist,* Number 24, Hamilton vividly sketched the precarious strategic situation of the United States, suggesting the danger in case the policies of Britain and Spain, heretofore coincidentally alike, should be formally concerted against its interests.[30] The position of the United States was undoubtedly insecure, but the initial threat came not from the concert of policies Hamilton predicted but from a falling-out between these two neighbors. The Nootka affair of 1790, which necessitated the first full-dress formulation of security policies by the new government under President Washington, raised the danger of a possible transfer of adjacent territories from weak Spain to powerful Britain.

29. Letter to the President of Congress, John Jay (Aug. 4, 1779), Wharton, *3*, 281.

30. Henry Cabot Lodge, ed., *The Works of Alexander Hamilton* (14 vols. New York, 1904), *11*, 191–94.

The Anglo–Spanish war scare which developed during the spring and summer of 1790 and profoundly affected the young United States arose out of apparently trifling events at Nootka Sound.[31] A small British fur-trading settlement had existed undisturbed for three years on this island, discovered and first explored by the Englishmen Cook and Vancouver, when in the late summer of 1789 two Spanish warships appeared, seized a British merchant vessel there and looted it, imprisoned the crew, and asserted Spanish sovereignty over the area. The Spanish government justified these high-handed actions by referring to their ancient claim to exclusive jurisdiction over the whole Pacific Ocean and its American shores, based on Papal Bulls and the Portuguese–Spanish treaty of Tordesillas dating from the fifteenth century.

The British government under Pitt, still smarting under the defeats of the war of the American Revolution and anxious to restore the damaged maritime prestige of England, chose to make this incident the occasion for challenging Spain's pretensions in the Pacific. The time was especially propitious, since Spain's ally France was in the throes of revolution. In February 1790 Britain dispatched a note to Spain demanding full reparation for the injuries done to British subjects and their property and denying the validity of Spanish claims to sovereignty in the region.

When worried Spain delayed a reply, Pitt applied pressure. On May 4 a great press of seamen took place in English seaports. The following day a message from the King revealed the extent of the crisis to Parliament, which responded by authorizing accelerated naval preparations. War appeared likely. Early in August, Spain yielded to the ex-

31. For the general history of the Nootka affair see W. R. Manning, "The Nootka Sound Controversy," *Annual Report of the American Historical Association, 1904*, Washington, 1905. Chap. 10 deals especially with America's relation to the controversy.

tent of acceding to British demands for reparation, and Pitt determined to turn the screw still tighter by requiring satisfaction in the question of the Pacific monopoly.

In desperation, Spain invoked French support under the terms of the Family Compact, but the equivocal assurances received from Montmorin made it clear that the traditional alliance had not survived intact the strains of the French Revolution. Then on October 2, confident that Spain would not fight, Pitt repeated the British demand in the form of an ultimatum. Spain submitted completely in the first Nootka Convention of October 28, 1790, which recognized the equal rights of Britain and Spain to trade, sail, and settle the Pacific Northwest above the line of San Francisco. Pitt had won an important diplomatic victory.

Surrounded as it was by territories of the contending European powers, the United States was necessarily deeply interested in the Nootka controversy. The possibility of an Anglo-Spanish war carried with it for the infant republic both an opportunity and a danger—the opportunity as a neutral to capitalize on its geographical position to secure advantageous commercial and political settlements from the belligerents, particularly Spain, and the danger that a war would result in the transfer of Spanish territory in North American to Britain, completely upsetting the balance of power on this continent, encircling the United States in an iron ring of land and sea power, and forcing it into another war for its very existence. It was in an attempt to contend with this serious threat to the national security that President Washington and his advisers gave the No-Transfer idea its first elaboration.

It was universally agreed that neutrality in the expected war was the only wise course for the United States, still war-weary and heavily in debt from the struggle for independence, and lately embarked on a still dubious adventure in governmental reorganization. Thomas Jefferson, recently arrived from France to assume his new duties as Secretary of State, hoped that the New World could "fatten on the follies of the old," by becoming the granary and carrier for warring Europe.[32] Clearly too, the benefits our neutrality would confer upon the prospective belligerents should not be given gratis but should be used to bargain for political and economic advantages. President Washington particularly emphasized the leverage a European war would give in dealing with feeble Spain on the Mississippi question.[33] The accommodation eventually suggested by the United States to Spain to assure our benevolent neutrality, or perhaps assistance, was the cession of the Floridas to the United States, to prevent the British conquest we feared as much as they. The war crisis ended too soon for this object to be realized, however, and the only true progress toward easing the situation in the Southwest was the pacific Treaty of New York, signed on August 7, 1790, with Alexander McGillivray, the half-breed leader of the Creeks.

With Britain, too, the Nootka controversy offered a chance to press for agreement on unsettled issues. In October 1789 Washington had written to Gouverneur Morris, then on private business in France, requesting him to undertake a mission to London to ascertain the attitude of that government on the questions of a commercial treaty and the northwest posts. Morris was coolly received at first, but as the crisis developed in April and May the Duke of Leeds became markedly more cordial, although Britain avoided definite commitments. Simultaneously, in New York, Anglo–American issues were the subject of discussion between members of the administration—particularly Hamilton—and Major George Beckwith, the unofficial representative of Lord Dorchester, the Governor of Canada. While the in-

32. Letter to Edward Rutledge, July 4, 1790, Paul L. Ford, ed., *The Writings of Thomas Jefferson* (10 vols. New York, 1892–99), *5*, 197.
33. Washington to Lafayette (Aug. 11, 1790), *GW*, *31*, 87–88.

formal nature of these talks precluded any actual settlement, they were most useful in preparing the ground for later negotiations with George Hammond, the first official British minister to the United States, who was appointed after the Nootka crisis.

If the opportunity for adjustment of other issues between the United States and Britain was lost when the war scare evaporated, the danger of transfer of Spanish Louisiana and Florida also temporarily abated, but not before the American government had determined upon a definite policy to prevent it. It is with this aspect of the Nootka affair that we are principally concerned here.

Anxiety over the possibility that Spain might cede her possessions on our border to a more formidable power had appeared before 1790. After the breakdown of the Jay-Gardoqui negotiations in 1786, a rash of rumors broke out across the United States that France was about to receive Louisiana or the Floridas or both in exchange for West Indian islands. So numerous and pressing were the inquiries from members of Congress that Louis Guillaume Otto, the French chargé in New York, felt constrained on December 21, 1786, to address a formal denial to John Jay in which he quoted instructions from Vergennes of August 25 which directed him to state that "the exchange of Louisiana for a French possession in the West Indies, has never been in question. And if anything should be again said of it, you will be pleased to deny it formally."[34] This letter was published in the New York *Packet* on January 19, 1787, after both the *Pennsylvania Journal* and the *Packet* had reprinted an item from a London newspaper alleging confirmation that the Floridas had been ceded to France. Otto's assurances failed to allay suspicion, however, and the rumor con-

34. F. P. Blair, ed., *The Diplomatic Correspondence of the United States, 1783–1789* (7 vols. Washington, 1833–34), *1*, 336.

tinued to crop up periodically until the outbreak of the French Revolution.[35]

In contrast to these vague, disquieting rumors the threat of 1790 was real, immediate, and appeared likely to necessitate forthright action. An Anglo–Spanish war loomed as a distinct possibility, and Britain was thought to have sea and land forces available to accomplish the conquest Americans dreaded.

A glance at the correspondence between the London government and its various representatives in North America, however, reveals that both Britain and the United States overestimated the capacity and readiness of the other to do them harm. In fact the British government was quite as apprehensive about an American expedition against the northwest posts as the Washington administration was about Louisiana and the Floridas. On May 6, the day following the King's message to Parliament and in many respects the key date in the Nootka controversy, Lord Grenville, the Secretary of State for Home Affairs, wrote to Lord Dorchester, Governor General in Quebec, informing him of the possibility of war with Spain, asking him to cancel his projected visit to England because of the emergency, and cautioning him of the danger that the United States might seize the opportunity to wrest the posts from Britain, possibly in alliance with Spain. Furthermore, because France might also join Spain, no troops might be expected as reinforcements in Canada. In a separate instruction written the same day, Grenville suggested steps for Dorchester to take to encourage the United States to remain neutral. Referring to the Morris mission as evidence of a disposition toward conciliation on Washington's part, it was suggested that Dorchester send "proper persons . . . though not authorized by any public commission" to explore the possi-

35. *Pennslyvania Journal* (Jan. 6, 1787) and *New York Packet* (Jan. 16), Burnett, pp. 533–34 and n. 565, 819.

bilities for agreement with the United States, and to keep watch for expeditions against the forts.[36]

Dorchester responded by sending to the United States his aide-de-camp Major George Beckwith, who had performed several previous missions as secret observer of American affairs. Beckwith departed for New York around the end of June 1790 equipped with two sets of instructions, one for public display which conveyed Dorchester's hopes for continued friendly relations between the two countries and which pointed out that the United States also had a stake in the termination of the Spanish monopoly, and a secret set which revealed British anxieties.[37] These directed Beckwith to report fully on all military preparations and dispositions, to ascertain the state of relations with Spain and France, and, after investigating American public opinion on the Mississippi question, to hint at the advantages of an alliance with Britain in this connection.

During the remainder of the year Beckwith carried out his mission with considerable tact and skill. Through his agency the two governments reassured each other in the matter of Indian affairs in the Northwest, and Hamilton was able to inform Britain that the United States had no commitments to Spain, although no discussion of an Anglo–American alliance could be undertaken on such an informal basis.[38] In this instance, as in the negotiation of Jay's Treaty in 1794, the relations of the Secretary of the Treasury with the British representative in this country were often more frank and cordial than was consistent with most effective bargaining by the United States. Hamilton's anglophilism and the dependence of his fiscal system upon duties levied on a high volume of trade (which he felt necessarily meant

36. Douglas Brymner, ed., *Report on Canadian Archives for 1890* (Ottawa, 1891), pp. 131–33.

37. Ibid., pp. 143–44.

38. Lodge, ed., *Writings of Hamilton, 4,* 300–1.

trade with England) help to account for, though they cannot entirely excuse, his indiscretions on these occasions.

The tone of comradely candor that marked these discussions was in disconcerting contrast to other measures undertaken by Britain to make certain that if the United States should determine not to be neutral, its effectiveness as an opponent would at any rate be largely neutralized. Chief among the measures was the encouragement given to separatist elements on the American frontier, a policy already tried with some success by Spain. These appeals to dissident elements in the United States strikingly emphasize one of the dangers that would result from a transfer of Spanish territory to Britain.

On April 17, 1790, the Lords of the Privy Council for Trade recommended to Grenville that special commercial concessions be given Vermont and Kentucky, to weaken their connection with the United States "or any . . . other foreign country" and draw them toward Great Britain.[39] The Home Secretary acted upon this suggestion in his instructions to Dorchester of May 6, proposing an extension of the privileges already given Vermont to include the export of flour down the St. Lawrence. The bait for Kentucky was free navigation of the Mississippi.[40]

No more attractive lure could be offered the frontiersmen, as President Washington well knew. In 1784, immediately after Spain closed the river to American use, he had expressed concern that the "touch of a feather" could induce western secession to Britain or Spain in return for free navigation.[41] The circumstances under which the Jay-

---

39. F. J. Turner, "English Policy toward America in 1790–1791," *American Historical Review*, 7 (1901–02), 707.

40. Brymner, pp. 132–33. Levi Allen was Vermont's commissioner in London at this period.

41. Washington to Governor Benjamin Harrison of Virginia (Oct. 10, 1784), *GW*, 27, 475.

Gardoqui negotiations had broken down had not made the West less restive. Now the Nootka crisis arose to provide a sharp contrast between the immediate advantages to the frontier settlements of joining Britain in direct action against Spain and the dubious prospect of awaiting results from the tortuous processes of American diplomatic negotiations with Madrid.

Evidence had not been lacking in New York that the British were actively pressing their cause in the West. In 1788 a British agent, Colonel John Connolly, had traveled from Canada through the western settlements inciting them to armed attack on Louisiana with weapons supplied by Britain. Connolly's mission accomplished nothing, partly because he unwisely chose to confide in General James Wilkinson—that consummate scoundrel who was receiving pay from Spain while serving as commander of United States forces in the West—and partly because little could be expected from a land attack on Louisiana without naval support against Spain in the Gulf. The Nootka controversy altered this situation, however, and gave rise to at least one projected attack on Louisiana from American territory with British aid. The South Carolina Yazoo Land Company, formed by a group of speculators with the intention of establishing a colony on lands claimed by Spain, had appointed as its general agent a certain James O'Fallon, on the strength of his glib tongue and his supposed influence at New Orleans. When the Spanish authorities refused consent for the project, O'Fallon turned to Britain. The war crisis ended too soon for anything to be done, however, and President Washington's declaration of August 26, 1790, against any settlements in the Yazoo region removed all respectable support from O'Fallon's scheme.[42]

42. On Connolly see Charles Gayarré, *History of Louisiana* (4 vols. New Orleans, 1903), *3,* 235–37; and A. P. Whitaker, *The Spanish–American Frontier* (Boston, 1927), pp. 140–44.

If the Connolly and O'Fallon affairs represented the double menace of western separatism and British encirclement through conquest of Louisiana, the Bowles affair rounded out the danger by including Florida and reviving the threat of Indian warfare in the Southwest, lately relieved by the treaty with McGillivray of the Creeks. Maryland-born William Bowles had sided with Britain in the Revolution, and served in Florida before being dismissed from the British army.[43] He lived for a time among the Creeks and Cherokees, and in 1788 returned to them as the agent of a Nassau mercantile firm, to challenge the leadership of McGillivray and his supporters, Panton, Leslie, and Company. Expelled from the Creek lands in 1789, he led a handful of followers to Canada, where he evidently persuaded Dorchester that he was the spokesman of a considerable segment of the Creek and Cherokee nations. In any case he was given transportation to London to present his case in person. Although he arrived after the Nootka affair was over, he proposed that Britain support the Indian nations in an attack under his leadership on Spanish Florida, Louisiana, and Mexico, pointing out at the same time how useful such an alliance would be in protecting the British West Indies from the United States. Grenville not only received Bowles' memorial but accorded him special trading privileges in the British Caribbean islands, although at the same time he strongly discountenanced any idea of hostilities against the United States.[44]

The full significance of British interest in Bowles' schemes becomes apparent in connection with Pitt's flirtation with the projects of the Venezuelan adventurer Fran-

43. For Bowles' activities at the time of the Nootka crisis see Turner, pp. 708, 726–34; and J. W. Caughey, *McGillivray of the Creeks* (Norman, Okla., 1938), pp. 47–48.

44. Turner, pp. 728–32. This project was particularly recommended to Grenville's attention by Dorchester. See Brymner, p. xliii.

cisco de Miranda, who devoted his life to a fruitless search
for foreign support in a war of liberation in Spanish
America.[45] In February 1790 when the Nootka crisis was
first taking shape, and again on the eventful sixth of May,
Pitt had interviews with Miranda, in which the latter unfolded his views on the readiness of the Spanish colonies for
emancipation, on military plans, and on the form of government to be established after independence was won. Not
only South and Central America but Cuba and Spanish
North America west of the Mississippi were included, with
Louisiana apparently reserved for British dominion.

Pitt's genuine interest in these projects is reflected in reports to him from various quarters on conditions in the
Floridas and Louisiana. In October 1790 Sir Arthur Campbell, who evidently was to command part of the expedition,
reported discouragingly on the feasibility of an overland
attack on Mexico from New Orleans. A secret agent in New
York who signed himself "R.D." urged Pitt not to lose this
opportunity to repossess his "Southern Farms" (the Floridas), with assurances that an army of American backwoodsmen could be hired cheaply for the job. Another view was
presented by the English consul in Charleston, who admitted the ease with which the Floridas could be taken but
advised against doing so because the Americans looked with
a "very jealous eye" on those provinces.[46]

Well might the United States regard with a "jealous eye"
the prospect of exchanging crumbling Spanish rule for the
British colossus to the west and south, delivering its military
position, its commercial fortunes, its territorial integrity,
perhaps even its political existence into the hands of a
single, enveloping power, the most formidable in the world.
The United States could not force the Mississippi outlet

45. The standard work on Miranda's career is W. S. Robertson,
The Life of Miranda, Chapel Hill, 1929.
46. Turner, pp. 716 and n., 721–26.

against British might; the West would then be lost, the fruits of independence gone. The seriousness of this situation was not lost on the American government, and the counsels taken on how best to prevent the transfer of Spanish possessions to British represent an important step in the formulation of the fundamental security policies of the United States.

THE NO-TRANSFER POLICY IN THE NOOTKA CRISIS

Word of the King's message to Parliament on the Nootka crisis arrived in the United States sometime around the middle of June. As we have seen, the first reaction of most American statesmen to this news was that their obvious course of policy in case war broke out was neutrality coupled with diplomatic pressure on Britain and Spain for concessions. Nevertheless, it was immediately apparent that participation in the war might become necessary to prevent a British conquest of the mouth of the Mississippi. In a conversation with President Washington on July 1, Vice President Adams voiced apprehensions that New Orleans would fall to the English, whose possession of it "would be very injurious to us," and advocated joining Spain in the war if public opinion supported it.[47]

Thomas Jefferson, the Secretary of State, was also deeply concerned. On July 11 he wrote to his fellow Virginian James Monroe that the United States must show itself prepared to fight if necessary, for there was evidence of a general British design on Louisiana and the Floridas which would place this country in the "tremendous position" of being entirely encircled by British power.[48]

Jefferson enlarged on these views in a memorandum he

47. J. C. Fitzpatrick, ed., *The Diaries of George Washington* (4 vols. Boston and New York, 1925), *4, 132.*

48. *GW, 5,* 198–99.

submitted to Washington the following day. Hamilton had
reported the substance of his interview of July 8 with Major
Beckwith to the President in Jefferson's presence, and
Washington had asked both men to "revolve the matter in
all its relationships in their minds" in order to be ready to
make policy recommendations.[49] Accordingly Jefferson,
assisted by James Madison, set down his views in the form
of an outline bearing the somewhat unwieldy title: "Heads
of consideration on the conduct we are to observe in the
war between Spain and Great Britain and particularly
should the latter attempt the conquest of Louisiana and the
Floridas."[50] Jefferson's strategic analysis opened with a consideration of the dangers involved in this conquest. Not
only would the acquisition strengthen Britain, it would
weaken the United States by seducing the West from the
Union. Similarity of language, laws, customs, and institutions as well as the economic magnets of free navigation and
the West Indian trade would suffice to accomplish this.
Great Britain would "encircle us compleatly, by these possessions on our land board, and her fleets on our sea-board.
Instead of two neighbors balancing each other, we shall
have one, with more than the strength of both." Jefferson
felt it worth going to war to prevent this eventuality even
though it would be a severe financial strain, but thought
victory impossible unless France joined Spain on our side.
The best policy was to delay crossing the bridge until we
came to it, on the chance that Britain might not attempt
this campaign, or might fail, or might be thwarted by the
continental allies. If the United States lost this gamble, it
would be better prepared for the inevitable war with Britain by having hoarded its strength. Meanwhile there were
two courses of action the United States could take which
might help deter Britain. The first was to suggest that Spain

49. Fitzpatrick, *Diaries, 4,* 139.
50. P. L. Ford, ed., *Writings of Jefferson, 5,* 199–203.

make the provinces independent, under a joint guarantee by Spain and the United States. This was of course an indirect threat of war. So was the second course of action, which was to inform Beckwith "that . . . we should view with extreme uneasiness any attempt of either power to seize the possessions of the other on our frontier, as we consider our own safety interested in a due balance between our neighbors."

Even this guarded statement of the No-Transfer idea, which emphasized the fact that the preservation of a North American balance of power was a vital interest of the United States, was considerably softened by Hamilton in his next meeting with Beckwith on July 22. He reported to Washington that in the course of the conversation "something was said respecting the probable course of military operations, in case of a war between Britain and Spain, which Mr. Beckwith supposed would be directed towards South America; alleging, however, that this was mere conjecture on his part. I hinted cautiously our dislike of any enterprise on New Orleans."[51]

Jefferson, to whom the Franco–American alliance was still the most important factor in our diplomatic position and who was not especially sensitive about speaking firmly to England, was in addition inclined to bluff his way through tense international situations. These tendencies are clearly reflected in the set of instructions to American diplomatic agents abroad which he prepared for delivery by Colonel David Humphreys, whom Washington had appointed as special courier.

On August 2 he wrote to the American chargé in Spain, William Carmichael, that the Nootka crisis offered an opportunity to reopen negotiations on the Mississippi question.[52] If war broke out he was to demand free navigation

51. Lodge, ed., *Works of Hamilton, 4,* 301–2.
52. P. L. Ford, ed., *5,* 216–18, 225–31.

and the right of deposit as a *sine qua non,* and was to threaten that the situation in the West left no choice but resort to force if negotiation failed. Such a war might be undertaken jointly with England, in which case the United States would receive Spanish possessions to the east of the Mississippi, Britain those to the west bordering Mexico. Perhaps the best solution, Carmichael was to suggest, would be for Spain to cede the Floridas and New Orleans to the United States at the outset, making a friend rather than an enemy. If Spain should not become embroiled in war with England, Carmichael was to continue pressing for the same concessions, but Jefferson cautioned that in this event "they must be pressed more softly, and . . . patience and persuasion must temper your conferences, till either these may prevail, or some other circumstances turn up, which may enable us to use other means for the attainment of an object which we are determined, in the end, to obtain at every risk." A week later the Secretary of State instructed William Short in Paris that in case of war he should attempt to induce France to persuade Spain to cede New Orleans to the United States.[53]

Using the threat of an alliance with Britain was all very well as an attempt to jar Spain into action on the Mississippi question, but Jefferson had no intention of putting his head in the Lion's mouth if he could escape it. To the informal agent in London, Gouverneur Morris, he wrote the following significant instruction to be conveyed to the British government in the event of war with Spain:

> These tamperings [Beckwith's mission] prove they view a war as very possible; and some symptoms indicate designs against the Spanish possessions adjoining us. The consequences of their acquiring all the country on our frontier, from the St. Croix to the St. Mary's, are

53. Jefferson to Short (Aug. 10, 1790), ibid., pp. 218–21.

too obvious to you to need development. You will readily see the dangers which then environ us. We wish you, therefore, to intimate to them that we cannot be indifferent to enterprises of this kind. That we should contemplate a change of neighbors with extreme uneasiness; and that a due balance on our borders is not less desirable to us, than a balance of power in Europe has always appeared to them. We wish to be neutral, and we will be so, *if they will execute the treaty* [of 1783] *fairly and attempt no conquests adjoining us.* The first condition is just: the second imposes no hardship on them. They cannot complain that the other dominions of Spain would be so narrow as not to leave them room enough for conquest. If the war takes place, we would really wish to be quieted on these two points, offering in turn an honorable neutrality. More than this, they are not to expect.[54]

This note is interesting in several respects. Here the No-Transfer principle is stated in much less equivocal terms than in the memorandum of July 12. Not only did Jefferson close the door on any possibility of an Anglo–American alliance, which reveals the element of bluff in his instructions to Carmichael and Short, but his assertion that the British government could not count on neutrality of the United States if they chose to disregard American rights and interests backs his No-Transfer statement with a definite threat of force. Jefferson consciously applied the concept of balance of power to this situation, recognizing the analogy between the fundamental security policy of Britain and the emerging No-Transfer idea here. Furthermore he advanced his second condition to Britain not as a claim of right but as an assertion of interest, which it was. Finally, his compla-

---

54. Jefferson to Morris (Aug. 12, 1790), ibid., pp. 224–25. Jefferson's italics.

cency before the possibility of British conquest of other Spanish colonies in the New World illustrates how restricted in extent and particular in application the No-Transfer concept still was. It was in no sense a hemispheric security policy in 1790. Jefferson strictly limited it to European territories adjacent to the United States.

There remains a final episode in the formulation of American policy during the Nootka crisis—that of the well-known "queries" put by President Washington on August 27 to the Vice President, the Chief Justice of the Supreme Court, and members of his Cabinet as to the course to follow in the event that Lord Dorchester asked permission to march troops across American territory against Louisiana, or in case he marched without asking.[55]

Washington took care to suggest what the full strategic implications of such a request from Dorchester would be, since New Orleans would undoubtedly be the ultimate objective: "The *consequences* of having so formidable and enterprising a people as the British on both our flanks and rear, with their navy in front, as they respect our western settlements which may be seduced thereby, as they regard the security of the Union and its commerce with the West Indies, are too obvious to need enumeration."[56] Actually, all the evidence now available makes it appear unlikely that an overland expedition against New Orleans was ever contemplated by Britain in 1790; only combined operations of land and sea forces from the Gulf were considered.

The Secretary of State and the Chief Justice responded the following day. Jefferson's letter was framed along the lines of his July 12 memorandum and emphasized strongly that a transfer of Louisiana and the Floridas must be pre-

---

55. Washington's letter and all the replies are conveniently printed in W. C. Ford, *The United States and Spain in 1790* (Brooklyn, 1890), pp. 43–106.

56. Ibid., p. 43.

vented at all costs, including war. He again counseled delaying entry into the war as long as possible, and in reference to the hypothetical Dorchester request advised giving no answer, reserving the question for future action.[57]

John Jay recommended consenting to the passage as preferable to suffering humiliation or being forced into a war by refusal which would be disregarded, particularly since Britain actually controlled the region involved, though it was ours by right. So impressed was the Chief Justice by the unpreparedness of the United States for war that he considered it better temporarily to let Britain take the Floridas, though he admitted "the danger of permitting any nation so to preponderate, as to endanger the security of others," which had "introduced into . . . politics the idea of preserving a balance of power."[58]

On August 29 John Adams and Henry Knox submitted their opinions. The Vice President argued that truly neutral conduct left no alternative but refusal; consent would constitute an injury to Spain. Defiance of our refusal must be dealt with by negotiation rather than a certainly disastrous war, but negotiation would have to await an exchange of regular diplomatic representatives.[59]

The Secretary of War counseled refusal, but without the threat or application of force. Knox felt Spain would not declare war unless joined by France, and in this case the United States might be forced to honor its commitments under the alliance of 1778. Meanwhile war should be avoided, mainly because it would involve the loss of our foreign commerce and consequently the destruction of Hamilton's fiscal policies.[60]

Hamilton delayed his reply until September 15, and then submitted a lengthy document, partly a legal analysis, partly

57. Ibid., pp. 56–58.
58. Ibid., pp. 50–55.
59. Ibid., pp. 45–49.
60. Ibid., pp. 103–6.

an essay in the principles of *Realpolitik* applied to the position in which the United States found itself. It contained no specific recommendation but explored the advantages and disadvantages connected with either consent or refusal. Admitting fully the danger inherent in encirclement by Britain, Hamilton argued that Spain was no less intractable on the Mississippi question than Britain would be, and that the only ultimate solution was the expulsion of all foreign power from the river mouth. Meanwhile, refusal alone would not hinder Dorchester from his designs, and war was undesirable. Hamilton argued at some length against the notion that this nation owed something to Spain for her aid during the revolution, stressing that in any case a nation must consult its interests, not sentiments, in matters of foreign policy. If consent were given to Dorchester, some attempt ought to be made to attach conditions, such as free navigation and the cession of New Orleans. In any case, consent ought to be accomplished by a "candid intimation that the expedition is not agreeable to us, but that thinking it expedient to avoid an occasion of controversy, it has been concluded not to withhold consent."[61]

The prevailing tone of all these communications is a pervasive conviction of weakness—a belief that the United States must for the time being avoid war at almost any cost. Actually, of course, Dorchester lacked the forces to launch the attack Washington feared, and in fact was concerned for the safety of his own border outposts. Under these circumstances, if the Nootka crisis had resulted in war Jefferson's strong statement of opposition to the transfer of Louisiana to England might have produced favorable results, provided no British counterthreat revealed the irresolution beneath it.

The deliberations provoked by the Nootka crisis represent the first general consideration of security policies

61. Ibid., pp. 68–100.

undertaken by the government of the United States, and they reflect emerging patterns of strategic thinking which were to serve as fundamental precepts in the future. The instinctive choice of neutrality in 1790 was not simply an admission of a temporary inability to make war, but grew out of a deep-seated aversion to becoming once again entangled in European wars alien to American interests, and out of a desire to be left alone to pursue the arts of peace in a bountiful land. So long as there were European possessions on its borders, the United States could not be indifferent to shifting combinations of power across the Atlantic which might directly affect its security, but as the Nootka crisis revealed, alliances were considered with extreme reluctance, and only to ward off dire calamity. The long-range aim of American diplomacy was the displacement of European sovereignty in North America entirely—continental expansion always had strategic overtones—and later on in South America as well, but meanwhile policy was directed toward preserving the colonial *status quo* or improving upon it. This meant if possible maintaining a balance of rival powers on our borders, preventing the displacement of a weak power by a stronger one, and remaining free of any engagements that would worsen our bargaining position when and if European conditions offered opportunities for the New World to "fatten on the follies of the old."

The No-Transfer policy took articulate though still rather tentative shape in the Nootka crisis as the keystone of this emerging grand strategy of American diplomacy. It was essentially a defensive policy—preventive diplomacy designed to guard against a contingent threat to the national security by a shift in or the destruction of the American balance of power. In the tumultuous years before the Hemisphere was virtually freed of European colonies the No-Transfer policy received many significant applications, not the least important of which was the fight to prevent the retrocession of Louisiana to Napoleonic France.

CHAPTER 2

The Federalists and Louisiana

The Nootka crisis was like the roll of distant thunder on a summer's day, threatening a storm that failed to come. But the real storm came soon enough. Beginning in 1792 a generation of tempestuous wars descended on the Old World, during which a shifting coalition of powers led by Britain grappled with the inspired armies of the French Republic and Empire which threatened to make themselves the masters of Europe.

The United States was determined from the outset to avoid involvement in the struggle, but after British entry extended the war to the high seas, the American desire to earn maximum profits from neutral carriage collided with the attempts by both major belligerents to achieve command of the sea. Controversies over conflicting interpretations of the laws of maritime warfare eventually contributed to the involvement of the United States in hostilities first with France in 1798 and later with England in 1812. Two fundamental objectives of American foreign policy, non-entanglement in the affairs of Europe and the promotion of foreign commerce, proved to be incompatible with each other under the stresses of world conflict, and each was compromised in turn.

Nor was neutrality entirely consistent with national security and the desire for territorial expansion. On the continent of North America the embroilment of Europe re-opened the momentous question of successorship to the declining power of Spain in the Mississippi Valley, the Floridas, and finally all of Spanish America. Once again, as in the great colonial wars of the past, the fate of regions vital to the peace and prosperous development of the American states depended on events in Europe. During the first decade of war, as rumors of revived French interest in American colonies gave way to the awful certainty that Spain had indeed retroceded Louisiana to Napoleonic France, the problem of devising means to prevent actual transfer of the province gradually emerged as the principal concern of American diplomacy.

Implementation of the No-Transfer principle in respect to Louisiana again raised questions which involved the entire future direction of American foreign policy. Should this nation attempt to uphold the policy independently or should it seek alliances? Should the principal reliance be placed on negotiation or on preclusive occupation by United States forces? If the latter, should the areas be permanently annexed to the Union? Would the Constitution permit this?

Resolution of these problems was complicated by the appearance on the American scene of organized political parties whose differences of opinion extended equally to matters of domestic and foreign policy. One fundamental distinction between Hamiltonian Federalists and Jeffersonian Republicans in the realm of foreign affairs lay in their attitudes toward the French Revolution. News of the revolution had at first been greeted with enthusiasm by nearly all Americans, who felt that the nation which had done most to support their own struggle for liberty was now paying them the additional compliment of imitation. Such unanimity on the subject of France was destined to be short-lived. Conservatives in the United States were shocked and repelled by the regicide, by the bloody excesses of the Paris mob, and by the ominous aggressiveness of French foreign policy. Opposed to any extension of democracy at home, and inclined to place the protection of property among the first purposes of government, the Federalists divined in Jacobinism the satanic shape of mob rule, godlessness, and social disintegration. Conversely, England, in whose aristocratic government they found so much to admire and on whose trade with the United States the success of the funding system depended, emerged in the Federalist view as the last citadel of traditional values, to be supported by every means consistent with American interests.

Jefferson and his party, on the other hand, took no such melancholy view of human nature. Convinced of the capacity of mankind for self-government, they explained the Reign of Terror as a temporary reaction to the sudden destruction of the old, repressive social order and confidently awaited the ultimate triumph of reason in France. The Republicans were not slavishly devoted to the cause of France any more than the Federalists were to that of England— both placed American interests foremost—but they were resolutely opposed to war with France or alliance with Britain except in the last extremity, and they abandoned their belief in the fundamental good will of France toward the United States with considerable reluctance and only in the presence of incontrovertible evidence to the contrary. Their education began with the affair of Citizen Genet, which threatened the transfer of Louisiana to France.

CITIZEN EDMOND GENET

Long before Genet's arrival in the United States, evidence of a renewed French interest in the colony ceded to Spain in 1763 was filtering in. In January 1789 Comte de Moustier, La Luzerne's successor as minister from France to

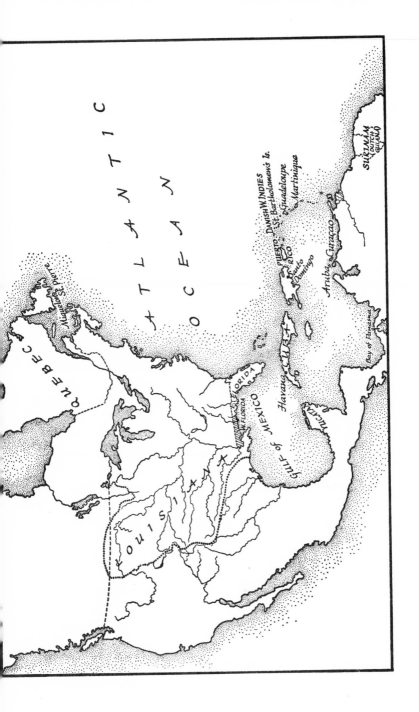

QUEBEC

Miquelon St. Pierre

A T L A N T I C

O C E A N

L O U I S I A N A

E. FLORIDA
W. FLORIDA

GULF of MEXICO

Havana CUBA

YUCATAN

Bay of Panama

DANISH W. INDIES
St. Bartholomew's Is.
Guadeloupe
Martinique

PUERTO RICO
Santo Domingo

Aruba Curaçao

SURINAM
DUTCH GUIANA

the United States, penned a lengthy memorandum to his government in which he set forth the economic and political advantages of repossessing Louisiana.[1] Jefferson, then Secretary of State, knew something of the contents of this document, and he alluded to it briefly in his instructions to Short in Spain during the Nootka crisis, though without expression of alarm at the idea.[2]

There was occasion for real anxiety soon enough, when in 1792 the French government initiated informal conversations with England in an effort to persuade that nation not to join the coalition forming against revolutionary France. One of the inducements offered by France was the prospect of partitioning Spain's empire in the New World. When these negotiations broke down, the French turned to the omnipresent Miranda, giving serious consideration to the projects he had advanced to Pitt in 1790.[3]

During the weeks while Edmond Genet was preparing to depart for his post as Minister to the United States, Paris buzzed with talk of extending the revolution to the Americas as soon as the expected war with Spain and England should begin.[4] Brissot de Warville, the most prominent

---

1. E. W. Lyon has published the outline of this memorandum and the full text of important parts of it in the *Mississippi Valley Historical Review*, 22 (1935), 251–66. For a general discussion of French interest in Louisiana see the same author's *Louisiana in French Diplomacy, 1759–1804*, Norman, Okla., 1935.

2. Jefferson to Short (Aug. 10, 1790), Lipscomb and Bergh, eds., *Writings of Thomas Jefferson, 8*, 78: "The Count de Moustier, during his residence with us, conceived the project of again engaging France in a colony upon our continent, and . . . he directed his views to some of the country on the Mississippi, and obtained and communicated a good deal of matter on the subject to his court."

3. Robertson, *The Life of Miranda*, chap. 6.

4. For the background of Genet's mission see F. J. Turner, "The Origins of Genet's Projected Attack on Louisiana and the Floridas," *American Historical Review, 3* (1898), 650–71.

Girondist leader, had been in America and favored the idea of liberation, as did France's great general, Dumouriez. Thomas Paine and a group of American expatriates chorused their encouragement. It is not surprising, therefore, that Genet's instructions ordered him to establish close relations with the government of the United States with a view to forwarding this plan.[5] The first moves were to be made in North America—beginning with New Orleans—as a prelude to the general liberation of Spanish America and the opening of its commerce to the allies. Free navigation of the Mississippi and the acquisition of Canada were to be offered as bait for the United States. Should the government at Philadelphia not fall in with his proposals, Genet was authorized to deal directly with the inhabitants of Kentucky to organize attacks on territories adjacent to the United States.

For the American government to have given countenance to this scheme, or to have permitted Genet to fit out privateers in American ports as he was also instructed to do, would obviously have been unneutral. France, in fact, wished the United States to remain neutral, so that American ships could supply the French West Indies after the British navy made its inevitable sweep of the French merchant marine. Therefore, the attacks were to assume the guise of spontaneous revolts among "inhabitants" of the Spanish colonies, recruited from the trans-Allegheny frontier with the connivance of the United States government.

President Washington ultimately frustrated these plans by his refusal secretly to tailor his neutrality policy to suit the purposes of France. Resolved to do justice to France, he had early in 1793 against Hamilton's advice supported Jefferson's contention that the new French envoy should be received without reservations, and that the French alliance

5. Ibid., pp. 657–58.

could not honorably be repudiated. But Washington was equally determined that the United States should not become entangled in the European war, and on April 22, 1793, issued a proclamation warning American citizens against unneutral actions.

The attitude of the Secretary of State was not so rigidly impartial. On February 20, 1793, some weeks before Genet's arrival, Jefferson had a talk with Colonel W. S. Smith, lately returned from France, who informed him in a general way of the French designs on lower Louisiana and Mexico, and who gave it as his understanding that France would not object if the United States took the Floridas.[6] Jefferson wrote to his commissioners in Spain revoking the offer he had made during the Nootka crisis to guarantee Spanish possessions in North America.[7] Presumably, he expected Louisiana to become independent—one sentence in the instruction suggests this—but if so it is difficult to account for his explicit prohibition of an American guarantee of Louisiana and the Floridas, either against independence or "indeed against any other nation." What "other nation" except France might take Louisiana? In like circumstances Jefferson had feared British encirclement in 1790, but for the present he was sufficiently persuaded of French benevolence to be able to view with equanimity the prospect of the transfer of Louisiana to that nation. This attitude was destined to change in time.

Genet landed in Charleston on April 8, 1793, and before he had even presented his credentials at Philadelphia busily engaged himself in carrying out his instructions. He placed Mangourit, the French consul at Charleston, in charge of plans for an expedition against the Floridas under the leadership of Elijah Clarke of Georgia, and arranged for the

6. P. L. Ford, ed., *Writings of Thomas Jefferson, 1*, 216.
7. Jefferson to Carmichael and Short (March 23, 1793), ibid., *6*, 206.

fitting out of privateers for France. Small wonder that when
he arrived in Philadelphia a month later he was coolly received. Only in Jefferson could he perceive any warmth.
The Secretary of State was indignant at the "pusillanimous"
neutrality proclamation, which Hamilton had drafted, and
considered it as evidence of the latter's desire to "make a
part in the confederacy of princes against human liberty."
France appeared to Jefferson to be a magnanimous nation
which "offers everything and asks nothing."[8]

Washington, however, could not be budged from his
policy of strict neutrality by Genet's arguments, and soon
the French envoy turned to intrigue and to direct appeals to
the American people over the heads of their government.
Conditions were not unfavorable to the success of these
tactics. Sympathy for France and hatred for Spain were
strong among the men of the western waters, and their
loyalty to the federal government had not been strengthened
by its excise taxes and its lack of success in opening the
Mississippi. George Rogers Clark responded to Genet's call
to arms, and there were many who were prepared to follow
him against Spain. French propaganda found ready listeners
among creoles in New Orleans who had never resigned
themselves to Spanish rule, and among French Canadian
malcontents.

Jefferson did not approve of Genet's highly improper
activities and wrote to Monroe that he was doing everything
in his power to "moderate the impetuosity of his movements, and to destroy the dangerous opinion which has been
excited in him . . . that the people of the United States will
disavow the acts of their government."[9] Nevertheless, a
week later when Genet unfolded to him as "Mr. Jefferson"
and "not as Secretary of State" his instructions to the French

8. Jefferson to Madison (May 19, 1793), Lipscomb and Bergh, 9,
96–98.
9. Jefferson to Monroe (June 28, 1793), ibid., p. 144.

botanist Michaux for forwarding the attack on Louisiana by American backwoodsmen and his appeal to the French Canadians to revolt, Jefferson's only remonstrance was against "putting halters around the necks" of American officers and soldiers who would be violating United States neutrality.[10] Furthermore, Jefferson rewrote at this time, without changing the date, an earlier letter of introduction for Michaux to Governor Shelby of Kentucky, although he now knew the Frenchman's journey was not the innocent "botanical expedition" he had previously thought it.

Jefferson's disloyalty to Washington's neutrality policy on this occasion is indefensible, but his apparent disregard of the security threat posed by a possible French expedition against New Orleans requires some explanation, especially in view of his stated opposition to retrocession when he was President in 1802. In the first place, he assumed that the attacking force would rendezvous outside the territory of the United States, technically preserving neutrality. Moreover, there was reason to believe, in the summer of 1793, that war with Spain was imminent.[11] Spanish intransigence on matters of the boundary and navigation of the Mississippi, combined with attacks by Spain's Indian allies on American settlements, had produced the belief that Spain meant to provoke hostilities. On June 14, 1793, President Washington even went so far as to request a military intelligence report on the strength and disposition of Spanish forces in the Floridas.[12] The possibility of war may have made the preservation of neutrality seem less important to Jefferson.

The Secretary of State also believed that the French in-

10. Memo of conversation with Genet (July 5, 1793), P. L. Ford, *1*, 236.

11. Jefferson thought it "inevitable": Jefferson to Madison (June 23, 1793), Lipscomb and Bergh, p. 139.

12. Secret letter to the Secretary of War (Henry Knox), *GW, 32,* 502.

tended to set up an independent state in Louisiana.[13] The evidence in French archives reveals no final decision as to the ultimate disposition of Louisiana, although any American statesman who gambled that the French would not keep it for themselves was taking a long chance.[14]

Genet's persistent misconduct caused Washington to request his recall and to take strong precautions against any expedition against neighboring territories. Jefferson had already deserted Genet, realizing that the inevitable result of his activities would be to force the United States into the war on the side of France. The new Jacobin government at Paris repudiated and replaced Genet, but, as we shall see, did not abandon the idea of repossessing Louisiana for France.

THE SHADOW OF WAR WITH FRANCE, 1795–1800

The announcement of Jay's Treaty with England marked the beginning of a serious deterioration in Franco–American relations which lasted for five years. This treaty, which was barely acceptable to the United States Senate because of Jay's failure to receive assurances of future British respect for neutral rights as interpreted by the United States, was anathema to the French government, which was relying heavily on American neutral carriage for vital supplies. France chose to treat Jay's Treaty not as a more or less uneasy compromise of maritime principles consented to under imperious necessity in exchange for substantial benefits on the boundary question, but as a deliberate violation of the provisions of the Franco–American treaty of 1778, which

13. P. L. Ford, ed., *1*, 236.
14. F. J. Turner, "The Policy of France toward the Mississippi Valley in the Period of Washington and Adams," *American Historical Review, 10* (1905), 261.

had defined neutral rights liberally. Worried at any signs of Anglo–American rapprochement and determined to bend American policy to French desires, France resorted to naval practices which outdid those of Britain in outrage, and cast about for other means to bring the independent United States to heel. To this end the French government relied partly on officious meddling in American domestic affairs, such as their insolent attempts to prevent the ratification of Jay's Treaty or their efforts to bring about the defeat of Federalist candidates. At the same time one of the most persistent arguments at Paris in favor of rebuilding the French empire in North America was the possibility it would offer of influencing the policies of the United States. French control of Mississippi navigation would be a tourniquet on the main artery of American trade; the slightest pressure would bring an instantaneous response to French demands. The United States might in that way be fashioned into the dependable puppet that French policy required. This line of reasoning was known and feared in America, and concern over the possibility that France might replace Spain at New Orleans is a leitmotiv running through all the disputes with France during the period. In truth, the sovereign independence of the United States was at hazard.

In 1795 it seemed for a brief interval that the Mississippi question had been at least temporarily laid to rest by Pinckney's Treaty with Spain, which accorded satisfaction to the United States on the boundary, the right to navigate the Mississippi, and maritime principles. Hopes raised by the treaty proved premature, however, for Spain delayed execution of its terms for over two years, under circumstances which seemed to point to France as supporting villain in the piece.

As far as Manuel de Godoy was concerned, the concessions he granted in his treaty with Pinckney were a bone thrown to the Americans to keep them pacified while he was engaged in the delicate and dangerous feat of changing sides in the European war. At Basel in 1795 he concluded a separate peace with France, deserting Britain, and in the autumn of the following year went all the way by declaring war on his former ally. The British, he correctly surmised, would not be pleased at this turn of events, and he sought to guard his flank by satisfying American demands so that the Yankees would be less tempted to join Britain in an attack on the Spanish possessions in North America. If he had to live up to his promises in Pinckney's Treaty he would do so, though reluctantly, to keep the United States neutral; if he could get away with not fulfilling these newly assumed obligations, covering his noncompliance with a thick fog of litigious casuistry, so much the better. This was, after all, the kind of diplomacy at which Spaniards had been taught by adversity to excel.

After Basel, Spain became in American eyes little more than a satellite of France, a situation which enhanced fears in the United States that Spain would be persuaded or forced to transfer Louisiana and the Floridas. These fears were not unjustified. At Basel, the French negotiator, Barthélemy, was instructed to get Louisiana for his country as the price of peace, but Godoy would yield only the Spanish half of Hispaniola. From 1795 to 1798 the French government constantly pressed Spain to cede Louisiana, and demanded West Florida as well. France argued that she needed these lands to supply her West Indian islands, so as to relieve them of their dependence on the United States, and to provide a base for their defense. Retrocession, the French pointed out, would also relieve Spain of the expense of guarding her frontier against American backwoodsmen. France in Louisiana would be, in Talleyrand's phrase, a "wall of brass" erected between Western aggressiveness and the riches of Mexico. Most of these arguments eventually reached American ears, and their effect was not calming.

Godoy was probably willing to part with Louisiana at any time after Pinckney's Treaty, provided he could exact a large-enough price, but the insubstantial offers which the Directory made were satisfactory neither to him nor to Urquijo, who succeeded him early in 1798.[15] Spanish diplomatists continued to fence skillfully with French negotiators while glancing nervously over their shoulders for signs of an Anglo–American concert against their North American possessions.

There was ample room for concern on this score. The persistent crisis in Franco–American relations played into the hands of the anglophiles who now composed Washington's Cabinet. The Secretary of State was Timothy Pickering, one of the high priests of New England Federalism, who had been appointed because no one better qualified could be found to accept the position. Pickering yielded to none in his hatred for France or his admiration of England, and looked to Hamilton for guidance in matters of policy. So also did the Secretary of War, James McHenry, and Oliver Wolcott, who had succeeded Hamilton as Secretary of the Treasury when the latter retired from public office, if not from politics. These men, who later served in President Adams' Cabinet as well, were important agents in effecting a closer alignment of American and British policies, and one of their most useful instruments was the widespread suspicion of French designs in Louisiana.

During the early fall of 1796 warnings of renewed French activity in Louisiana and Canada reached Philadelphia from American representatives abroad. From his listening-post at The Hague, John Quincy Adams informed his father, the Vice President, of new French negotiations for the retrocession of Louisiana, to be paid for by returning Santo

15. A. P. Whitaker, "The Retrocession of Louisiana in Spanish Policy," *American Historical Review, 39* (1934), 454–76.

Domingo to Spain.[16] Coupled with this, news of the appointment of Mangourit, Genet's former lieutenant, to replace Adet as minister to the United States seemed to indicate a sinister threat to American interests.[17] At Paris, Monroe heard similar rumors, and sounded out members of the Directory on their aims in Louisiana and Canada. The answers were hardly reassuring. He was told that France had no designs on Canada for herself but wished it independent; as for Louisiana, France would take it only in case of war between Britain and Spain, to prevent Britain from getting it.[18]

Not only did war soon break out between Britain and Spain to make this possibility come alive, but Franco–American relations took an abrupt turn for the worse when France dramatically severed relations on the eve of the American presidential elections in an attempt to frighten voters into defeating the Federalists. John Quincy Adams even suspected that the real cause of the rupture went deeper, and that it was connected with a projected attack on Canada and possession of New Orleans by France.[19]

These reports from abroad, together with the evidences of French hostility at home, evoked fresh statements of the No-Transfer principle. A few days before he left office President Washington suggested to the Secretary of State that Spain be warned of American opposition to the transfer to

16. J. Q. Adams to John Adams (Aug. 13, 1796), W. C. Ford, ed., *Writings of John Quincy Adams* (7 vols. New York, 1913–17), 2, 20.

17. Ibid., p. 19. Monroe at Paris argued successfully against the appointment of Mangourit.

18. Monroe to Pickering (Aug. 27, Sept. 10, 21, 1796), W. R. Manning, ed., *Diplomatic Correspondence of the United States: Canadian Relations, 1784–1860* (3 vols. Washington, Carnegie Endowment for International Peace, 1940–43), *1*, 475–77 (cited as Manning, *CR*).

19. J. Q. Adams to Pickering, Oct. 16, 1796, W. C. Ford, ed., *Writings of Adams, 2*, 31 n.

France of her possessions adjoining us, and inquired: "might it not be advisable to let Mr. Pinckney know how unpleasant to this country it would be, that the French should be possessed of Louisiana and the Floridas."[20] Pickering thought it would also be well to advise Rufus King, the American minister at London, of this policy, and did so the following day.[21] These instructions were in the nature of standing orders to do whatever was possible to prevent the French from becoming neighbors, without any indication of how far the United States was prepared to go in support of the policy. Clearly it was hoped that warnings would suffice.

Shortly after John Adams assumed office on March 4, 1797, ominous signs made it clear that France was not yet prepared to modify her policies toward the United States. General C. C. Pinckney, sent to Paris to replace Monroe, was not received, and after news of Adams' election reached France the American envoy was ordered out of the country. The rupture was complete. Adams determined to give negotiation another try and sent John Marshall and Elbridge Gerry to join Pinckney in a special mission to France, but he also took steps to prepare for war, if it should come to that.

Meanwhile, Federalist indignation against France was fired by evidence confirming the existence of the long-suspected French plot to incite a revolt in Canada. Rufus King had written Pickering in December 1796 about British seizure of a shipload of arms purchased on the continent by Ira Allen of Vermont, which were thought to be destined

20. Washington to Pickering (Feb. 14, 1797), *GW, 32, 328.*
21. Pickering to King (Feb. 15, 1797), Manning, *CR, 1, 101–2.* The transfer of eastern Santo Domingo to France in 1795 brought no objections from the United States. It was not until 1808 that the No-Transfer principle was extended beyond the continent, and then the object was Cuba.

for Canada.[22] The following spring news arrived from Quebec of the arrest of two Americans who were part of a French conspiracy to preach sedition among the Canadians.[23] Pickering glimpsed the outlines of a monstrous reversion to the strategic situation of 1756:

> The discovery corresponds with prior facts and circumstances indicating the designs of France to repossess Canada, by a force from Europe, an insurrection of the Canadians, and aid from numerous adherents in the United States. . . . We are not without apprehensions that France means to regain Louisiana, and to renew the ancient plan of her monarchs of *circumscribing* and encircling what now constitute the Atlantic States. To the execution of such a plan so dangerous to our union and peace, every real American must be firmly opposed.[24]

Pickering asserted his belief in this letter that none but a few "desperate adventurers" among Americans could be recruited by France for such schemes, but he was whistling in the dark, for the recent revelation of the "Blount Conspiracy" had demonstrated how restive the frontiersmen still were under the continued closure of the Mississippi. This affair concerned the project of a certain Chisholm for an attack by American backwoodsmen on Louisiana with British financial aid. The British minister at Philadelphia, Robert Liston, sent Chisholm to London to unfold his plan, but the home government gave it no support. The Spanish minister, Yrujo, got wind of the affair from General Collot, who had himself been recently engaged in a not unexcep-

22. King to Pickering (Dec. 15, 1796), Manning, *CR, 1,* 478.
23. Documents relating to the Canadian plot are to be found in Douglas Brymner, ed., *Report on Canadian Archives for 1891* (Ottawa, 1892), Note D.
24. Pickering to King (June 20, 1797), Manning, *CR, 1,* 111–12.

tionable tour of exploration of the Mississippi Valley arranged for by the French minister Adet, in anticipation of the hoped-for acquisition of Louisiana by France. Yrujo seized upon the Chisholm plot as a further justification for Spain's failure to evacuate the Mississippi posts as required by Pinckney's Treaty. Pickering accepted Liston's denials of British complicity and proceeded to engage Yrujo heavily in an epistolary duel on the subject of Spain's unfulfilled obligations.[25]

Spain's stubborn refusal to open the Mississippi or to run the new boundary aroused Federalist tempers to fever pitch and led them to the conclusion that France must be behind it all. Rufus King saw in Spain's attitude evidence that Louisiana had already been ceded to France.[26] Pickering must have agreed that France was the key, for during conversations with Yrujo he pressed questions about the status of Louisiana with such warmth that the Spanish minister was moved to send off worried dispatches to his government, warning that if retrocession were contemplated it must be kept a profound secret until France could occupy the province with a sizable force, for the Federalist administration was prepared to go to war rather than to permit the transfer to take place.[27]

Under the pressure of mounting difficulties with France and her Spanish ally, the No-Transfer principle was subtly acquiring a more militant cast. It was also beginning to

25. Liston's letter introducing Chisholm to Lord Grenville (March 16, 1797) reveals that it was concern over the possible transfer of Louisiana to France that moved him to refer the project home. He felt that temporary, preclusive occupation of Louisiana by England might be advantageous; see F. J. Turner, "Documents on the Blount Conspiracy," *American Historical Review*, 10 (1905), 582.

26. King to Pickering (Aug. 5, 1797), C. R. King, ed., *Life and Correspondence of Rufus King* (6 vols. New York, 1894–1900), pp. 208–9.

27. Yrujo to Godoy (July 20, 1797), cited in A. P. Whitaker, *The Mississippi Question, 1795–1803* (New York, 1934), p. 122.

figure strongly in partisan politics. Chafing for an excuse for war with France, the Federalists discovered in the retrocession question the means they sought to seduce the Republican West from its pro-French sympathies. After 1797 they lost no opportunity to raise the specter of the "Gallic Peril" at New Orleans, attempting, not without sporadic success, to steal the West from Jefferson by arrogating to themselves the role of chief defender of the right to free navigation of the Mississippi. Not that the Republicans for a moment relaxed in their support of the frontiersmen's principal objective, but the means by which they proposed to gain it were pallid beside those of the Federalists. Hamilton and his followers declared that the time for negotiation, for talk, was past, and preached a war of conquest against France's ally. In July 1797 "Peter Porcupine," the Federalist editor, sounded the new note with unmistakable clarity: "A war with Spain is absolutely necessary to the salvation of this country, if a war with France takes place, or if the Spaniards have ceded Louisiana to France. They must both be driven into the Gulf of Mexico, or we shall never sleep in peace."[28] When, a few months later, hostilities with France actually began, the Federalist policy of preclusive conquest of Louisiana emerged full-blown.

THE UNDECLARED WAR WITH FRANCE

John Adams' dogged determination to exhaust every means for a peaceful settlement of the disputes with France before resorting to force eventually dealt the death blow to his party's hopes for war and popular support, but the President was not unrealistically optimistic about the results his special mission might produce. On January 24, 1798, before any word had arrived from Marshall, Pinckney,

28. *Porcupine's Works, 6,* 123 n., cited in Whitaker, p. 121.

and Gerry, he consulted his Cabinet on the policy to be followed in case of war with France.[29] Only the answer of the Secretary of War survives, but it is most important because it reflects the ideas of Hamilton, to whom McHenry submitted the President's queries for fear he himself might make "poor or dangerous recommendations."[30] Hamilton considered war with France undesirable at the moment, because the people opposed it and because there was no territory to be gained from it. Spain should be pressed, but not to the point of war. The United States must negotiate with France from a position of strength, however, and to that end the army and navy ought to be enlarged, the latter perhaps with British assistance, and merchantmen should be armed and authorized to capture French armed vessels, while the treaties with France should be abrogated. It will be seen that this was exactly the course of action actually adopted after the "XYZ affair."

Hamilton approved of cooperation with Britain, but was strongly opposed to an alliance with that power, and his reasons illustrate how qualified in fact his anglophilism was. The British Isles were in peril of invasion by Bonaparte's armies and might fall, he thought, in which case we should be better off not to be entangled in their fate. It was in their interest to cooperate with us in any case, and we should seek no agreement except that all territory to the east of the Mississippi River must be ours. Thus Hamilton advised using a crisis with France to stake out a claim to the Floridas and New Orleans, but without any definite plan for acquiring them. It was not long before he supplied this omission.

Word of Talleyrand's insulting attempt to extort a bribe for peace with the United States reached Adams on March

29. C. F. Adams, ed., *Works of John Adams, 8,* 561–62.
30. McHenry to Adams (Feb. 15, 1798), B. C. Steiner, *Life and Correspondence of James McHenry* (Cleveland, 1907), pp. 291–95.

4, 1798, and on March 16 he revealed it to the nation in the famous "XYZ" message. The war fever that swept the nation following this news carried Hamilton's program into effect, but there was no declaration of war against France, although some engagements between American and French armed vessels occurred on the high seas. The Federalists found themselves in the novel situation of being almost popular, but could not capitalize on their good fortune by leading the nation into a full-fledged war. The President and Republican members of Congress opposed any such drastic step, and besides there was no way to attack French territory. No way, that is, except by attacking Spain, France's ally.

Godoy, however, had just deprived them of this opportunity. At the end of February, Spain informed the United States that it would execute the terms of Pinckney's Treaty, and by the end of March the posts were in American hands and trade on the Mississippi reopened. The West relaxed, remained loyal to the Republican party, and supported Adams' future attempts at a negotiated settlement of Franco–American disputes.

The Federalists didn't give up easily. On March 25, Pickering had an inspiration which he communicated to Hamilton: "What ought we to do in respect to Louisiana . . .? Perhaps those orders [to evacuate the posts] may have resulted from Spain's seeing or fearing the necessity of ceding Louisiana to France, and hence concluding that she might as well do a grateful thing to us before the surrender. . . . The Spanish force in Louisiana is small."[31] Here was a way of keeping the Mississippi question politically alive in the West. Whether one argued, as Rufus King had the previous December, that France was to blame for Spanish obstinacy,

31. Pickering to Hamilton (March 25, 1798), J. C. Hamilton, ed., *Works of Hamilton, 6,* 275–76, cited in Whitaker, *Mississippi Question,* p. 119.

or as Pickering now did that France was behind Spanish yielding, the important thing was not to lose sight of the fact that France controlled Spain and that France sought the transfer of Louisiana.[32] The way to prevent transfer, Pickering suggested, was to attack before France could occupy the province.

This course of direct action offered a solution not only to a tactical problem in domestic politics but also to a familiar security problem in foreign policy. The fruits of war against France would be territorial expansion on the continent at the expense of Spain. Under ordinary circumstances there was no need to seize New Orleans from Spain; the day was not far off when that weak power could be easily dislodged, and the United States could afford to wait. But France, the greatest land power in the world, aggressive and overbearing, was another matter. The end Pickering sought was not new. It was the grand design of ridding North America of European influence. But the means he chose—preclusive conquest in the face of a highly contingent danger—were certainly novel.

Pickering enlarged on his views a week later when he instructed Rufus King in London on the policy to be pursued in case of war with France.[33] The United States considered an alliance with Britain to be inexpedient, but looked toward a concert of measures in certain operations. Specifically, King was to ask if Britain would "lend, or sell on credit" six ships of the line, or perhaps six frigates, and

32. It is quite probable that by this time Liston had shown to Pickering intercepted dispatches of Fauchet and Adet, French Ministers to the U.S., in which they urged the acquisition of Louisiana by France for the purpose of influencing American policy. Liston had these documents as early as Nov. 1796. See Brymner, ed., *Report on Canadian Archives for 1891,* Note D, pp. 62–63. See also Whitaker, *Mississippi Question,* p. 119 n.

33. Pickering to King (April 2, 1798), Manning, *CR, 1,* 136–39.

to request that the British squadron on our coasts be strengthened. The *quid pro quo* offered was American protection against a French invasion or insurrection in Canada.

King was also to inform Britain of his government's policy regarding neighboring possessions:

> We have been perfectly satisfied that Spain should hold Louisiana: but we are unwilling that it should be transferred to France: from various considerations . . . we fear the cession may be already made. If we come to a rupture with France, the treaty of alliance between her and Spain will necessarily involve us with the latter: and it may become expedient, perhaps necessary, for us to seize on Louisiana, and West Florida, that we may hold the key to the Western world; without which, our possessions on the waters of the Mississippi and its numerous and extensive branches will lose more than half their value; and to avoid this evil, the inhabitants may be induced to separate from the United States and unite with France, who will doubtless have Louisiana, if we do not prevent them; and this prevention should be an early capture of the Spanish posts, down to the mouths of the Mississippi.[34]

War with France would not, of course, "necessarily involve us" with Spain at all, unless the issue were forced by an American assault on Spanish territory, and this was something France would clearly be interested in avoiding. The woefully undermanned Spanish garrisons at New Orleans and in the Floridas were incapable of defending their own positions, much less of launching a counterattack to carry the war to the Americans. France had much to lose and nothing to gain by calling her ally to arms in a war against the United States.

34. Ibid., p. 138.

Pickering's policy looked less like defense than like cold aggression. He suggested no definition of the circumstances under which United States forces would occupy the "key to the Western world"—no yardstick of degrees of danger. Even assuming, as he did, the probability that France already held title to Louisiana, might not American occupation have been made conditional on news of the expected attack on the British Isles, whose navy could then no longer prevent French operations across the Atlantic? Or at least might not the occupation have been carried out subject to future negotiations on the status of the mouth of the Mississippi? Since the opening of the Mississippi and the evacuation of the posts by Spain, the United States had no legitimate cause for war with that power. No satisfactory proof existed that an imminent transfer of Louisiana to France placed vital American interests in mortal danger. War with France and Spain meant entanglement in the European struggle to the end, at a time when the United States could ill afford the cost, for objectives which might well have been achieved by a bloodless diplomatic victory had diplomacy been tried.

The Federalist leaders were impatient with overnice attention to forms, however, as they ceaselessly sounded the tocsin against the French menace and proclaimed the hoary military dogma that the best defense is the swift offensive.[35] In a series of articles published by the New York *Commercial Advertiser,* using the pen-name "Titus Manlius," Hamilton fanned the flame of public indignation over the XYZ affair with furious denunciations of French depravity. At the same time, however, he presented a characteristically realistic analysis of the interest of the United States in preserving the balance of power in Europe. He defined the

35. King to Hamilton (July 31, 1798), C. R. King, ed., *Life and Correspondence of Rufus King, 2, 375.* Washington to John Trumbull (June 25, 1799), *GW, 37, 250.*

supreme objective of French policy as the destruction of
Great Britain, "which had repeatedly held the balance of
power [in Europe] in opposition to the grasping ambition
of France."[36] Should Britain fall and France become supreme at sea as well as on land, the entire world would become vassals of the new Rome. With Louisiana in French
hands, as it probably already was, Hamilton warned, "the
foundation will be laid for stripping [Spain] of South America and her mines; and perhaps for dismembering the
United States. The magnitude of this mighty mischief is
not easily calculated."[37]

Hamilton acquired a personal stake in war with France
when he was appointed Inspector General and second in
command under Washington of the new army authorized
by Congress in the national emergency. Fired by visions of
the military reputation and glory he had always hungered
for, Hamilton's imagination ranged far beyond the confines
of simple defensive operations to embrace dazzling schemes
for the liberation of the Hemisphere. Rufus King had written Pickering and Hamilton that Miranda was back in
England, where Pitt was once again giving ear to his projects and urged his friends to promote the idea of American
cooperation in them.[38] Hamilton was enthusiastic, but
President Adams remained sturdily opposed to any unnecessary war for chimerical objectives.[39] Military preparations
languished as growing antiwar sentiment came to Adams'
support, but even after the President's decision to send a
fresh mission to France to seek peace, Hamilton did not
entirely abandon his hopes. In June 1799 he described to

36. April 12, 1798, Lodge, ed., *Works of Hamilton, 6,* 282.

37. Ibid., p. 284.

38. King to Pickering (Feb. 7, 1798), C. R. King, ed., *Life and Correspondence, 2,* 281.

39. Ibid., pp. 658–59. C. F. Adams, ed., *Works of John Adams, 8,*
569–72; *10,* 134–58.

the Secretary of War the need for an enlarged military establishment: "Besides eventual security against invasion, we ought certainly to look to the possession of the Floridas and Louisiana, and we ought to squint at South America."[40]

Among the first generation of American statesmen, Alexander Hamilton was the pre-eminent exponent of *Realpolitik,* capable of formulating policies on the coldest calculation of the national interest, stripped bare of sentimentality. His cabinet papers on the occasions of the Nootka crisis in 1790 and the neutrality decision in 1792 are eloquent testimonials to his clear appreciation of the role of power in international affairs and the primacy of self-interest in the conduct of states. Yet in 1798 he failed signally to balance the capacities and interests of the nation and to assess the chances for success of his bold enterprises. His vision clouded by personal ambition, considerations of party, and an unreasoning hatred of France, he would have engaged the nation in a quixotic adventure in Spanish America which could only have ended in disaster. Hamilton possessed remarkable gifts of intellect and energy, but he was humanly fallible. One sees in his enthusiasm for Miranda's schemes the same defects in character—the false sense of honor and the warmth of spirit—which caused him to accept Burr's challenge. If it had not been for John Adams, these qualities might have sealed his country's fate as well as his own.

Secretary of War James McHenry probably knew about the Miranda business, but he was not one of the inner circle in the affair. During the summer of 1798, while talk of cooperation with Britain was prevalent, he became concerned about ensuring American interests at the mouth of the Mississippi, and apparently unaware of Pickering's instructions

40. Hamilton to McHenry (June 27, 1799), Lodge, ed., *Works,* 7, 97.

to King nearly three months before suggested to the Secretary of State that the United States should stake out its claim. "Is it right that measures taken by our government which may eventuate in putting Great Britain in possession of the French West India Islands should be productive of no equivalent to the United States? . . . Ought not Mr. King to inform the British cabinet, without loss of time, that the United States can in no event permit New Orleans to pass from the hands of Spain, unless to become a part of the United States?"[41] McHenry's formulation of the No-Transfer concept is interesting because it was generalized, so far as New Orleans was concerned, to apply to any transfer, to Britain as well as France, and it is clear that he was not without his suspicions of both powers.

McHenry's suggestion in this instance was not acted upon, nor was another noteworthy recommendation he made a short time afterward. Early in November, General Washington raised the question of whether the army had automatic authority to act in case of the transfer of Louisiana and the Floridas to France.[42] McHenry felt that all doubt should be removed, and in his recommendations to President Adams for the annual message he urged that Congress be requested to pass a resolution vesting full power in the President to take possession of Louisiana and the Floridas on behalf of Spain in case of danger of their being seized by France.[43] This is substantially the course actually followed by President Madison in 1810 in connection with East Florida, which led to the famous No-Transfer Resolution of 1811. The phrase "on the behalf of Spain" suggests that McHenry looked upon preclusive occupation largely as

41. McHenry to Pickering (July 22, 1798), Steiner, ed., *Life and Correspondence of James McHenry*, pp. 315–16.
42. Washington to Generals Hamilton and Pinckney (Nov. 10, 1798), *GW, 37*, 14–15.
43. McHenry to Adams (Nov. 25, 1798), Adams, ed., *Works, 8*, 604 n.

a device for protecting American interests while holding the territories in trust for Spain pending a final disposition by peaceful negotiation after the danger had passed.

Expectations of war and hopes for Federalist victory at the polls dimmed, however, when Adams nominated Murray, Ellsworth, and Davie as commissioners to treat with France, and flickered out completely when he peremptorily ordered them off to Paris after months of delay by Pickering. The President had "pulled down the pillars" of Federalism, courageously sacrificing partisan advantage on the altar of peace. The elections of 1800 removed the Federalists from power and elevated to the presidency Thomas Jefferson, the friend of France.

CHAPTER 3

The Republicans and Louisiana

The new President entered upon his duties hopeful of improved relations with France. The previous September Adams' commissioners had concluded with Bonaparte, now First Consul, the Convention of Mortefontaine, which promised to remove all causes of discord arising from French depredations on American commerce. Jefferson confidently slashed the budget for the army and navy to a little over a quarter of the figure reached under Adams, despite the fact that disquieting rumors about the retrocession of Louisiana to France still circulated. These were nothing new, however, and Jefferson saw in them no reason for postponing his measures for reducing the national debt.

Jefferson was due for a rude awakening, because this time the rumors were true. The very day following the Franco–American agreement, Napoleon had struck the bargain with Spain which promised him Louisiana in return for the delivery of the Kingdom of Etruria to the Duke of Parma, kinsman of the Spanish monarchs.

Napoleon was under no illusion that the United States would accept this momentous news gratefully, nor for that matter were the Spanish. Spain was aware of the advantages in economy and security for her other colonies to be gained by trading off her white elephant in North America, but with Spanish Ambassador Yrujo's warnings in mind, the government thought it best not to move until the French were free to direct their whole attention to the New World. Some months before the Treaty of San Ildefonso, the Spanish prime minister outlined his reasons for awaiting the pacification of Europe before ceding Louisiana to France. If this were not done,

> the Americans, who know how important it is that Louisiana should remain in our hands, would prevent the cession and transfer and would even go to the point of declaring war on us, as they have already threatened to do on another occasion when they suspected [retrocession], and nothing would be accomplished but to turn the world upside down again and expose us to a mortal blow in the Americas. On the other hand, if this were arranged at the general peace, the Americans would find themselves without any power to aid them in their designs.[1]

Retrocession, then, was to wait upon the conclusion of peace between France and her enemies, including Britain, so that the United States in its time of great peril would find itself in a position of diplomatic isolation. Although the Treaty of San Ildefonso preceded the French treaties of peace with Austria (Lunéville, Feb. 9, 1801), and with Britain (Amiens, Oct. 1, 1801), Spain safeguarded herself against American wrath by making retrocession secret and also conditional on the fulfillment of terms by France which delayed the actual orders for French occupation another two years. Thus by the time the United States awoke to discover that its nightmare was at last a fact, there was no nation to appeal to for support. It confronted the menace of the French colossus alone, without the prospect of British aid which Adams had enjoyed and, as a result of Jefferson's

1. Urquijo to Muzquiz (June 22, 1800), cited in A. P. Whitaker, "The Retrocession of Louisiana in Spanish Policy," *American Historical Review, 39* (1935), 469–70.

economies, with only a fraction of the military strength he had commanded.

The threat began to assume substantial proportions in the spring of 1801. Back in September David Humphreys, the American minister at Madrid, learning from leaks in Paris newspapers that negotiations for retrocession were in progress, had demanded and secured denials from Urquijo.[2] A dispatch from the United States minister in London, Rufus King, the following March reported a number of circumstances which lent credence to the prevalent opinion that France had at length succeeded in getting Louisiana.[3]

However well-disposed he may have been toward them, Jefferson never wished the French in Louisiana. He considered these portents "very ominous," but seemed unsure that anything could be done about them.[4] Four years before, when the Federalists were just beginning to beat the drum for war, Jefferson had expressed a belief that his old standby, economic coercion, might prevent the cession of Louisiana to France, but now he seemed at a loss for a policy:[5] "We consider her [Spain's] possession of the adjacent country as most favorable to our interests, and should see with extreme pain any other nation substituted for them.... Should France get possession of that country, it will be more to be lamented than remedied by us."[6]

2. Henry Adams, *History of the United States during the Administration of Thomas Jefferson and James Madison* (9 vols. New York, 1889–91), *1*, 368.

3. King to Madison (March 29, 1801), C. R. King, ed., *Life and Correspondence of Rufus King, 3*, 414–15.

4. Jefferson to Monroe (May 26, 1801), P. L. Ford, ed., *Writings, 8*, 58.

5. Jefferson to Thomas Pinckney (May 29, 1797), Lipscomb and Bergh, eds., *Writings, 9*, 388.

6. Jefferson to Governor W. C. C. Claiborne of the Mississippi Territory (July 13, 1801), cited in Henry Adams, *History of the United States, 1*, 403–4.

It is not difficult to understand this indecision in a man who had opposed by instinct and conviction the war policy of the Federalist regime, and who must now dimly perceive that the safety of the nation might demand a resort to force. The Secretary of State, James Madison, shared his chief's dilemma, and cast about for reasons to explain an action which Napoleon must realize would jeopardize American friendship for France. While he did not discount the possibility that France meant to use her new territories to exert pressure on the policies of the United States, he at first inclined to the view that the French had moved to make certain that Britain did not get there first.[7] Madison sought to remove this cause for concern in instructions to Pinckney at Madrid, stressing the fact that the United States opposed any transfer whatsoever, to Britain or to France, and wished Spain to retain the territory.[8] Shortly afterward, he reminded Rufus King in London of American opposition to any change of neighbors in the southwest, adverting particularly to the danger of British encirclement, which made that nation "the last of neighbors that would be agreeable to the United States."[9] The means he proposed to prevent a change—"peace and persuasion"—were not, however, very formidable under the circumstances.

The tone which the Secretary of State adopted toward France could not be described as imperious, either. Robert R. Livingston, who was about to embark on his eventful tour of duty as American minister at Paris, received copies of King's and Pinckney's instructions, and in addition Madison urged him to impress upon the French government

7. Madison to Wilson Nicholas (July 10, 1801), Gaillard Hunt, ed., *The Writings of James Madison* (9 vols. New York, 1900–10), *6*, 427 n.
8. Madison to Pinckney (June 9, 1801), *Annals of Congress, 1789–1824* (42 vols. Washington, 1834–56), *7*, 1013–14.
9. Madison to King (July 24, 1801), C. R. King, ed., *Life and Correspondence, 4*, 85 n.

the "anxiety of the United States to maintain harmony and
confidence with the French Republic, the danger to which
those will be exposed by collisions, more or less inseparable
from a neighborhood under such circumstances [French
possession of the outlet of the Mississippi] . . . It cannot be
the interest of this country to favor any voluntary or com-
pulsive transfer of the possessions in question from Spain to
France."[10]

If the First Consul proved insensitive to delicate suggestion, however, it would be well to speak softly and bow to
the inevitable: "Should it be found that the cession from
Spain to France has irrevocably taken place, or certainly will
take place, sound policy will require . . . that nothing be
said or done which will unnecessarily irritate our future
neighbors, or check the liberality which they may be disposed to exercise in relation to the trade and navigation
through the mouth of the Mississippi." In these instructions
also there appears the first suggestion that the cession of the
Floridas—particularly West Florida, through which the
Mobile River flows—to the United States would do much to
relieve hostility toward the holder of New Orleans. This
idea illustrates how narrowly the Jefferson administration
based its No-Transfer policy upon concern over a commercial outlet for the West. Madison mentioned in his catalogue
of reasons for objecting to retrocession that it would endanger America's peace by placing her between the possessions of the great antagonists of Europe, but the cession of
the Floridas would no more remedy this security problem
than it would remove the threat of French interference in
domestic affairs. Nor did Jefferson entertain any visions of
expansion to the westward at this time, if he was prepared
to acquiesce in the occupation of Louisiana by France. At
no time before the fortuitous Louisiana Purchase did the

10. Madison to Livingston (Sept. 28, 1801), *Annals of Congress*, 7,
1015.

administration seriously object to French control of the lands to the west of the Mississippi.

Bonaparte was not likely to be deterred by Madison's mild caveats, for even as Livingston was preparing to sail for France the First Consul was taking the first steps toward consolidating his new empire in North America. Immediately after making peace with Britain, Napoleon dispatched General Leclerc with an army to subdue Toussaint L'Ouverture, leader of the revolted blacks in Santo Domingo. This island, marked along with Guadeloupe as the wealth-producing heart of the French overseas empire, was to be supplied with foodstuffs and lumber from Louisiana, which would be occupied as soon as Santo Domingo was subjugated. In early 1802 only Toussaint's small and ill-equipped army barred France's road to New Orleans, and there was little reason to believe the obstacle would long delay Leclerc. That Santo Domingo did eventually provide the critical delay in Napoleon's timetable owed little to support from the United States.

Meanwhile, across the Atlantic, King and Livingston were acting together in an effort to find a way to avert the impending crisis in American affairs. Separated by a six-weeks' voyage from their capital and often without fresh instructions for several months at a time, these men bore a more important responsibility in policy-making than is the case with their modern counterparts. Without specific instructions in the matter, both agreed that an effort must be made to enlist the support of Britain against the transfer of Louisiana and the Floridas (which they mistakenly thought were included in Napoleon's bargain) to France.

In June 1801, while his nation was still at war with France, Lord Hawkesbury, now British foreign minister, had shown a lively concern over the rumors of retrocession. His anxiety extended to the security not only of Canada but of the British West Indies, in case the Floridas were included in the cession. His vehemence had moved King to remind him that the United States opposed any transfer of the Floridas, except to themselves.[11] After he had signed the preliminary articles of peace with France, however, Hawkesbury's tone underwent a marked change. He refused to raise the retrocession question at Amiens, despite King's urging, and discounted the danger from an empty wilderness or from Leclerc's expedition.[12] Clearly Britain had no intention of allowing the Louisiana issue to disturb the fragile peace just achieved in Europe.

Soon after Livingston arrived at Paris he concluded with King that British support was essential. The fact of retrocession was common knowledge—King had sent copies of the Treaty of San Ildefonso to Madison on November 20— yet Livingston found the French government extremely evasive on the subject.[13] Unfortunately for the firm stand he hoped to be able to take later, Livingston temporarily subsided into the "soft policy" his instructions authorized and declared "that as long as France conforms to the existing treaty between us and Spain, the government of the United States does not consider herself as having any interest in opposing the exchange."[14]

Having thus retired from the field without having drawn his sword, Livingston appealed to King to persuade Britain to come forward as champion.[15] King replied that he had done what could be done already but that, even though he was convinced that Britain was concerned about the security of her trade and possessions in the New World, she was not

11. King to Madison (June 1, 1801), C. R. King, ed., *Life and Correspondence, 3,* 469.

12. King, memo of conversation (Nov. 25, 1801), ibid., *4,* 17–19.

13. Livingston to Madison (Dec. 10, 1801), *Annals of Congress, 7,* 1018.

14. Livingston to Madison (Jan. 13, 1802), ibid., p. 1020.

15. Livingston to King (Dec. 30, 1801), ibid., p. 1019.

disposed to act at present. He closed with a recommendation calculated to stiffen Livingston's spine, but it came a little late:

> My principal reliance would . . . be placed upon a temperate, plain and explicit representation to the French government . . . of the mischiefs which we may be made to suffer from the completion of the cession, accompanying the same by assurances of our earnest desire to live in harmony with France . . . concluding with direct insinuation that foreseeing as we do the pernicious influence of the measure upon our political and social happiness, it will be impossible for us to see it carried into effect with indifference.[16]

King realized that this sort of pronouncement might ultimately have to be backed up by force, and he had no illusions about the chances of the United States in single combat with France, now that British seapower was neutral, but he also saw clearly that the principle of opposing the transfer of Louisiana must on no account be abandoned. He reminded Livingston that American interests were primarily involved, and that the United States could depend on no one else to fight her battles for her.[17] King had no sympathy for Jefferson's apparent complacent optimism and visible military unpreparedness:

> No policy in my opinion has so often proved to be pernicious as that of shutting our eyes upon what we cannot avoid seeing, and of putting off exertions to prevent injury, and thereby leaving the public welfare either to the government of chance, or in the hands of the adversary; a mode of administration which always

16. King to Livingston (Jan. 16, 1802), C. R. King, ed., *Life and Correspondence, 4,* 57–59.
17. King to Livingston (March 23, 1802), ibid., *4,* 86–90.

amounts to a confession of weakness. . . . The truth
should not be disguised from ourselves or others; that
we are the first power in our own hemisphere, and that
we are disinclined to play the part of the second.

King's preference for an attitude of sturdy self-reliance
anticipates the defiant nationalism displayed by John
Quincy Adams under somewhat analogous circumstances in
1823, but Adams suspected that Britain could be counted on
to help prevent French intervention in the New World,
while King knew that temporarily at least his nation stood
alone. Therefore, King counseled negotiations from a position of strength, looking toward the procurement of Louisiana and the Floridas in return for credit guarantees for
French purchases of supplies for their armies in the Caribbean. This was the first suggestion that all of Louisiana be
bought, and Livingston acted upon it later.

King's estimate of Jefferson's initial handling of the retrocession crisis was not far from the mark, but soon the President veered off sharply on another tack. His bright expectations that Franco–American relations would be cordial and
candid once the Federalists were out of office had been
gradually corroded by experience. The French government
continued to deny that it had acquired Louisiana, even after
Jefferson held in his hands copies of the Treaty of San
Ildefonso sent him by King. In addition to this exhibition
of duplicity there was the unpleasant arrogance that General
Leclerc had displayed in confiscating American property in
Santo Domingo, and the rising concern in the West caused
by falling prices and persistent rumors of an imminent
French occupation of New Orleans.[18] Jefferson decided the
time had come to brandish the mailed fist.

18. Dunbar Rowland, ed., *The Official Letterbooks of W. C. C.
Claiborne,* 6 vols. Jackson, Miss., 1917; see Claiborne to Madison
(Dec. 20, 1801; Jan. 20, 1802), *1,* 31, 35.

The return to France of his good friend Pierre Samuel Du Pont de Nemours afforded Jefferson the occasion he sought to reach the inner councils of the French government, which Livingston had apparently failed to do. The President asked Du Pont to impress upon Bonaparte the seriousness with which the United States regarded the retrocession of Louisiana, and for his guidance made him the bearer of new instructions to Livingston, which were left unsealed so that the Frenchman might acquaint himself fully with their contents.[19]

Nothing could have shocked the old Physiocrat more than the tone of this celebrated letter to Livingston, which breathed a thundering defiance which the Federalists had scarcely dared to match when they were assured of British support:

> There is on the globe one single spot, the possessor of which is our natural and habitual enemy. It is New Orleans, through which the produce of three-eighths of our country must pass to market . . . [Spain is so weak as not to disturb us. She can be induced to give it up some day, but not so France.] The day that France takes possession of N. Orleans fixes the sentence which is to restrain her forever within her low water mark. It seals the union of two nations who in conjunction can maintain exclusive possession of the ocean. From that moment we must marry ourselves to the British fleet and nation. . . . This is not a state of things we seek or desire. It is one which this measure, if adopted by France, forces on us. . . . The change of friends, which will be rendered necessary if France changes that position, em-

19. Jefferson to Du Pont (April 25, 1802), Gilbert Chinard, ed., *The Correspondence of Jefferson and Du Pont de Nemours* (Baltimore, 1931), p. 46.

barks us necessarily as a belligerent power in the first war of Europe. In that case France will have held possession of New Orleans during the interval of peace, long or short, at the end of which it will be wrested from her. . . .

If France considers Louisiana however as indispensable for her views she might perhaps be willing to look about for arrangements which might reconcile it to our interests. If anything could do this it would be the ceding to us of the island of New Orleans and the Floridas.[20]

Du Pont was appalled at Jefferson's apparent assumption that Napoleon Bonaparte would retreat before a blustering barrage of threats. The natural reaction to the demand "Cede this country or we will take it," he wrote the President, was the answer "We will defend it."[21] The United States must be prepared to offer some solid equivalent, and gold was the only one available. Du Pont reached the same conclusion that King had arrived at—the best course open to the United States was to offer to purchase New Orleans and the Floridas—and this was the direction his conversations took when he got to Paris.[22] Apparently this reasoning carried weight in Washington, for Madison's next instructions to Livingston and Pinckney spoke of payment.[23]

It is impossible to say how seriously Jefferson meant his proposal of marriage to the British fleet and nation, but it is safe to say he would have acted upon it only in the last

20. Jefferson to Livingston (April 18, 1802), P. L. Ford, ed., *Writings*, 7, 144–46.

21. Du Pont to Jefferson (April 30, 1802), Chinard, ed., *Letters*, p. 52.

22. Ibid., p. 53.

23. Madison to Livingston (May 1, 1802), and Madison to Pinckney (May 11, 1802): *Annals of Congress*, 7, 1027–28, 1031.

extremity of desperation, for he was already firmly wedded to the ideal of the political separation of the New World from the Old and devoted to the preservation of peace to the exclusion of every value except survival and liberty. In any event, it takes two to make a marriage, and Britain remained coyly evasive on the subject of Louisiana.[24]

Jefferson's blast had no visible effect on French policy. Du Pont's arrival in Paris coincided with the receipt of news from Leclerc that Toussaint had been taken, and Napoleon's reaction was to press Spain for the order to deliver Louisiana to France and to demand West Florida as well. During the late summer he began preparing an expedition under General Victor destined for New Orleans. Livingston observed these activities with mounting alarm, and tried desperately to secure an agreement from France to cede or sell New Orleans and the Floridas to the United States, but to no avail. Aware now that France had not received West Florida as part of the original bargain with Spain, he sent warnings home that Napoleon would probably order Victor to seize it, and perhaps Natchez too, if the United States did not prepare to defend it.[25] Disconsolately, Livingston described his fruitless efforts on behalf of his country: "There never was a government in which less could be done by negotiation than here. There is no people, no legislature, no counsellors. One man is everything. He seldom asks advice and never hears it unasked. . . . Though the sense of every reflecting man about him is against this wild expedition, no one dares to tell him so."[26]

Jefferson shared Livingston's disillusionment with the Consulate, but not his despair. In a private letter to his minister at Paris he admitted that he stood "compleately

24. King to Madison (May 7, 1802), ibid., pp. 1028–29.
25. Livingston to Madison (Nov. 11, 1802), ibid., pp. 1056–57.
26. Livingston to Madison (Sept. 1, 1802), ibid., pp. 1052–53.

corrected of the error, that either the government or the nation of France has any remains of friendship for us." In spite of this knowledge, and in spite of the fact that his *démarche* of the previous April had produced no results, Jefferson had reverted to the high ground of strict neutrality in the European rivalry, which for all his fulminations was probably where he had stood all along:

> In this state of things, we shall so take our distance between the two rival nations, as, remaining disengaged until necessity compels us, we may haul finally to the enemy of that which shall make it necessary. . . . No matter at present existing between them [France] and us is important enough to risk a breach of the peace; peace being indeed the most important of all things to us, except the preservation of an erect and independent attitude.[27]

Jefferson's failure to request an increase in the army and navy, the lack of any instructions to King looking toward alliance with Britain, and his cautious behavior in the future all sustain the conclusion that this letter to Livingston, rather than the one sent by Du Pont earlier, reflects his real policy in the retrocession crisis. The Du Pont letter had been a bluff; French occupation of New Orleans appeared more likely in October than it had the previous April, and yet this was not a matter "important enough to risk a breach of the peace." Jefferson was taking a long chance that something would turn up to deliver New Orleans into his hands before he was forced into a war and into alliance with Britain. His luck held—but before he emerged safely he underwent a trying experience.

27. Jefferson to Livingston (Oct. 10, 1802), P. L. Ford, ed., *Writings, 8,* 173.

THE FINAL CRISIS—CLOSURE OF THE MISSISSIPPI

On October 16, 1802, the Spanish Intendant at New Orleans, Juan Ventura Morales, announced the suspension of the right to deposit cargoes for trans-shipment which Americans had enjoyed for almost four years under the terms of Pinckney's Treaty. Once again the West was inflamed at the blocking of its artery of trade, and once again the Mississippi question became urgently bound up with the retrocession question. Although it cannot be shown that France had anything to do with the order closing Mississippi navigation, Americans at the time almost universally suspected French influence, and the Federalist party hurriedly dusted off the Gallic Peril. Jefferson soon found himself in a situation where action was necessary if the Republicans were not to lose western support.

The President's first concern was to keep the retrocession and the suspension questions separate, so as not to give the war party an issue to exploit. In his second annual message, Jefferson touched on retrocession only lightly, as a measure which, if carried into effect, would "make a change in the aspect of our foreign relations which will doubtless have just weight in . . . deliberations of the legislature."[28] On the subject of suspension he was silent.

The Republicans knew better than to try to suppress this issue, and on December 17, two days after the President's message, John Randolph of Virginia offered a resolution in the House of Representatives requesting that all the Department of State correspondence on the violations of Pinckney's Treaty be laid before the House.[29] A few days later the President complied, and all seemed peaceful until January 4, when Roger Griswold, Federalist from Connecticut, opened the offensive for the opposition by introducing a

28. Ibid., p. 183.
29. *Annals of Congress*, 7, 281.

resolution requesting delivery to the House of all official
documents relating to the cession of Louisiana to France, if
such transmission were not deemed improper by the Executive. Here was the expected attempt to link the two issues,
and Randolph led the attack against Griswold's motion,
which was defeated on January 11.[30]

Republican party discipline had held up under this test,
but Jefferson recognized the need for dramatic action to
keep the situation in hand. In a surprise move on January
11 he sent to the Senate the nomination of James Monroe
as Minister Extraordinary and Plenipotentiary to join
Livingston in France and, if necessary, Pinckney in Spain to
negotiate a convention "for the purpose of enlarging, and
more effectually securing, our rights and interests in the
river Mississippi, and in the territories eastward thereof."[31]
In the opening sentence of his special message, Jefferson
alluded to the questions of both suspension and retrocession
as special objects of interest to the mission, combining them
now for the purpose of removing them from the political
arena.

Monroe was the idol of the West, and the Senate's approval of his mission did much to appease the frontiersmen.
Jefferson, however, delayed actually sending Monroe to
France, and within a month the Federalists had evolved
another tactic for embarrassing the administration. On February 16 Senator Ross of Pennsylvania introduced a resolution which began with a recital of the need for securing the
suspended rights of deposit and navigation, and proceeded
to this substantive clause: "That the President be authorized to take immediate possession of such place or places,
in the said island [New Orleans], or the adjacent territories,
as he may deem fit and convenient for the purposes aforesaid; and to adopt such other measures for obtaining that

30. Ibid., pp. 312, 366.
31. Ibid., pp. 22–23.

complete security as to him in his wisdom shall seem meet."[32] The Resolution also would authorize the President to use the regular army and navy and militia from the western states and called for the appropriation of five million dollars to defray the expenses of the expedition.

There was little novelty to this proposal; it was essentially a reversion to the preclusive war policy of 1798–99, with the familiar aim of converting the West to Federalism by a promise of direct action. The Ross Resolution provoked a heated ten-day debate along strictly partisan lines before it was amended to death by the Republicans. The debate centered about the question of whether war should be a first or a last resort; if it served no other purpose, it jogged Jefferson into sending Monroe off, to prove that negotiations were at least getting under way.

While the instructions to Monroe and Livingston contained the form of a treaty with France for the cession of New Orleans and the Floridas to the United States, for which payment up to two million dollars was authorized, the *sine qua non* of a peaceful settlement was really nothing more than secure possession of a right to deposit and of navigation on the Mississippi.[33] In the last analysis, Jefferson had shown himself unwilling to make an issue of the transfer of Louisiana to France; he would allow New Orleans to pass to Napoleon, risking the welfare of the West on the dubious supposition that the First Consul would perform his engagements in good faith until such time as unpredictable circumstances should deliver the mouth of the Mississippi into American hands. These instructions were secret, of course, and outwardly the administration assumed a belligerent posture. Pichon, the French chargé in Washington, communicated to Paris his anxiety over signs that

32. Ibid., pp. 95–96.

33. Madison to Livingston and Monroe (March 2 and April 18, 1803), ibid., pp. 1095–1108, 1135–39.

an Anglo–American *rapprochement* was developing out of the crisis.[34]

It is true that when Monroe departed for France he carried with him a letter of introduction from the British minister in Washington to Lord Whitworth, the British ambassador at Paris.[35] Shortly thereafter, Madison sent supplementary instructions to the commissioners in Paris which dealt with the possibility of an alliance with Britain.[36] Monroe was to communicate with the British government on the subject of an alliance if it became clear that France intended war, or if no satisfaction could be had on the navigation of the Mississippi. The suggested terms of alliance indicate how gingerly Jefferson approached Britain, and have an interesting bearing on the development of the No-Transfer policy. Jefferson offered Britain nothing except the privilege of fighting America's battle for her. The United States was not prepared to grant anything beyond a promise not to conclude a separate peace with France, and Monroe was expressly forbidden to agree to any guarantee of British territories. Moreover, he was to issue a warning that the United States opposed the transfer of Louisiana to Britain (as it did to France) as "altogether repugnant to . . . sound policy."[37] If Jefferson were finally forced into war by Napoleon's obstinacy, he intended to take the occasion to assert the paramount interest of the United States in the trans-Mississippi West; he had no intention of allowing Britain to replace France as a hazard to American security.

34. Pichon to Talleyrand (Feb. 13, 1803), quoted in Lyon, *Louisiana in French Diplomacy*, pp. 181–82.

35. Ibid., p. 181.

36. Madison to Livingston and Monroe (April 18, 1803), *Annals of Congress*, 7, 1135–39.

37. Madison to Livingston and Monroe (April 18, 1803), ibid., pp. 1136–37.

Actually, there was at this time some likelihood that Britain might acquire Louisiana. In mid-March 1803 it became evident in Europe that the resumption of war between France and England was imminent. Alarmed at reports that Britain had revived Miranda's projects, Rufus King reminded the Prime Minister that the United States could not view with indifference the transfer of New Orleans to either France or Britain.[38] Addington replied that Britain had no desire to possess the country and would take it only to prevent French occupation, but that if the United States failed to obtain it from France, Britain might be forced to occupy it.

The fact of the matter was that the Addington government, after considerable prodding, had at length become convinced that British interests in the West Indies and Canada demanded that Bonaparte be prevented from occupying New Orleans and Louisiana. Since early 1802 William Cobbett and William Windham had been urging the government to take positive action against this transfer of territory, not only on the grounds of a direct threat to the security of British possessions, but also because of the additional leverage French occupation of New Orleans would give that nation in influencing the policies of the United States.[39] Their efforts were ably seconded by Edward Thornton, the British chargé at Washington, who was impressed by Jefferson's apparent determination to fight rather than see New Orleans go to France, in the President's words to "throw away the scabbard" if it should come to war. Both Thornton and Windham advocated that the British seize New Orleans and then turn it over immediately to the United States, ending a serious strategic threat to themselves while making a grand gesture toward the

38. King to Madison (April 2, 1803), ibid., p. 1125.
39. For British policy at this period see Bradford Perkins, *The First Rapprochement* (Philadelphia, 1955), pp. 161–67.

Americans which would bind them by ties of gratitude to Britain. As long as Addington and Hawkesbury retained any hope that the peace of Amiens with France might be made permanent, they turned a deaf ear to such counsels, but when in early 1803 war appeared imminent, they turned, though with characteristic languor, to the consideration of a preventive occupation of New Orleans. The No-Transfer declarations Rufus King had made to Britain had left their mark, however, for Addington, in suggesting the possibility of such a move to the American envoy, volunteered assurances that Britain regarded American possession as the best ultimate solution to the problem. None of this passed the stage of tentative discussion, for a few weeks later, contrary to the expectations of every American official, Napoleon ceded to the United States not only New Orleans but the whole of Louisiana.

It is clear that Napoleon's decision to sell Louisiana rested more on a series of fortuitous circumstances over which Jefferson exercised no control than on concern generated by American statements of the No-Transfer policy. The American people owed much to the yellow fever and native insurrections which decimated Leclerc's forces in Santo Domingo and to the unseasonable frosts in Holland which held Victor's relief expedition icebound throughout the winter of 1802–03. By the time the spring thaws came, tension between England and France was mounting swiftly, and Victor's troops were held in Europe for service in the war everybody knew was at hand. Under these circumstances Napoleon abandoned his dreams of empire in North America, ridding himself of a province he had never occupied and now probably could not occupy or defend, in return for American gold which he needed. Certainly there could be no advantage in driving the United States into the arms of his enemy by holding on to a worthless wilderness. On April 30, 1803, therefore, the dazzled American commissioners set their hands to a document which secured forever the navigation of the Mississippi to the West, which removed North America a step farther from the arena of European conflict, and which opened the way for American settlement as far as the Rocky Mountains.

For Jefferson the Louisiana Purchase was a piece of good luck beyond his most extravagant imagining. In a letter to his friend John Bacon, written before he received the momentous news from Paris, he revealed what little result he expected from Monroe's mission:

> Although I am not sanguine in obtaining a cession of New Orleans for money, yet I am confident in the policy of putting off the day of contention for it, till we are stronger in ourselves, and stronger in our allies, but especially till we shall have planted such a population on the Mississippi as will be able to do their own business, without the necessity of marching men from the shores of the Atlantic 1500 or 2000 miles thither, to perish by fatigue and change of climate.[40]

As he wrote some months later, his policy was to "palliate and endure, if Messrs. Ross, Morris, etc. did not force a premature rupture," until the tide of fortune turned.[41] How long or how brief a period this might be he had no way of judging; how much more difficult it might be to eject the French once they were established at New Orleans than to prevent their gaining a foothold by timely military preparations in support of a firm diplomatic stand against occupation he did not sufficiently consider. From the information in his possession at the time he sent Monroe to France, he had no reason to suppose that Victor's army would not proceed with the occupation as planned.

40. Jefferson to Bacon (April 30, 1803), P. L. Ford, ed., *Writings*, 8, 229.
41. Jefferson to Joseph Priestley (Jan. 29, 1804), ibid., pp. 294–95.

Jefferson, the philosopher-statesman, the moralist in politics who believed that the precepts which govern the conduct of individuals ought to operate in the relations between states, often spoke and wrote as realistically as Hamilton about the fact that diplomacy and war are inseparable, that force underlies all political relationships. But Jefferson's thought was anything but predictable. A spirit as generous as his, with a curiosity as wide-ranging and free, is difficult to categorize; he can be quoted on either side of almost any philosophical position. He was, furthermore, never doctrinaire in the actual exercise of power, but pragmatic, accommodating, and quite willing to be inconsistent in small things to achieve his larger ends. The most consistent strain in Jefferson's nature was his unlimited optimism, his faith in the fundamental goodness and progressiveness of mankind, the sense of a benevolent guidance in the world's destinies, a disinclination to view life as a tragedy.

Engaging though such a sense of cosmic well-being may be, it can tempt a leader away from action into the comfortable paralysis of decision that comes from an escape from biological into geological time. Things may assuredly work out in the long run, but, as Lord Keynes once remarked, everyone lives in the short run. Jefferson's diplomacy in the retrocession crisis often seems not a considered plan based on an analysis of immediate national interest but a series of improvisations hastily formulated without a serious appreciation of the realities of the international situation. It was less a course of action than a means to delay taking action. While Britain was at peace with France it was idle to talk about an alliance that might never be possible, just as it was foolhardy not to sacrifice considerations of economy to placing the country in a decent posture of defense. Plenty of Britons thought that a French occupation of New Orleans would be desirable as a means of making the United States

more docile, of curbing the growth of that turbulent republic as a commercial rival and as a power in the New World.[42]
Curiously enough, if Hamilton and Jefferson had exchanged policies, each would have behaved more appropri-
ately under the circumstances in which they found themselves. During the period of America's quasi-war with
France, while Britain was an active belligerent, eager to
cooperate with any enemy of Napoleon, strong diplomatic
pressure against the transfer of Louisiana coupled with
threats of an alliance with Britain would have been an eco-
nomical and effective method of securing the western interest. But after Amiens only military strength in the
field and a respectable navy could certainly have deterred
Bonaparte.

Both political parties, no matter how they differed in the
means they chose, believed firmly that the United States
must some day control Louisiana and the Floridas, and both
preferred Spain as the most likely candidate for future
expulsion. As Rufus King remarked to Lord Hawkesbury,
quoting Montesquieu, "it is happy for the trading powers
that God has permitted the Turks and Spaniards in the
world, since of all nations they are the most proper to possess
a great empire with insignificance."[43] Both the Federalists
and the Republicans issued repeated No-Transfer declarations to prevent the substitution of a stronger colonial
power for Spain, declarations which tended to confirm the
policy in American practice. There was not yet, however
(nor would there be for a half century), any sense of continuity in these applications for the policy, any reference to
precedent—for example to the Nootka crisis. Moreover, the
No-Transfer idea was still strictly limited to contiguous
continental territory. Spain's cession of Santo Domingo to
France and Britain's occupation of Trinidad during this

42. Perkins, *Rapprochement*, p. 162.
43. C. R. King, ed., *Life and Correspondence, 3*, 469.

period were not considered threats to American safety, and passed unprotested. Americans still defined the geographical extent of their vital interests in fairly narrow terms.

The Louisiana Purchase vastly enhanced the security of the United States. The threat of encirclement by European possessions was gone, at least for the time being. Westward expansion was free to proceed through thousands of miles of vacant wilderness now under the sovereignty of the United States. The mouth of the Mississippi, the "key to the Western World," as Pickering had called it, which had been so acute a focus of diplomatic concern, was at last in American hands. But its acquisition was clouded by the lingering danger of Spanish possession of West Florida. It was to this troubled province that the No-Transfer policy was next applied.

CHAPTER 4

The "Madison Doctrine" of 1811

The acquisition of the Floridas had been one of the main objects of Monroe's mission to France in 1803, and his failure to secure them considerably dimmed the luster of the Louisiana Purchase in the eyes of his countrymen. During the next fifteen years the inclusion of East and West Florida in the Union remained a major objective of American foreign policy, and until the Floridas were safely annexed the United States sought to keep them in Spanish hands through repeated assertions of the No-Transfer policy. Of all these the most noteworthy from the point of view of the history of the policy is the congressional Joint Resolution of 1811, which has generally been considered, though inaccurately, as the genesis of the No-Transfer principle, and because it was inspired by a special message from the President has been christened by one historian the "Madison Doctrine."[1]

A glance at the map shows why the United States was vitally interested in obtaining the Floridas. New Orleans could never be made militarily secure so long as a foreign power held West Florida, which extended to the Mississippi above the city in the vicinity of Baton Rouge. The "pan-

1. Herbert Kraus, *Die Monroedoktrin in ihrer Beziehungen zur amerikanischen Diplomatie und zum Völkerrecht* (Berlin, 1913), p. 59.

handle" of East and West Florida below 31° closed off the natural river transportation routes to the Gulf of Mexico for the produce of eastern Tennessee and the Mississippi Territory, while the excellent harbors of Mobile and Pensacola bays, if in the possession of the United States, were natural naval bases for the protection of the coasting trade from the Mississippi, or in the possession of a hostile maritime power for the interdiction of that indispensable traffic. Spain was too weak herself to menace the security of New Orleans, but her very weakness was in itself a danger, creating a political vacuum into which might flow the power of Britain or France, whose maritime practices as belligerents created a sustained crisis in their relations with the neutral United States.

If not a major threat, Spain's presence in the Floridas was a constant irritation to Americans, and led to a desire to speed her departure from the Gulf Coast of the Mississippi. Spanish authority was strong enough to prevent trade down the Tombigbee–Alabama–Mobile river system, but not strong enough to police the provinces properly. Spanish Florida became a species of no-man's land, a haven for fugitive slaves and hostile Indians who kept settlers on the American side of the border in constant dread of scalping parties or servile rebellion. The Floridas were also a busy center of the smuggling trade, particularly during the Embargo period.

To the logic of geography and of economics which determined American interest in the Floridas was added the logic of nationality as settlers from the United States moved across into Spanish territory to take up lands. It was these Americans who eventually created the occasion for the occupation of West Florida and expeditions in East Florida by United States forces.

From the time of the Louisiana Purchase until the Spanish situation was reduced to chaos by the Peninsular War, the Jefferson administration resisted the temptation to wrest the Floridas from Spain by force, and relied instead upon diplomacy at Paris, Madrid, and London. The United States sought to exchange East Florida for claims against Spain arising out of spoliations of American commerce by Spanish warships or by French warships in Spanish territorial waters, and out of losses suffered by American citizens as a result of the closure of the Mississippi in 1802. To West Florida, Jefferson and his successors claimed a direct right, on the grounds that it had been included in the Louisiana Purchase.

This latter claim was the inspiration of Robert R. Livingston, who knew better than any other American that Napoleon had tried and consistently failed to persuade Spain to cede West Florida along with Louisiana. Nonetheless, he converted his colleague Monroe to his views, and together they persuaded Madison and Jefferson to take the stand that the United States had purchased the land between the Iberville and the Perdido rivers from France. This exercise in auto-suggestion was compelled by the importance of West Florida to the United States and the danger of its transfer to Britain, and the vague definition of boundaries in the treaty of cession as well as the apparent willingness of Napoleon to approve a certain elasticity of interpretation gave further impetus to it.[2]

Jefferson tried a variety of approaches to the problem of how to acquire the Floridas without the cost and risk of a

2. On the danger of transfer to Britain see Monroe to Madison (May 18, 1803), S. M. Hamilton, ed., *The Writings of James Monroe* (7 vols. New York, 1898–1903), *4*, *25*. The treaty ceded to the United States "the colony or province of Louisiana, with the same extent as it now has in the hands of Spain, and that it had when France possessed it [before 1763]; and such as it should be after the treaties subsequently entered into between Spain and other states." This was the wording of the treaty ceding the province to France in 1800.

war, all of which met with a uniform lack of success. In the Mobile Act of 1804 he essayed finesse, but Yrujo's heated protest against an administrative absorption of West Florida through customs legislation forced him to retreat. Monroe's special mission to Spain to try to exchange pecuniary claims for Spanish Florida fared no better. Finally, acting upon hints from Talleyrand which recalled the unsavory XYZ affair, Jefferson pushed through Congress the secret "Two Million Act," which granted that sum to the Executive to use for "diplomatic purposes." This devious project for bribing France to force Spain to cede the Floridas had hardly got under way before Talleyrand fell from favor, and Napoleon, victorious over Austria and Prussia and at peace with the Tsar, decided to put an end to Godoy's restless flirtations with London. In early March 1808 French armies poured over the Pyrenees and Joseph Bonaparte mounted the throne of Charles IV. But on the famous *dos de mayo* the Spanish nation rebelled against the "intruder King," and the provisional government that appeared allied itself with Great Britain. Thus began the Peninsular War, which kept alive resistance to Napoleon on the Continent, which made Wellington's name a household word throughout Europe and America, and which marked the beginning of the end for the First French Empire.

These momentous events opened broad new avenues of policy for the United States, in respect not only to the Floridas but to all of Spanish America as well. In the welter of confused reports and rumors about the Spanish situation, Jefferson pursued a series of volatile and often directionless policies, reacting impulsively to every fresh intelligence from abroad, darting up some of the avenues of approach only to beat a hasty retreat, catching glimpses of the breathtaking vista of Latin America independence—now confining himself to the narrow objective of obtaining the Floridas, now looking outward to Cuba and, on one occa-

sion, far beyond all the Americas, scattering No-Transfer
statements as he went.

THE "LARGE POLICY OF 1808"[3]

From time to time discouraged American diplomats
charged with the unhappy task of trying to acquire the
Floridas from Spain had counseled their government to
seize the territory first and negotiate afterward.[4] Although
this was the course eventually adopted by President Madison in West Florida, it did not appeal to Jefferson's pacific
disposition, especially after the brilliant success of his
Louisiana diplomacy, the peculiar European circumstances
behind which he never fully appreciated. It was not until
HMS Leopard attacked an American naval vessel in the
Chesapeake outrage, bringing the United States to the verge
of war with England, that Jefferson entertained the possibility of a forcible settlement of the Florida issue. In case
of war he saw that Britain would at once try to occupy the
Floridas as a *"point d'appui* to annoy us."[5] To prevent this
the United States must take over the Floridas in self-defense,
in which case he felt that Cuba would probably join the
United States also.[6] The basis for his supposition about
Cuba is unclear, but this marks the first appearance in
Jefferson's expansionist plans of the island which was never
afterward absent from them. Cuba would in future be the
most consistent object of application of the No-Transfer
principle in American diplomacy.

3. The phrase is A. P. Whitaker's; see his *The United States and the
Independence of Latin America, 1800–1830* (Baltimore, 1941), chap. 2.
4. Monroe and Pinckney to Madison (May 23, 1805), *ASPFR*, 2,
667. See also Bowdoin to Madison, in I. J. Cox, *The West Florida
Controversy, 1798–1813* (Baltimore, 1918), p. 267.
5. Jefferson to General Armstrong at Paris (July 17, 1807), Lipscomb
and Bergh, eds., *Writings of Jefferson, 11*, 284.
6. Jefferson to Madison (Aug. 16, 1807), ibid., p. 327.

Napoleon, naturally not displeased with the deterioration of Anglo–American relations, attempted to make the United States commit itself to war on the side of France, using Florida as bait. In February 1808, on the eve of his invasion of Spain, the Emperor expressed his approval of an occupation of Florida by the United States to prevent a forcible transfer to Britain, and offered his assistance in securing a cession of the territory to the United States on the condition that they conclude an alliance with France. The American minister, General Armstrong, transmitted Napoleon's offer with an angry reminder to Madison of the continued depredations practiced by France against American shipping and the recommendation that the United States choose either France or Britain as an enemy, but at all events to waste no time in laying hold of the Floridas.[7] With the war crisis safely passed and the Embargo substituted for more forceful measures, Madison replied serenely that his country saw no reason at present for departing from its policy of neutrality, but that "should circumstances demand from the United States a precautionary occupation against the hostile designs of Great Britain, it will be recollected with satisfaction that the measure has received his Majesty's approbation."[8] Bonaparte received this rebuff with ill humor and ordered Champagny to inform Armstrong that no occupation of the Floridas was permissible without the approval of the King of Spain, who was now Joseph Bonaparte in Napoleon's view at least, if not in that of the Spanish people.[9]

This episode in the Florida question occasioned by the war scare with Britain only served to illustrate the unfavorableness of the situation in Europe for an early solution of

7. Armstrong to Madison (Feb. 22, 1808), *ASPFR, 3,* 250.
8. Madison to Armstrong (May 2, 1808), ibid., p. 252.
9. Champagny to Armstrong (June 22, 1808), Henry Adams, *History, 4,* 311.

the problem. Until the middle of 1808 there appeared to Jefferson and Madison no way to achieve their aims in West Florida without becoming involved in the European war. But suddenly, with the French attack on Spain, the uprising of the *dos de mayo,* and the landing of a British army in Portugal, opportunity seemed to dawn for just such a bloodless victory in Florida as had been achieved in Louisiana.

The importance of the Spanish revolution extended in fact much farther than Florida. During the five years in which Spain was the battleground of warring factions supported by foreign armies, the Spanish colonies in the New World, left largely to their own devices, experienced a new political and commercial freedom that set in motion independence movements which eventuated in the expulsion of Spanish authority from the continental possessions. No one caught this wider significance of the Spanish civil war more quickly than Jefferson, who, like every American statesman of his generation, was devoted to the ideal of separation of the political systems of the New World and the Old—to which Washington and Hamilton had given classic expression in the Farewell Address of 1796. The formation of independent republics throughout Latin America could achieve that separation on a scale that had hitherto seemed only a remote possibility. Spain was powerless to prevent the liberation of the Americas; only the intervention of the great powers of Europe could do so. It was a desire to forestall this possibility that later evoked Monroe's message of December 2, 1823, in which the doctrine of the two spheres was restated and implemented with caveats against European intervention or colonization in the New World. Monroe spoke after his country had recognized the independence of several Latin American states; in 1808 the revolts had not begun and the problem was one of preserving the essential conditions under which independence might be sought and won. Jefferson therefore turned once again to the No-Transfer policy, which had already seen much service in attempts to prevent an increase of European power in North America, and extended its application explicitly to Cuba and Mexico and by implication to the whole of Latin America. The No-Transfer policy did not appear in Monroe's message, for reasons we shall examine in the next chapter, but its application to the new situation in Spanish America in the famous cabinet resolution of October 22, 1808, shows it to have been the fundamental instrument of the policy in preserving the conditions that made the Monroe Doctrine possible.

It is not surprising that the early news of Napoleon's invasion of Spain directed Jefferson's attention, momentarily at least, back to Cuba, in which he had evinced earlier interest. On May 10 Albert Gallatin, the Secretary of the Treasury, wrote the President of late word from Spain brought by "young Rittenhouse," suggesting that while these new developments might mean the loss of Spain's colonies to Britain, they would on the whole be favorable to the aims of the United States, even though it would now be necessary to deal with Napoleon on the Florida issue.[10] Jefferson saw no such advantages in a change of ownership in the Spanish colonies. "I shall sincerely lament Cuba's falling into any hands but those of its present owners. Spanish America is at present in the best hands for us. '*Chi sta bene, non si muove*' should be our motto."[11]

Jefferson's immediate concern, however, remained more narrowly focused on the Floridas, and when he learned that British armies were supporting the Spanish patriots and

10. Gallatin to Jefferson (May 10, 1808), Henry Adams, ed., *The Writings of Albert Gallatin* (3 vols. Philadelphia, 1879), *1*, 387.

11. Jefferson to Gallatin (May 17, 1808), Lipscomb and Bergh, *12*, 57. On the quotation: John Adams wrote to John Marshall in 1800 that this was the motto of the Hotel de Valentinois in Passy, where he had stayed during his mission to France.

Ferdinand VII against Joseph Bonaparte, he perceived an opportunity to secure that prize once and for all without entanglement with either of the great belligerents of Europe. His hopes rested on a dispatch from William Pinkney of June 5, which indicated that Britain might be willing to make some concession to the United States on the corrosive issue of impressment and neutral rights. In this event Jefferson saw a "favorable occasion of doing ourselves justice in the south."[12] Accordingly, the President instructed the Secretary of War to make plans for using the new levies authorized by Congress in the war crisis for the occupation of both East and West Florida.[13]

Jefferson did not scruple at forcible land-grabbing if there was no risk of war involved, but Pinkney's letter proved a false hope. When it became evident that there would be no settlement with Britain, the President abandoned for the time being his project of seizing the Floridas. He had other strings to his bow, and one of these was encouragement to the peoples in neighboring Spanish dominions to declare their independence of Spain. The application of this policy to the Floridas was a by-product of the "large policy" of the Cabinet resolution on the danger of transfer of the Spanish dominions in America generally.

For a brief moment in 1808 Jefferson caught a dazzling vision of the opportunity now opening up for the liberation of all the Americas from European domination. The British victories over French armies at Bailén and Vimeiero and the retreat of Joseph Bonaparte and his court behind the Ebro

12. Jefferson to Gallatin (Aug. 11, 1808), P. L. Ford, ed., *Writings of Jefferson*, 9, 203. Gallatin, in a letter of Aug. 5 to Jefferson, had suggested seizing West Florida to prevent British occupation: Adams, ed., *Writings of Gallatin*, 1, 400.

13. Jefferson to Dearborn (Aug. 12, 1808), Ford, 9, 203–4. At this same time Jefferson wrote to the other members of his Cabinet in the same vein.

focused the attention of the American government on the broader implications of the Spanish war for the Americas. On October 22 the Cabinet unanimously agreed on "sentiments which should be unauthoritatively expressed to influential persons in Cuba and Mexico":

> If you remain under the dominion of the kingdom and family of Spain, we are contented; but we should be extremely unwilling to see you pass under the dominion or ascendency of France or England. In the latter cases should you choose to declare independence, we cannot now commit ourselves by saying we would make common cause with you but must reserve ourselves to act to the then existing circumstances, but in our proceedings we shall be influenced by friendship to you, by a firm belief that our interests are intimately connected, and by the strongest repugnance to see you under subordination to either France or England, either politically or commercially.[14]

These "sentiments" were to be carried to Havana by the new consul, Anderson, and to Mexico City by Hughes and Burling, both ostensibly going in search of men from Zebulon Pike's exploring party, lost in the Rocky Mountains. Jefferson also sent instructions to Governor Claiborne at New Orleans to communicate these views to "proper characters." In his instructions to Claiborne the President included a most significant statement of the assumption underlying his whole No-Transfer and independence policy: "We consider their interests and ours as the same, and that the object of both must be to exclude all European influence from this hemisphere."[15] Here, explicitly stated,

14. Memo by Jefferson of Cabinet meeting, in the Anas: Ford, *1*, 334–35.
15. Jefferson to Claiborne (Oct. 29, 1808), ibid., *9*, 212–13.

is the political axiom which formed the basis for the whole policy of the United States toward the independence of Latin America, later to be summed up in the Monroe Doctrine. In its broadest form it is the "Grand Design" of American hemispheric policy; in its narrower application to adjacent borderlands it had long been the implicit foundation of the development of the No-Transfer policy as applied to Canada, Louisiana, and the Floridas.

The "large policy" of 1808 was abandoned by Jefferson and his successors almost at once, and they reverted to the smaller one of acquiring the Floridas. It had been an impulse too sweeping to be followed up, too easily subordinated to the more pressing issues with Britain and France.[16] Not for another decade would support of the independence of Latin America command a place in the official policies of the United States government.

Jefferson's anxiety about the designs of Britain and France on the Floridas led him to take steps to prevent a transfer of those vital provinces. The garrison at New Orleans had been increased to four thousand, ostensibly to help enforce the Embargo and to nip any rival of the Burr conspiracy in the bud, but in reality, as we have seen, to be ready to seize West Florida, should a European power threaten to move in close to the Mississippi lifeline. A large British squadron at Halifax which was rumored destined for the West Indies particularly worried Americans in the late weeks of 1808. At this time the President appointed two commissioners to communicate his views on Florida to the Spanish officials concerned and to learn what they could of the attitudes of those officials toward events in their homeland.

The first of these commissioners was that tarnished war-

16. Whitaker has done an autopsy on the policy in his *United States and the Independence of Latin America,* chaps. 2 and 3 passim.

rior General James Wilkinson, a man of large ambition, small fortune, and conveniently ambivalent loyalties, long a secret pensioner of Spain and now lately emerged from an official investigation of his conduct in relation to the Burr conspiracy. Prior to the Cabinet meeting of October 22 Wilkinson had warned Jefferson of the danger that Britain might "cajole or frighten" Someruelos, the Captain General at Havana, out of Cuba and the Floridas. Wilkinson suggested himself as candidate for a mission there to forestall the catastrophe and also incidentally to furnish himself with "irrefragable evidence to strike dumb his slanderers and revilers."[17]

Wilkinson's journey to Havana was delayed by bad weather, so that his interview with Someruelos actually took place after Jefferson had left office. The Captain General's notes of the conversation indicate that Wilkinson gave assurances that the concentration of troops at New Orleans implied no menace to Spanish territory and that for the present the claim to West Florida would not even be reopened. If, however, an unfriendly power should take over that territory or East Florida as a base from which to attack American possessions, the United States would "regard itself as authorized (without any hostile view against Spain or its interests) . . . by natural law and the law of nations, to oppose such an attempt . . . by such movements and seizures as circumstances should dictate."[18]

This was fair warning that any attempted transfer of the Floridas to Britain would result in their swift absorption by the United States. The contingency is almost exactly the same as that provided for in the later No-Transfer Resolution of 1811.

While Wilkinson was thus engaged, Jefferson's second

17. Wilkinson to Jefferson (Oct. 1, 1808), Cox, *West Florida*, pp. 286–87.

18. Cox, *West Florida*, pp. 291–92.

special commissioner, Governor Claiborne of the Orleans Territory, had a most encouraging conversation with Governor Folch of West Florida, which he reported to the Secretary of State on April 21, 1809.[19] According to Claiborne, Folch assured him that the Spanish colonies in America would never submit to Bonaparte, and if Napoleon should be victorious in Spain, Mexico and Cuba would declare their independence, in which case they would prefer to be allied with the United States. To Claiborne's declaration that the United States would dislike seeing any of the Spanish dominions fall politically or commercially under the influence of either France or England, Folch replied that England had strong claims on their affections, but that he thought there was no likelihood of transfer to that power. The Spaniard then volunteered the opinion that the Floridas being of more importance to the United States than to any other power, they must eventually become a part of the Union. Whether or not Folch made this last statement only in order to ward off any immediate move by the United States in West Florida cannot be determined, but it is a precedent for the actual offer of the Floridas he made late the following year, which formed an important part of the background of the Joint Resolution of 1811.

Jefferson was intent upon acquiring the Floridas and perhaps Cuba for the United States, but only if the risk of entering the European war could be avoided. The imposition of this latter condition resulted in a mercurial policy which reacted quickly and radically to the latest intelligences from Europe. Thus in August 1808 he had considered forcible seizure if Pinkney arrived at a settlement with England; by October he had shifted his hopes to an independence movement in Spanish America, buttressed by the No-Transfer policy, and had sent commissioners to

19. Claiborne to Robert Smith, private (April 21, 1809), Rowland, ed., *Claiborne Letterbooks*, 4, 342–44.

Spanish officials to sound them on common action in pre
venting occupation of their provinces by Britain or France
Before their missions had actually begun, he had changed
course again. Recent tidings of French victories on the
peninsula aroused expectations in the President that Bonaparte would now seek to assert his authority over Spain's
American colonies, and would be willing to purchase American neutrality toward these designs by ceding the Floridas
to the United States.[20] A short time later the ex-President
suggested to his successor that Cuba might also be included
in the bargain, and that the United States ought to take it
and mark it *ne plus ultra,* since any further acquisitions
would require a navy to protect them.[21] Jefferson's willingness to give Napoleon a free hand in the rest of Spanish
America in return for immediate gain in the Floridas reveals how superficial his devotion really was to the wider
implications of the Cabinet resolution of 1808 for the
political and commercial separation of Europe and the
Americas.

Shortly after his assumption of office, President Madison
appeared to have abandoned his predecessor's forward policy in Florida. Early in April 1809 the French minister in
Washington, already angered by the repeal of the Embargo
and having learned of the Wilkinson mission and troop
concentrations at New Orleans, heatedly demanded an
explanation of the American government's policy toward
Florida. Madison at once dispatched Gallatin with assurances to still the apprehensions. According to Turreau, Gallatin informed him that President Madison had no designs
on the Floridas—"that was Mr. Jefferson's hobby"—and
that the administration would not take Cuba even if it were

20. Jefferson to James Monroe (Jan. 28, 1809), Ford, *9,* 243.
21. Jefferson to Madison (April 27, 1809), Lipscomb and Bergh, *12,*
276–77. See also his letter to Madison (April 19, 1809), Ford, *9,* 251–
52; and to W. C. Nicholas (May 25, 1809), ibid., p. 252.

offered as a gift.[22] Gallatin was generally opposed to the Florida intrigue, and there may have been as many of his own ideas in this statement as of Madison's, but there can be no doubt that for the time being the administration was following a strictly hands-off policy in Florida. To General Wilkinson, eager to seize the Floridas or bribe Spanish officials to hand them over, the Secretary of War wrote on June 22 that no interference in the affairs of the Spanish colonies would be encouraged or permitted by any persons, civil or military, under United States authority.[23]

More significant than Turreau's complaint for the future development of Madison's Florida policy was the statement presented by the newly arrived British minister, Francis James Jackson, a few months later, to the effect that His Majesty's Government could not "see with indifference any attack upon" Spain's possessions.[24] Jackson received assurances no less categorical than those given Turreau, but within a year the American government had re-embarked on a forward policy in the Floridas for which the threat of British intervention provided a convenient justification.

THE NO-TRANSFER RESOLUTION OF JANUARY 15, 1811

In June 1810 the attention of the Madison administration was urgently redirected to the Floridas by events in Europe and in Spanish America. In the Peninsular War the British armies had been forced back into Portugal while the Spanish patriots held only Cadiz and its immediate vicinity. To observers in the United States it seemed that

22. Henry Adams, *History*, 5, 37–38. Shortly afterward Smith gave similar assurances to the British minister: J. Fred Rippy, *Rivalry of the United States and Britain over Latin America, 1808–1830* (Baltimore, 1929), pp. 32–34.

23. Cox, *West Florida*, pp. 302–3.

24. Rippy, *Rivalry*, pp. 32–34.

Britain and her Spanish allies would soon part company, and when in April and May 1810 revolts against Spanish authority took place at Caracas and Buenos Aires, the hand of England was discerned behind them. After Trafalgar assured the supremacy of the Royal Navy at sea, Britain was the only European power capable of pursuing an independent policy in the New World, and remained in consequence the chief threat to United States interests there. Before the Embargo British and American merchants rivaled each other in a brisk clandestine trade with the Spanish American colonies, but after Jefferson adopted his policy of commercial coercion the British enjoyed virtually a clear field. In the favorable commercial concessions made to Britain by the rebel governments in Spanish America the Yankees saw the first steps toward British economic and political hegemony over the rest of the hemisphere. These evidences that Britain was playing a "deep game" in Spanish America, coupled with the steadily increasing acerbity of the quarrel over neutral rights and impressment, caused the Republicans to recollect the interest of the South and West in the Floridas and to take steps to ensure these important provinces against British influence.

Madison quickly determined upon a three-pronged offensive to counteract London's designs: a direct warning to keep hands off the Floridas, the dispatch of agents to Spanish America, and the encouragement of a revolt against Spanish authority among American residents of West Florida.[25]

---

25. Gallatin took care of the arrangements for sending Joel R. Poinsett to Buenos Aires, Chile, and Peru. At the time that Poinsett was preparing for his departure, Gallatin suggested to Madison that George Erving or some other person also be sent to Havana to guard against undue British influence there and in the Floridas. His suggestion was not acted upon, however. Adams, ed., *Writings of Gallatin*, *I*, 490–91.

On June 13 Secretary of State Robert Smith directed William Pinkney in London to warn the British government "that any steps on the part of Great Britain interfering with [the Floridas] will necessarily be regarded as unjust and unfriendly, and as leading to collisions, which it must be the interest of both nations to avoid."[26]

The day following Smith's instructions to Pinkney, Governor Claiborne, who was in Washington conferring with administration leaders, wrote to William Wykoff, a member of the Orleans Territory executive council, requesting him to visit West Florida for the purpose of informing its inhabitants that they would be welcomed into the Union should they ask American intervention on their behalf.[27] Claiborne expected an independence movement to develop in West Florida like those occurring elsewhere in the Spanish dominions, in which case American interests would demand annexation of the territory. But it would be best if the intervention of the United States were requested rather than imposed, if some show of spontaneity accompanied the annexation. The Governor asked, "Can no means be devised to obtain such request?"

Madison was expecting the West Florida revolt at least two months before it actually occurred, but feared that Britain might strike beforehand. On July 17 he wrote Smith to alert Governor Holmes of the Mississippi Territory to act "in the event of foreign interference with West Florida or of internal convulsions . . . to take care of the rights and interests of the United States by every measure

26. Robert Smith to William Pinkney (June 13, 1810), W. R. Manning, ed., *Diplomatic Correspondence of the United States Concerning the Independence of the Latin American Nations* (3 vols. New York, 1925), *1*, 5–6 (cited as Manning, *LA*).

27. Claiborne to Wykoff (June 14, 1810), Rowland, ed., *Claiborne Letterbooks, 5*, 31–34. See also Cox, *West Florida,* chap. 9 passim.

within the limits of the Executive authority."[28] The question of the limits of executive authority soon became an acute one for President Madison. The anticipated uprising in West Florida took place on September 23, when settlers of American origin in the four parishes between the Mississippi and the Pearl rivers overwhelmed the tiny Spanish garrison at Baton Rouge, raised the flag of the West Florida Republic, and within a fortnight applied for incorporation in the American union.[29]

No man was better acquainted with the Constitution than James Madison, one of its chief architects and exponents, and upon receiving word of the insurrection he was doubtful whether he had to wait over a month until Congress convened before taking action. He was strongly moved to act at once, but he knew that the President possessed no authority to annex foreign territory. Furthermore, in this case intervention could be construed as an act of war against Spain. Only an imperative emergency would justify such a usurpation of the war-making power of Congress. In a letter describing his dilemma to Jefferson, Madison suggested that such an emergency might in fact exist in the form of a possible transfer to Britain, a "dangerous party . . . whose conduct at Caracas gives notice of her propensity to fish in troubled waters."[30]

The invitation of the insurgents came in due time, and Madison decided to act without Congress. On October 27 he issued a secret proclamation annexing West Florida as far east as the Perdido River, subject to future "fair and

28. Madison to Smith (July 17, 1810), Hunt, ed., *Writings of Madison, 8,* 105–6.

29. *ASPFR, 3,* 395. American forces took no part in the insurrection, but a number of Americans appear to have crossed the border to aid the rebels. See Julius Pratt, *Expansionists of 1812* (New York, 1925), p. 72 n.

30. Oct. 19, 1810, Hunt, ed., *Writings, 8,* 110.

friendly negotiation and adjustment" with Spain.[31] His legal justification rested on the familiar claim that the territory formed a part of the Louisiana Purchase, that acts of Congress (e.g. the Mobile Act) had looked forward to its eventual incorporation, and that the present unrest there constituted a serious menace to the rights and interests of the United States. On the same day, the Secretary of State instructed Claiborne to occupy the territory but not to use force against Spanish troops still in possession of any part of it.[32] The town of Mobile thus remained for a time in Spanish **hands.**

Madison was apprehensive that Britain might retaliate, and on October 30 he instructed Pinkney to issue another warning to Britain about the transfer of nearby Spanish possessions:

> East Florida also, is of great importance to the United States, and it is not probable that Congress will let it pass into new hands. It is to be hoped Great Britain will not entangle herself with us by seizing it, either with or without the privity of her allies in Cadiz. The position of Cuba gives the United States so deep an interest in the destiny, even, of that island, that although they may be inactive, they could not be a satisfied spectator at its falling under any European government, which might make a fulcrum of that position against the commerce and security of the United States.[33]

Madison would not go to war to prevent the transfer of Cuba to Britain, but he would soon have congressional au-

---

31. *ASPFR, 3,* 397–98.

32. Smith to Claiborne (Oct. 27, 1810), ibid., pp. 396–97. Claiborne entered Baton Rouge on Dec. 7.

33. Madison to Pinkney (Oct. 30, 1810), Hunt, *8,* 121–22.

thority in the Joint Resolution and Act of January 15, 1811, to do so in case of foreign attack on the portions of East and West Florida which remained unoccupied by the United States.

In explanations to France, the prevention of the transfer of West Florida to Britain was alleged as the motive for the intended occupation of that territory by the United States.[34] Napoleon in fact welcomed a move which might bring the United States into further conflict with Britain at the moment when Madison had announced his intention of reinstituting nonintercourse with that nation.[35] In any case the French Emperor was powerless to prevent the annexation.

The British threat to the Floridas was not explicitly brought forward in Madison's secret annexation proclamation as a reason for his action, but as we have seen, it contributed to his decision to move without waiting for Congress to convene, and it served also to explain the annexation to the French. The same danger was kept before the public eye to gain popular acceptance of Madison's policy. In November and December 1810 the *National Intelligencer,* frequently a sounding-board for the opinions of the administration, printed letters stressing the danger of foreign intervention in the Floridas and urging American intervention, not only in West Florida to the Perdido, but also in Pensacola and St. Augustine if necessary to preclude their occupation by a hostile force.[36]

Madison revealed his West Florida proclamation to the nation in his annual message at the opening of the final session of the Eleventh Congress, blandly asserting the legality of his action, while making only a passing reference to "a

34. Henry Adams, *History,* 5, 313.
35. Cadore to Serurier (Dec. 20, 1810), Cox, *West Florida,* p. 535.
36. *National Intelligencer* (Nov. 27, Dec. 1, 27, 1810). Cox, *West Florida,* pp. 491–93.

situation . . . exposing the country to ulterior events which might essentially affect the rights and welfare of the Union."[37] In the Senate, Pickering led the Federalist attack on a bill to include West Florida in the Orleans Territory, but received little for his pains except a vote of censure for reading a letter of Talleyrand's from which the injunction of secrecy had not been removed. West Florida was accepted as a territory, and in August 1812 a thorny question was settled by dividing it between the new state of Louisiana and the Mississippi Territory, though in theory at least it was subject to future negotiation with Spain.

While Congress was wrestling with the question, the President's attention was directed to the territory east of the Perdido, for which no provision had yet been made. In the summer of 1810 the Secretary of War had sent General George Matthews of Georgia on a mission similar to Wilkinson's of the year before, to sound out Governor Folch on the idea of a union of American forces and the small Spanish garrison, to ward off any foreign attack on the Floridas.[38] Possibly out of a genuine despair of his position but more probably as a device to delay American occupation, Folch made a tentative offer to surrender his entire province in case he had not received reinforcements by January 1, 1811.[39] As soon as he heard of Claiborne's occupation of Baton Rouge, Folch indignantly withdrew his offer, but word of this did not reach Washington before Madison had employed Folch's letter to get authorization from Congress to annex the remainder of the Floridas under certain contingencies.

On January 3, 1811, the President delivered a secret message before a joint session of Congress, at which time he laid before that body Folch's letter and also a protest from Mor-

37. *Annals of Congress, 11,* 12.
38. Cox, *West Florida,* pp. 522–25.
39. Folch to the Secretary of State (Dec. 2, 1810), *ASPFR, 3,* 398–99.

ier, the British chargé in Washington.[40] Coached by Luis de Onís, the unrecognized representative of the Cadiz government in the United States, Morier caustically attacked the validity of American claims to West Florida, suggesting that Madison's professions of friendship for Spain might better have been supported by aiding Spanish authorities in suppressing the revolt of "desperadoes and land-jobbers" than by occupying the province. At the close of his note Morier declared that because of the ties that bound her to the government of Spain, Britain could not see with indifference any attack upon Spain's interests in America.[41]

Madison emphasized this last statement in his message, interpreting it as a threat of "interposition which might . . . materially affect the United States." He then asked Congress for a No-Transfer declaration:

> Taking into view the tenor of these several communications, the posture of things with which they are connected, the intimate relation of the country adjoining the United States eastward of the river Perdido to their security and tranquillity, and the peculiar interest they otherwise have in its destiny, I recommend to the consideration of Congress, the seasonableness of a declaration that the United States could not see, without serious inquietude, any part of a neighboring territory, in which they have, in different respects, so deep and so just a concern, pass from the hands of Spain into those of any other foreign Power.[42]

The President concluded his message with a request for enabling legislation to provide for the possession and gov-

40. The message and the secret deliberations of Congress which ensued are conveniently printed in D. Hunter Miller, *Secret Statutes of the United States*, Washington, 1918.

41. Morier to Smith (Dec. 15, 1810), *ASPFR, 3*, 399.

42. Miller, *Secret Statutes*, p. 11.

ernment of any part of these territories pursuant to arrangements desired by the Spanish authorities and to provide authority to act against the danger of transfer to another foreign power.

After deliberating and voting behind closed doors for a little over a week, the Senate and the House came to agreement on a joint resolution and an enabling act which received the President's signature on January 15.[43] In view of their importance, the secret resolution and statute are worth quoting at length:

> Taking into view the peculiar situation of Spain, and of her American provinces; and considering the influence which the destiny of the territory adjoining the southern border of the United States may have upon their security, tranquillity, and commerce: Therefore,
>
> *Resolved by the Senate and House of Representatives of the United States of America, in Congress assembled,* That the United States, under the peculiar circumstances of the existing crisis, cannot, without serious inquietude, see any part of the said territory pass into the hands of any foreign power; and that a due regard to their own safety compels them to provide, under certain contingencies, for the temporary occupation of the said territory; they, at the same time, declare that the said territory shall, in their hands, remain subject to future negotiation.
>
> *An Act to enable the President of the United States, under certain contingencies, to take possession of the country lying east of the river Perdido, and south of the state of Georgia and the Mississippi territory, and for other purposes.*

43. The vote in the Senate on the bill was 23 to 7, in the House, 78 to 21: ibid., pp. 17, 29.

Be it enacted by the Senate and House of Representatives of the United States of America, in Congress assembled, That the President of the United States be, and he is hereby, authorized, to take possession of, and occupy, all or any part of the territory lying east of the river Perdido, and south of the state of Georgia, and the Mississippi territory, in case an arrangement has been, or shall be, made with the local authority of the said territory, or any part thereof, to occupy the said territory, or any part thereof, by any foreign government; and he may, for the purpose of taking possession, and occupying the territory aforesaid, and in order to maintain therein the authority of the United States, employ any part of the army and navy of the United States which he may deem necessary.[44]

These are notable documents in many respects. Not again until the so-called Pittman–Bloom joint resolution of June 18, 1940, expressing opposition to the cession of French and Dutch possessions in the Caribbean to Nazi Germany, would Congress authorize in advance presidential action to prevent a threatened transfer of territory in this hemisphere from one European sovereign to another, and in 1940 the use of force was not expressly contemplated.

The action of Congress in 1811 conferred upon the No-Transfer idea an air of permanence and tokens of dignity which it had hitherto lacked. A precedent had been set which could be referred to later, as it was in 1818 when negotiations with Spain over the Floridas reached another crisis. What had previously been a more or less casual device for dealing with particular security problems began after

44. Miller, pp. 5–6. Secs. 2 and 3 of the enabling act provided $100,000 to defray the expenses of taking possession, and authorized the executive to set up a temporary government in the territory with due regard for the civil liberties of the inhabitants.

1811 to assume the self-conscious aspect of a settled policy, ready at hand to be applied to analogous situations in regions other than the Floridas. American diplomatists began to show that awareness of a common pattern in events which is the necessary condition for the crystallization of a principle from a policy.

The measures adopted by Congress in 1811 were not justified principally as a claim of right, but rather by a claim of inescapable self-interest dictated by geographical and economic necessity. In notifying the British government of the new policy, Secretary of State Smith candidly admitted that eventual possession of the Floridas was contemplated by the United States. "This motive of national interest is supported and strengthened by the obvious policy of the measure. Although this government does not wantonly seek an extension of territory, it frankly avows the pursuit of an object essential to its future peace and safety upon honorable and reasonable terms. The United States cannot see with indifference a foreign power, under any pretext whatever possess itself of the Floridas."[45]

Whatever the magnitude of the British threat to the Floridas that Madison had found it convenient to suggest to Congress, the language of Morier's protest was certainly vague on the subject of what, if any, action Britain might take on behalf of Spain. And as a matter of fact Morier's superiors in London, while they approved the chargé's conduct, were explicitly unwilling even to threaten the use of force, much less to undertake direct military action in the Floridas. The British Foreign Minister warned Augustus Foster, his newly appointed minister to Washington, against any "hostile or menacing language," and to confine his representations "within the limits of a friendly and candid exposition of the unjust and ungenerous nature of

45. Smith to Pinkney (Jan. 22, 1811), Manning, *LA, 1*, 9–11.

the proceedings of the government of the United States against the foreign possessions of Spain, in the present situation of the Spanish government and nation."[46] "Great Britain cannot," Wellesley continued, "view such proceedings against her ally [the occupation of West Florida], without regret and pain; but it is not a necessary consequence of those sentiments, that this government should proceed to vindicate the rights of Spain by force of arms." As long as the British government entertained this view, there was little likelihood that they would provide Madison with a justification for occupying East Florida because of a threat of transfer, as authorized in the congressional No-Transfer resolution. The President in fact hoped for little on this score, and directed his immediate attention to the possibility that the local authorities would deliver the remainder of the province to the United States.

THE ACT OF 1811 APPLIED TO EAST FLORIDA

Armed with the law of January 15, Madison hastened to take advantage of Folch's offer to surrender the rest of West Florida. On January 26 Secretary Smith drafted instructions to General Matthews and Colonel John McKee appointing them commissioners to receive the province from Folch and reminding them also of the second contingency specified by Congress under which the territory might be occupied, namely the "undoubted manifestation of the approach of a force" for the purpose of substituting another foreign power for Spain there.[47] Finding Folch obdurately unwill-

46. Wellesley to Foster (April 10, 1811), Bernard Mayo, ed., "Instructions to the British Ministers to the United States, 1791–1812," *Annual Report of the American Historical Association for 1936* (3 vols. Washington, 1941), 3, 321.

47. Smith to Matthews and McKee (Jan. 26, 1811), *ASPFR, 3,* 571–72.

ing even to discuss the purpose of his mission until American forces had been withdrawn from the part of West Florida which they had occupied, and unable to descry any British squadrons on the horizon, Matthews made his way to the East Florida border in accordance with discretionary authority in his instructions to try his luck at acquiring this territory by agreement with the "local authorities."

The history of Matthews' activities is a familiar one and need not detain us.[48] Unsuccessful in his attempts to persuade the governor of East Florida to surrender his province voluntarily, Matthews stirred up a revolt among American settlers near the St. Mary's River. Aided by gunboats of the United States Navy and army regulars who crossed the border as "volunteers," the insurgents took Amelia Island on March 18, 1812, and proceeded to besiege St. Augustine. Matthews accepted the northern portion of East Florida in the name of the United States from these "local authorities."

Although the President and the Secretary of State had been kept informed by Matthews of the progress of his intrigues, they had made no remonstrance, and in fact had ordered the military and naval commanders in the area to cooperate with him. Probably this meant cooperation after the revolution had taken place, not in bringing it about. Nevertheless their commissioner had some right to suppose his actions had his superiors' tacit approval, and it seems highly likely that the President was not unwilling to make use of Matthews' methods for obtaining the province under an attenuated interpretation of the limitations on executive action imposed by Congress.

Matthews' stroke against Spanish authority in East Florida was ill-timed from the point of view of the Republican

48. For the best account of events in East Florida at this time see Pratt, *Expansionists of 1812,* chap. 2 passim.

administration, however, and Madison was forced to repudiate his agent's actions. The recently published correspondence of John Henry, which had exposed an alleged intrigue between New England Federalists and British authorities in Canada, made Matthews' machinations in Florida politically embarrassing to Madison, who did not want a Republican scandal to neutralize his partisan advantage.[49] On April 4, 1812, Secretary of State James Monroe, who had replaced the incompetent Robert Smith a year before, wrote to inform Matthews that he had exceeded his powers under the laws of Congress, and that he was relieved of his assignment.[50]

As it turned out, the recall of Matthews did not signify a retreat from East Florida. Madison appointed Governor D. B. Mitchell of Georgia, another ardent annexationist, as the general's successor; and although Mitchell received instructions to restore the status quo ante Matthews, he was ordered not to return the occupied territories to Spanish authority until he had guarantees of amnesty for the native insurgents, whom he was not to remove from power.[51] Difficulties arising out of these conditions promised to delay the withdrawal of American troops indefinitely.

Anxiety lest the province should fall a prey to Great Britain undoubtedly supported the determination of the American government to stay in East Florida, particularly since the likelihood of war with that power was increasing almost daily. When the British minister demanded an explanation of Matthews' subversive agitation among the subjects of Spain below the St. Mary's and affirmed the "deep interest which His Royal Highness the Prince Regent takes in the security of Florida," Monroe responded in a note which admitted no exception to the assertion of paramount Ameri-

49. Ibid., pp. 109–14. Adams, *History,* 5, 174–86.
50. *ASPFR, 3,* 572.
51. Monroe to Mitchell (April 10, 1812), ibid.

can interests in that region.[52] After adverting to the long-unsatisfied claims against Spain, for which East Florida might be the only possible indemnity, the Secretary pointed out that "situated as East Florida is, cut off from the other possessions of Spain, and surrounded in a great measure by the territory of the United States, and having also an important bearing on their commerce, no other power could think of taking possession of it, with other than hostile views to them."

On the eve of the declaration of war against Great Britain, Monroe reminded Governor Mitchell of the duty of the executive under the law of 1811 and advised him that he was "authorized to consider the entrance, or attempt to enter, especially under existing circumstances, of British troops, of any description, as the case contemplated by the law, and to use the proper means to defeat it."[53]

After the war had begun, the British did not oblige the administration by attacking East Florida, but Mitchell prolonged his quarrel with the Spanish governor and hung on, confidently expecting, as did most Southerners, that Congress would legalize the occupation in the near future. A House proposal to occupy both the Floridas petered out in July, however, while Indian attacks threatened to dislodge the slender American garrison entirely. Madison gave control of the occupation to Major General Thomas Pinckney in October, resting his hopes for authorization of his actions on a bill sponsored by administration supporters in the Senate. On January 14, 1814, at the request of the Senate, the President submitted a report of the Secretary of State on the status of the East Florida question in which Monroe referred to the danger of a British attack on the province and recommended legislation authorizing the occupation

52. Foster to Monroe (Sept. 5, 1811), Monroe to Foster (Nov. 2, 1811): ibid., pp. 543–45.
53. Monroe to Mitchell (May 27, 1812), ibid., p. 573.

of all of Florida, since nothing could be accomplished by negotiation while Spain remained the satellite of Britain or France.[54]

The administration's hopes foundered when Federalists, northern Republicans, and personal foes of the President joined forces to strike out those sections of the bill pertaining to the territory east of the Perdido. As passed on February 12, the law authorized the occupation of no new territory except Mobile, which Wilkinson took on April 13. General Pinckney was ordered to evacuate East Florida, and the last American forces withdrew on May 16.

Meanwhile the question of British designs on the Floridas had arisen in another connection. Following the acceptance by the United States of the Russian mediation offer, Albert Gallatin and James Bayard received appointments to join John Quincy Adams in Europe to conduct peace negotiations. In his instructions Monroe ordered the commissioners to press the claim of the United States to West Florida (title from the Louisiana Purchase) and East Florida as well (indemnity for unsettled claims). He informed them of the imminent occupation of Mobile under the terms of the recent act of Congress, and reminded them that the law of 1811 still authorized the preclusive occupation of East Florida in case of an attempt by a foreign power to gain possession of it.[55] Gallatin had never favored the aggressive designs of Jefferson and Madison on the Floridas, and questioned the necessity or the wisdom of occupying Mobile when the result might be to draw Russia and Britain together against the aggressor and so jeopardize the peace negotiation.[56] Monroe replied curtly that the Mobile question was settled, but that East Florida had been ordered

54. Pratt, *Expansionists of 1812*, p. 227.
55. Monroe to the American Commissioners (April 27, 1813), Adams, ed., *Writings of Gallatin*, I, 539 n.
56. Gallatin to Monroe (May 2, 1813), ibid., pp. 539–40.

evacuated.[57] Then in an official letter to both commissioners and in a private communication to Gallatin, the Secretary disclosed that "reliable information" had reached
Washington of the cession of the Floridas to Britain by the
Cadiz government:

> Whether, if this be true, she will attempt to take pos-
> session of it, we know not. It is known however that a
> considerable force is collecting at Bermuda, and that
> an embarcation had been made at Cadiz of a strong
> reinforcement destined for this continent. Florida may
> be the object, tho' it is more probable, that its destina-
> tion will be, either Canada, or some part of our coast.
> You known the contingency on which a power is vested
> in the President by law to take possession of this prov-
> ince.[58]

To Gallatin, Monroe added his private opinion that possession of both the Floridas by the United States would
greatly facilitate negotiations for peace by showing Britain
what could happen to Canada if she failed to meet American demands on impressment and other issues.[59] Gallatin
remained unimpressed with Monroe's rumor, and amiably
recorded his dissent from the Secretary's views, urging an
immediate evacuation of East Florida as the surest way to
remove any pretext for a British occupation.[60]

The British neither attacked East Florida nor made an
issue of the American occupation of West Florida during
the peace negotiations at Ghent, despite Spanish urging.

57. Monroe to Gallatin (May 5, 1813), ibid., pp. 540–41.

58. Monroe to Gallatin and Bayard (May 1813), Elizabeth Donnan,
ed., *Papers of James A. Bayard,* Vol. 2 of *Annual Report of the American Historical Association, 1913* (Washington, 1915), pp. 222–23.

59. Monroe to Gallatin (May 6, 1813), Adams, ed., *Writings of Gallatin, 1,* 543–44.

60. Gallatin to Monroe (May 8, 1813), ibid., p. 545.

In any event, Jackson's victory at New Orleans would have settled the issue so far as Britain was concerned. Madison had failed to acquire East Florida, despite the hopeful expectations which had accompanied the Act of 1811 and the declaration of war in 1812. Peace had come to Europe and America, ending any immediate danger of transfer to either Britain or France, though this was not always clearly understood in the United States. The territory west of the Perdido remained occupied "subject to future negotiation," and although the incorporation of the area into the Union with the admission of Louisiana, Alabama, and Mississippi lent an air of unreality to the proceedings, the American government reverted to the weary business of diplomatic bargaining with Spain for the cession. Until Spain finally ratified the Adams-Onís treaty in 1820, the shadow of Britain continued to loom menacingly over the Floridas, with the result that the United States kept the anti-transfer trigger of the Act of 1811 in constant readiness for use to back up American occupation if necessary. Oddly enough, its only application was against not Britain but a band of freebooters without proper authority from any foreign government.

THE THREAT OF TRANSFER AND THE FLORIDA NEGOTIATIONS

Pakenham's operations against New Orleans from West Florida during the War of 1812 served dramatically to emphasize the long-appreciated fact that in the hands of a hostile major power the Spanish province was a lethal weapon pressed against the arterial Mississippi waterway. The treaty of Ghent by no means put an end to anxieties on that score. The awakened sense of American nationality which was one of the permanent legacies of the war carried with it an intensified hatred and suspicion of England, which was alert for sinister designs on the part of that nation in the New World. Command of the seas gave her the power, alliance with Spain the justification, and the prospect of commercial advantages and acquisition of the Floridas and perhaps Cuba the motive, for intervening to quell the revolts in the Spanish colonies and to contain the growing power of the United States. So it seemed to Americans at any rate. Actually, Castlereagh's policy was to cultivate good relations with the United States (the Rush-Bagot Treaty for neutralizing the Great Lakes and the boundary settlement in 1818), but to try to prevent them from becoming the first nation to recognize the revolted Spanish colonies and so to diminish the prestige and trade of Britain there. Meanwhile he maneuvered skillfully to avoid a flat refusal to aid Spain in forcibly subduing her colonies, which would in turn—as finally happened in 1820—reveal to his continental partners in the Concert of Europe the ideological gulf between Britain and the champions of armed intervention in the name of "legitimacy."

After the close of the Congress of Vienna the United States suffered from an epidemic of rumors that Spain had ceded the Floridas to Britain.[61] Monroe called these reports to the attention of his minister at London, John Quincy Adams, and directed him to inform the British government that any move to occupy the province "must of necessity produce war" with them.[62] The United States had a claim to West Florida by right and to East Florida by necessity. In any other hands it constituted an intolerable menace by virtue of its command of the Gulf and the rivers so important to western commerce and because of the opportunity it gave for influence over the Creeks and other Indians.

61. See E. H. Tatum, *The United States and Europe, 1815–1823* (Berkeley, 1936), pp. 158 ff.

62. Monroe to J. Q. Adams (Dec. 10, 1815), Hamilton, ed., *Writings of Monroe, 5,* 381.

The Indian question was particularly touchy at this time. Many rebellious Creeks had taken refuge in Florida to escape General Jackson's avenging armies in 1813, and the British had organized them during their campaign there. After the war, Colonel Nicholls, a British officer who had been engaged in this work, and a certain Captain Woodbine remained among the Creeks, encouraging them to resist the division of Creek lands imposed by the Treaty of Fort Jackson in 1814. In 1815 Nicholls concluded an alliance with the Indians in the name of Great Britain. The British government quietly repudiated the work of these self-appointed agents, but to the American frontiersman the continued presence in Florida of British subjects who presumed to make representations on behalf of the savages and who were openly supplying them with firearms made it easy to believe that Britain had designs on the territory.

Upon receiving Monroe's letter, Adams took up the Florida question with Lord Castlereagh.[63] In response to the American minister's request for a more formal disavowal of Colonel Nicholls and his treaty than the verbal statements of Lord Bathurst, the Foreign Secretary merely repeated that there was no such document among the papers he was to carry down to Parliament. Adams explained that rumors about a cession of the Floridas to Britain had heightened the concern aroused by the Nicholls affair. On this point Castlereagh declared himself happy to be able to set Adams at ease:

> There is not and never has been the slightest foundation for it whatsoever. It never has been even men-

63. Diary entry dated Jan. 25, 1816, C. F. Adams, ed., *Memoirs of John Quincy Adams* (12 vols. Philadelphia, 1874–77), *3*, 289–91. Adams reported the conversation briefly to Monroe on Jan. 31, Manning, *CR, 1,* 783, and in more detail on Feb. 8, W. C. Ford, ed., *Writings of John Quincy Adams, 5,* 502–5.

tioned. . . . We have no desire to add an inch of ground to our territories in any part of the world. We have as much as we know how to manage. . . . Do you only observe the same moderation. If we should find you hereafter pursuing a system of encroachment upon your neighbors, what we might do defensively is another consideration.

This mixture of assurances and admonitions was not calculated to relieve the anxieties of the American government. In all probability the Foreign Secretary had no real intention at any time of making an issue of peace or war out of American efforts to acquire the Floridas, but was merely doing his duty to Spain and to his own country by strewing disturbing insinuations in the restless path of United States expansionism in North America and influence in Spanish America. At any rate, by late 1817 Castlereagh had come to the conclusion that Spain must inevitably cede the Floridas to the United States, though he cloaked his conviction with a spiritless offer to mediate in the dispute.[64]

As Secretary of State, Monroe had reopened negotiations with Spain for a cession of the Floridas, but he had got no further than Spain's unacceptable offer to exchange those provinces for Louisiana minus New Orleans. On the same day the Virginian was inaugurated as President of the United States, his friend Andrew Jackson wrote to make certain Monroe had not lost sight of this important object of foreign policy. Arguing in favor of opening the former Creek lands for sale, Jackson urged the necessity of populating the southern borderlands as rapidly as possible in the interests of national security. The revenues lost would be "but as a drop in the bucket when brought in competition with the value of that country to the Union, or when compared with

64. Castlereagh to Bagot (Nov. 10, 1817), C. K. Webster, *Britain and the Independence of Latin America* (2 vols. London, 1938), 2, 489.

the amount which it would cost the United States to retake it, should it once fall into the hands of an enemy possessing a superiority on the ocean."[65] Monroe did not lose sight of the Floridas, and he remained agitated during his first year in office by a fear that Britain intended soon to intervene in the struggle between Spain and her colonies. Such a development, "fraught with importance to the United States," could involve them in a war which would "decide the fate of our free government, and of the independence of Spanish America."[66]

It was not to do battle at Armageddon that American forces were presently mobilized, however, but to clear Amelia Island and the Seminole country of a band of freebooters. In the late summer of 1817 Fernandina, on Amelia Island—the scene of Matthews' exploits a few years earlier—was captured by Gregor McGregor, a Scottish adventurer lately come from expeditions in Mexico. McGregor (who bore an unauthorized commission from the unofficial representative in the United States of the revolutionary government of Venezuela!) proceeded to dispatch privateers against merchant shipping, some of it American, while he continued the profitable contraband trade with American territory. On October 30 President Monroe presented his Cabinet with a query as to the expediency of sending an expedition to break up this nest of pirates and smugglers, and receiving an affirmative answer ordered General Gaines to proceed there for that purpose.[67] Upon his arrival,

65. Jackson to Monroe (March 4, 1817), J. S. Bassett, ed., *The Correspondence of Andrew Jackson* (7 vols. Washington, 1926–35), 2, 277–78.

66. Monroe to Jackson (June 2, Oct. 5, 1817), ibid., pp. 296, 332. Monroe resorted to hyperbole here for the purpose of persuading Jackson not to retire.

67. See Charles C. Griffin, *The United States and the Disruption of the Spanish Empire, 1810–1832* (New York, 1937), p. 140; and S. F. Bemis, *John Quincy Adams and the Foundations of American Foreign Policy* (New York, 1949), p. 344.

Gaines found that McGregor had been supplanted by Luis Aury, Venezuelan patriot and sometime associate of Jean Lafitte, the Baratarian buccaneer. Gaines had no difficulty in occupying the town, however.

In his first annual message Monroe revealed his orders to Gaines, and asserted his belief that the acts of McGregor and Aury had no official sanction from any revolutionary government in Spanish America—adding, significantly, that if such authority had in fact been given, "it would be difficult to reconcile it with the friendly relations existing between the United States and the colonies."[68] The implications of this statement rapidly became apparent when Henry Clay, now beginning to make political capital out of the popular cause of recognizing the independence of Spain's revolted colonies, used the expulsion of revolutionary forces from Amelia Island as an issue with which to discredit the administration before the electorate.[69]

Monroe was on secure ground politically, for Clay would win few votes in the South by advocating leaving a foreign force in possession of a part of coveted East Florida, but the President took no chances on a stampede in Congress toward precipitous recognition of Spain's colonies. Early in January 1818 the administration released for publication the No-Transfer resolution and enabling act of 1811, hitherto undisclosed to the public, and on January 13 the President delivered a special message on the occupation of Amelia Island before a joint session of Congress in which he declared that Gaines had been ordered to act under the provisions of that legislation.[70] After insisting that Mc-

68. Manning, *LA, 1,* 50–51.
69. Bemis, *Adams,* p. 345.
70. See *Niles' Weekly Register, 13* (Jan. 10, 1818), 315–16. On Jan. 26 the *National Intelligencer* published the old protests of Morier and Foster against the original occupation of West Florida, with no apparent purpose beyond re-creating the suspicion of Britain which had led to the original passage of the Act of 1811.

Gregor and Aury were private adventurers engaged in piracy and an illicit traffic in slaves, Monroe went on to declare that their pretensions to rule over Fernandina infringed on the larger rights and interests of the United States in East Florida:

> The path of duty was plain from the commencement. . . . The law of 1811, lately published, and which it is therefore proper now to mention, was considered applicable to the case from the moment the proclamation of the chief of the enterprise was seen. . . .
>
> For these injuries, especially those proceeding from Amelia Island, Spain would be responsible if it was not manifest that . . . she was utterly unable to prevent them. . . . The territory of Spain will nevertheless be respected so far as it may be done consistently with the essential interests and safety of the United States. In expelling these adventurers from these parts it was not intended to make any conquest from Spain or to injure in any degree the cause of the colonies. Care will be taken that no part of the territory contemplated by the law of 1811 shall be occupied by a foreign government of any kind, or that injuries of the nature of those complained of shall be repeated.[71]

The Amelia Island occupation was the first and only application of the anti-transfer provisions of the Act of 1811, and it was in several respects a peculiar one. For one thing its applicability to the case in question appears to have been distinctly an afterthought, regardless of what Monroe said in his special message. No mention of the Act occurs in any surviving account of the Cabinet meeting of October 30, or in the Secretary of War's orders to Gaines. Probably Monroe invoked it belatedly to head off criticism in Con-

---

71. Hamilton, ed., *Writings of Monroe, 6,* 36 n.

gress of his intervention, since it provided statutory authorization for what might have been considered an act of war against Spain. This seems more than likely in view of the questionable identification of McGregor's and Aury's bands of rascals as a "foreign power" within the contemplation of the Act, particularly when Monroe was at such pains to prove they had no legitimate connection with any Spanish American government. Even had he admitted the connection, the fact that these governments remained unrecognized by the United States or any other nation might have presented legal difficulties in itself. Monroe's inconsistencies reflect the delicate situation he faced in trying to prevent the recognition issue from becoming acute in Congress, and at the same time preserving the Floridas for the United States. He was no more anxious to see Spanish American rebels in Amelia Island than to see Great Britain there. Notwithstanding the strained construction of the law of 1811 which Monroe resorted to, his course of action was undoubtedly in line with the original intention of Congress in enacting it: to keep the Floridas in the hands of weak Spain until such time as the United States could secure them, if possible by peaceful means.[72]

The Amelia Island episode hastened the decision of Luis de Onís to open the negotiation with Secretary of State John Quincy Adams which culminated in the celebrated "Transcontinental Treaty" of 1819, by which the United States received not only the two Floridas but title to vast reaches of prairie, mountain, and forest extending above the line of 42° north latitude to the Pacific. One of the

72. When in May 1818 David de Forest, the agent of the Buenos Aires government in the United States, revealed to Secretary of State Adams that his government was considering taking the Floridas, Adams referred to the Act of 1811 and the Amelia Island episode as evidence of his government's attitude toward the matter. Adams, ed., *Memoirs of J. Q. Adams, 4,* 89.

most important elements contributing to this spectacular achievement of American diplomacy was General Jackson's capture of St. Marks and Pensacola in Florida during the Seminole war early in 1818, and the accompanying execution of Arbuthnot and Ambrister, Britishers who like Woodbine and Nicholls had been counseling and supplying the Indians. Jackson's exploits demonstrated again to Spain that the United States could seize the Floridas at will, and encouraged Madrid to expedite a peaceful settlement of the question, especially after it became clear that Great Britain had chosen to make no protest about Ambrister and Arbuthnot. Although public sentiment in England ran so high against Jackson's actions that, as Castlereagh later told Rush, there might have been war had the Ministry but "held up a finger," the British government held fast to its belief that its "true policy" in the war-weary years after Vienna was "to appease controversy, and to secure, if possible, for all states a long interval of repose."[73] Spain's hopes for British interposition in the Florida question and in the Spanish colonial revolts were completely dashed when a short time later Castlereagh disclosed that he would oppose any such policy at the forthcoming Congress of Aix-la-Chapelle.[74]

Even though evidences of the conciliatory disposition of the British government toward the United States multiplied in the years after Ghent, they failed to allay the suspicions of the American people and of Secretary Adams that all of it was somehow calculating and insincere. Therefore when Spain delayed ratification of the Adams-Onís treaty, British influence was immediately assigned as a cause. In July 1819

73. Rush, *Memoranda of a Residence at the Court of London* (Philadelphia, 1833), p. 140. Castlereagh to Bagot (Nov. 10, 1817), cited in Rippy, *Rivalry,* p. 66.

74. Castlereagh to Wellesley (Sept. 1, 1818), Webster, *Britain and Latin America,* 2, 369–70.

Hezekiah Niles published in his *Register* portions of the debate in the House of Lords on the Florida treaty, particularly a speech by Lord Lansdowne attacking the government for jeopardizing the balance of power in the vicinity of the British West Indies by not requiring from Spain a pledge against a cession of the Floridas to the United States.[75] This sort of statement recalled the old protests of Morier and Foster in 1810 and 1811, published the year before, and echoed a recent rumor that the British had declared to Spain that they wanted an option on the Floridas.[76] Spanish diplomacy encouraged these suspicions by citing British displeasure as a reason for delaying ratification, disingenuously invoking the shadow of British power when Castlereagh's policy of noninterference denied Spain the substance of it.[77]

Final ratification of the Transcontinental Treaty by Spain somewhat belatedly followed the revolution of January 1820 there; and on February 19, 1821, ratification for a second time in the United States Senate put an end to the Florida question forever. In the years of mounting crisis that preceded the War of 1812 and in the lingering bitterness that followed it, the fear that the world's first sea power might secure a lodgment in the vicinity of New Orleans, with all that such a contingency threatened for the safety and commerce of the southern and western United States, had been the primary element in the American determination to possess the Floridas. Jefferson had considered seizing them outright, but had also invited a voluntary annexation through the Wilkinson and Claiborne missions, meanwhile losing no opportunity to proclaim his government's opposition to any transfer of the provinces except to the United States. After an insurrection there which had his hearty

75. *Niles' Weekly Register, 16* (July 8, 1819), 316.
76. Ibid., *13* (Nov. 15, 1817), 181–82.
77. Forsyth to Adams (Aug. 22, 1819), Manning, *LA, 3,* 1986.

approval, Madison ensured West Florida against a Spanish transfer to Great Britain by annexing it, and in effect proclaimed his power to do the same in East Florida with the famous Resolution and Act of 1811. The sectional nature of concern over Florida became clearly evident in the failure of the annexation bills in Congress during the war. After Ghent the commercial rivalry with Britain in Latin America helped to promote a more broadly national support for the anti-British Florida policy of Monroe and Adams.

The nationalism forged in the flames of the war with Britain accepted as axiomatic the superiority of American republican institutions over those of the decadent monarchies of Europe, and defiantly predicted the eventual triumph of liberty throughout the world. As a necessary precondition it postulated the creation of a separate American system of republican states in the Western Hemisphere, headed by a North American republic of continental pro-proportions. More than any other American of his day, Secretary of State John Quincy Adams personified the truculent republicanism and expansionism of his countrymen. Exasperated by Spain's failure promptly to ratify the Transcontinental Treaty, he confided to his diary thoughts on American policy, past and future, which he would not long keep from the world:

> Great Britain, after vilifying us twenty years as a mean, low-minded, peddling nation, having no generous ambitions and no God but gold, had now changed her tone, and was endeavoring to alarm the world at the gigantic grasp of our ambition. . . . Nothing that we could say or do would remove this impression until the world shall be familiarized with the idea of considering our proper dominion to be the continent of North America. From the time when we became an independent people it was as much a law as that the Mississippi

should flow to the sea. Spain had possessions upon our
southern, and Great Britain upon our northern border.
. . . It is a physical, moral and political absurdity that
such fragments of territory, with sovereigns at 1500
miles beyond the sea, worthless and burdensome to
their owners, should exist permanently contiguous to a
great, powerful, enterprising and rapidly growing
nation.[78]

The "law" Adams referred to is the concept of national
interest which the United States had so far applied succes-
sively to Louisiana and Florida. Adams himself next invoked it—to prevent a transfer to Great Britain—though in
regard to the adjacent island of Cuba rather than the continent of North America.

78. Adams, ed., *Memoirs of J. Q. Adams, 4,* 438–39.

CHAPTER 5

Cuba and the Monroe Doctrine

The extension of the No-Transfer policy to Cuba was a logical outgrowth of the acquisition of New Orleans and the Floridas, to which it had already been successfully applied. Just as the security of the "key to the Western world" at the mouth of the Mississippi made it imperative that adjacent Spanish territories not fall into the hands of a great maritime power, so the safe continuance of American sea-going commerce in the Gulf of Mexico required that neither Britain nor France should establish herself in Havana harbor, virtually impregnable if properly fortified, and so situated that from it a first-class sea power could command the commerce of the entire Caribbean region. More than that, Cuba could be a self-sustaining base (so far as foodstuffs were concerned) from which a hostile force could mount an offensive against Florida or Louisiana.

In addition to the strategic necessity for preventing the transfer of Cuba, the United States had a strong commercial interest in the island which developed greatly during the trials of Spain in the Peninsular Wars, when the ancient system of commercial exclusion broke down under the pressures of necessity, even in the colonies like Cuba which remained loyal to Spain. In 1821 out of the 1,322 vessels entering the port of Havana 655 were American, as compared with 385 Spanish and 128 English ships.[1] That same year the value of exports from the United States to Cuba stood at over four and a half million dollars, or two-thirds the value of the entire trade with Spanish America, while in return the island constituted an important source of specie and supplied much of the coffee and other tropical products consumed in the United States.[2] Furthermore, commercial interest in Cuba was not sectional; New England and the Middle Atlantic states had a larger stake in it than had the South.

The same cannot be said for the slavery issue, which began to figure prominently in the Cuban question after the Missouri Compromise of 1820, and continued to do so until the American Civil War. Southerners urged the annexation of Cuba to the United States as a permanent solution to the persistent threat to national security posed by the failing power of Spain: they were eager to add another slave state to buttress their strength in Congress; they feared a revolution in Cuba which would result in slave insurrections that would serve as an example to their own Negroes; and they worried that Great Britain might acquire the island and free the slaves there, exposing the Southern states to the contagion of emancipation.

These strategic and economic considerations moved Secretary of State Adams in 1823 to describe Cuba as "an object of transcendent importance to the political and commercial interests of our Union . . . an importance in the sum of our national interests with which that of no other foreign territory can be compared, and little inferior to that which

1. Joel R. Poinsett, *Notes on Mexico* (London, 1825), pp. 288–89. Poinsett made a brief stopover in Cuba on his return from his well-known journey to Mexico.

2. Whitaker, *United States and Independence of Latin America*, pp. 128–31.

binds the members of the Union together."[3] When he wrote
this, Adams had long since firmly established the policy of
opposing the transfer of Cuba from Spain to any other European power, believing that the island must someday become a part of the United States through the workings of
the "laws of political gravitation"—the imperative logic of
Cuba's geographical position. During 1823 the danger that
Cuba might be transferred to Britain or France was as important an anxiety in Washington as was the threat of intervention by the Holy Alliance in the struggle between Spain
and her colonies; and the No-Transfer policy stood in a position of equal importance among the hemispheric security
policies of the United States and the newly conceived principles of Noncolonization and Nonintervention announced
by President Monroe in his celebrated message of December 2.

Opposition to the transfer of territory in this hemisphere
from one European sovereign to another was the fundamental security policy of the United States as long as there were
no other independent nations in the Americas, and even
after Latin America gained its independence, the policy
continued to apply to the crucially important European
colonies remaining in the New World. After this time there
was no longer any danger (except in Cuba, the Guianas, and
a diminishing number of Caribbean islands) of a transfer of
colonial sovereignty in such a way as seriously to disturb the
American balance of power. From 1822 on, the threat came
from intervention by European powers to restore Spanish
authority. This is the threat the Monroe Doctrine was
directed against, and its principles were in effect variations
of the No-Transfer principle, devised to meet a new situation. Historians of the Monroe Doctrine have failed fully to
appreciate this. It will be the purpose of the present chapter

3. Adams to Hugh Nelson (April 28, 1823), W. C. Ford, ed., *Writings of J. Q. Adams, 7, 372.*

to examine the relation of the Cuban question and the No-Transfer policy to the events that led to the Message of 1823.

BEYOND THE FLORIDAS LIES CUBA

It will be recalled that Cuba was one of the objects of Jefferson's "large policy" of 1808, prominent features of which were a stated opposition to the transfer of the island to another European power, and a declaration of common interest in excluding all European influence from this hemisphere. Jefferson made a permanent convert to this policy in Governor Claiborne, who in the years before the War of 1812 constantly urged upon the Madison administration the strategic and commercial importance of preventing a British acquisition of Spanish Cuba, "the real mouth of the Mississippi."[4]

Manifestations of a general concern over the fate of Cuba appeared only after news arrived of Spain's delay in ratifying the Adams-Onís treaty of 1819. This revived suspicions of British plots to check the growth of the United States. Rumors circulated to the effect that Britain was applying pressure at Madrid to prevent the cession of the Floridas to the United States, or to obtain them for herself, or at least to secure a cession of Cuba to Britain as compensation for American aggrandizement.[5] When British newspapers and parliamentary opposition began publicly to urge these policies on the government, American fears seemed justified.

Passage of the British Foreign Enlistments Act of 1819 aroused particular uncertainty across the Atlantic about Castlereagh's real motives, because this move to curb clandestine aid to the Latin American revolutionists seemed so directly opposed to Britain's interests and past practice.

4. Claiborne to Robert Smith (Dec. 24, 1810), Rowland, ed., *Letterbooks, 5,* 62–63. See also ibid., pp. 65, 290–91, 396, and *6,* 21, 27–28.
5. *Niles' Weekly Register, 16* (May 22, June 2, 1819), 210–11, 381.

Actually, as became clear in time, Castlereagh had no intention of enforcing the Act, and privately sponsored expeditions continued to depart unmolested from Britain after it was passed. The measure was a sop to Spain—an attempt to delay Ferdinand's inevitable appeal to the continental powers for aid in subduing his revolted colonies.

American diplomatic representatives in Europe who tried to fathom the mysteries of British policy did not come up with very encouraging explanations. True, Gallatin at Paris could see no threat to the United States in the Foreign Enlistments Act, but Alexander Everett, the American chargé d'affaires at Brussels, speculated to his friend the Secretary of State that the only way to account for Castlereagh's sponsorship of a measure so unpopular and so opposed to previous British policy, was to suppose that it represented part of a bargain which gave Cuba to Britain in return.[6] In London, Richard Rush approached Castlereagh directly on the subject of Britain's attitude toward the Florida cession, and received the not entirely reassuring reply that while the British government would have preferred that Spain had not made the cession, they now favored ratification of the treaty rather than a disturbing war between Spain and the United States.[7]

Neither Monroe nor Adams was much alarmed about British policy at this time; in fact the Secretary of State was so sure that Castlereagh would not support Ferdinand that he recommended seizing the Floridas if Spain further delayed ratification of the treaty of 1819 with the United States. He was confident it could be done without the risk of war.[8]

6. Gallatin to John Forsyth in Madrid (July 9, 1819), Adams, ed., *Writings of Gallatin*, 2, 109–11. Everett to Adams (Aug. 8, 1819), Manning, *LA, 3*, 1711–12.

7. Tatum, *United States and Europe*, pp. 161–62.

8. April 8, 1820, J. Q. Adams, *Memoirs, 5*, 60.

The atmosphere of calm assurance that prevailed at the Department of State was in sharp contrast to the excited tone of the American press, which reflected the hostility provoked by anti-American writings in British newspapers and periodicals. Hezekiah Niles, for example, took particular and violent exception to an editorial in the *Times* of London which declared that the inevitable annexation of the Floridas by the United States "brings with it the invincible necessity for the acquisition of Cuba by the British crown. . . . The two transactions are necessary parts of the same whole, and must be, if possible, put out of hand together."[9] The Baltimore editor retorted that "there is an 'invincible necessity' to *us* that this grand island should become independent, or remain as it is, in the possession of some weak power, such as Spain." A few days later Niles reprinted an article from the *National Advocate* which contained excerpts from the work of an English pamphleteer, J. Freeman Rattenbury, entitled "Remarks on the Cession of the Floridas to the United States of America, and on the Necessity of Acquiring the Island of Cuba by Great Britain."[10] This article contained scarcely a line which was not offensive to American sensibilities. Rattenbury characterized Adams' conduct of negotiations for the Floridas as having been carried on in the "petty spirit of a tradesman," and alluded to the "unexpiated murder of Arbuthnot and Ambrister" as a "foul charge against the American character."[11] He emphasized the threat to British interests in the Caribbean of the growing power of the United States by describing at length the commanding position occupied by Cuba over ocean commerce in that region, and submitted his opinion

9. *Niles' Weekly Register, 17* (Jan. 8, 1820), 305–6.

10. Ibid. (Jan. 22, 1820), p. 353. The Rattenbury article was printed originally in *The Pamphleteer, 15,* London, 1819–20. See also Tatum, pp. 165–66.

11. *The Pamphleteer,* pp. 264–65.

that control of the island must pass into British hands by peaceful cession if possible, but forcibly if necessary.[12]

The American editor responded to this challenge with the promise that if Spanish resistance to British attempts to obtain Cuba should fail, "there is another power who will aid in preventing Great Britain from obtaining a commanding control at the mouth of the Mexican Gulf."

In the person of Andrew Jackson the United States possessed a commander more than willing to lead its forces in a war to prevent the transfer of Cuba to Britain. Two years previously Jackson had expressed to the President his conviction that the island must someday belong to the United States.[13] Now in the midst of the uncertainty surrounding British policy in the Florida question, he voiced his concern about Cuba to John C. Calhoun, the Secretary of War. Calhoun's answer revealed that he considered Cuba no less important to the security of the United States than did Jackson: "[Cuba] is, in my opinion, not only the first commercial and military position in the world, but is the key stone of our Union. No American statesman ought ever to withdraw his eye from it; and the greatest calamity ought to be endured by us, rather than it should pass into the hands of England."[14]

In case Spanish obstinacy forced the United States to seize the Floridas, and in case Spain then declared war, Calhoun favored a permanent conquest of Cuba. Should Spain not declare war, he thought no move against Cuba ought to be made by the United States, "unless the designs of England on it . . . should become sufficiently manifest." Calhoun's concern over the fate of the "key stone of the Union" did not diminish during the next three years, nourished as it

12. Ibid., pp. 278–79.
13. Jackson to Monroe (June 2, 1818), Bassett, ed., *Correspondence of Jackson*, 2, 378.
14. Calhoun to Jackson (Jan. 23, 1820), ibid., *3*, 12.

DECEMBER						
S	M	T	W	T	F	S
						1
2	3	4	5	6	7	8
9	10	11	12	13	14	15
16	17	18	19	20	21	22
23	24	25	26	27	28	29
30	31					

Success

Cuba 160

was by his fear that Cuba's slaves would be freed by their own or British agency.[15]

American anxiety about Cuba abated quickly after news arrived from Spain of the successful liberal revolt against Ferdinand, which had begun on New Year's Day among the troops assembled at Cadiz for operations against the Spanish–American insurgents. The people of Spain forced their monarch to accept the Constitution of 1812, which vested much of the authority formerly wielded by the King in the new constitutional Cortes. It was generally believed in the United States that the Cortes would now speedily approve the Adams-Onís treaty, and that Cuba would be rendered proof against a British attack by the enthusiastic loyalty of its people to the liberal regime in Spain. Spain's final ratification on the treaty in February 1821 put an end to the Florida question, and with it Cuba, too, passed momentarily out of the public mind.

SUSPICION OF BRITISH DESIGNS REVIVED

Early in 1822, with the passage in Congress of a bill authorizing the appointment of diplomatic missions to the former colonies of Spain, the United States took the lead in recognizing the independence of Latin America. This was a bold move but not precipitously taken or particularly risky. Practically every vestige of Spanish control had disappeared from the American continent, and the government of the Cortes, nearly bankrupt, branded a pariah by the Holy Allies' Troppau Circular and Laibach Manifesto, and without hope of British support, could not re-establish its authority on the mainland. Like the unilateral pronouncement of the Monroe Doctrine the following year, recogni-

---

15. See Adams' report of Calhoun's remarks on Cuba (Sept. 1822), C. F. Adams, ed., *Memoirs, 6,* 70.

tion of the new states enhanced the prestige of the United States in Spanish America, and was calculated to retard the growth of European influence there.

In the United States Congress the opponents of recognition used Cuba as an argument.[16] In the House, Robert Garrett of Virginia suggested the alarming possibility that Spain, about to lose her colonies, would sell them to a power able to retain them:

> Now, suppose Spain should cede Cuba to England, or even the Havana. . . . It is a universal opinion in the United States that it is utterly incompatible with our best interests that England should possess Cuba. . . . [Recognition] will not only prevent us from possessing it in the only safe and peaceful way, but in all probability, produce the very event we have the most reason to deprecate.[17]

These scare tactics produced some genuine alarm. Senator DeWolf of Rhode Island came in great agitation to John Quincy Adams with the tale that Britain would take possession of Cuba within a month, and it was with some difficulty that the Secretary calmed the Senator's fears.[18]

As he amply demonstrated in the course of the next few months, Adams had as keen an appreciation of the importance of Cuba to the Union as any other American, but he

---

16. It is Herminio Portell-Vilá's contention that while the example of American independence fired the rest of Spanish America with revolutionary fervor and the United States favored their wars of liberation, annexationist sentiment in this country stood opposed to Cuban independence. That this was not invariably true was amply demonstrated during 1823, as the present chapter shows. H. Portell-Vilá, *Historia de Cuba en sus relaciones con los Estados Unidos y España* (4 vols. Havana, 1938–41), *1, 159.*

17. *Annals of Congress, 17,* 1521–22.

18. Adams, *Memoirs, 5,* 486.

was not the man to be panicked into ill-considered action by unsubstantiated rumors. In a series of Cabinet meetings in September he again had occasion to apply cold reason to the subject of Cuba in discussion he described as "of deeper importance and greater magnitude than had occurred since the establishment of our independence."[19] President Monroe called the meetings to consider what answer should be returned to a group of Cuban patriots who had requested assurances of annexation to the United States before they launched a revolution against Spain. Calhoun showed himself most anxious for the annexation of Cuba to avert the twin dangers of its transfer to Britain or a slave rebellion there, adding that Jefferson believed the island should be taken even at the cost of a war with Britain. He himself felt that since the United States was not yet prepared for such a war, the Cubans should be dissuaded from any action for the time being.

Adams remarked pointedly, on the notion of taking Cuba at the cost of war with Britain, that for the present, and for a long time to come, such a war would "result in her possession of that island, and not ours." He could not, moreover, agree with the idea of urging the Cubans to remain loyal to Spain, which in his view "would expose them to be transferred to Great Britain by Spain, of which there is a double danger: first by the present revolutionary government of Spain, to purchase support against the Holy Alliance; and secondly, by Ferdinand, to purchase the aid of Great Britain to consummate a counter-revolution in his favor."

Adams' advice prevailed, and the answer as sent bore assurances of the friendly disposition of the United States toward the people of Cuba, while declining to undertake any commitment for the uncertain future. The Secretary of

19. The meetings are reported by Adams, *Memoirs, 6,* 69–74, Sept. 26–Oct. 1.

State denied Calhoun's charge that this was indirect incitement to rebellion; but then, Adams was not so sensitive to the slavery side of the Cuban question as his colleague. Adams' chief concern was clearly for the continued good will of the Cuban people, with an eye to the day when this island, so important to the United States, should cast off the yoke of Spanish sovereignty.

During the next month or so the administration achieved a degree of calm confidence in the stability of the Cuban situation which permitted it to pass over almost without discussion a rumor that Britain was engaged in negotiation with Spain to exchange Gibraltar for Cuba.[20] This mood was shattered in December, however, by the news that a British fleet had been ordered to Cuban waters with instructions to land marines on the island, if necessary, to eradicate nests of pirates preying on shipping in the Spanish Main. Americans immediately suspected that this "police action" masked sinister British designs on Cuba.

These fears were not wholly without foundation, for the new British foreign minister, George Canning, considered Cuba no less vital to British interests in the Caribbean than did the United States on its part. In a meeting of the British Cabinet held on November 15, 1822, he expressed a conviction that if the United States obtained Cuba "it may be questioned whether any blow, that could be struck by any foreign Power in any part of the world would have a more sensible effect on the interests of this country or on the reputation of its Government."[21] Warned by his secret agent in Havana of American designs on Cuba, the Foreign Secretary instructed his cousin Stratford Canning, British

20. Ibid., p. 112. Crawford said he had received the information in confidence from the French minister.
21. Memo for the Cabinet (Nov. 15, 1822), Webster, *Britain and the Independence of Latin America*, 2, 393.

minister at Washington, to inquire discreetly into the matter and to report.[22] Aware that British maneuvers in the vicinity of Cuba would generate alarm in the United States, Canning belatedly gave assurances that any "partial and temporary trespass upon Spanish territory" would be "limited by the necessity which produces it"—that is, clearing out the pirates.[23] This British disavowal of any intention of permanently occupying the island arrived too late to prevent a serious wave of anxiety in Washington.

Under the new circumstances Adams was inclined to attach some importance to the rumors that Britain was negotiating in Madrid for possession of Cuba. He therefore ordered the United States minister in Spain to ascertain the truth in the matter, and in case he found such talks in progress to express the sentiments of his government on the subject, "which are favorable to the continuance of Cuba in its connection with Spain."[24]

Shortly after the Secretary of State finished drafting this cautious No-Transfer admonition, the House of Representatives began debating a resolution introduced by Representative Trimble of Ohio, asking the Executive for estimates on the cost of building a naval base at Key West. Defending his motion, Trimble made it evident that the source of his interest in the matter was the "important purpose of defending the commerce of the United States against the island of Cuba, if that island should ever fall into the

---

22. Canning to Stratford Canning (Oct. 11, 1822), Rippy, *Rivalry,* p. 79. Bemis, *J. Q. Adams,* p. 373.

23. Canning to Sir Charles Stuart at Paris (Dec. 1, 1822), Webster, *Britain and the Independence of Latin America,* 2, 109–10. Canning forwarded a copy of the assurances he had sent to France to Stratford, to be read to Adams: Bemis, *J. Q. Adams,* 373.

24. Adams to John Forsyth (Dec. 17, 1822), J. B. Moore, *A Digest of International Law* (8 vols. Washington, 1906), *6,* 379–80.

hands of a Power hostile to the United States."[25] Evidently
Trimble shared the conviction expressed by Adams in the
September Cabinet meetings that the United States had
insufficient naval strength to prevent a British occupation of
Cuba. Adams' recourse under the circumstances was an
attempt to forestall the test by diplomatic means, while
Trimble's was to build up a countervailing naval power in
the strategic passage between Cuba and Florida. This combination of policies was well suited to the limited capabilities of the United States at the time.

Stratford Canning reported to his government the excitement produced in the United States by British operations in
Cuba, enclosing newspaper discussions of the advisability
of seizing Cuba to prevent "so formidable an increase of
British power" as would result from a permanent occupation of the island.[26] An American squadron sailed from
Norfolk early in 1823 to hunt pirates, and the presence of
the two potentially hostile fleets in Cuban waters only increased the explosiveness of the situation.

At this critical juncture two new developments partially
relieved Anglo–American tension. The first was Stratford
Canning's disavowals of any ulterior British designs on
Cuba, and the second was news of the intended invasion of
Spain by France as agent of the Holy Alliance, which in-
fused a fresh element of doubt into the question. Suspicion
flared briefly in February 1823 that France's price for re-
storing Ferdinand to absolute power might be Cuba, but
the old apprehension about British policy toward the island

25. *Annals of Congress,* 17th Cong., 2d Sess. (Dec. 19–20, 1822), pp.
425, 435–37. Secretary Thompson reported on Dec. 29 that the administration had already occupied Key West and had a garrison of Marines there. He strongly recommended its fortification. Tatum, *U.S.
and Europe,* p. 172.

26. Stratford Canning to Canning (Jan. 1, 22, 1823), Rippy, *Rivalry,*
p. 84.

soon returned.[27] The mistress of the seas was known to have opposed intervention in Spain at the Congress of Verona. Might not England defend the government of the Cortes and get Cuba in return? Or might she not seize Cuba to prevent its cession to France? The fact remained that Britain was the only power now capable of taking the Pearl of the Antilles—the only possible threat to American interests in the island. It is significant, in the light of the issuance of the Monroe Doctrine a few months later, that the immediate danger perceived by the American government from French intervention in Spain focused more on Cuba than on the revolted colonies, and that it was Britain and not the continental powers which posed the threat. The spectacular success of French arms in Spain heightened concern about an intervention by the Holy Allies to restore Ferdinand's lost colonies to him, but throughout the famous Cabinet discussions on Canning's proposals in November 1823 the danger that Cuba might be transferred to Britain remained an important object of concern.

In mid-March of 1823 President Monroe once again assembled his Cabinet for a series of indecisive conferences on the Cuban question. The immediate occasion for these meetings may well have been a dispatch from Gallatin in France received on March 11. Gallatin was certainly not by nature an alarmist, nor was he an ardent expansionist, as his attitude toward the Floridas had proved, so that when he warned his government that Britain might be making serious attempts to obtain Cuba as compensation for aiding the Spanish government against France, his words carried weight in Washington.[28]

Little transpired at the first meeting on March 14, but the following day the debate was, in Adams' phrase, "most

27. Tatum, pp. 104–6, 173–74.
28. Gallatin to Adams (Jan. 6, 1823), Whitaker, *U.S. and Latin America*, pp. 402–3.

warm,"[29] Calhoun declaring himself in favor of war with England to prevent her obtaining Cuba, and Secretary of the Navy Thompson advising that the people of Cuba be urged to declare their independence if they could maintain it. Adams insisted they could not, and repeated his former judgment that the United States could not win a war with Britain over Cuba. He refused to treat seriously the suggestion that Congress be called into special session. It must have been a stormy meeting, for Adams wrote himself a memorandum in his diary "to keep cool on this subject."

Monroe attempted to solve the question by proposing on March 17 to offer Britain a joint pledge not to take Cuba. Adams and Calhoun joined in opposing this suggestion, probably because neither was willing to forswear the possibility of acquiring Cuba for the United States, although Adams' recorded reason was an aversion to plunging "into the whirlpool of European politics." On this inconclusive note the Cabinet abandoned its attempts to arrive at a concerted policy to meet the menace of a transfer of Cuba to Britain.

Public antipathy to Britain's supposed designs on Cuba was running high. On April 5 Niles reported that "the feelings of the people of the United States are much excited by an apprehension that the 'occupancy' of this island may be transferred to Great Britain, under some pretence, in consequence of the war for 'legitimacy' that France, no doubt, has made on Spain."[30] During the same week a communication to the Boston *Columbian Centinel* urged annexation by the United States if necessary to keep Britain from acquiring the island, both because of strategic considerations and because loss of the valuable Cuban trade would be a

---

29. Adams' notes on these discussions are to be found in his *Memoirs, 6,* 137–39.

30. *Niles' Weekly Register, 24* (April 5, 1823), 72–73.

serious blow, and "the greatest sufferers would be the New England states."[31]

Members of the administration continued to regard the Cuban problem as one of first importance. Writing to his sympathetic friend Andrew Jackson, Calhoun reaffirmed his view that "the country ought to be prepared for the worst. Without Cuba our confederacy is not complete; and with it in the hands of the English, the best line of communication between the entrance ports, would be intercepted."[32] President Monroe, meanwhile, suffered some second thoughts on his proposal of a joint guarantee of Cuba to Spain by Britain and the United States. In case of a revolution in Cuba—he asked Jefferson, who favored the joint guarantee—would this require the United States to suppress it? If we were not willing to promise this, would Great Britain and Spain accept the proposal at all?[33] Monroe must have appreciated that such a pledge was inconsistent with the national interest and with the precedent established in the case of the continental colonies.

Adams' contribution in recent deliberations of the Cabinet had been largely negative; he had confined himself to restraining the reckless belligerence displayed by Calhoun and opposing the President's suggested self-denying ordinance, which might have embarrassed the United States in case of a Cuban offer of annexation in the future. The Secretary of State entertained no illusions about the outcome of a naval war to prevent the transfer of Cuba to Britain, but short of a disastrous war he recognized that the administration was "called upon, in the performance of its duties

31. *Columbian Centinel* (April 2, 1823), cited in Whitaker, *U.S. and Latin America*, p. 404.

32. Calhoun to Jackson (March 30, 1823), Bassett, ed., *Correspondence of Jackson, 3*, 193–94.

33. Monroe to Jefferson (April 14, 1823), Hamilton, ed., *Writings of Monroe, 6*, 307.

to the nation, at least to use all the means within its competency to guard against and forfend it."[34] The means Adams chose to employ was a powerful statement to the Spanish government of the No-Transfer policy, which went far beyond the mild caveat he had uttered the previous December. This declaration he embodied in instructions to Hugh Nelson, newly appointed American minister to Spain.[35] It is a particularly significant document, because it reveals the estimate Adams and his colleagues had formed of the European situation and shows how exclusively they were preoccupied by the British threat to Cuba at the time the French invasion of Spain began. Of the fifty printed pages of the instruction, twelve are devoted to the Cuban question and the remainder is taken up with protests against piratical depredations on American commerce, the use of the United States Navy to suppress them, and other matters. The threat of intervention by the Holy Allies in Spanish America is scarcely mentioned, and then only as a remote and unlikely contingency, given the opposition of the British government and their command of the seas.

Adams began his instruction to Nelson by denying that an assertion of interest in the impending war between France and Spain constituted a departure from the traditional American policy of abstention from the politics of Europe. He still believed firmly that the "first and paramount duty of the government" was to "maintain *peace* amidst all the convulsions of foreign wars, and to enter the lists as parties to no cause, other than our own." But like the Freedom of the Seas, the fate of adjacent European colonial possessions was a cause "peculiarly our own." The continental colonies Adams considered irrevocably lost, but Spain still retained the "power of transferring her own dominion" over Cuba to

---

34. W. C. Ford, ed., *Writings of J. Q. Adams,* 7, 379.
35. Adams to Hugh Nelson (April 28, 1823), ibid., pp. 369–81.

another nation, and therefore the power to do the political and commercial interests of the United States serious harm. "Such indeed are, between the interests of that island and of this country, the geographical, commercial, moral and political relations, formed by nature . . . [that] it is scarcely possible to resist the conviction that the annexation of Cuba to our federal republic will be indispensable to the continuance and integrity of the Union itself." No annexation would take place in the determinate future; for the present Spain could be assured that the United States had no designs on Cuba whatsoever and would act only to prevent a transfer of the island to another European power.

In Adams' opinion Britain was the only power to be feared in this connection. No matter what plans France and the Holy Allies might have for stifling constitutional liberty in Cuba, Britain could be counted on to resist them. But therein lay the chief danger, for with or without the permission of Spain, Britain might take permanent possession of the island, as had been so often rumored in recent months.

The Secretary of State gave little credence to past rumors, but he also placed little trust in Britain's future adherence to the disavowals of designs on Cuba presented to him by Stratford Canning two months before. "The war between France and Spain changes so totally the circumstances under which the declaration . . . was made, that it may, at its very outset, produce events under which the possession of Cuba may be obtained by Great Britain without even raising a reproach of intended deception against the British government for making it." In case Britain came to the aid of the constitutional government, Adams thought it likely that a British guarantee of Cuba would be included in the terms of alliance, in which case a "temporary and fiduciary" British occupation of the island might turn into a "permanent and proprietary possession."

To forestall any such contingency, Adams applied the No-Transfer policy to Cuba, coupled with the most formidable threat he could make under the circumstances:

> You will not conceal from the Spanish government the repugnance of the United States to the transfer of the island of Cuba by Spain to any other power. . . . In casual conversation, and speaking as from your own impressions, you may suggest the hope, that if any question of transferring the island to any other power is, or shall be in agitation, it will not be withheld from your knowledge, or from ours; that the condition of Cuba cannot be changed without affecting in an eminent degree the welfare of this Union, and consequently the good understanding between us and Spain; that we should consider an attempt to transfer the island, against the will of its inhabitants, as subversive of their rights, no less than of our interests; and that, as it would give them the perfect right of resisting such transfer by declaring their own independence, so if they should, under these circumstances, resort to that measure, the United States will be fully justified in supporting them to carry it into effect.

Adams was anxious to avoid provoking war—his policy was not to be stated officially, but as the private opinions of the American minister—but he wanted it made clear that the United States would resort to force if diplomacy failed.

The Secretary of State now hastened to establish a special agent in Cuba, with instructions to watch for signs of either an impending transfer or an independence movement.[36] Far from wishing to incite the Cubans to rebellion, Adams hoped they would remain under Spanish authority, and desired them to be informed of this fact. He would foster

36. Adams to Thomas Randall (April 29, 1823), Manning, *LA, 1*, 185–86.

rebellion against a threatened transfer to Britain, and support it with all the resources at his command, but there is not the slightest indication that he intended to make Spain's current distresses in Europe the occasion for stripping her of her most valuable remaining possessions.[37] Some day, Adams believed, the "law of political gravitation" would accomplish the annexation peacefully.

After the first of May, Anglo–American relations took a turn for the better, and the Secretary of State, at least, relaxed a bit. Word arrived from the American chargé in Madrid that no negotiations on Cuba had taken place between Britain and Spain, although he added the mildly disquieting intelligence that the Spanish government counted on the United States to save the island if it were endangered.[38] More important in clearing the air was receipt of George Canning's warning to France against any permanent occupation of Spain, or an attempt to appropriate any of her American colonies, and the harmonious preparations for fresh negotiations on such long-standing Anglo–American difficulties as the fisheries question, suppression of the African slave trade, and trade with the British West Indies.[39] Stratford Canning remarked on the "improved tone of public feeling," adding that "even Adams has caught something of the soft infection."[40]

37. In this connection Monroe wrote to Jefferson that the United States had advised the Cubans to "cling to Spain . . . as long as they can, and to resist by force any attempt to get possession of the island, by England." If they then appealed to the United States, the matter would be laid before Congress, probably with favorable results. Monroe to Jefferson (June 30, 1823), Hamilton, ed., *Writings of Monroe*, 6, 312.

38. John Appleton to Adams (March 20, 1823), ibid., *3*, 2035–37.

39. Canning to Sir Charles Stuart at Paris (March 31, 1823), Webster, *Britain and the Independence of Latin America*, 2, 111–12.

40. Stratford Canning to Canning, private (May 8, 1823), Dexter Perkins, *The Monroe Doctrine, 1823–1826* (Cambridge, 1932), p. 60.

That the Secretary of State was not entirely converted from his habitual suspicion of Great Britain became evident during the famous Cabinet discussions precipitated by Canning's proposal for an Anglo-American declaration against intervention by the Holy Allies in Spanish America. Some of the decisions taken at these meetings were embodied in Monroe's annual message of December 2, 1823, later to become known as the Monroe Doctrine.

THE NO-TRANSFER POLICY AND THE MONROE DOCTRINE

French armies, invading Spain early in April 1823, reached Madrid six weeks later, and within three months had returned the entire country, except for the traditional redoubt of Cadiz, to the absolute sway of Ferdinand VII. News of this phenomenal success caused a spasm of anxiety in the United States that the Holy Alliance would next move to extinguish liberty in its last stronghold—the Americas. Fear for the independence of the new states in Spanish America, and even for the safety of the United States itself, temporarily submerged in the public minds the threat that Cuba might be transferred to another European power. Little about Cuba appeared in the public press in the fall of 1823 when the Monroe Doctrine was being formulated, but it figured somewhat more prominently in the Cabinet discussions themselves.

The spectacular progress of French arms in Spain aroused concern in England as well as in the United States, and moved Canning to propose to the American minister that the two nations join in a declaration of policy on Spanish America:

1. We conceive the recovery of the Colonies by Spain to be hopeless.

2. We conceive the question of the Recognition of them, as Independent States, to be one of time and circumstances.
3. We are, however, by no means disposed to throw any impediment in the way of an arrangement between them and the mother country by amicable negotiation.
4. We aim not at the possession of any portion of them ourselves.
5. *We could not see any portion of them transferred to any other Power with indifference.*[41]

In Point 5 Canning offered to endorse the No-Transfer policy, with all the power of the British navy behind it, and in Point 4 to reinforce it with assurances that Britain was included within its scope.

This was a tempting proposition for Rush, but he was disturbed by the discrepancy between the positions of Britain and his own country revealed in Point 2. The United States had already committed itself by recognizing several of the former Spanish colonies as independent states. He was aware in a general way of the important distinction Adams later more fully elaborated: that these nations, now independent, were no longer subject to transfer (the word itself implied that they were still in a colonial status), and although he was prepared on his own responsibility to join Canning in the proposed declaration, he refused to do so unless Britain first followed the United States in recognizing the independence of the former Spanish colonies. Meanwhile Rush referred the matter to Washington for further instructions.

Canning proved unwilling to take the step of immediate recognition, and no amount of flattery or persuasion could

41. Canning to Rush, private and confidential (Aug. 20, 1823), Manning, *LA*, *3*, 1478. Italics inserted.

cause the American minister to alter his position. Abandoning any expectation of collaboration with the United States, the Foreign Secretary turned directly to France for an explanation of French policy in respect to Spanish America, and rather to his surprise received categorical assurances on October 12, 1823, from the French minister, Polignac, that his government had no intention or desire to appropriate any part of the Spanish dominions to itself, or to act by force of arms against them.

Canning did not inform Rush of the Polignac memorandum until November 24, and news of it arrived in Washington only after Monroe had made his historic declaration of policy, but the American minister, noticing in interviews early in October that Canning was avoiding the subject of South America which he had so warmly pressed a few days before, wrote to Adams that he considered "that all further discussion between us in relation to it is now at an end."[42] Rush finally guessed that the motive behind Canning's proposal was that England "having ends of her own in view has been anxious to facilitate their accomplishment by invoking my auxiliary offices as minister of the United States at this court. . . . It is France that must not be aggrandized, not South America that must be free." This dispatch arrived in Washington in the midst of the November Cabinet meetings, and effectually ended any consideration of a joint declaration with Britain, to which Adams had stood opposed from the first.

The famous deliberations in Monroe's Cabinet occasioned by receipt of Rush's August dispatches are a familiar chapter of American history. Canning's written proposals produced no special sense of urgency in the administration, although their importance was immediately appreciated. Monroe soon after left for a three-weeks' vacation at his

42. Rush to Adams (Oct. 10, 1823), ibid., p. 1501.

home in Virginia, carrying with him copies of the proposals for further study. While at Oak Hill he wrote to the surviving Virginian ex-Presidents, Jefferson and Madison, asking their advice on what answer to return to Canning. Monroe made it clear that he favored departing from the traditional policy of nonentanglement in this important instance to make the joint pronouncement with Britain.[43]

Jefferson wrote that he considered the question raised by Rush's dispatches "the most momentous which has ever been offered to my contemplation since that of Independence."[44] He agreed with Monroe that the joint statement ought to be made, in order to detach Britain from the continental allies for the purpose of liberating the New World from European influence. "Great Britain is the nation which can do us the most harm of any one, or all, on earth; and with her on our side we need not fear the whole world." Jefferson assumed that British and American interests coincided in the Spanish–American question, and it was not Point 2 but Point 4, the self-denying ordinance, which gave him momentary pause:

> De we wish to acquire to our own confederacy any one or more of the Spanish provinces? I candidly confess that I have ever looked on Cuba as the most interesting addition which could ever be made to our system of states. . . . Yet as I am sensible that this can never be obtained, even with her own consent, but by war; and its independence, which is our second interest (and especially its independence of England) can be secured without it, I have no hesitation in abandoning my first wish to future chances and accepting its independence

43. Monroe to Jefferson (Oct. 17, 1823), Hamilton, ed., *Writings*, o, 323–25.
44. Jefferson to Monroe (Oct. 24, 1823), ibid., pp. 391–93.

with peace and the friendship of England, rather than its association at the expense of war and her enmity.

Madison was also inclined to make the joint declaration, although he was more distrustful of British motives than Jefferson.[45] Point 4 worried him also: "Does it exclude future views of acquiring Puerto Rico etc. as well as Cuba?" Both the elder statesmen felt immediate doubts as to the expediency of pledging the United States not to obtain Cuba, but both considered the removal of the threat of its transfer to Britain worth the temporary sacrifice. In the final analysis their expansionism proved to be based chiefly on strategic grounds.

The Secretary of State had qualms about Point 4, but he used them to argue against a joint declaration with Britain during the first Cabinet meeting called on November 7 to discuss Canning's proposals. Adams contended that the proposal appeared to be "to obtain some public pledge from the Government of the United States, ostensibly against the forcible interference of the Holy Alliance between Spain and South America; but really or especially against the acquisition to the United States themselves of any part of the Spanish–American possessions."[46] He could not agree with Calhoun's inclination to give Rush discretionary powers to join Canning in a declaration against the Holy Allies, if necessary, even at the cost of a pledge not to take Cuba or Texas. Like Jefferson, the Secretary of War saw considerable advantage in securing a like disavowal from Britain, the power most able to seize the provinces. In Adams' view the United States was giving a lot and receiving nothing in return. He would not waive the possibility of receiving

45. Madison to Monroe (Oct. 30, 1823), ibid., *6*, 394–95.
46. Adams, ed., *Memoirs of J. Q. Adams, 6,* 177. Unless otherwise indicated, the quotations on the following pages dealing with the Cabinet meetings in Nov. are from the *Memoirs, 6,* 177–216.

Cuba from a revolutionary government there which might request annexation to the United States, a thing they would never, he was certain, request of Britain.

It was Adams who set the tone of the meetings in which the Monroe Doctrine was formulated, and most of his opinions eventually prevailed, although at times only after considerable modification. When at first the major question was whether a joint or an independent declaration should be made, Adams stoutly opposed coming in "as a cockboat in the wake of the British man-of-war." To follow Britain would diminish the prestige of the United States in Spanish America. Furthermore, the Secretary of State did not take the menace of intervention by the Holy Allies as seriously as did Calhoun, whom Adams described as "perfectly moonstruck" at the fall of Cadiz, and who felt that Britain must at all costs be detached from the continental powers. Adams declared that he no more believed "that the Holy Allies will restore the Spanish dominion upon the American continent than that the Chimborazo will sink beneath the ocean." In his opinion Britain was already committed by her interests to preventing a French intervention in America, and needed no encouragement by the United States to pursue them. It was equally evident to him that British and American interests were not necessarily identical in the Spanish–American question, and when in mid-November he learned from Rush that Canning had apparently abandoned his proposals, he was confirmed in his suspicions. In this new state of affairs Calhoun argued the danger of making any declaration of policy whatever, but Monroe supported Adams' determination to put the United States on record, and it was the President's idea to do so not only in diplomatic correspondence but also publicly in his annual message. The Monroe Doctrine, as issued on that occasion, applied equally to the Holy Allies and to Britain.

Adams' suspicions of Canning's motives centered in part around Cuba, as we have seen, but they were also aroused by the Foreign Secretary's present unwillingness to recognize the new states as the United States had done. This fact produced a fundamental distinction between the British and American positions which precluded any possibility of joint action so far as Adams was concerned, necessitating both an independent statement and a completely new formulation of hemispheric policy by the United States.

The celebrated Cabinet discussions of November 1823 revolved about the drafting of three documents: the President's Message, instructions to Rush, and the reply to certain communications from the Russian government, the most important of which was a circular note in which Nesselrode triumphantly reviewed successful interventions by the Holy Allies to suppress liberal revolutions in Italy and Spain, pointed with approval to the successful counter-revolution in Portugal, and seemed to promise the extension of the blessings of reaction to remaining portions of the civilized world where they were not being enjoyed.[47]

Adams was aware that the situation required of the administration a major decision on hemispheric policy, and he insisted that all the documents being drafted be "part of a combined system of policy and adapted to each other."[48] Monroe agreed, and the three papers were considered throughout the meetings as part of a single policy decision. In view of this, the fact that a statement of the No-Transfer policy occurs in the reply read to Baron Tuyll, the Russian

47. Count Nesselrode to Baron Tuyll (Aug. 30, 1823). This and other materials relating to the policy discussions in the Cabinet are printed in W. C. Ford, "Some Original Documents on the Genesis of the Monroe Doctrine," *Proceedings of the Massachusetts Historical Society,* 2d ser. *15* (1901–02), 373–436. The Russian note is on pp. 402–5.

48. C. F. Adams, ed., *Memoirs of J. Q. Adams, 6,* 179.

minister, in the early drafts but not in the final draft of the instructions to Rush and not at all in the President's message requires some explanation.

Because of the opportunity it afforded Adams to address a militant declaration of republican principles to the guiding spirit of the Holy Alliance, he considered the reply to the Russian minister "the most important state paper that ever went from my hands." "The paper itself," he wrote, "was drawn to correspond exactly with a paragraph of the President's message . . . which was entirely conformable to the system of policy which I have earnestly recommended for this emergency."[49] The note to Tuyll did not contain the Noncolonization principle which the message contained; Adams had already told the Russian minister the previous July that the United States assumed the principle "that the American continents are no longer subjects for any new European colonial establishments."[50] The principle of Abstention—that it is the intention of the United States not to interfere in purely European affairs—he stated at some length, in much the same terms as in the message. Adams also coupled the principle of Nonintervention with the No-Transfer concept, now stated in such broad terms as to elevate it to the status of a general principle:

> The United States of America, and their government, could not see with indifference, the forcible interposition of any European power, other than Spain, either to restore the dominion of Spain over her emancipated Colonies in America, or to establish Monarchical Governments in those countries, or to transfer any of the possessions heretofore or yet subject to Spain in

49. Ibid., p. 199.
50. July 17, 1823, ibid., p. 163.

the American Hemisphere, to any other European Power.[51]

Adams here applied the No-Transfer principle broadly to the whole hemisphere, not to a specific locality as had always been the case before. Its application to possessions "heretofore subject to Spain" is remarkable, in view of the careful distinction between loyal and emancipated colonies that he had made in his draft of instructions to Rush, written during the same period.

The keynote of Adams' reply to Canning's proposals is the insistence that Britain take the step of recognizing the independence of the revolted Spanish colonies, "that measure being taken, we may then harmonize in all the arrangements and acts which may be necessary [for preserving the independence of the new states]. It is upon this ground alone, as we conceive, that a firm and determined stand could now be jointly taken by Great Britain and the United States."[52] The government concurred in Canning's Point 5 (that it "could not see any portion of [the Spanish possessions] transferred to any other power, with indifference"), but Adams felt the necessity of explaining that this applied only to the loyal colonies (i.e. Cuba and Puerto Rico), and no longer to the independent states of Spanish America, for the protection of which the new principles of Noncolonization and Nonintervention were devised. In the first draft of his instructions to Rush he elaborated upon this distinction:

> The ground of resistance which we would oppose to any *interference* of the European Allies, between Spain and South America, is not founded on any partial interest of our own or of others. If the Colonies belonged to Spain we should object to any transfer of

51. Nov. 27, 1823, W. C. Ford, "Genesis of the Monroe Doctrine," p. 408.

52. Adams to Rush (Nov. 29, 1823), Manning, *LA, 1,* 210–12.

them to other nations, which would materially affect our interests or rights. . . . Our present opposition to the disposal of any part of the American Continents by Spain, with her European allies, is that they do not belong to Spain, and can no more be disposed of by her than by the United States.[53]

This paragraph shows that the principles of the Monroe Doctrine sprang from the same roots as the No-Transfer principle, now no longer applicable to the independent nations which had appeared in the New World. When the rest of the two continents belonged to Spain, the No-Transfer principle had been, in Adams' view, theoretically applicable throughout the hemisphere. It was the original policy of hemispheric security, although threats to the rights and interests of the United States as defined to date had been confined to adjacent Spanish territories in North America and the island of Cuba.

In his original draft of instructions to Rush, Adams specifically applied the No-Transfer principle to both Cuba and Puerto Rico: "Our own interest and wish would be that they should continue in their political connection with Spain under the administration of a free Constitution, and in the enjoyment of their Liberties as now possessed; we could not see them transferred to any other Power, or subjected to the antient and exploded dominion of Spain, with indifference. We aim not at the possession of them ourselves."[54] In his amendment of Adams' draft, Monroe avoided this extension of the definition of transfer to include an attempt to restore the old regime in Cuba. He preferred to leave action to the Cuban people themselves, with no positive commitment by the United States to act.[55]

53. W. C. Ford, "Genesis of the Monroe Doctrine," p. 386.
54. Ibid., p. 387.
55. Ibid.

The President agreed with Adams that a firm general statement of the No-Transfer principle ought to be included in the reply to the British government. He considered placing directly after the concurrence in Canning's Points 4 and 5 a statement of the Nonintervention principle, together with a statement of the No-Transfer principle which suggested that American interest in a change in the territorial status quo might vary inversely with the distance from the United States:

> In both these portions [Points 4 and 5] we fully concur—and we add that we could not see with indifference any attempt by one or more powers of Europe, to restore these new states to the Crown of Spain, or to deprive them, in any manner whatever, of the freedom and independence which they have acquired. *Much less could we behold with indifference the transfer of those new governments, or of any portion of the Spanish possessions, to other powers, especially of the territories bordering on, or nearest to the United States.*[56]

In the final form of the instructions to Rush, all these statements of the No-Transfer principle were omitted, but the early drafts indicate how closely Monroe and Adams associated it with the principles of the Doctrine and how much the threat to Cuba and Puerto Rico occupied their minds at the time. The fact of its omission in the instructions and in the Message does not mean that the importance of the No-Transfer principle had diminished, but rather that a fresh statement at the moment seemed unnecessary and inexpedient. As recently as the preceding April the administration had gone on record at both Madrid and London as opposing the transfer of Spanish territory in the hemisphere to another European power. Furthermore, its concurrence in Point 5 was a sufficient re-emphasis of its

56. Ibid. Monroe's italics.

stand in November, in view of the fact that Canning had by proposing it in effect given assurances that he had no designs on the loyal colonies, and that no immediate threat of a transfer was apparent at the moment. To stress the No-Transfer principle in the instruction to Rush would only blur the essential distinction Adams wished to make between the fact that the United States viewed the former Spanish possessions as independent nations while Britain viewed them as colonies in revolt. For Adams, his opposition to the transfer of these nations was not only an assertion of interest by the United States but also, now, a matter of right—as independent states they could no longer legally be disposed of by another power. Until Britain joined us on this ground, Adams wrote to Rush privately, no concerted policy was possible because "Great Britain negotiating at once with the European Alliance and with us, concerning America, without being bound by any community of principle (but only a casual coincidence of interest with us) would still be free to accommodate her policy to any of those distributions of power, and partitions of Territory which have for the last half century been the *ultima ratio* of all European political arrangements."[57] Only if the European states recognized the former Spanish colonies as independent could the hemisphere be further freed of the combinations and collisions of the European balance of power. This was the ultimate objective of Adams as it had been for all his predecessors.

Some years ago Edward H. Tatum advanced the thesis that the Monroe Doctrine was aimed primarily at England, not the Holy Allies. He based his argument largely on Anglo–American tensions between 1815 and 1823 arising out of commercial rivalries, vituperative duels in the press, and the Florida and Cuba questions.[58] It is unquestionably

57. Adams to Rush (Nov. 30, 1823), ibid., p. 391.
58. Tatum, *The United States and Europe.*

true that Britain presented the greatest concern to the United States until early 1823, but one must ignore all the records of the November Cabinet meetings to deny that the Holy Alliance was at least equally the objective of the Noncolonization and Nonintervention principles of the Monroe Doctrine. To support this thesis Tatum contends that because the danger of transfer of Cuba to Britain was constantly on the minds of Monroe and his advisers, the No-Transfer principle was "implicit in the very spirit" of the Monroe Doctrine.[59] But if Monroe and Adams had drafted the annual message of 1823 chiefly as a warning to Britain to keep hands off Cuba, they need not have left their meaning to be implied. Each of them had long since applied the No-Transfer principle in the course of the controversies over Florida and Cuba, and, as we have seen, considered and rejected another specific statement in the instructions to Rush.

Far from being an extension of the Monroe Doctrine, or even having its origins in that document, the No-Transfer principle had been from the beginning of our independence a fundamental bulwark of American security, the original political device for preserving the status quo of colonies in the New World until they gained independence. Invoked continuously throughout the first half century of our national history, it was the fountainhead of the new principles articulated by John Quincy Adams and proclaimed by President Monroe in his message of 1823 to meet the altered circumstances produced by the independence of Latin America. Until it was formally joined to the Monroe Doctrine by President Grant and Secretary of State Fish in 1869 and 1870, the No-Transfer principle was continuously and independently applied to prevent unwelcome intrusions of European power into the Western Hemisphere.

59. Ibid., p. 277.

CHAPTER 6

The Congress of Panama

The Cuban problem, which had been temporarily sub-merged by the Holy Alliance scare in 1823, quickly re-emerged as a major issue in United States foreign policy, and remained for the rest of the century a tantalizing mixture of threat and promise for American statesmanship. In July 1825 the London *Courier* described Cuba as the "Turkey of trans-Atlantic politics, tottering to her fall, and kept from falling by those who contend for the right of catching her in her descent."[1] To the familiar roster of contestants—Spain the possessor and the United States, Great Britain, and France the traditional, would-be successors— were now added the new states of Mexico and Colombia, with Russia an interested spectator. It was the opposing pressures of selfish, contending, political forces that kept the Pearl of the Antilles in Spanish hands: many nations coveted Cuba, but all preferred a continuation of the status quo to its transfer to another maritime power.

Certainly Spain's retention of Cuba and Puerto Rico owed nothing to the wisdom of Spanish policy. During the crisis of 1825 and 1826 the world was again treated to an awesome display of Spanish obtuseness to their own best interests. The government of Ferdinand the "Well-Beloved,"

1. Quoted in *Niles' Weekly Register, 28* (Aug. 6, 1825), 354.

with French armies bolstering the weak allegiance of his people, stubbornly refused to face the hopelessness of the situation in America and end the war with a recognition of the independence of Spain's former colonies. With what angry statesmen in Washington and London could only view as a quixotic retreat into unreality, Spain clung tena ciously to a melancholy belief that some miracle would re store the empire, and continued to plan suicidally extrava gant projects for reconquest that bore no relation to the international facts of life. By late 1825 the last remnants of Spanish power had been driven from the American con tinents, and Mexico and Colombia stood poised, if not en tirely prepared, to attack the strongholds in loyal Cuba and Puerto Rico from which Spain still threatened their secure enjoyment of independence. Neither John Quincy Adams nor George Canning regarded these proposed expeditions with relish, and both strove mightily though unrewardingly to drive some sense into Ferdinand, in order to save the islands for Spain.

United States interest in Cuba continued to rest on the strategic position of the island, on economic considerations and on the slavery question. Although the slavery issue swelled to a deafening crescendo in the years preceding the American Civil War and threatened to obliterate the others all three factors remained operative. Accordingly, the three part policy laid down by Secretary of State Adams in 1823 prevailed up until 1898, namely (1) that the United States was content to see the island remain in the hands of Spain (2) that it could not see with indifference its transfer to an other European power, and (3) that it would not renounce the chance of acquiring Cuba for itself. Every President from Jefferson to McKinley, with the sole exception of Abraham Lincoln, believed that Cuba must some day be joined to the American union, and most of them made some effort to effect that juncture. All believed equally firmly that Cuba must not pass from Spain to any other power, and if, as is surely the case, the No-Transfer principle has been the most frequently repeated foreign policy of the United States, the overwhelming majority of those statements have been in connection with Cuba.

When President John Quincy Adams and his Secretary of State, Henry Clay, assumed office in March 1825, they had immediately to deal with the crisis raised by the likelihood of early Mexican and Colombian expeditions against Cuba. The course of action they adopted was to try to get Spain to make peace and to recognize the independence of Latin America, by direct appeals to Mexico and Colombia for forbearance and to Spain for sanity, and by indirect attempts at persuading Spain to this policy through the intercession of Tsar Alexander of Russia and, secondly, of Britain and France. Their chief supporting argument was that Spain ran a grave risk of losing Cuba and Puerto Rico entirely if she persisted in her folly, and each American appeal was accompanied by a statement of the No-Transfer principle to define United States interest in the matter.

None of these strictures against transfer was directed specifically against Mexico and Colombia. If it had been, it would have represented a sharp break with past practice and placed the No-Transfer principle in a completely novel political context. For the principle had always been primarily a security policy, designed and used to prevent unwelcome changes in the local American balance of power through the substitution of a stronger for a weaker European maritime nation as sovereign in colonies adjacent to the United States. Like the Noncolonization and Nonintervention principles of the Monroe Doctrine—which, as we have seen, developed out of it—the No-Transfer principle was originally an instrument of American isolationism, resting on the doctrine of the two spheres—the assumption that Europe and America did in fact represent distinct political systems, and ought to remain politically separated as they were geographically separated. It was a power-political policy employed to minimize European influence in the New World, with the eventual aim of banishing it from the Americas entirely in the interests of peace.

Obviously objections to the transfer of Cuba to Mexico or Colombia could not have been explained on these grounds. If the United States had flatly opposed Mexican or Colombian possession of Cuba in and of itself, the conclusion would be inescapable that the No-Transfer principle had become an engine of Manifest Destiny, and that professed security considerations were a mask for territorial aggrandizement. There were overtones of expansionism, of course, in its applications to Louisiana and the Floridas, but they were muted, and subordinate to imperious requirements of national safety. Besides, no other American state then existed to claim interest in those territories. Was the United States playing dog in the manger in Cuba?

The answer to this question is certainly negative, though a slightly qualified negative. There is no evidence that the acquisition of Cuba was an immediate or primary objective of the Adams-Clay policies, no matter what may have been their ultimate and remote expectations from the working of Adams' "law of political gravitation." This administration was genuinely content, as they constantly reiterated, to see Cuba remain in the hands of Spain, as long as its ports remained open to American commerce. And, as Clay instructed Joel Poinsett, who was departing for his post as United States minister to Mexico, this country would welcome an independent Cuba as a solution to its problem, if that independence could be sustained. To this end the United States was willing to consider committing itself with other American states to a joint guarantee of Cuba's independence once it was won, a degree of entanglement this nation had cautiously evaded when approached a year previously by Colombia and Brazil for defensive alliances.[2] The principal objection to a Mexican or Colombian occupation of Cuba from the viewpoint of the United States was that the new states had neither the military nor the naval power to defend the island. Under their rule it would be even more likely to fall to some European power than under Spain's.[3] Thus it was the time-honored strategic and commercial concern over intrusions of European influence which operated after all, and not imperialistic cupidity. In addition to this, Washington somewhat later became concerned about the repercussions in the South of a possible slave rebellion in connection with a Mexican or Colombian attempt on Cuba, but a discussion of this factor can be deferred for the moment.

Shortly after taking office, Adams and Clay launched into their campaign to avert the danger to Cuba. Having outlined their position to Mexico and Spain, they turned to what was to be their chief reliance: an appeal to the Tsar to use his influence in Madrid to persuade Spain to end the war. Clay's instruction to Henry Middleton in St. Petersburg, which runs over 3,000 words, is an exhaustive summary of the American view of the situation.[4] As far as Spain's chances of recovering her continental colonies was concerned, wrote the Secretary of State, "the reconquest of the United States by Great Britain would not be a more hopeless enterprise." If Spain persisted in fighting, Mexico and Colombia would attack Cuba and Puerto Rico and almost certainly take them. The United States itself had no designs on the islands, but their position, their commercial importance, and the character of their population made them necessarily objects of supreme interest to this country.

2. Clay to Poinsett (March 26, 1825), Manning, *LA, 1,* 229–33.
3. Clay to Alexander H. Everett, United States Minister to Spain (April 27, 1825), ibid., p. 243.
4. Clay to Middleton (May 10, 1825), ibid., pp. 244–50.

All the great maritime powers, including the United States, opposed the transfer of Cuba to any of the others, so that any change in its political condition would bring with it the threat of general war. Cuba, given the nature of its population, probably could not maintain its independence, so that the most satisfactory solution all around would be for it to remain under Spanish sovereignty. This could only be done, however, if Spain terminated hostilities against her former colonies and recognized their independence.

Clay transmitted copies of Middleton's instructions to London and Paris, urging those governments to second the Tsar's anticipated interposition at Madrid.[5] But the overture to Alexander turned out to be a fruitless diplomatic venture. Whether John Quincy Adams overestimated the friendship he had established in those warm talks on the windy banks of the Neva when he was serving as United States minister at St. Petersburg, or whether he was misled by the enthusiasm of Baron Tuyll for his project, his expectations for support from the architect of the Holy Alliance were eventually dashed.[6] It was at best a forlorn hope that the monarch who had so recently issued a state paper which Adams indignantly described as "an Io Triumphe over the fallen cause of revolution" could be induced to persuade Ferdinand to recognize his revolted colonies in America, even to save Cuba and Puerto Rico. It is doubtful under any circumstances whether Ferdinand could have been moved from his stubborn insistence on continuing the struggle, but Alexander never made the attempt. The French government considered the situation hopeless, and when Adams and Clay finally heard from Russia, Nessel-

5. Clay to Rufus King, United States Minister to Great Britain (May 11, 1825), ibid., pp. 250–51. Clay to James Brown, United States Minister to France (May 13, 1825), ibid., pp. 251–52.
6. Memo of conversation, Adams to Tuyll (May 19, 1825), J. Q. Adams, *Memoirs,* 7, 9–10.

rode's reply ought to have (though it did not) immediately deflated any hopes still entertained in Washington.[7] The Tsar felt he could not act until he had ascertained the "ulterior views of Spain" on this subject. This was the kiss of death, for no progress could be made by deferring to Ferdinand's obduracy, and as if this were not enough, the Russian foreign minister deftly tossed back the ball by expressing hopes that the United States would do everything in its power to defeat any enterprises against Cuba and Puerto Rico. Any chance of success ended completely with Alexander's death at the end of the year, for even had his brother Nicholas been disposed to intercede with Spain, he was too engrossed in the crisis caused by the Decembrist uprising to do so immediately.

While Adams and Clay were awaiting the outcome of their policy of indirect pressure on Spain, a new factor entered the picture which brought into play an alternative British attempt at dealing with the problem of the Spanish Antilles. Both London and Washington were disturbed about reports of an outburst of French activity in the Caribbean during the summer of 1825. In late May Governor Donzelot of Martinique furnished a naval convoy for a shipment of Spanish troops bound for Havana, and toward the end of July the French squadron in the Caribbean was abruptly and heavily reinforced by the addition of twenty-eight vessels. Added to the continuing threat to Cuba from Mexico and Colombia, these seemingly ominous developments precipitated a fresh attempt by George Canning at a concert of policy with the United States.

Canning's sensitive arrogance had never recovered from the rebuff he had suffered in the proposals to Rush two years before, or from the march Adams had stolen on him in

7. Brown to Clay (July 15, 1825), Manning, *LA, 3,* 1412. Nesselrode to Middleton (Aug. 20, 1825), ibid., p. 1875.

their rivalry for prestige in Latin America by persuading President Monroe to issue his Doctrine independently. Stung at being overreached, the Foreign Secretary had ordered Addington to destroy all correspondence relating to that humiliating episode and to renumber his files to obliterate all evidence of it for posterity. He had circulated the Polignac memorandum to point up for Latin America the priority of British action in curbing Holy Alliance intervention on behalf of Spain. When, early in 1825, Canning launched Britain on a policy of recognizing the independence of Latin America, the stage was at last set for the necessary re-establishment of British ascendancy in the new states, and with it the prevention of the development Canning most feared—the creation of a closed political system in the New World under the domination of the United States.[8] For in Canning's intricate mind the preconditions of a safe reversion to traditional British isolationism, of the policy of manipulating the balance of power free of prior commitments, were on the one hand the disruption of the European Concert and on the other the political fragmentation of the Americas. Canning's view of international affairs postulated a political continuum, but a continuum of interacting discrete sovereignties.

Whatever the contradictions in their long-range policies, the short-run objectives of Canning and Adams provided some basis for joint, or at least parallel, action. Both were concerned about Cuba and Puerto Rico, neither relished the prospect of a descent on the islands by the new states (though Canning was careful to conceal his attitude from Mexico and Colombia), and both preferred to maintain the status quo there rather than see them transferred to any

8. For a perceptive analysis of Canning's policies at this period see William W. Kaufmann, *British Policy and the Independence of Latin America, 1804–1828* (New Haven, 1951), chap. 10.

other power. Canning's first move was a sharp demand to France for an explanation of the convoy episode, which resulted in prompt disavowals from Paris of any intent to land troops or to intervene in the war, and in a reprimand to Donzelot for his unauthorized action.[9] The British Foreign Secretary learned with discomfort in this exchange, however, that the French commander in the Caribbean had standing orders to aid Spain in defending her island possessions. Here was the raw material for an explosive international incident, and Canning determined to arrive at some arrangement for neutralizing the danger of someone's blundering into war.

When he learned of the Adams-Clay appeal to Russia and France, Canning's reaction was one of contempt, tinged with disbelief that the Americans could be so "childish" and disingenuous as to embark on so sterile an approach. Fleetingly, he even suspected "the Yankees" of being not fools but knaves engaged in a sinister deception, of being "just the rogues that we have always taken them to be, but which I was willing to hope they were resolved to be no longer."[10] His own solution was to revive the proposal for a tripartite "guarantee" of Cuba to Spain which he had advanced in 1823. This time it was to take the form of a self-denying pledge by Britain, France, and the United States, renouncing any designs on the island for themselves, but without any understanding in regard to possible attacks by the new states. This, Canning believed, would at once relieve Ferdinand's mind as to any threat from the major

9. Granville to Canning (July 18, 1825), Webster, *Britain and the Independence of Latin America*, 2, 186–87; (Aug. 1, 1825), ibid., pp. 187–88.

10. Canning to Lord Liverpool (Aug. 6, 1825), E. J. Stapleton, *Some Official Correspondence of George Canning* (2 vols. London, 1887), *1*, 283.

maritime powers, and better dispose him toward making peace with Latin America.[11]

Once decided on this policy, Canning pressed for its acceptance with his characteristic vigor and impetuosity, but he was doomed to disappointment. From France he at first received encouragement, and then, unexpectedly, a flat rejection of his project, as being an embarrassment to the Family Compact between France and Spain.[12] The veteran American diplomat Rufus King expressed interest in Canning's proposals, but found a defect in them that made him feel it necessary to refer the matter back to Washington. King wished to make the three-power pledge conditional on a recognition by Spain of her revolted colonies, a change Canning was unwilling to make because, he said, it implied that if Spain refused the condition, the three maritime powers would be in effect threatening a move against Cuba.[13] Adams and Clay agreed with King that removing Spain's concern about the major powers would only encourage Ferdinand to continue his foolhardy prosecution of the war and thus provoke the attack on Cuba by the new states that the United States wished to avoid.[14]

The collapse of his scheme, especially in a manner so unpleasantly analogous to the conversations with Rush, did nothing to improve Canning's temper. If nothing could be done directly to remove the danger of a change of status in Cuba, at least something might be salvaged from the fiasco to improve Britain's position in Latin America at the expense of the United States. Canning accordingly subsided

11. Canning to Rufus King (Aug. 7, 1825), Canning to Granville (Aug. 23, 1825): Webster, *Britain and the Independence of Latin America*, 2, 194–95, 520–24.

12. Granville to Canning (Aug. 29, 1825), ibid., 2, 196.

13. King to Clay (Aug. 11, 1825), Manning, *LA*, *3*, 1558–60. Canning to King (Sept. 8, 1825), Webster, 2, 526–28.

14. Clay to King (Oct. 17, 1825), Manning, *LA*, *1*, 254–60.

into a cunning watchfulness, scanning Washington's moves for ammunition to use when the occasion presented itself. He had not long to wait; Adams and Clay soon provided him with the ammunition, and Simón Bolívar the occasion, when he issued Britain an invitation to send an observer to the forthcoming Congress of Panama.

The Washington government was worried about the French refusal to adhere to the Tripartite Agreement. Earlier in the summer, when he was still hoping for French support in persuading Ferdinand to come to his senses, Clay had sent the mildest of inquiries to Paris about the convoy episode in the Caribbean, and had received vague reassurances in reply. Now he felt the time had come to make the kind of statement about Cuba which would leave no doubt in the French mind as to where the United States stood. Canning, who was provided with a copy, called Clay's note "as pert a paper as a French Minister can desire to hear."[15] So it was. Clay insisted that the United States be informed in advance of any such large fleet movements as the French had made the previous summer.[16] He repeated Adams' formulation of policy toward Cuba and restated the No-Transfer principle in vigorous language: the United States "would not consent to the occupation of these islands by any other power than Spain under any contingency whatever."

Clay invited Canning to join in these representations to the French, whereupon the Foreign Secretary waspishly retorted that he had communicated the views of the British government to this effect as long ago as July, and that to repeat them now "would have been to take at the suggestion of a third Power, and as subsidiary to the declarations of that Power, a step which the British Government had al-

15. Kaufmann, *British Policy*, p. 209.
16. Clay to Brown (Oct. 25, 1825), Manning, *LA, 1*, 260–61.

ready taken long before, singly and of their own accord."[17]
By this display of ill-tempered independence Canning was
soothing his wounded vanity, but he had made little advance toward mastery of the situation.

Adams and Clay were not aware, of course, that Canning's
interest in the Cuban situation had transformed itself into a
search for ways to score on the United States in a rivalry for
influence in Spanish America. If they had been, they might
have proceeded more circumspectly than they did in the
next few weeks, although the prevention of a change in the
status of Cuba would have remained an objective of the
first magnitude in their policy regardless of British man-
euverings. In any case, they took a step which appeared to
Canning to give him the advantage at long last, when they
sent identical notes to Mexico and Colombia asking them to
suspend for the time being any plans for an expedition
against Cuba, pending the results of the Tsar's endeavor on
behalf of peace.[18] The dispatch of these communications
was prompted by news of the surrender of the fortress of
San Juan de Ulloa at Vera Cruz, the last stronghold of Spanish resistance in Mexico, and by Baron Tuyll's concern for
fear a Mexican thrust at Cuba would ruin the effects of
Russia's anticipated persuasion.[19]

These notes were not No-Transfer statements by any
stretch of the imagination. They were a request, not a
demand, a suggestion rather than a warning. They contained no hint that Washington would interfere under any
circumstances with what it considered to be a legitimate
operation of war, although there was in fact one set of

17. King to Canning (Jan. 9, 1826), Canning to King (Jan. 13,
1826): Webster, 2, 538, 540–41.

18. Clay to José Maria Salazar, Colombian Minister to the United
States (Dec. 20, 1825), Manning, *LA, 1*, 263–64.

19. Memo of conversation between Adams and Clay (Dec. 20, 1825),
C. F. Adams, ed., *Memoirs, 7*, 88.

contingencies under which the Adams administration felt it would be necessary to act. Clay disclosed to the Tsar that the United States would interpose only if Mexico and Colombia endangered this country's internal security by conducting their attack in a "desolating manner" by fomenting race warfare.[20] Transference to another European power would never be countenanced; transference to another American nation under the circumstances could be opposed only if it appeared likely to incite a slave rebellion in the South.

Canning learned of the American *démarche* with the greatest satisfaction, for in the Cuban problem he was now convinced he had a means of contrasting for the edification of Spanish America the disinterested benevolence of Great Britain with the selfish covetousness of the United States. One measure of the hopes he entertained for this stratagem is his acute irritation at the impression he received that his representative in Washington had supported Clay's policy of leashing Mexico and Colombia.[21] "If the United States," he wrote Vaughan, "think that particular interests of their own require that a certain operation of war should not be undertaken by one of the belligerents, it is a question, and a very nice one for them, how they will prevent the undertaking of it."[22] With acid sarcasm he delivered his reprimand: "if it had been intended that you should treat with the Secretary of State of the United States in a matter so delicate . . . you would not have been left without instructions upon a point of as much novelty as delicacy and importance." The unfortunate Vaughan, who was in no better position than Adams and Clay to divine the sinuosities of the Foreign Secretary's policies, gave what lame assurances he could. Canning, relieved, proceeded to pre-

20. Clay to Middleton (Dec. 26, 1825), Manning, *LA*, *1*, 265–66.
21. Charles Vaughan to Canning (Dec. 21, 1825), Webster, 2, 536–37.
22. Canning to Vaughan (Feb. 8, 1826), ibid., pp. 542–43.

pare his case against the United States for deployment at
the Congress of Panama.

THE CONGRESS OF PANAMA

The Congress of Panama was the brain child of the Liberator, Simón Bolívar, president of Colombia. Since 1822 he
had been planning an "Amphyctionic Assembly" of American nations, the main purpose of which was to be the formation of a league or confederation of the sovereign states of
the New World for mutual defense and cooperation. It was
hoped that the United States, which had so far refused to
enter into the system of bilateral defensive alliance which
the new states were fashioning, could be induced to sign an
all-inclusive multilateral pact in support of the Noncolonization principle recently announced by President Monroe.
It was also hoped that Great Britain, whose supremacy at
sea impressed the military imagination of the Liberator,
would informally guarantee the political and territorial
integrity of the former Spanish colonies.[23]

The Congress of Panama has always and rightly been
regarded as a milestone in the history of the Monroe Doctrine, but it is also an important chapter in the development
of its preceding security policy, the No-Transfer principle.
The attempt to "pan-americanize" the Doctrine in 1826
failed; it was not until a century later that the United States
decided in favor of an international partnership with Latin
America. John Quincy Adams made it clear that the traditional policies of nonentanglement and no prior commitments applied, though perhaps not with equal rigidity, to
Latin America as well as to Europe. Isolationism was not yet
hemispheric but continental, and the Monroe Doctrine, far

23. For general accounts of the Congress of Panama see Joseph B.
Lockey, *Pan-Americanism: Its Beginnings,* New York, 1926; and Bemis, *Adams,* pp. 543–61.

from being the automatic engine of general defense that Latin America might have wanted it to be, was to be applied or not solely in accordance with the national interest of the United States in any particular situation.

Through all the deliberations in Washington on the great question of an entangling alliance, there ran in a continuous skein the more immediate, pressing, and critical problem of the future of Cuba and Puerto Rico. One of the announced objects of the meeting at Panama was the coordination of plans by the nations at war with Spain for expanding their operations, certainly to the Spanish Antilles and perhaps even beyond the two great oceans to the Canaries and the Philippines, in order to force Ferdinand to make peace. While discussion of these matters was supposed to be confined exclusively to the belligerents, the interest of the neutral United States in Cuba made it seem imperative to bring whatever influence possible to bear against such military ventures. The record of the Cabinet meeting called by President Adams after receiving the first, tentative overtures from Colombia on attending the Congress shows that the Cuban situation had a strong influence on the decision to participate.[24]

Adams and Clay delayed taking formal action until they received a more specific agenda, but when this arrived early in November 1825 the President promptly sent to the Senate the names of Richard C. Anderson of Kentucky, United States Minister to Colombia, and John Sergeant of Pennsylvania, for approval as envoys to the Assembly of American Nations at Panama. Among the subjects listed on the agenda for discussion by the neutral states, one, a proposed codification of international law for the Americas, was clearly designed to appeal to the United States, which would be attracted by the prospects of securing agreement

24. May 7, 1825, Adams, *Memoirs, 6,* 542.

to its principles of neutral maritime rights. The others were bound to be controversial: the conditional alliance, abolition of the African slave trade, and determination of a uniform rule of conduct toward Haiti. In his brief special message to the Senate accompanying the nominations of Anderson and Sergeant, John Quincy Adams referred delicately to the "indirect influence" the United States might exercise upon "any projects or purpose" growing out of the war between the American Republics and Spain, "which might seriously affect the interests of this Union."[25] This, of course, meant Cuba.

To those who in recent years have been persuaded by abuses of the discretionary powers of the Executive that true democracy implies legislative direction of foreign affairs, the debates in Congress on the mission to Panama should be instructive. Seldom in our history has there been so little discussion of the intrinsic merits of the case, and so much sheer partisanship. For this issue gave the opponents of the Adams administration their first opportunity to display the massive obstructionism which paralyzed the President's program through his tenure in office. The Era of Good Feelings disintegrated as the Jackson forces, determined to avenge the "corrupt bargain" of 1824 and to ensure victory for the newly forming Democratic party in the next election, used every means at their disposal to discredit Adams and Clay. The President eventually won the battle over Panama, but it was the only significant legislative contest he did win.

In the Senate, the opposition opened its campaign with an unfavorable report from the Committe on Foreign Relations on the Panama mission. The situation in Cuba and

25. Message from President Adams to the Senate of the United States (Dec. 26, 1825), *The Executive Proceedings of the Senate of the United States on the Subject of the Mission to the Congress of Panama,* 19th Cong., 1st Sess., No. 68 (Washington, 1826), p. 4.

Puerto Rico, according to the report, was one of the commanding reasons for not attending the Congress of Panama. Rather than suffer the inevitable embarrassment of having either to approve or to disapprove the proposed expeditions against the islands, the United States would do better to stand aloof and maintain uncertainty both in Europe and in America over what action it might take in any contingency. Encouragement to the new states not only would be undesirable in itself but might easily provoke European aid to Spain, with a resulting danger of the transfer of Cuba to one of the major maritime powers.[26]

It rapidly became apparent to Adams' adversaries that the Cuban question offered one of the most promising avenues of attack on the administration. On January 30, 1826, Senator Van Buren introduced a resolution asking the Chief Executive to transmit all papers relating to the request for Russian interposition to end the war, and all correspondence with Spain on the subject.[27] Adams complied at once, and henceforward scarcely a speaker neglected to touch on Cuban policy. The level of debate was not notably high. Notwithstanding the President's specific pledge of his opposition to entering any entangling alliances or abandoning a position of neutrality, there was an interminable wrangle over the supposed departure from traditional isolationist policy. The slavery senators missed no opportunity to inveigh against sitting in conference with persons of "mixed race," against any recognition of the Negro republic of Haiti, and against encouraging any descent upon Cuba by the new states, imbued as they were with the "genius of universal emancipation."

But it is the Cuban question that concerns us here. It is interesting that with the lone exception of Senator Wood-

26. Report of the Senate Committee on Foreign Relations (Jan. 16, 1826), ibid., pp. 70–71.
27. Resolution introduced by Van Buren (Jan. 30, 1826), ibid., p. 77.

bury of New Hampshire there was no voice raised in opposition to the No-Transfer principle itself. On the contrary, the burden of the opposition arguments was that the principle had not been applied broadly or effectively enough in Cuba. Woodbury missed the point by treating the principle in legal terms, when he asked what right the United States had to protest against the acquisition of the island by, say, France.[28] Like the principles of President Monroe's message of 1823, the No-Transfer principle was an assertion of interest, not of right; in essence it was political, not legal. Those who, like Van Buren, the leader of the anti-administration forces, opposed the mission to Panama attacked Adams and Clay as "political busybodies," who out of a passion to cut a great figure in international affairs had fettered themselves by declaring to Russia that they could not interfere with attacks by the new states unless the Cuban slaves were encouraged to murder their masters.[29] Van Buren's own policy, he declared, would have been to apply the No-Transfer principle equally to Latin America and to Europe in connection with Cuba.

It is doubtful whether this radical suggestion represented a settled conviction on the part of the Little Magician. To a certain extent it was opposition for its own sake. There is an illuminating remark ascribed to him after the battle over Panama had been lost: "Yes they have beaten us by a few votes . . . but if they had only taken the other side and refused the mission, we should have had them."[30] At any rate, when Van Buren was serving as Secretary of State four years

28. Speech of Mr. Woodbury in the Senate (March 1, 1826), pamphlet, Washington, Gales and Seaton, 1826.

29. Speech of Van Buren in the Senate (March 1826) and of Hague in the Senate (March 1826), pamphlets (Washington, Gales and Seaton, 1826), pp. 22–26.

30. Carl Schurz, *Life of Henry Clay*, American Statesmen Series (2 vols. Boston, 1887), *1*, 273.

later, his policy was indistinguishable from his predecessors' which he had attacked so vehemently.[31]

Whichever side the speaker took, there was fairly general agreement that the proposed Mexican and Colombian expeditions were unwelcome. Senator Johnston of Louisiana favored the Panama mission in order to be able to prevent the attacks by acting behind the scenes—"advise them—remonstrate—menace them if necessary"—to avert the catastrophe of a slave rebellion in Cuba.[32] Speaking in opposition, John Randolph painted a horrifying and hyperbolic picture of emancipated slaves who could invade our South from Cuba "in row boats."[33] This debate gave full scope to Randolph's impressive powers of vituperation. He attacked Henry Clay's long-standing affinity for the Latin-American cause by referring to the Panama mission as a "Kentucky cuckoo's egg laid in a Spanish-American nest." It was at this time also that he delivered himself of his celebrated thrust at the supposed bargain by which Clay had thrown his influence behind Adams when the selection of the President went to the House of Representatives in 1824, allegedly in order to receive a Cabinet post in reward, when he spoke of the "combination of Blifil and Black George—the combination, unheard of until then, of the Puritan with the black-leg."[34] Clay challenged Randolph as a result of these remarks, but the meeting, described appreciatively by Thomas Hart Benton as "about the last high-toned duel that I have witnessed," was happily bloodless.

Finally on March 14, 1826, the Senate confirmed the nominations of Anderson and Sergeant. The battle was not

31. Van Buren to Cornelius Van Ness, United States Minister to Spain (Oct. 13, 1830), Manning, *LA, 1,* 313–14.

32. Speech of Johnston in the Senate (March 1826), pamphlet (Washington, Gales and Seaton, 1826), pp. 16–18.

33. *Niles' Weekly Register, 30* (1826), 1–16.

34. *Register of Debates,* 19th Cong., 1st Sess., *2,* 401–3.

yet finished, however, for the House of Representatives debated over a month longer before making the necessary appropriation for the mission. In a special message accompanying the transmission of documents requested by the House, President Adams openly emphasized the Cuban question as a reason for participating in the Congress, in contrast to the veiled references on the subject in his communication to the Senate earlier.[35] No longer so cautious about matters which were supposed to concern belligerents alone, he warned that the plans of Mexico and Colombia, involving as they did the danger of a slave rebellion or of transfer to a European power, must necessarily engage the attention of the United States.

Congressional criticisms of their Cuban policy must have had an effect upon the administration, for in his instructions to Anderson and Sergeant, Clay assumed a considerably firmer attitude toward the Mexican and Colombian projects than formerly.[36] For the information of the envoys he not only stated the familiar opposition to Cuba's transfer to any other European power but also declared flatly that "we are unwilling to see its transfer or annexation to either of the new American states." If friendly persuasion did not suffice to induce them to abandon or suspend their plans, they would have to be warned that the United States would consider a move by them to annex Cuba as a war of conquest rather than of self-defense. If in this instance European powers with an interest in the "balance and stability of power in the West Indies" decided to intervene for the purpose of preserving the status quo, the United States, "far from being under any pledge at present to oppose them

35. Message of the President of the United States to the House of Representatives (March 15, 1826), Executive Document 129, 19th Cong., 1st Sess. (Washington, 1826), p. 9.

36. *International American Conference: The Congress of 1826 at Panama* (4 vols. Washington, 1890), *4*, 138–43.

might find themselves, contrary to their inclination, reluctantly drawn by a current of events to their side." The United States, then, might help Europe maintain Spanish sovereignty in Cuba, not because possession of Cuba by the new republics constituted a threat in itself—except for the slavery question—but because Mexico and Colombia lacked the naval power to defend the island, and their occupation threatened to create a power vacuum which would intensify the danger of a transfer of the island to a major maritime nation which Washington dreaded.

If George Canning had been able to read Clay's instructions, he would have been overjoyed, for they fitted perfectly the unflattering image of the United States he was preparing to present at the Congress of Panama. When Bolívar invited the British government to send an observer to the Congress, Canning marshaled all his powers in an effort to prevent the formation of an American hemisphere confederation under United States leadership, separated from and possibly hostile to the European state system. For this purpose he relied heavily—probably too heavily—on an exposure of Washington's Cuban policy to discountenance the United States in the eyes of Latin America. The Foreign Secretary's instructions to his agent, Edward J. Dawkins, reveal the contrast he wished to draw between British and American policy:

> The British Government, indeed, are so far from denying the right of the New States of America to make a hostile attack upon Cuba . . . that we have uniformly refused to join with the United States in remonstrating with Mexico and Colombia against the supposed intention, or in intimating that we should feel displeasure at the execution of it. We should indeed regret it, but we arrogate to ourselves no right to control the military operations of one belligerent against another.

The Government of the United States, however, professes itself of a different opinion. It conceives that the interests of the United States would be so directly affected by either the occupation of the Havannah by an invading force or by the consequences which an attack upon Cuba, even if unsuccessful, might produce in the interior of the island, that the Cabinet of Washington hardly disguises its intention to interfere directly, and by force, to prevent or repress such an operation.[37]

Canning urged the new states to attempt a fresh negotiation for peace with Spain, because since "neither England nor France could see with indifference the United States in occupation of Cuba," any military assault by Mexico and Colombia on the island would lead to a chain reaction of disastrous war.

Of course Canning exaggerated the length to which Adams and Clay were prepared to go in Cuba. At the most, they contemplated concerted action with the European powers to secure Cuba to Spain. He also, like the American government, overestimated the strength and resolve of Mexico and Colombia to undertake the expedition. Nevertheless, as a debating stratagem, Canning's point was most useful. Shortly after his arrival at Panama, Dawkins felt a distinct chill enter into his relations with Don Pedro Gual, the Foreign Minister of Colombia. At a loss at first to account for the change, Dawkins soon discovered that it arose from Gual's having read certain dispatches of the United States minister at Madrid, recently made available to the Senate by President Adams. In them Everett had declared that he believed Britain to be interested in a continuation of war between Spain and her former colonies, in order to

37. Canning to Dawkins (March 18, 1826), Webster, *Britain and the Independence of Latin America*, *1*, 408–9.

clinch her monopoly of commerce with Latin America. With the aid of a sheaf of correspondence that Canning's foresight had provided, Dawkins was able to dispel the notion that Britain had suspended efforts at Madrid on behalf of peace and to press Canning's new plan for negotiations.[38]

Dawkins won an easy victory in re-establishing British influence at Panama. In fact it is doubtful whether the task was ever as great as Canning imagined. The superiority of the Royal Navy and the pre-eminence of Britain as a manufacturing nation combined to give that country a natural advantage over the United States in any race for political and commercial influence in Spanish America. In any event, there was no contest at Panama, for Dawkins found himself unopposed. The United States envoys never arrived; Anderson died of fever on his way to the Isthmus, and Sergeant, fearful of the pestilential climate, delayed sailing so long that he missed the conference entirely. A second meeting, scheduled at Tacubaya in the federal district of Mexico, never convened, and the Congress of Panama passed into history without important issue. Although rumors of a possible Mexican or Colombian expedition against Cuba occasionally circulated as late as 1829, the internal condition of those states made such ventures increasingly improbable.

As concern about the new American states waned, the familiar rumors of a British design on Cuba reappeared. When in late 1826 a war scare blossomed over British irritation at Spanish meddling in Portugal, Albert Gallatin in London tried vainly to get "positive assurances" from Canning that Britain would not strike at Cuba. Worried by Canning's evasiveness and never much of an expansionist, the veteran American diplomatist felt it to have been a mistake to have turned down the tripartite agreement offered by Britain and France the year before, but Gallatin

38. Dawkins to Canning (July 7, 1826), ibid., pp. 413–20.

in this instance had to content himself with a firm reitera-
tion of the No-Transfer principle.[39] Clay in turn sent off a
secret agent to Havana to report the temper of the people
there.[40]

The question was, as always, how far the United States
was prepared to go to prevent the transfer of Cuba. Since
the No-Transfer Resolution of 1811, Congress had not provided the Executive with specific authorization to use force
to prevent the transfer of territory in the New World from
one European sovereign to another. And the war-making
power constitutionally resided in Congress. In Madrid the
ebullient American Minister, Alexander H. Everett, hear-
ing of alleged plans for British-sponsored uprisings in the
Canary Islands and Cuba, went so far as to suggest to the
Spanish Secretary of State for Foreign Affairs that if London
persisted in its machinations, the United States "would feel
called upon to aid the King [of Spain] in maintaining the
existing state of things" in Cuba.[41] This went beyond his
instructions, and beyond the powers of the President to
commit the nation to a course of action. Clay felt constrained to reprove Everett for his indiscretion, and in his
instructions to Cornelius Van Ness, who shortly succeeded
Everett, he was careful to point out that if Spain again inquired about the use of force in support of the No-Transfer
principle, Van Ness was to reconfirm the policy itself, but
also to emphasize the traditional American aversion to entangling commitments. Spain would have to rely not on any
direct pledge of assistance but on reasonable suppositions

39. Gallatin to Clay (Dec. 22, 30, 1826), Gallatin, *Writings*, pp. 345–
47, 352–53.

40. Clay to Daniel P. Cook (March 12, 1827), Manning, *1*, 282. See
also Rippy, *Rivalry*, pp. 89–90, and Bemis, *Adams*, p. 542.

41. Everett to Clay (Aug. 17, 1827; April 4, 1828), Manning, *3*,
2146–47, 2152–56. See also the private letter of Everett to Adams,
cited in Bemis, pp. 542–43 n.

drawn from the known attitudes of the Congress and people of the United States toward any threatened transfer of Cuba.[42] This Adamsonian caution and regard for the niceties of constitutional law remained the rule in United States policy for a few years more, until with the assertiveness that accompanied the spirit of Manifest Destiny and the increasing intensity of the slavery question, it was replaced by a habitual resort to threats of force coupled with attempts to purchase the island from Spain.

42. Bemis, *Adams,* p. 543; Clay to Van Ness (Oct. 2, 1829), Manning, *LA, 1,* 305–8.

CHAPTER 7

Slavery Expansionism and No Transfer

During the thirty years before the outbreak of the Civil War the institution of slavery came to epitomize the extensive and extraordinarily complex social, economic, and emotional differences between the sections. The slavery question pervaded every political issue, domestic or foreign, tinging it with the struggle for power between North and South, obscuring and distorting the national interest. It was a tragic time, when great talents were squandered on casuistry, and second-rate men increasingly found their way to high office in Washington and in diplomatic missions abroad. Partisanship invaded the realm of foreign affairs to an extent unknown since the days of Jefferson and Madison, touching even the No-Transfer principle, though very slightly compared with other policies.

Slavery had always been one of the foundations of American interest in Cuba, but in these years it threatened to become the only one. Commercial interest somewhat declined as the natural result of a renewed tariff war with Spain which seriously impaired American trade with Cuba, and while consideration of military security continued to figure prominently in discussions of Cuban policy, particularly among moderate Democratic expansionists from the

North, slavery came to overshadow all other questions.[1] The American slave states lived in constant dread of the "Africanization" of Cuba, through either internal revolt or external intervention which would erect a Negro republic on the model of Haiti. Any such development, accompanied as it must be by shocking scenes of devastation and blood-letting reminiscent of Napoleon's day, loomed as a persistent threat to the safety of southern planters and their "peculiar institution."

There was ample reason for alarm. By 1843 Negroes outnumbered the white population of Cuba by a margin of 58 to 42 per cent, and the illegal continuation of the African slave trade to Cuba widened this gap annually. Emancipation of the slaves in the British West Indies in 1833 and in the French West Indies in 1848 heightened unrest in Cuba, where a rash of local slave rebellions broke out in the thirties and forties.[2]

The existence of slavery in Cuba tended to keep the island in Spanish hands. Although both the Polk and Pierce administrations made serious attempts to purchase Cuba, rising northern antislavery sentiment produced a formidable opposition to annexation as a solution for the Cuban problem, and to American slavery expansionists Madrid could always declare with chilling effect that "Cuba must be either Spanish or African." Powerful interests in both Spain and Cuba supported the continuation of slavery there, but the threat of emancipation could always be counted on to dampen annexationist ardor in the United States.

The shadow of Great Britain in the slavery question heavily reinforced the application of the No-Transfer prin-

1. Basil Rauch, *American Interest in Cuba, 1848–1855* (New York, 1948), pp. 30 ff.

2. H. H. S. Aimes, *A History of Slavery in Cuba* (New York and London, 1907), pp. 125–221 passim.

ciple in Cuba. To all the familiar aspects of Britain as a
threat to American interests—Britain the tyrant of the seas,
the insatiable imperialist power, the commercial rival, the
controller of the world's money market—there was now
added Britain the leader of world abolitionism. Antislavery
not only caught up the British populace in the evangelical
fervor of reform but received the sanction of official policy.
As early as 1817 London launched a campaign to outlaw
the African slave trade and to authorize visit and search by
member naval forces of the others' merchant vessels to de-
tect and punish illicit traffickers in human misery. The
United States refused to adhere, not because it condoned
the trade, which was outlawed in 1808, but because the
British refused to give satisfaction on the impressment issue,
as required by Washington. The question of the African
slave-trade treaty was a continuous source of irritation in
Anglo–American relations, because a good many American
vessels were illegally stopped by British cruisers, and because the American flag was undoubtedly used to cover
slavers' activities. None of these vexations, however, compared with direct British abolitionist activity in and near
the United States. British antislavery men were known to be
in close touch with their American counterparts, and there
was a widespread and not ill-founded belief among slavery
men in the United States that British officials were pressing
abolition on the government of Texas. There was no room
for doubt that Britain opposed the annexation of Texas to
the United States. As we shall see, suspicions of similar
British activity in Cuba prompted grave anxiety in
Washington.

President Jackson had little to do with Cuba during his
eight years in office, except to negotiate ineffectually with
Spain for a reduction of the prohibitively high tariffs on
foreign goods imported into the island. The single statement to issue from his administration reflected the new,

more belligerent tone that was henceforward to mark Democratic applications of the No-Transfer principle. In September 1832 Secretary of State Edward Livingston wrote to William Shaler, the first American consul to be received in Cuba, that "the great objects of our Government in relation to Cuba are, a free and untrammeled trade, on its present footing, eased of discriminating duties—to preserve it in the hands of Spain *even at the expense of a war*—and only in the event of finding that impossible, to look to its annexation to our confederacy."[3]

Between 1833 and 1839 Spain was convulsed by civil strife that seemed to threaten new danger of a transfer of Cuba, partly because England and France intervened on behalf of the infant Queen Isabella and the Queen Regent Maria Christina against the Carlist pretenders, and partly because of the exhaustion of the Spanish treasury as a result of the struggle. American diplomatic representatives at Madrid warned Washington that British arms shipments to the Spanish government and the control of the Spanish debt by British creditors might lead to demands by London for the cession of Cuba. Even though the British ambassador to Spain disclaimed any such intentions, the American minister, Mr. Eaton, advised his government to remind London of our opposition to the transfer of the island.[4]

There was, in fact, a highly secret negotiation between a representative of Maria Christina and Louis Philippe early in 1836 for the sale of Cuba, Puerto Rico, and the Philippines to France for forty million reals, to replenish depleted Spanish coffers. The citizen-king haggled over price, how-

3. Livingston to Shaler (Sept. 1, 1832), W. R. Manning, *Diplomatic Correspondence: Inter-American Affairs, 1830–1860* (12 vols. Washington, Carnegie Endowment for International Peace, 1932–39), *11*, 6–7 (cited as Manning, *IA*). Italics inserted.

4. Van Ness to Forsyth (Dec. 10, 1836), Eaton to Forsyth (April 29, Aug. 10, 1837): ibid., pp. 300–2, 305–6, 307.

ever, and the offer was withdrawn.[5] No intimation of this reached Washington, where Britain continued as chief villain in the piece. When, some months later, the United States chargé at Paris inquired about a rumored French loan to Spain, he was blandly informed that France was considering no loan and preferred to see Cuba remain in the hands of Spain, or if not to be independent. Mr. Anderson took the occasion to reaffirm American opposition to any transfer of Cuba, and gathered from the interview that France was distrustful of British designs on Cuba.[6]

The deepest suspicions of Britain appeared to be justified when in 1838 agents of British antislavery societies approached the Spanish regent to urge emancipation in Cuba. The United States minister hastened to submit a lengthy defense of slavery to the foreign ministry, concluding with the now customary No-Transfer statement, in which he declared that a cession of Cuba would be regarded by the United States as a "departure from friendship" on the part of Spain and an evidence of "hostility" on the part of the receiver.[7] Rumors the following year that British bankers were considering a private loan to the Spanish government, with the proviso that the British and French governments guarantee the revenues of Cuba, Puerto Rico, and the Philippines as security, caused the American minister at London to state categorically that "it was impossible that the United States could acquiesce in the transfer of Cuba from the dominion of Spain to any of the great maritime powers of Europe."[8]

As a result of ten years of agitation over British designs on Cuba, the American government in 1840 took the very step

5. James M. Callahan, *Cuba in International Relations* (Baltimore, 1899), pp. 173–74.

6. Anderson to Forsyth (June 6, 1837), Manning, *IA, 6,* 507–8.

7. Eaton to the Count de Ofalia (March 10, 1838), ibid., *11,* 312–13.

8. Andrew Stevenson to Forsyth (June 16, 1839), ibid., *7,* 239–41.

John Quincy Adams had previously declined to take—a pledge of armed support to Spain in retaining the island. Secretary of State Forsyth's instructions to the American chargé in Madrid therefore represent a significant milestone in the development of the No-Transfer policy.[9] The Secretary of State began by apologizing for repeating a position the Spanish government had "often been apprised of," but he desired to restate the No-Transfer formula "for fear . . . that the subject should be lost sight of in the frequent changes or modifications of the Spanish Cabinet." Forsyth was understating the need, for in eight years there had been nineteen changes in the Spanish ministry of foreign affairs, a condition which led Washington Irving to remark after brief service as American minister that "to carry on negotiations with such transient functionaries is like bargaining at the window of a railroad car—before you can get a reply to a proposition, the other party is out of sight."[10]

The immediate threat to Cuba was from Britain, and arose from two circumstances, as Forsyth saw it. The first was the Spanish debt owed to British creditors, which could lead to a British occupation of Cuba if that country realized its object of getting the island's revenues pledged as collateral. The second was the strengthened slave trade treaty concluded in 1835 between Britain and Spain. It was common knowledge that Spain had failed to suppress the trade in Cuba, as she had contracted to do in the treaty of 1817, and it was apprehended that Britain would use this as a pretext to occupy the island. Forsyth therefore instructed Vail to tell the Spanish government, informally and if possible only verbally, of the "fixed resolution" of the United States government, "taken after long and mature deliberation," never to permit such an occupation. "Should you have

9. Forsyth to Aaron Vail (July 15, 1840), ibid., *11*, 23–24.
10. Callahan, *Cuba in International Relations*, p. 181.

reason to suspect," the Secretary of State concluded, "any design on the part of Spain to transfer voluntarily her title to the island, whether of ownership or possession, and whether permanent or temporary, to Great Britain or any other power, you will distinctly state that the United States will prevent it, at all hazard, as they will any foreign military occupation for any pretext whatsoever—And you are authorized to assure the Spanish government that in case of any attempt from whatever quarter, to wrest from her this portion of her territory, she may securely depend upon the military and naval resources of the United States to aid her in preserving or recovering it."

During the next two years rumors multiplied that British abolitionists were fomenting a revolt in Cuba with promises of the assistance of a British naval force in setting up a Negro republic. All this reached its climax early in 1843 when Secretary of State Daniel Webster wrote to Robert Campbell, the American consul in Cuba, asking him to get the facts. In this crisis the Whig administration endorsed and restated the pledges given by their Democratic predecessors, Webster repeating Forsyth's exact language in his letter to Campbell and presumably also in conversation with the Spanish minister in Washington.[11]

Campbell discredited the notion that the British government had any immediate plans for occupying Cuba, but he was unable to give any reassurance about the abolitionists there. Much of the anxiety about British antislavery agitation arose from the fact that Britain by treaty right had established in places like Brazil and Cuba mixed commissions to adjudicate cases involving alleged slave-trading vessels. As a result, a great many Britishers with strong

11. Vail to Forsyth (Jan. 15, 1841), Vail to Webster (Nov. 30, 1841): Manning, *IA, 11,* 314–16, 326–30. Webster to Campbell (Jan. 14, 1843), *Writings and Speeches of Daniel Webster* (18 vols. Boston and New York, 1903), *14,* 460–63. Callahan, pp. 183–84.

abolitionist views were introduced into localities where their enthusiasm could have full run. This was the case with David Turnbull, a notorious abolitionist and former member of an antislave trade mixed commission in Cuba, who served as British consul in Havana for two years under the regime of Captain General Valdés, one of the few Cuban governors who enforced the prohibition of the slave trade and therefore failed to enrich himself in office. Turnbull was expelled from Cuba in 1842 by Valdés' successor, Leopoldo O'Donnell, but not until he had given a bad fright to both Americans and Cuban creole planters by his flagrant antislavery agitation.[12]

By 1843 Cuba and Texas had become inextricably entwined in the minds of the slavery expansionists. They coveted these areas for an extension of slave territory and as a means of maintaining their power in Congress; they knew of British abolitionist activity in both and suspected more, and they were persuaded that Britain meant to snatch either or both prizes from their grasp through emancipation, as a preliminary to a frontal attack on the institution in the United States. John C. Calhoun privately suggested to Secretary of State Upshur that a joint guarantee of Cuba to Spain by the United States and France might thwart British plans.[13] Upshur instructed Irving to report any evidence that the British were dropping the poison of abolition into the ears of the Spanish court, and early in 1844, after reports of insurrections from consuls in Cuba, Secretary Calhoun actually dispatched an American warship to the island, while the indefatigable Campbell again searched for signs

12. St. George L. Sioussat, "John C. Calhoun," in Samuel Flagg Bemis, ed., *American Secretaries of State and Their Diplomacy* (10 vols. New York, 1928), 5, 139–40. Rauch, *American Interest in Cuba*, pp. 38–40.

13. Calhoun to Upshur (Aug. 27, 1843), Sioussat, "Calhoun," p. 144.

of British complicity.[14] In their hysteria the slavery interests even imagined that the British were playing the game both ways—that they were not only working for emancipation directly but also conniving at the continuation of slave trade in Cuba in order to foster an explosive social situation that would end in a slave revolt. From London, Edward Everett reported with relief Lord Aberdeen's declaration that this was not the case.[15]

POLK'S PURCHASE PLAN

James K. Polk of Tennessee was borne into the White House on a wave of militant nationalism and expansionist fervor which enlarged the territory of the United States by the addition of Texas, New Mexico, California, and Oregon, and which caused covetous glances to be cast toward further acquisitions in Mexico, the Sandwich Islands, Yucatán and Cuba. Polk's was the first serious American bid for Cuba, but as we shall see, his purchase proposal broke against the obstinate refusals of Spain to consider it, and this particular solution of the Cuban problem had to be temporarily abandoned.

As one would expect, the heightened consciousness of the power and dignity of the United States which accompanied the rise of Manifest Destiny made Americans especially resentful and suspicious of European meddling in the affairs of the New World and of European territorial ambitions there. British activities in Texas actually hastened its annexation to the United States, though they were designed to retard it, and while Polk probably had no intention of fighting Britain over the Oregon question or seriously demanding more than the final 49° boundary line, the pop-

14. Upshur to Irving (Jan. 9, 1844), Manning, *IA, 11,* 31–32. Calhoun to Campbell (Jan. 8, 1844), Sioussat, "Calhoun," p. 140.
15. Everett to Calhoun (Aug. 2, 1844), Manning, *IA, 12,* 260–61.

ular appeal of the grossly assertive "54 40 or Fight" is indicative of the national temper. Rumors of British moves in California elicited instructions from Secretary of State James Buchanan to the American consul at Monterey, Thomas O. Larkin, to be vigilant against any attempts at seizure, for the United States "could not view with indifference the transfer of California to Great Britain or any other European Power."[16] Here is a modified version of the No-Transfer principle applied not to the classic situation of transfer from one European sovereign to another but to transfer from an American to a non-American state. Strictly speaking, it falls somewhere between the Noncolonization principle of the Monroe Doctrine and the No-Transfer idea as defined for the purposes of this study, but its kinship to the whole nexus of hemispheric defense policies is the obvious and important thing, rather than any niggling refinement of argument about proper classification. The same may be said for the reoccupation by Britain in 1883 of the Falkland Islands, which had been under Argentine rule in the interval. In this instance the United States government took no official notice of a transfer that certainly might have been regarded as a challenge to avowed American policies, but that, because of its remoteness and the preference of American whalers for British ownership, was not.[17] Scattered American statements of interest in preserving Hawaiian sovereignty, particularly against French inter-

16. Buchanan to Larkin (Oct. 17, 1845), J. B. Moore, ed., *The Works of James Buchanan* (12 vols. Philadelphia, 1908–11), *6*, 275–78. See also R. W. Kelsey, "The United States Consulate in California," Academy of Pacific Coast History, *Publications, 1*, No. 5 (June 1910), 101.

17. The dispute between Britain and Argentina over the Falklands, which continues to the present day, has been exhaustively studied in Julius L. Goebel, *The Struggle for the Falkland Islands*, New Haven, 1927.

ference, made during the Whig administrations also fall within this uncertain category.[18]

Dexter Perkins, in his distinguished history of the Monroe Doctrine, draws particular attention to Polk's annual message of December 2, 1845, as signaling the revival of Monroe's principles after a period of "quiescence" of over twenty years.[19] The message is important in the history of the No-Transfer principle too, not only because, as Perkins suggests, it seems to contain a tentative linking of the hitherto separate Monroe Doctrine and "Madison Doctrine," but also because the President delivered himself of remarks about balance of power politics which apply to all the American hemispheric security policies. Polk's statement was stimulated directly by a speech delivered six months before by the French prime minister, Guizot, in answer to demands by the opposition for an explanation of French policy in Texas. Guizot asserted that French interests required the support of independent states in the New World to create a balance of power there which would prevent any single state from becoming predominant.[20] Here, explicitly—and one might add imprudently—stated is the intention Americans had long suspected France and especially Britain of having, of "Balkanizing" North America to put a check on the growth of the United States.

Polk's reply to Guizot was a strong reaffirmation of the Nonintervention and Noncolonization principles of the

18. See, e.g., Secretary of State Daniel Webster to George Brown, American Commissioner to the Sandwich Islands (March 15, 1843), Webster to William C. Rives (June 19, 1851): Webster, *Writings and Speeches, 14,* 434, 436–37. For Clayton's statement see Mary W. Williams, "John Clayton," in Bemis, ed., *American Secretaries of State, 6,* 14.

19. Dexter Perkins, *The Monroe Doctrine, 1826–1867* (Baltimore, 1933), chap. 2, pp. 62–125.

20. Ibid., pp. 70–72.

Monroe Message of 1823, accompanied by references to the possible annexation of adjacent territories which could certainly apply to Cuba as well as to Mexican lands:

> The American system of government is entirely different from that of Europe. Jealousy among the different sovereigns of Europe, lest any one of them might become too powerful for the rest, has caused them anxiously to desire the establishment of what they term the "balance of power." It cannot be permitted to have any application on the North American continent, and especially to the United States. We must ever maintain the principle, that the people of this continent alone have the right to decide their own destiny. Should any portion of them . . . propose to unite themselves with our Confederacy, this will be a question for them and us to determine, without any foreign interposition. We can never consent that European Powers shall interfere to prevent such a union because it might disturb the "balance of power" which they may desire to maintain upon this continent.

Then follows the passage that Perkins considers to be a reference to the No-Transfer principle in connection with the principles of Monroeism.

> Existing rights of every European nation should be respected, but it is due alike to our safety and our interests that the efficient protection of our laws should be extended over our whole territorial limits, and that it should be distinctly announced to the world as our settled policy that no future European colony or dominion shall with our consent be planted or established on any part of the North American continent.[21]

21. Ibid., pp. 89, 93–94.

This might refer to Cuba, but it more probably, as Perkins suggests, refers to California, and if so presents a statement of the No-Transfer principle only in the special case of transfer from an American to a European power which we have discussed above, and which lies outside the mainstream of the policy. The positive joining of the No-Transfer principles with the principles of Monroe by President Grant and Secretary of State Fish in 1869 and 1870 (which will be treated in the next chapter) must be taken as the definitive fusion under one rubric of all these policies for hemispheric security.

Whatever else may be said of Polk's message of 1845, it certainly does not represent a "revival" of the No-Transfer principle as it does of the Monroe Doctrine of 1823. The older policy had been in continuous and significant application to Cuba throughout the intervening years, and no matter how firmly Polk restated Monroe's dicta, he failed to apply them to the European intervention in the La Plata region, to British extensions of their protectorate over the Mosquito Indians in Central America, or to the isthmian transit when he looked forward to British and French adherence to Elijah Hise's treaty of guarantee with Nicaragua.

While the nation's attention and energy were absorbed in the War with Mexico, the Cuban question was temporarily submerged in the tide of larger affairs. It did not, however, disappear entirely. The attention of the Washington government was caught in July 1847 by a speech of Lord George Bentinck, who suggested in the House of Lords on behalf of British holders of Spanish bonds who had suffered from repeated defaults that the British government seize Cuba and Puerto Rico as security for the debt. Lord Palmerston replied for the government that British action on the case was not a matter of power, of which there was plenty, but of expediency. He did not feel that at the moment such action was wise, but he did not rule it out as a possibility for the future.[22] American diplomatic representatives in Spain searched assiduously for information about any Anglo–Spanish agreement on this subject, finally concluding that while occupation of Cuba for the debts was actively debated in Britain, for the time being the use of force was not contemplated by London.[23] Bentinck's speech nevertheless remained a convenient bugbear for the use of American annexationists for a number of years to come.

Interest in Cuba revived, curiously enough, because of a crisis in Yucatán. This peninsula was a semi-autonomous part of the Mexican confederation, independent enough to remain neutral during Mexico's war with the United States. Early in 1847 the native Mayan population rose up against the white ruling class, who in terror of annihilation in a race war appealed to the United States and also to Great Britain and Spain for annexation in return for protection. The prospect of European intervention in Yucatán worried American expansionists, so that with the end of hostilities in Mexico, President Polk carried the matter to Congress in a special message on April 19, 1848.[24]

Polk's message on Yucatán lacked his customary precision. He offered no specific recommendations for action but presented the proposal of the Yucatánese government in such a way as to make clear the dangers of European occupation. According to "established policy," the President declared, the United States could not consent to a transfer in Yucatán of "dominion and sovereignty either to Great Britain,

22. Hansard, *Parliamentary Debates*, third series, *93*, 1285–98, 1305–6.

23. See the series of dispatches in July and Aug. 1847 from Reynolds and Saunders in Spain to the Secretary of State, Manning, *IA, 11*, 407–29.

24. J. D. Richardson, ed., *Messages and Papers of the Presidents* (10 vols. Washington, 1896–99), *4*, 582.

Spain or any other European power." Here once again Polk invoked a modified version of the time-honored policy, in this instance to cover the unique case of voluntary offer of annexation by an American to a non-American state. Whatever violence Polk's opposition to the transfer of Yucatán did to his own insistence in the message of 1845 on the right of American states to determine their own destinies, the President's concern clearly arose from the strategic problem such a move would pose for the United States. Yucatán, Polk pointed out, is "situate in the Gulf of Mexico, on the North American continent; and from its vicinity to Cuba, to the capes of Florida, to New Orleans, and indeed to our whole southwestern coast, it would be dangerous to our peace and security if it should become a colony of any European nation."

Responding to Polk's lead, Senator Hannegan of Indiana, Chairman of the Senate Foreign Relations Committee, introduced a bill on May 5 authorizing the President to occupy Yucatán "temporarily" with military forces to repel the Indian attacks.[25] The ensuing debate turned into a general shindy between expansionists and anti-expansionists, involving Cuba fully as much as it did Yucatán. Hannegan argued that Britain would occupy Yucatán if the United States failed to act, and that in five years more she would have Cuba too, holding the "lock and key" to declare the Caribbean *mare clausum*, and to control the mouth of the Mississippi as absolutely as she controls the mouth of the Thames."[26] Jefferson Davis agreed with Hannegan's strategic analysis, as did his colleague from Mississippi, Senator Foote.[27] Westcott of Florida introduced the slavery issue, charging that Britain sought to emancipate the slaves in Cuba to strike at the South and that they would populate

25. *Congressional Globe*, 30th Cong., 1st Sess., pp. 596–97.
26. Ibid., p. 599.
27. Ibid., pp. 599–600.

Yucatán with manumitted slaves from Jamaica, "surrounding" Florida with a cordon of Negro freemen.[28]

Lewis Cass of Michigan, representing the Northern Democratic expansionists, dwelt at great length on the insidious dangers of creeping British domination in the Caribbean. First the Bahamas and Jamaica, then Belize and the Mosquito Coast, and now Yucatán and Cuba—all a prey to the insatiable British appetite for empire.[29] That a few days after he made this speech Cass was nominated for the presidency by the Democrats gives his remarks a special interest, particularly since the party split over the expansion issue, the dissident elements turning to Van Buren. Cass went resoundingly on record in favor of a public declaration of the No-Transfer principle in connection with Cuba: "We owe it to ourselves to avow distinctly to the world that the attempt to procure the transfer of Cuba from Spain to any other nation, whether peaceably or forcibly, would be resisted by the whole power of this country. To others it may be a question of territorial aggrandizement, or of mercantile cupidity; but to us it is a question of necessity—I had almost said of political life or death."

John C. Calhoun of South Carolina, speaking with all his prestige as a veteran champion of the southern cause, and filled with disillusionment at the bitter fruits of expansionism in sectional conflict, opposed the Yucatán bill.[30] His speech of May 15 is famous now, because in it the last survivor of Monroe's Cabinet argued against the extension, and particularly against the notion of automatic application of Monroe's principles. Each challenge to them should be considered separately, on its merits in terms of the immediate national interest, Calhoun declared, and the Doctrine ap-

28. Ibid., appendix, p. 608.
29. Ibid., pp. 614–17.
30. Ibid., p. 712, appendix, pp. 631–32.

plied or not as circumstances warranted. This is interesting because it is precisely the position adopted by the Whigs and anti-expansionist Democrats toward the No-Transfer principle a few years later, at the time of the Cass Resolutions. In 1848, however, Calhoun was not in favor of introducing elements of flexibility into the application of the No-Transfer principle as he was of the Monroe Doctrine. There were cases in which he would resort to war. "Am I asked for one? I will answer. I designate the case of Cuba." Britain must not be allowed to take over Cuba and emancipate the slaves. Here the national interest was well-defined and enduring.

The Senate debate on Yucatán made it abundantly clear that the opponents of expansion were formidable, so that when news arrived of a peace in the peninsula a few weeks later Senator Hannegan seized the opportunity to withdraw his bill. The surge of enthusiasm for the extension of American territory which had brought Polk to office had partially spent itself, and the Wilmot Proviso brought sober second thoughts about the complications for national policy inherent in the acquisitions recently made. Thus it was that when in the last stages of the Yucatán discussion the President came to the conclusion that it was necessary to try to acquire Cuba, he proceeded with the most profound secrecy.

On May 10, 1848, Polk was paid a visit by John L. O'Sullivan, accompanied by Senator Stephen A. Douglas of Illinois, who seconded O'Sullivan's arguments in favor of purchasing Cuba. O'Sullivan was one of the New York Barnburners (the splinter group of the Democratic party that in the early forties championed liberal reforms), but he returned to support Polk in 1844 and became a chief dispenser of patronage for the administration.[31] As editor of the *Democratic Review* and the New York *Morning News,* he coined the phrase "Manifest Destiny," advocated expan-

31. Rauch, *American Interest in Cuba,* pp. 48 ff.

sionism, and seems privately to have accepted slavery if not defended it, though this was not part of his public façade. After 1847 Cuban annexation became a ruling passion in his life, and in league with the Cuban junto in the United States and other annexationists he worked tirelessly to effect his end, whether by legal means or otherwise.

O'Sullivan worked on Secretary of State Buchanan first, and found him, as everyone did, indecisive and evasive, his influence with Polk steadily and palpably declining.[32] Finally O'Sullivan went straight to the President himself, and after their interview left a lengthy memorandum in which he stressed, as he often had with Buchanan, the danger of transfer to Britain as a reason for purchasing Cuba. Polk didn't entirely trust O'Sullivan—but then that narrow, tough, and suspicious man trusted no one entirely—and during their interview said nothing, but later confided to his diary that he favored the purchase scheme.[33] The die was cast.

Polk opened the subject of purchase in a Cabinet meeting on May 30. Everyone present admitted the British threat. Secretary of the Treasury Walker, a Mississippi planter, and Secretary of the Navy John Y. Mason of Virginia were immediately favorable to the proposal, but Buchanan equivocated, saying that he was ultimately in favor of annexation but that he doubted the wisdom of attempting anything at the moment, partly because of the danger of war with Britain and France and partly because the purchase attempt, if found out, might hurt Cass in the forthcoming presidential election.[34] General Cass dispelled the latter objection a few days later when he told Polk he

32. Ibid., pp. 65, 67.
33. M. M. Quaife, ed., *The Diary of James K. Polk* (4 vols. Chicago, 1910), *3*, 446.
34. Ibid., pp. 468–69.

favored "amicable purchase" and would be willing to campaign on that issue.[35]

The strategy that Polk hammered out in a series of Cabinet meetings finally brought the Secretary of State around from his original truculent wish to dissociate himself entirely from the enterprise to a reluctant acquiescence in the scheme, although Polk continued to suspect Buchanan of presidential ambitions and of wanting to save the purchase of Cuba to adorn his own administration.[36] In essence, the approach advocated by the President was to take advantage of the recent rupture of relations between Britain and Spain to stress the danger from Britain to Cuba, while at the same time giving tangible evidence of American good will toward Spain, in hope that this along with an offer of up to $100,-000,000 would persuade Spain to part with her prized possession.

The European situation indeed looked promising. Sir Henry Bulwer had been given his passports by the Spanish government a few weeks before, because of Spanish indignation at British suggestions that the monarchy introduce liberal reforms to avoid the fate of Louis Philippe and because of Bulwer's personal services to Spanish liberals. The lines between London and Madrid had been angrily pulled down. On the other hand, Polk found it possible to demonstrate in two documents the friendly solicitude of the United States government for Spanish sovereignty in Cuba. The first of these were instructions to Robert Campbell, the United States Consul in Cuba, who had recently reported an incipient annexationist revolution brewing there, in which Campbell was cautioned to give no encouragement by word or deed to the intrigue, and was reminded that the Spanish government "is well aware that we will resist to the

35. Ibid., pp. 476–77.
36. Ibid., pp. 497, 485–88.

last extremity [Cuba's] transfer to any European power."[37] A second part of this letter, not intended to be shown to the Spanish foreign minister, encouraged Campbell to hope that the island might soon become American through peaceful negotiation. Campbell's information about the plot was accurate, and was corroborated by O'Sullivan, who was in constant touch with the Cuban junta here.[38] The revolutionary movement was led by Narciso Lopez, a Venezuelan who had distinguished himself in the military service of Spain and who had now devoted his life to the cause of Cuban independence. Buchanan went further than the letter to Campbell in proving his loyalty to Spanish interests; he exposed Lopez' plans to the Spanish Minister in Washington.[39] Lopez escaped to the United States, to spend the next few years organizing the filibustering expeditions to Cuba that plagued Polk's Whig successors.

The second earnest of good intention toward Spain was the order Polk dispatched to General Butler, prohibiting United States soldiers from joining a Cuban revolutionary movement on their way back from Mexico.[40] This was designed to nip in the bud General Worth's reported scheme for leading an American force in support of Lopez.

Perhaps because he distrusted Buchanan, Polk determined to conduct his negotiations through the American minister to Spain, Romulus M. Saunders. The instructions sent to Saunders meticulously outlined the procedure he was to follow and are particularly emphatic on the point of secrecy.[41] The Spanish Cortes was to know nothing of the American proposal, and all Saunders' dispatches were to be sent to Washington by special messenger directly to the

37. Buchanan to Campbell (June 9, 1848), Manning, *IA, 11,* 53.
38. *Polk Diary, 3,* 476–77.
39. Rauch, *American Interest in Cuba,* p. 77.
40. *Polk Diary, 3,* 485–86.
41. Buchanan to Saunders (June 17, 1848), Manning, *IA, 11,* 54–64.

Secretary of State. In order to make certain that no word about the negotiation leaked out, Polk withheld all correspondence relating to it from the Department of State files until his administration was on the point of leaving office, and even refrained from telling O'Sullivan about it.[42]

In the negotiation itself, Saunders was to begin by mentioning the revolutionary unrest in Cuba, and then show the instructions to Campbell and Butler to demonstrate American good faith. He was to stress the British menace, repeat the familiar No-Transfer formula of United States policy, and only then, and in the most delicate way, unfold the question of sale to this country, using arguments supplied him from Washington.

Romulus Saunders was perhaps not the perfect instrument for this subtle task. A faithful if not particularly successful party hack, he had received his post as a reward for the parliamentary ingenuity he had employed on Polk's behalf at the Democratic Convention in 1844. Certainly his personal qualifications for a diplomatic appointment were unimpressive; John Quincy Adams once remarked of him that "there is not a more cankered or venomous reptile in the country."[43] He spoke neither the language of the country to which he was accredited nor French—no language in fact, as Buchanan later conceded, "except English, and even this he sometimes murders."[44] But perhaps Saunders' chief defect as a negotiator was the conviction he speedily developed that Polk's strategy was mistaken and that he himself had a better one.

Saunders felt that as long as the United States gave Spain copious assurances about Cuba, Madrid would never be disposed to sell. He found Spain still relying on the pledges of support to Spanish sovereignty in the island given by

42. *Polk Diary, 3,* 493.
43. Rauch, p. 85.
44. Buchanan to Clayton (April 17, 1849), Moore, ed., *Works, 8,* 361.

Forsyth in his instructions to Vail in 1840. Unlike his principals in Washington, Saunders thought Spain should be made uneasy about American support if they were to be induced to make concessions.[45] His first feelers after receiving his instructions convinced Saunders that the Spanish government would not consider cession except in the event of an imminent danger of revolution or of an English attempt on the island.[46] The American minister thereupon retreated from the firm assurances of support in case of a threatened transfer of Cuba to Britain—cunningly, as he believed, suggesting that in such an event the United States would rather purchase Cuba from Spain than fight England to retain it for Spain.[47] The Duke of Sotomayor replied that no cession was possible without a radical change of circumstances, and indeed from this time forward no Spanish government was able to consider ceding the island. The retention of Cuba became in the minds of Spaniards of every political complexion deeply involved with the honor of Spain, and every American purchase attempt was therefore doomed to failure.

Despite the elaborate precautions taken to ensure secrecy, some hint of Polk's purchase proposal leaked out. On December 18, 1848, Senator Jacob Miller, a New Jersey Whig, introduced a resolution calling upon the President to communicate to the Senate any correspondence with Spain relating to the purchase of Cuba. A Polk Democrat, Senator Dickinson of New York, managed to have the embarrassing Miller Resolution tabled a few weeks later, but the respite was brief.[48]

45. Saunders to Buchanan (June 27, 1848), Manning, *IA, 11*, 440–41.
46. Saunders to Buchanan (July 29, 1848), ibid., pp. 443–47.
47. Saunders to Buchanan, (Aug. 18, 1848), ibid., pp. 449–50.
48. *Senate Journal*, 30th Cong., 2d Sess., pp. 67, 104.

CHAPTER 8

The Rise and Decline of the Whig "New Look"

What James K. Polk wanted he usually got, but his administration closed on a discordant note of frustration on two counts: he had failed to acquire Cuba, and he had not been able to prevent the election of a Whig war hero to the Presidency. Zachary Taylor chose as his Secretary of State John M. Clayton of Delaware, a successful lawyer and ardent political partisan, whose personality contained a volatile blend of caution and impetuosity which did not ideally suit him for the first office in the Cabinet.

The new Secretary of State was determined on a change in Cuban policy. There would be, for one thing, no renewal of Polk's attempts at purchase. Stimulated by his party's victory at the polls, Clayton indulged in a little playful malice at the expense of his predecessor in the State Department. "What will you give me," he inquired of Buchanan, "to recall Romulus Saunders from Spain? Shall I try to buy Cuba after you have made such a botch of that business? Do you still wish like Sancho to have an island?"[1] Buchanan tried to keep his reply light, but could not resist declaring

1. Clayton to Buchanan (April 14, 1849), Buchanan, *Works, 8,* 359–60.

fervently that "we can't do without Cuba, and above all we must not suffer its transfer to Great Britain."[2]

The Whigs had no intention of abandoning the No-Transfer policy, of course, but in line with their general attitude that the operation of the Monroe Doctrine should be not continuous and automatic but rather a matter to be considered separately on its merits when each challenge arose, they wished to revoke the pledges of assistance to Spain that had characterized Cuban policy since 1840. Clayton outlined this change in policy to Daniel Barringer, Saunders' replacement in Madrid:

> The President cannot comprehend or appreciate the motives or expediency of openly declaring to Spain that the whole power of the United States would be employed to prevent the occupation in whole or in part of Cuba, from passing into other hands; because he has reason to believe that this declaration on our part has led to counterdeclarations being made by Spain against us, of a similar character, by other interested powers.[3]

The United States was determined to oppose the transfer of Cuba, but the Taylor administration did not intend to "utter any threat or enter into any guarantees to Spain" on the matter. For Barringer's private guidance, however, Clayton declared that "news of the cession of Cuba to any foreign power would, in the United States, be the instant signal for war." Here was the threat all right, but to be reserved for an actual crisis, not to be issued in a generalized form.

Whig hopes that they could pursue a passive policy of watchful waiting toward Cuba were blasted by unforeseen events, however, and before President Fillmore left office Whig policy had come full circle, with the old pledges to

2. Buchanan to Clayton (April 17, 1849), ibid., p. 361.
3. Clayton to Barringer (Aug. 2, 1849), Manning, *IA, 11*, 69–70.

Spain renewed, in the face of threats of European intervention in the Cuban problem. The trouble began with the filibustering expeditions launched against Cuba from American ports, which provoked Britain and France first to dispatch additional fleet units to the Caribbean, and then to offer once again an unwelcome proposal for a tripartite guarantee of Cuba to Spain.

To rabid expansionists the Whig policy was anathema. If the government were no longer going to try to acquire Cuba, the extremists determined to take matters into their own hands by supporting Narciso Lopez' plan for freeing Cuba of Spanish control by force. Lopez organized four expeditions, two of which were broken up by the federal government before they could sail and two of which succeeded in reaching Cuba. In May 1850 he held the town of Cárdenas briefly before being driven back to Key West, and in 1851 he landed at Bahia Honda with over four hundred men, many of them American citizens, and actually penetrated into the interior of the island. As before, however, there was no spontaneous rising among the Cubans, and Spanish forces captured most of the filibusters, some of whom were summarily executed on the spot. Lopez was garroted in the public square at Havana.

The Whig administration enforced the neutrality laws with all the vigor at their command, but in the South, where the filibusters were regarded as heroes rather than as lawbreakers, it proved difficult to secure indictments and impossible to secure convictions from sympathetic juries. After the failure of the last Lopez expedition, in fact, angry mobs in New Orleans protested the execution of the Crittenden force by attacking Spanish shops and the Spanish consulate, an outrage for which Secretary of State Daniel Webster made written apologies to the Spanish government and for which, after the release of American prisoners in Cuba, the United States paid a sum in reparation.

The news of Lopez' Cárdenas expedition naturally produced a sensation in Madrid. Barringer, though hampered by a lack of instructions, felt it necessary to give immediate assurances to the Spanish government that the United States government was doing its utmost to prevent a recurrence of the raid.[4] The result of his interview with the Minister of Foreign Affairs failed to leave anyone feeling very comfortable, as it worked out. Pidal sounded out the American minister on a United States guarantee of Cuba to Spain, saying that Saunders had indicated he had authority to negotiate such a treaty. Whether Saunders' ineptitude had left this erroneous impression or whether Pidal deliberately distorted the facts to draw Barringer in, the American minister found it necessary to deny his own powers to treat on this question. He purposely confused the issue by stating that the United States would resist "at all costs" the transfer of Cuba to any other power and that at the same time he was "not authorized" to repeat and continue assurances that "the whole power of the United States" would be used to defend Cuba for Spain. This unhappy and contradictory combination of the "new look" and the "old look" in American Cuban policy could only leave Pidal thoroughly bewildered.

The Spanish Foreign Minister thereupon resorted to veiled intimations that England and France, which also had interests in the Caribbean area, had given Spain some form of guarantees of Cuba, though he declined to be explicit about details. Thus was born a bogey that agitated Washington for several years to come. Barringer tried to discover whether there were formal agreements between Spain and Britain and France, but got nowhere with the British Minister at Madrid. He was inclined to conclude that there might have been verbal assurances given to Spain, but no

4. Barringer to Clayton (July 19, 1850), *ibid.*, pp. 500–8.

more.[5] Actually, there were none, but not because of Spain's failure to solicit them. During the next year Madrid addressed no less than five separate pleas for guarantees of Cuba to London and Paris, all of which fell on deaf ears. Palmerston refused even to discuss the question unless Spain was prepared to institute reforms in Cuba and to take measures to suppress the African slave trade there.[6]

Britain and France did take positive action of an alarming sort after Lopez' ill-fated Bahia Honda expedition in 1851. On September 27 the British chargé informed the Department of State that British naval vessels on the West Indian Station had been ordered to prevent, by force if necessary, landings in Cuba by adventurers of whatever nationality.[7] President Fillmore at once wrote to Secretary Webster, who was not in Washington, telling him of this ominous development and of fresh rumors reported by Mr. Rives from Paris of an Anglo–French guarantee of Cuba to Spain. Webster agreed with Fillmore that the British naval orders might inflame the long-standing quarrel with Britain over peacetime visit and search, but was more concerned about the danger of a British occupation of Cuba.[8] A week later when the French Minister revealed that similar orders had been given to the French squadron in the Caribbean, American suspicions of Anglo–French collusion to set up a protectorate in Cuba intensified. Acting Secretary Crittenden drafted a strong warning to France against any visit and search of American merchantmen, re-

5. Barringer to Webster (Oct. 3, 1850), ibid., p. 569.

6. Amos A. Ettinger, "The Proposed Anglo–Franco–American Treaty of 1852 to Guarantee Cuba to Spain," *Transactions of the Royal Historical Society*, 4th ser. *13* (1930), 151.

7. Crampton to Acting Secretary of State Crittenden (Sept. 27, 1851), Manning, *IA, 7,* 441–42.

8. Fillmore to Webster (Oct. 2, 1851), Webster to Fillmore (Oct. 4, 1851): Moore, *Digest of International Law, 6,* 458–59.

gretting the gratuitous implication that the United States would not enforce its own neutrality acts, and pointedly reminding Sartiges that France had been "long since officially apprized by this Government that the United States could not see without concern [Cuba] transferred by Spain to any other European State."[9] The French minister acted quickly to calm American concern with assurances that the orders were "spontaneous, isolated, and an exclusive case," but in the same breath, and with a point of view that foreshadowed the European reaction to the Everett note a year later, he denied any American claim to paramount interest in a region where European nations held colonies which formed a part of "their general system of policy."[10] So much for the Nonintervention and No-Transfer principles.

The haunting specter of an Anglo–French concert of policy on Cuba persisted. Louis Napoleon hinted as much in a speech, and it was known that a secret meeting had been held at Lord Palmerston's estate, attended by the French ambassador and the Spanish minister, to which Sir Henry Bulwer, lately minister to the United States, had been called in consultation. Neither Barringer in Madrid nor Abbott Lawrence in London believed that the matter had arrived at the stage of a formal joint guarantee of Cuba by the two great maritime powers, but something was certainly in the works.[11]

The administration's opposition to British and French intervention in the Cuban situation received support from Congress in a form that significantly underlined American determination to command the situation. In December the

9. Crittenden to Sartiges (Oct. 22, 1851), Manning, *IA, 6,* 460–64.

10. Sartiges to Crittenden (Oct. 27, 1851), ibid., pp. 628–31.

11. J. C. B. Davis, United States chargé at London, to the Secretary of State (Sept. 19, 26, 1851), Barringer to Webster (Oct. 14, 1851), Lawrence to Webster (Nov. 7, 1851): ibid., 7, 439–41; *11,* 625–26; 7, 442–43.

House adopted a resolution requesting the President to communicate, if not incompatible with the public interest, all information on any treaty between Britain, France, and Spain about Cuba, about the relative strengths of the British, French, and United States naval forces in West Indian waters, and about whether additional appropriations were needed to increase American forces on that station.[12] A few weeks later the House unanimously requested transmission of all diplomatic correspondence relating to the island of Cuba.[13] President Fillmore forwarded the documents and published them in full, an act greeted with anguished outcries from the Democrats, since Polk's ill-fated purchase attempt was now made public for the first time.

Whatever doubts were entertained in Washington, the British and French governments had no wish to provoke a clash with the United States over Cuba. Nor had they been acting in perfect unity. Each had reasons for conciliating Spain, however, and for discovering a way to tranquilize the Caribbean area. The solution attempted was a revival of the tripartite treaty of guarantee Canning had proposed a generation earlier. After Palmerston's dismissal from the Foreign Office, which removed his truculent voice from British policy, and after Louis Napoleon's *coup d'état* of December 2, 1851, which necessitated attention to domestic problems rather than to a forward foreign policy in France, the time was ripe for an attempt at a general agreement on Cuba. No one in London, Paris, or Madrid except the enthusiastic Count Walewski, French ambassador to Britain, seems to have expected the United States to accept this bid, but it appeared at least to be worth a try.[14]

12. Resolution introduced by Mr. Meade (Dec. 15, 1851), *Journal of the House of Representatives*, 32d Cong., 1st Sess., pp. 94–95.

13. Resolution presented by Mr. Faulkner (Feb. 2, 1852), ibid., p. 304.

14. Ettinger, pp. 158 ff.

The project for a three-power agreement which the British and French ministers at Washington presented in identical notes on April 23, 1852, aimed at a generalization of the No-Transfer principle, the acceptance by the United States of a self-denying ordinance in regard to Cuba, and a pledge to curb the filibusters:

> The high contracting parties . . . disavow individually and collectively, for the present as well as for the future, all intention of obtaining possession of the island of Cuba, and they engage respectively to prevent and to repress, so far as may lie in their power, every attempt undertaken toward this end by any power or individual whatsoever.
>
> The high contracting parties declare individually and collectively that they will not assume or maintain, either for all or one of them, any right of exclusive control over the said island, and that they will not assume nor exercise any authority there.[15]

In conversation with Crampton and Sartiges following the presentation of their notes, Secretary Webster indicated his "entire concurrence" with the views of their respective governments concerning Cuba, but he held out little hope of adherence by the United States to the tripartite pact.[16] An election year was a bad time to raise this controversial issue, he cautioned, not to speak of the deep-seated aversion to entangling agreements generally felt by Americans. Webster's formal answer to Britain and France a few days later did not altogether close the door to a multilateral agreement on Cuba, but it is certain that he had no intention of

15. Manning, *IA, 6,* 637.

16. Crampton to Malmesbury (April 25, 1852), Sartiges to Turgot (April 25, 1852): Ettinger, pp. 166–67.

accepting.[17] To Barringer in Spain he sent instructions which revived the pledges revoked by Clayton at the beginning of the Whig period. A British and French partnership for the protection of Cuba threatened American interests, Webster wrote, and if Spain would agree not to cede Cuba to any European power, the United States would give her every assistance in protecting the island.[18] Faced with the threat of foreign intervention, the Whigs had abandoned the caution of John Quincy Adams, and returned to Forsyth's blanket commitment.

Daniel Webster's lingering fatal illness delayed a final answer to the Anglo–French proposal until December, after the Whigs had lost the election. It fell to Edward Everett to draft the United States reply, and the new Secretary of State, after a long day's work at the Department, stood at a sideboard in his room in Willard's Hotel and swiftly sketched out a state paper which is a minor masterpiece of its kind.[19] The Everett Note was enthusiastically endorsed by men of both parties at the time because it accurately caught the mood of America in the fifties—the buoyant nationalism, the new sense of power, the swelling pride in past achievement; and the nervous optimism about a future at once clouded by the ugly controversy over slavery and glinting with hope after the Compromise of 1850. Without resorting to the bombast which had characterized campaign oratory in the recent election, but in a calmly judicial tone, firmly secured by ligatures of the logic of national interest, Everett gave satisfying expression to the fundamental propositions of American hemispheric policy in a way that they had not been set forth before.

17. Webster to Crampton, identical note to Sartiges (April 29, 1852), Manning, *IA*, *7*, 75.

18. Callahan, *Cuba in International Relations*, p. 232.

19. Everett to Crampton and Sartiges (Dec. 1, 1852), Manning, *IA*, *6*, 466–75.

In the last analysis, Everett's statement of the American position on Cuba was essentially the same as John Quincy Adams' formulation: the United States was content to see the island remain in the hands of Spain, it could not see with indifference its transfer to any other European power, but it would not renounce Cuba if future circumstances should permit honorable annexation. Everett's special contribution was to make explicit the basic postulate of American paramount interest which had always tacitly underlain statements of the No-Transfer idea as well as the principles of the Monroe Doctrine: to state the doctrine of the two spheres in terms of overriding strategic concern.

The Secretary of State reaffirmed support of the No-Transfer principle as traditionally applied to Cuba, not because the United States objected to increases in the power and territory of European nations in other parts of the world but because the transfer of Cuba in particular to another European state could not take place "without a serious derangement of the international system now existing, and it would indicate designs in reference to this hemisphere which could not but awaken alarm in the United States." In other words, the American balance of power would be adversely affected, and this balance was a particular concern of the United States. Britain and France, through the proposed convention, wished to establish general adherence to the principle that Cuba should not be transferred to *any* power, including the United States. This principle Everett declined to accept. "The President does not covet the acquisition of Cuba for the United States. At the same time he considers the condition of Cuba as mainly an American question, and to a limited extent only a European question. The proposed Convention proceeds on a different principle." While equal in its terms, it was by the nature of the situation unequal in operation. Everett reviewed the strategic, commercial, and, very lightly, slavery aspects of American interest in Cuba, and to dramatize his point inquired how Britain and France would view the relative disabilities incurred if the United States should propose to them a similar self-denying ordinance applying to a Spanish island guarding the mouth of the Thames or Seine.

Everett advanced other arguments against the tripartite agreement—that the Senate would never accept it, that Americans had an aversion to entangling alliances, that there existed a constitutional question as to the power of an administration to impose a permanent disability on its successors, and that the agreement would probably intensify filibustering activity rather than halt it—but essentially the American rejection rested upon a disinclination to allow Europe to set limits on American freedom of action and territorial expansion in this hemisphere. The Secretary of State reviewed at considerable length the expenditures of blood and treasure by which the American people had progressively expanded their dominion and loosed themselves from the bonds of European control. This was for Everett and for his countrymen an irreversible process, which Europe must acknowledge and accept. Europe was not yet prepared to accept this, as their replies to the Everett Note showed, but the growth of American power made it only a matter of time until American predominance in this hemisphere became an unblinkable fact of international political life.

Taylor and Fillmore had conducted a Cuban policy of caution and restraint so far as circumstances permitted, mindful of the explosiveness of sectional rivalries, unresponsive to the acquisitive clamor of the slaveholding interest, and dedicated to a course of moderation both at home and abroad, in the interest of preserving the Union. The nation repudiated the Whig policy in a Democratic landslide that gave Franklin Pierce the electoral votes of every state except Kentucky, Tennessee, Massachusetts, and Vermont. In his annual message of December 1852, the outgoing President defended his policies for the last time, and once again recorded his opposition to the immediate annexation of Cuba as "a very hazardous measure" which "might revive those conflicts of opinion between the different sections of the country, which lately shook the Union to its center, and which have been so happily compromised."[20] Fillmore's advice was sound, as events proved, for the Cuban question added its tremors to the seismic disturbances that deepened and widened the political chasm between the sections in the next eight tragic years.

THE TRIUMPH OF SLAVERY EXPANSIONISM

Pierce's victory was widely regarded as a mandate for the resumption of territorial expansion, although the candidate himself had skirted around the subject in the campaign, as well he might. His following was a shaky coalition of Free Soilers, Unionists, States' Righters, Anglophobes, slavery expansionists, and "Young America" zealots which unhappily proved, as his critics charged, to be bound together by no common principles except the distribution of the patronage. While the President-elect kept his counsel, expansionist fever swept the nation, and in Congress the lame-duck session between the election and Pierce's inauguration was devoted in great part to discussions of projects of territorial extension, particularly Cuba. Most of the speakers were primarily concerned with the question of annexation *per se* and not with the danger of transfer to a European power, but there were frequent attempts to raise the bogey of British and French designs, and this is the aspect of the debate that interests us here.

20. *Congressional Globe,* 32d Cong., 2d Sess., pp. 7–11.

The abolitionists in Congress sniffed the wind, scented danger approaching, and decided that the best defense was a swift offensive. Joshua Giddings of Ohio told the House that Britain could have the island; anything was preferable to adding to the slave power in this country.[21] In the Senate, John P. Hale of New Hampshire, the Free Soil presidential candidate in the recent election, twitted the Democrats about Pierce's reticence in informing them when they should be able to "plant the standard of republican liberty . . . and extend the area of freedom" in Cuba.[22]

It was not, as one might have expected, the fire-eaters who opened the annexationist campaign, but the moderate Democrats in the person of Senator Mason of Virginia, Chairman of the Committee on Foreign Relations, who presented a resolution asking the Chief Executive for all correspondence relating to the tripartite pact, which Fillmore had referred to in his message.[23] Mason favored annexation but, like the moderates generally, opposed filibustering or any but an "honorable" acquisition of Cuba by cession or purchase. It was this group who felt most pressingly the need to keep the bogey of a British and French conspiracy against Cuba alive, in contrast to extremists like Pierre Soulé of Louisiana, who needed no touchstone but slavery. To Mason the three-power proposal was a covert and sinister warning of Anglo–French determination to prevent the annexation of Cuba by the United States, a trumped-up offer they knew we would never accept. They knew also, declared the Senator, lapsing into the flamboyant spreadeagle-ism of the day, that "if ever any ambitious or grasping potentate should attempt, either by rapine or by treaty, to take the island of Cuba from the possession of

21. Ibid., appendix, pp. 39–40.
22. Ibid., pp. 109–10.
23. Ibid., pp. 139–46.

Spain, it would become this country, cost what it might, to interpose and prevent it."

The aging Democratic war horse, Lewis Cass, arose to support Mason, declaring that the No-Transfer policy should be defended in Cuba "by all means God has given us."[24] Cass had been the particular target of charges of "Old Fogyism" from the Young Americans in the campaign, and he was at pains to disprove the libel. Young America was the activist wing of the Democracy, militantly and equally devoted to intervention in the cause of liberalism in Europe and to the territorial expansion of the United States. Not all Young Americans were active advocates of the extension of slavery, but none of them opposed it. Their principal organ was the *Democratic Review,* lately the property of John L. O'Sullivan and still under his editorial influence, which jogged Cass after his speech to join openly in the demand that Cuba be annexed at once.[25]

In the House of Representatives the subject of Cuba cropped up, not surprisingly, in the debate on proposed fortifications at Key West and Tortuga. Mr. Cabell of Florida argued in a speech on December 21 that the construction of Fort Taylor and Fort Jefferson would ensure that the Morro Castle no longer commanded Gulf commerce, and would provide a convenient staging area for forces sent to ward off an attempted European occupation of Cuba.[26] After the Christmas recess Representative Howard of Texas elaborated on Mason's suspicions of Britain, by recalling besides the tripartite pact the recent fleet movements and the protean encroachments of the Mosquito protectorate in Central America. These suggestions were shortly taken up in the Senate.

---

24. Ibid.
25. Callahan, *Cuba in International Relations,* pp. 243–44.
26. *Congressional Globe,* 32d Cong., 2d Sess., appendix, p. 51.

On January 15, 1852, General Cass surprised the Senate by presenting two resolutions which turned debate away from Mason's request for information on the tripartite pact and toward a positive policy for the future. The first resolution was a general restatement of the Noncolonization principle of the Monroe Doctrine, and the second was a No-Transfer resolution applied specifically to Cuba and armed with the threat of force:

> *And be it further resolved,* That while the United States disclaim any designs upon the island of Cuba inconsistent with their duties to Spain, they consider it due to the vast importance of the subject, to make known, in this solemn manner, that they should view all efforts on the part of any other Power to procure possession, whether peaceably or forcibly, of that island which, as a naval or military position, must, under circumstances easy to be foreseen, become dangerous to their southern coast, to the Gulf of Mexico, and to the mouth of the Mississippi, as unfriendly acts, directly against them, to be resisted by all the means in their power.

It would be a mistake, certainly, to take the Cass resolution too seriously as a stage in the evolution of the No-Transfer policy. Judging from the fact that avowed annexationists like Stephen A. Douglas opposed it, it appears to have been a strategic move on Cass' part to escape from the ranks of the Old Fogies and to surfboard on the wave of the future with the Young Americans. Douglas had been the idol of Young America, but concerted opposition of the other candidates at the Democratic National Convention in 1852 had cost him the nomination and given it to the dark horse Pierce. Disgruntled, Douglas took a leaf from Whig doctrine and opposed the resolution not because he did not favor "resisting such transfer at all hazards," but because there was no immediate crisis, and he saw no reason for making a general statement "based on contingencies that may never happen."

On the other hand Pierre Soulé of Louisiana, the most unrestrained advocate of forcible acquisition in the Senate, supported the Cass resolution even though it specifically disclaimed any design on the island. This was a bow from the extreme Southern faction of Young Americans in the direction of the effort the Michigan Senator was making on their behalf. Soulé took the occasion to announce his conviction that purchase was now an obsolete policy because of Spanish pride, and to defend the filibusters. This was the man President Pierce saw fit to appoint minister to Spain four months later! Such moderate Southern Democrats as Butler of South Carolina dissented on much the same grounds as Douglas, and Clemens of Alabama coolly reproved Cass for failing to consult in advance with his Democratic colleagues in the Senate, and especially with the President-elect, before advancing his proposal.

Of course Northern antislavery men attacked the measure as a piece of planter imperialism. Senator Hale lampooned Cass by introducing an amendment adding a No-Transfer resolution applying to Canada, and inquired with biting sarcasm why the principle was not announced in connection with Vancouver Island or Jamaica or the Bahamas, and why when boundary disputes arose territory was inevitably cut off in the north and added on in the south. Seward, no opponent of expansion then or afterward when Secretary of State, made it clear that for him the slavery question made the annexation of Cuba a dead issue.

Cass, in defending his resolution, strove mightily to reconstitute the Anglo–French menace. England had practically turned the Mediterranean into a British lake, he warned, and now seemed bent on doing the same in the Caribbean, which they would establish as *mare clausum*. He reached back five years to remind his listeners of Lord George Bentinck's speech in Commons to prove that the British coveted Cuba. So, too, did France, and only the rivalry of the two great European maritime powers had so far saved it for Spain. But if, as appeared certain from the tripartite proposal, they had made a deal about Cuba, the situation was serious indeed for American interests. Amplifying the remarks he had made on the occasion of Mason's resolution, the Michigan Democrat repeated his conviction that Britain and France had offered the three-power pact in full knowledge that it would be turned down, in order to have a free hand for their nefarious designs on Cuba.

Had the Cass Resolution been adopted, it would have been one of three such congressional sanctions of the No-Transfer principle, the first being the "Madison Doctrine" of 1811 and the last the Pittman-Bloom Resolution of 1940. Cass invoked the 1811 resolution as a precedent for his own, and argued that its publication in 1819 had exerted a salutary pressure on Spain to ratify the Adams-Onís treaty. Whatever the historical validity of this argument—and it is highly dubious—it weakened Cass' emphasis on the transfer danger, for he now seemed to be urging his resolution not so much as an open caveat to Britain and France as a device for persuading Spain to cede Cuba to the United States.

Annexation was of course the main issue, as everyone knew—annexation not to prevent a British or French occupation of Cuba but for its own sake. Military strategy was fading out as a determinant of Cuban policy, and slavery was king. There was no other issue connected with Cuba. Here, in microcosm during the debate on the Cass No-Transfer resolution, before Franklin Pierce had entered the White House and before the Kansas-Nebraska Act, can be seen the operation of those tendencies that later rent the Union—the emergence of slavery as the only issue, and the gravitation of moderates toward extremist positions that eroded national parties and made communication and compromise between the sections increasingly difficult.

Franklin Pierce broke his long silence on the expansion issue in his First Inaugural, delivered from memory on March 4, 1853.[27] As if in answer to Fillmore's last annual message, the new President boldly declared that "the policy of my Administration will not be controlled by any timid forebodings of evil from expansion. Indeed, it is not to be disguised that our attitude as a nation and our position on the globe render the acquisition of certain possessions not within our jurisdiction eminently important for our protection; if not in the future essential for the preservation of the rights of commerce and the peace of the world. Should they be obtained, it will be through no grasping spirit, but with a view to obvious national interest and security." Pierce hereby served notice that he intended to revive Polk's purchase scheme, which he did after some delay, but only after the repeal of the Missouri Compromise had so inflamed the North that any attempt to join Cuba to the United States would have split the Democratic party and torn the Union to tatters.

Efforts to revive the British and French threats, the only motive for taking Cuba that had any appeal in the North, proved unavailing. In May, Barringer reported from Madrid that it was absolutely certain that Spain had received no guarantees of Cuba, and that neither London nor Paris cared to risk American displeasure by giving them.[28] To Buchanan and Soulé, the newly appointed ministers to

27. Ibid., respectively, pp. 80–81, 90 ff., 172–73, 118–23, 96, 156–58, 90, 97–99, 125–27, 92 ff., 244.
28. Barringer to Marcy (May 7, 1853), Manning, *IA, 11,* 701–2.

Britain and Spain, Secretary of State Marcy sent instructions to repeat the No-Transfer policy, including opposition to intervention by Britain in any Cuban rebellion, but
these standing orders grew out of no particular, immediate
threats.[29]

Indeed, as the Near Eastern crisis deepened and the Crimean War drew on, Britain and France paid little attention
to Cuba. The chief concern in the southern United States
about the island after the autumn of 1853 was over the
"Africanization" policy that Spain was allegedly pursuing.[30] Don Juan de Pezuela, the Captain General, issued a
series of decrees in December ordering strict enforcement
of laws prohibiting the African slave trade, allowing the
importation of free Negroes as "apprentices" to alleviate
the chronic labor shortage on Cuban plantations, and taking steps to give immediate freedom and full rights to the
emancipados, slaves illegally imported since 1835. The
American slave states recoiled at the prospect of another
black republic like Haiti near their shores, and suspected
the Spanish of acting under British pressure to abolish
slavery in order to render Cuba unattractive to American
annexationists.

The Spanish government was not above using this threat,
especially in their desperate isolation during the Crimean
War, but there were too many influential Spaniards as
well as Cuban creoles with an interest in maintaining slavery on the island for any general policy of emancipation
to succeed. Americans suspected British and French pressure on Spain, but what there was came largely from private
abolitionist societies; any official suggestions about emancipation were urged among other reform measures to im-

29. Marcy to Buchanan (July 2, 1853), Marcy to Soulé (July 23,
1853): Manning, *IA, 6,* 454; *7,* 92–95.

30. Marcy to Alexander M. Clayton, United States Consul at Havana (Oct. 26, 1853), Manning, *IA, 11,* 166–67.

prove conditions in Cuba, not with a view to the "Africanization" of the island.[31]

Senator Cass donned his fright-wig again on February 25, this time drawing attention to a speech in which the British Foreign Secretary, Lord Clarendon, had asserted that British and French understanding was not confined to the Eastern Question but had "become general on all matters of policy, and extends to all parts of the world."[32] This, said Cass, meant Cuba, and to meet the challenge he introduced two vaguely worded resolutions against European interference. The Senate received this intelligence with indifference, except for a few languid remonstrances against Cass' propensity for tilting at "abstract dangers." Marcy asked Buchanan to inquire into Clarendon's statement, and the Foreign Secretary, expressing astonishment that his remarks should have been misinterpreted, assured the American minister that he was referring only to the La Plata region, and once again categorically denied any understanding with France about Cuba.[33]

The outbreak of the Crimean War and reports of political unrest in Spain emboldened President Pierce to renew attempts to purchase Cuba. Extremists in the South, however, were inclined to put more hope in the filibustering expedition being openly organized by John A. Quitman of Mississippi. In mid-March the Louisiana legislature presented a joint resolution to Congress in which they pointed with alarm to the "Africanization" program in Cuba, and asked for immediate action on annexation. Their representative in the upper house, Senator Slidell, followed up this move with a proposal to unleash Quitman by giving the President authority to suspend the Neutrality Acts for not

31. Allan Nevins, *Ordeal of the Union* (2 vols. New York, 1947), 2, 353.

32. *Congressional Globe*, 33d Cong., 1st Sess., pp. 483–84.

33. Marcy to Buchanan (March 11, 1854), Buchanan to Marcy (March 17, 1854): Manning, *IA*, 7, 102–4, 533–34.

more than twelve months.[34] Slidell cited as "proofs" of
British and French complicity in a program to Africanize
Cuba the familiar tripartite pact argument; the fact that
Lord Howden, the British minister at Madrid, had acted
as second to M. Turgot, the French minister, in his recent
duel with Pierre Soulé; and certain alleged evasions and
untruths in letters from British officials in answer to inquiries from private citizens in the United States about
their policy in Cuba!

During the month of July purchase was on every tongue,
with Buchanan in London and Mason in Paris aimlessly
speculating as to whether Britain or France or both would
object to a Spanish cession of Cuba to the United States,
and Soulé openly cultivating the rebels before they came
to power in Madrid, only with his inimitable tactlessness to
alienate them almost immediately after they assumed office.
President Pierce came up with the incredible notion of a
conference of these American diplomatists in Europe on
the subject of Cuba. They met in August, labored, and
brought forth the "Ostend Manifesto," that clarion call for
forcible seizure to counter the threat of "Africanization,"
which alone would have killed any prospect of purchase if
any Spanish government had been willing to consider it,
and which seemed calculated to invite the very European
intervention everyone professed to be trying to prevent.
Marcy repudiated the document, to be sure, but the dam-
age was done.

The expansionists never said die, but any real hope of
acquiring Cuba or any other territory to the southward
had long ago flickered out. Early in 1855 Mason and Cass
again took up the Senate's time with a lengthy "documen-
tion" of an Anglo–French conspiracy against American
interests in the New World, but it was all the old charges
rehashed. Senator Clayton brought them up short by in-

34. *Congressional Globe,* 33d Cong., 1st Sess., pp. 1021–25.

quiring irritably of the Democratic majority that if the danger were as great as they pictured it, where were the appropriations for a larger army and navy and for fortifications?[35]

Along with myriad other projects for expansion, the purchase of Cuba was an object of the foreign policy of James Buchanan, who, Polk suspected, had been trying to save this achievement for himself in 1848. In January 1859 the Senate Committee on Foreign Relations reported favorably on a bill to appropriate $30 million to "facilitate acquisition of Cuba by negotiation."[36] Senator Slidell of Louisiana delivered the report, in which he urged as a supporting argument the danger of transfer, which the United States "have declared incompatible with their safety, and have announced to the world that attempt to consummate it would be resisted by all means in our power." In a similar vein, the spokesman for the House Committee on Foreign Affairs the same day urged the adoption of a counterpart measure by the lower chamber, suggesting the usefulness of a No-Transfer resolution like that of 1811 to speed the cession.[37]

All this was in vain—choked by the growth of the slavery issue, which paralyzed American politics and nearly destroyed the Union before it was ruthlessly excised by the sword. The threat to Cuba from Britain and France during the fifties was an ephemeral bogey raised by slavery expansionists for their own ends. Even while the United States was torn by civil war, there was no attempt by the major maritime powers to take the island. In the new vigor of the post-Appomattox years the nation again looked outward, and the No-Transfer principle was revived as a fundamental security policy of the United States.

35. Ibid., 2d Sess., pp. 826–27.
36. *Senate Report 351*, Committee on Foreign Relations, relating to bill for acquisition of Cuba (S.497), 35th Cong., 2d Sess.
37. *Congressional Globe*, 35th Cong., 2d Sess., appendix, pp. 96–100.

CHAPTER 9

Predominance in the Caribbean

The United States emerged from the Civil War full of national vigor and ridden with debt, confronted by the gigantic problems of reconstruction and the challenge of consolidating the power of the Union lately restored in battle. This war, like so many others, released rather than exhausted national energies, and proved to be the preface to a chapter of explosive growth in population and economic activity which made the United States by the end of the century the first industrial nation in the world and a great power in international politics. For thirty years after Appomattox foreign affairs were a minor concern of the American people whose attention was absorbed—in a period of almost complete military security—by the immense labors of developing the resources of a continent, peopling the West, building the railroads, and organizing the great basic industries which are the cornerstone of American national strength.

During this period the urge for territorial expansion languished, despite the enthusiasm of Seward and Grant, because the temper of the times opposed it. Except for the purchase of Alaska, Congress frustrated every expansionist proposal, turning down Seward's treaty for the purchase of the Danish West Indies and Grant's project for the annexation of Santo Domingo. This opposition was, of course, partly a function of the struggle for primacy between the executive and legislative branches, for the Radical Republican leadership was certainly not against expansion in principle. Charles Sumner had caught the vision of a continental republic stretching from Pole to Isthmus, and his notorious attempt to get Canada from Britain in compensation for the "consequential" *Alabama* claims suggests the Homeric scope and boldness of his acquisitiveness. He was not alone in this; but for most Republicans these were ultimate, not immediate, objectives. The South must be subjugated first, and with it the Chief Executive; the debt must be liquidated, and the economy stimulated by loosing any bonds of government restraint on the individual enterpriser.

There was little enthusiasm in particular for the acquisition of Caribbean islands, all of which had large colored populations that would only add to an already difficult national problem, and over which lingered the faint, unpleasant aura of slavery imperialism. Arguments from Civil War experience that the nation needed coaling stations for commercial and military use, in order to give naval protection to commerce in the Caribbean or maintain a blockade in the Gulf, made little impression on a Congress that was not navy-minded. The United States fleet withered away, its officers frequently on half-pay for lack of duty assignments, until by 1880 the American navy was inferior to that of Chile.

The threat of European intrusion was still, as it had always been, the most effective agent for arousing interest in the Caribbean area, although for some time even this consideration evoked only listless debate, for it was difficult to make the danger seem real. Anglophobia in the United States was certainly not reduced by British negligence of neutral duties during the war, or by the evident consideration given by the London government to the recognition of Confederate independence. Feeling ran high against France for the Maximilian episode in Mexico, and against

Spain for trying to reimpose Spanish rule in Santo Domingo and for meddling in Chile and Peru—all in disregard of the Monroe Doctrine. An aroused nationalism resented these affronts, and given the growing strength of the United States it is not surprising that after the Civil War there were increasingly frequent declarations to the effect that eventually all European power and influence must be expelled from the New World. This had always been the implicit goal of the No-Transfer policy and of Monroe's principles, based as they were on the doctrine of separate political systems, European and American, but until the latter part of the nineteenth century there was little realistic prospect of implementing it.

After 1890 these tendencies were heavily reinforced by a growing conviction that the paramount interest of the United States in an isthmian canal had rendered obsolete the principle of joint control established in the Clayton-Bulwer Treaty of 1850, and that this nation must not only exercise exclusive control of the transit, but also establish an effective screen of defensive outworks along its approaches. Since all of the Antilles were the property of European powers before the Spanish-American War, there was an obvious American interest in preventing their transfer either to a stronger European sovereign or to one which had not yet established itself in the Caribbean. As the American defense perimeter broadened, new applications of the No-Transfer principle delimited the area in which the United States asserted its claim to predominant interest.

PUBLIC MARRIAGE OF THE NO-TRANSFER PRINCIPLE TO THE MONROE DOCTRINE

Professor Samuel Flagg Bemis used to say in his lectures at Yale that the No-Transfer principle and the Monroe Doctrine lay together in the same bed for years, until Presi-

dent Grant and his Secretary of State, Hamilton Fish, sol-
emnized their union. This noteworthy marriage was first
recorded by Dexter Perkins in the third of his brilliant
volumes on the history of the Monroe Doctrine, where
there is one of the very few, and certainly by far the best,
systematic accounts of a portion of the development of the
No-Transfer principle.[1] Since Perkins has covered the
ground thoroughly from 1867 to 1893, there is no purpose
to be served here by repeating his narrative at length, but
it is necessary to highlight the principal events and to offer
some additional interpretation of their significance.

Perkins' interest in the No-Transfer principle is of course
confined to the period after it had been firmly linked to the
Monroe Doctrine in official statements, when it becomes
identified in the public mind and in policy with the principles of 1823. This identification took place in 1869 and
1870, for reasons it is difficult to assign, and thenceforward
the No-Transfer idea is nearly always cited in a Monrovian
context. Although he is aware of the "Madison Doctrine"
of 1811 and of Adams' application of the principle to Cuba
before the Monroe message, Perkins repeatedly calls the
No-Transfer principle an "extension" or "corollary" of
the Monroe Doctrine.[2] In the sense that it was at a late
date incorporated into the Doctrine, this is not an inexact
statement of the fact, but in terms of historical provenance
it is, as we have seen, inaccurate and misleading. The No-
Transfer principle, the Nonintervention and Noncolonization principles, and the pledge of abstention from European politics all sprang from a common defensive reflex,
the desire to isolate the New World from the illiberalism,
the dynastic rivalries and alliances, and most particularly
the wars of Europe. Abstention and No-Transfer are as old
as the Republic itself, and without the appearance of other

1. Perkins, *The Monroe Doctrine, 1867–1907*, pp. 4–39.
2. Ibid., pp. 4–5.

independent nations in the New World during the Age of Liberation, there would have been no need whatever for the Nonintervention principle. In the early years of our national existence, when the United States was surrounded by European possessions, had the No-Transfer reflex not existed it would have been necessary, to paraphrase Voltaire's *mot* about God, for someone to have invented it. An opposition to transfers of territory that threaten adverse changes in the local power situation is the most elementary kind of political wisdom. The reflex did in fact exist from the beginning, and was in continuous application during the half-century before Monroe's message and afterward.

From the point of view of the history of the No-Transfer principle, the interesting thing about the Grant and Fish formulations is not only that they joined it to the Monroe Doctrine but that they represent the first generalized statements of the policy. Before this time it had invariably been applied to specific European possessions: Canada, Louisiana, Florida, Cuba. In a small way Seward anticipated his successors in instructions to the American minister at Copenhagen in 1867 when he warned that "no transfer of colonies in the West Indies between European powers can be indifferent to the United States."[3] But he had the Danish West Indies in mind, and this declaration hardly had the public character of the later ones.

President Grant's pronouncement was also occasioned by a specific concern, in this case the outbreak in 1868 of what proved to be a decade of revolutionary disturbances in Cuba. Nothing in the years intervening since the Pierce administration had reduced the traditional American vigilance in matters connected with Cuba. Seward had seen fit to repeat the Adams formula to the Spanish minister at about the same time he sent the instructions cited above,

3. Seward to Yeaman (May 16, 1867), Charles C. Tansill, *The Purchase of the Danish West Indies* (Baltimore, 1932), p. 52.

and now in the President's annual message of 1869 Grant used the Cuban situation as the occasion for advancing the No-Transfer doctrine as a general principle of policy:[4]

> The United States have no disposition to interfere with the existing relations of Spain and her colonial possessions on this continent. They believe that in due time Spain and other European powers will find their interest in terminating those relations and establishing their present dependencies as independent powers— members of the family of nations. These dependencies are no longer regarded as subject to transfer from one European power to another. When the present condition of colonies ceases, they are to become independent powers, exercising the right of choice and self-control in the determination of their future condition and relations with other powers.[5]

Grant's remarks about the future withdrawal of Europe from the New World are revealing, not only because they make explicit an ultimate, unstated objective of all the hemispheric defense policies from the beginning but also because the very fact that they could be publicly expressed tells us something about the confident mood of the times, which asserted with increasing insistency the principle of America for the Americans. This is a theme on which Secretary Fish expanded significantly the following year.

The President did not mention the Monroe Doctrine in his annual message of 1869; its association with the No-Transfer principle occurred in a special message sent to Congress in May 1870, in a vain attempt to jog reluctant senators into accepting the annexation of Santo Domingo, which Buenaventura Baez had offered in a desperate and

4. Confidential interview of Seward with Corci (May 7, 1867), Moore, *Digest of International Law, 6,* 456.

5. Richardson, ed., *Messages and Papers of the Presidents, 6,* 3986.

despicable attempt to save his political skin. Grant, an honest if morally obtuse man with a regrettable affinity for scoundrels, had his heart set on consummating this unsavory deal and tried, as had many expansionists before him, to resurrect the bogey of European intervention to further his purposes. He had information, he warned Congress, that a European power stood ready to offer $2,000,000 for Samaná Bay alone.[6] The President urged annexation as a preventive measure, but repeated the No-Transfer caveat to Europe anyway, coupling it with the Monroe Doctrine: "The doctrine promulgated by President Monroe has been adhered to by all political parties, and I now deem it proper to assert the equally important principle that hereafter no territory on this continent shall be regarded as subject to transfer to a European power."

Obviously Grant intended to lay down a general rule of policy in this statement, but it is not quite so obvious as Perkins would have it that he intended finally to attach the No-Transfer principle to the Monroe Doctrine.[7] Polk had mentioned both together in 1845, and the Cass resolutions of 1853 linked the Noncolonization with the No-Transfer principle, but in neither case, although the kinship of the policies must have been evident to the speaker, was there an intention of joining them formally. We may, I think, take Grant's message as a formal juncture, not so much because his intention is unmistakable as because from this time forward the No-Transfer principle is with increasing frequency treated as a part of the Doctrine.

It will be observed that Grant did not assert the No-Transfer principle in its classic form. Instead of specifying "European colonies," he said "no territory," which includes territory in the possession of American states as well. This of course makes sense in the light of his immediate interest

6. Ibid., 5, 4016.
7. Perkins, p. 16.

in Santo Domingo, and it makes equally good sense in terms of the precedents established in the cases of Yucatán and California. He also seems to limit the application of the No-Transfer principle to "this continent"—although knowing Grant, and in the absence of positive evidence that the phraseology was deliberately chosen, it may be assumed that this was either careless drafting or that "this continent" meant for him the entire area in which European nations held colonies in the Americas.

Perkins raises the question of the expediency and wisdom of making such a generalized statement of the No-Transfer principle, which would lead to expectations in the public mind that action would be taken to oppose *any* transfer of territory, regardless of size or importance, or whether the new owner was a weaker power. Surely for an historian of the Monroe Doctrine these cannot be serious concerns. Monroe's principles have always been stated in generalized terms, and yet no matter what the theoretical position of an administration on the question of automatic operation versus *ad hoc* application, invocations of the Doctrine have in practice always been taken after considering the individual case in terms of the national interest. Whether under Whigs, Republicans, or Democrats, the Monroe Doctrine has been honored in the breach as well as in the observance. Where is the danger in a general policy statement if it need not be invoked by name during European interventions in the La Plata region or in Mexico, at British reoccupation of the Falkland Islands or extension of the protectorate over the Mosquito Indians, or even the installation of Maximilian I as emperor of Mexico? The case of St. Bartholomew's Island, which we shall consider presently, shows that the No-Transfer principle need not be applied with absolute rigidity either.

Grant continued to cite the danger of foreign intervention in urging the annexation of Santo Domingo, though to no avail.[8] But the administration had another opportunity to assert the No-Transfer principle when Congress requested information on the state of commercial relations with Latin America. On July 14, 1870, Secretary Fish submitted a memorandum which dealt rather briefly with commerce but quite extensively with the political separation of Europe and America as a policy goal not only of the United States but of all the nations of the New World.[9] After a lengthy review of American expansion, the achievement of independence by Latin America, and the development of the Monroe Doctrine, Fish cited with approval President Grant's statement of the No-Transfer principle in his annual message the preceding December, and offered the following gloss on it:

> This policy is not a policy of aggression; but it opposes the creation of European dominion on American soil, or its transfer to other European powers, and it looks hopefully to the time when, by the voluntary departure of European governments from this continent and the adjacent islands, America shall be wholly American.
>
> It does not contemplate forcible intervention in any legitimate contest; but it protests against permitting such a contest to result in the increase of European power or influence.

Fish's incorporation of the principle into the Doctrine is definite, as is his statement of the ultimate object of these policies. In a most significant passage, swelling with a sense of national power and betraying more than a hint of condescension toward the other American republics, the Sec-

8. T. C. Smith, "Expansion after the Civil War," *Political Science Quarterly, 16* (1901), 430.

9. 41st Cong., 2d Sess., Senate Executive Document 112, pp. 1–13.

retary of State went Edward Everett one better in asserting the paramount interest of the United States in the New World as regards not only European states but the other American nations as well. The seeds of the later Roosevelt Corollary are in these sentiments:

> It will not be presumptuous . . . to say, with entire consideration for the sovereignty and national pride of the Spanish American republics, that the United States by the priority of their independence, by the stability of their institutions, by the regard of their people for the forms of law, by their resources as a government, by their naval power, by their commercial enterprise, by the attractions which they offer to European immigration, by the prodigious internal development of their resources and wealth, and by the intellectual life of their population, occupy of necessity a prominent position on this continent which they neither can nor should abdicate, which entitles them to a leading voice, and which imposes on them duties of right and honor regarding American questions, whether those questions affect emancipated colonies or colonies still subject to European dominion.

Up to the time they left office early in 1877, Grant and Fish gave constant reminders to Europe of this American claim to predominant interest in the Caribbean area. This assertion of interest did not at that time take the form of United States colonization or protection; Congress blocked the Santo Domingo scheme, Seward's Danish West Indies treaty was not revived, and the United States uttered frequent disclaimers of any designs on troubled Cuba. While the Washington government abandoned expansion for itself, it was hypersensitive to rumors of possible transfers of territory to European powers, particularly Germany, which enters the scene as a possible threat after the Prussian victory over Austria at Sadowa. Most of those rumors involved the possibility that Denmark was willing to trade her West Indian islands for the return of North Schleswig, taken by Prussia in 1864, and between 1871 and 1877 the United States addressed no less than seven inquiries to Copenhagen and Berlin, all of which met with honest, if increasingly weary, denials.[10] Bismarck never believed in colonial ventures for Germany, and when he finally yielded to middle-class pressure for at least a token empire, he took care as far as possible not to alienate Britain or the United States.

Very few of Fish's "inquiries" contained actual No-Transfer statements, in contrast to past American practice. Fish addressed one caveat about Cuba to Britain in 1870 in connection with a British loan to Spain, and another to Denmark and Germany in regard to a rumored cession of St. Thomas and St. John, but all the rest, including requests for information about alleged German interest in Puerto Rico and Santo Domingo, were just that and nothing more.[11] Europe understood the American attitude, however, and Fish knew it.

ST. BARTHOLOMEW—THE EXCEPTION
THAT PROVES THE RULE

The retrocession of St. Bartholomew island by Sweden to France in 1877 is the only actual violation of the No-Transfer principle in its long history, thereby giving importance to an episode that is in every other respect of trifling significance. Napoleon never actually took possession of Louisiana before it was sold to the United States, and the seizure

---

10. Tansill, *Danish West Indies,* pp. 154–75.
11. Fish to Moran (Dec. 1, 1870), Moore, *Digest of International Law, 6,* 457. Fish to Schenck (Jan. 5, 1874), Tansill, pp. 162–63.

of St. Pierre and Miquelon by the Free French on Christmas Day 1941 from the Vichy government did not involve a technical change of sovereignty, but St. Bartholomew was undoubtedly transferred from one European sovereign to another under the nose of the United States, and without so much as a by-your-leave.

A tiny speck in the Leeward group, eight square miles in area, having a population in 1877 of a little over 2800, St. Bartholomew lies about 150 miles due east of the Virgin Islands. Gustavus III acquired it from France just after the War of the American Revolution, but after his death the Swedish monarchy found the island an expensive burden and spent nearly a century in sporadic efforts to unload its white elephant in the West Indies.[12] In 1798 the Swedish minister at Berlin approached John Quincy Adams with an offer to sell St. Bartholomew at a bargain price to the United States. Adams forwarded the offer to his government for a formal reply, anticipating the reaction at home by saying that the American system of government was not suited to the possession of colonies, and that he doubted whether the United States would accept any West Indian island as a gift.[13] Twenty years later *Niles' Register* reported without comment rumors that Sweden was trying to sell the island to some European power, but apparently the United States government took no official cognizance of the story.[14] The Stockholm government made offers of cession to Washington again in 1825, when Adams and Clay proved

12. Unless otherwise indicated, this account is taken from a study by R. H. Luthin, "St. Bartholomew: Sweden's Diplomatic and Colonial Venture in the Caribbean," *Hispanic American Historical Review, 14* (1934), 307–24.

13. Adams to Pickering (Dec. 24, 1798), W. C. Ford, ed., *Writings of J. Q. Adams, 2,* 381–82.

14. *Niles' Weekly Register, 15* (Aug. 29, Nov. 14, 1818), 8, 197.

unresponsive, and in 1845, at which time Secretary of State Buchanan replied that "the acquisition of distant insular possessions for colonial dependencies has never been deemed desirable or expedient by the United States."[15]

Thus discouraged, Sweden waited another twenty years before opening the subject again, but this was in 1868 while the Senate was elaborately ignoring Seward's Danish West Indies project, so that the prospects were dim for St. Bartholomew. The Swedes found a way to generate interest in Washington, however, when they started negotiations with Italy, which wanted the island for a naval station. Secretary Fish at once remonstrated, gently to be sure, but firmly. In 1870 Sweden again broached the subject of sale to the United States, drawing attention to Italy's interest as an incentive, to which Fish pointedly replied that while "we would prefer to avoid any controversy with a friendly power which acceptance by Sweden and Norway of the offer of Italy above referred to might involve, an acceptance which might be construed as adverse to that cardinal policy of the United States which objects to new colonies of European governments in this hemisphere, it is hoped that it might comport with the views of your government to postpone for the present any definite disposition of the subject."[16] Seldom has a No-Transfer warning been more delicately put.

Probably because Italy was never seriously interested, the Stockholm government turned to France. In May 1877 the American minister in Sweden got wind of these discussions and reported them to Washington. The Acting Secretary of State, Frederick Seward, instructed Mr. Andrews to tell

15. Memo of conversation between Adams and Clay (April 25, 1825), J. Q. Adams, *Memoirs, 6,* 528. Buchanan to Ellsworth (July 28, 1845), Buchanan, *Works, 6,* 212.

16. Fish to Count Lewenhaupt (Feb. 14, 1870), Luthin, p. 320.

Sweden that it seemed "improbable" that a "friendly government" would consider such a transfer without prior consultation with the United States. Sweden did not, however, consult Washington further, and on August 10, 1877, concluded a treaty ceding St. Bartholomew to France. Presented with a *fait accompli,* Secretary of State Evarts failed to lodge a formal protest, although Andrews on his own initiative expressed his view to the Swedish Foreign Office that there would be "dissatisfaction in Washington" because "opinion in the United States has always been sensitive to acquisitions of territory in our neighborhood by European states."[17]

It is perhaps regrettable, but it is understandable that this single affront to the integrity of the No-Transfer principle should have been suffered to pass unprotested. In the first place the newly installed Hayes administration was swamped in a welter of thorny domestic problems. And certainly the transfer of this minuscule dot of land was hardly worth a quarrel with Sweden. The United States had had ample opportunity to buy the island and had refused. Sweden wanted to unload a financial burden, and France was in the last analysis probably the most acceptable European buyer as far as the United States was concerned. It had been the original owner, so that Washington could and did treat this incident as a reversion rather than as a transfer of sovereignty. This acquisition would add nothing to the strength of the nation that already controlled Martinique and Guadeloupe, while if Italy had purchased the island, a new naval power would have established itself in the Western Hemisphere. The Hayes administration had not abandoned the No-Transfer principle, but on the contrary after this blow proceeded to assert it with renewed vigor.

17. Andrews to Evarts (Aug. 21, 1877), ibid., p. 322.

CANAL DIPLOMACY AND NO TRANSFER

Applications of the No-Transfer principle have always been closely related to the security of the continental United States, and it is difficult to account for its extension to the far-flung islands of the Antilles without understanding that for Americans after the Civil War the Isthmus was another coastline, the vital link between the eastern and western seaboards. Behind American Caribbean policy in all its ramifications lay a fundamental concern about the military security of the isthmian transit and its strategic approaches. Before the advent of the air age, this was a naval problem, and the overwhelming majority of No-Transfer statements arose from a negative determination to prevent the establishment of new European naval bases in the area and a positive determination to acquire American naval bases as a defensive screen around the canal route.

The Clayton-Bulwer treaty of 1850 had established Anglo–American agreement on the principle that neither nation would seek exclusive control of an isthmian transit, but as early as 1852 such bold assertions of the priority of American national interest in the Caribbean as the Everett Note and in 1870 the Fish memorandum indicated that the United States would not accept this arrangement indefinitely. When in 1879 a company predominantly French in ownership and management was formed to construct a canal across the Isthmus of Panama, President Hayes sounded a note that was never afterward absent from American isthmian policy. "The policy of this country is a canal under American control. The United States can not consent to the surrender of this control to any European power or to any combination of European powers."[18]

18. Message to Congress (March 8, 1880), Richardson, ed., *Messages and Papers*, 7, 585–86.

As a result of the French purchase of St. Bartholomew and the venture of French capital on the Isthmus, the American mind was sensitized to threats from this power, so that when rumors reached Washington in the summer of 1880 that France was dickering for the purchase of the Danish West Indies, Secretary Evarts at once made inquiries at Paris. The rumor proved, as usual, to be without foundation, but a report of the incident in the New York *Herald* illustrates how much of an impression Grant's general statements of the No-Transfer principle had made:

> During the Presidency of General Grant it became necessary to inform the Danish government that any attempt to transfer her colonial possessions on this continent to another European nation would be regarded as an unfriendly act and treated as such. It has been necessary since the present administration came into power to reiterate the so-called Grant doctrine, and if necessary it will be done again.[19]

It was done again in 1885 and 1886, in warnings to France and Britain of American opposition to their leasing the Môle St. Nicholas in Haiti, an excellent anchorage which the United States itself sought in 1891 to acquire as a naval base.[20]

These events, like the modest naval building programs authorized between 1883 and 1889, were isolated, early harbingers of the convulsive martial fervor and enthusiastic expansionism of the "large policy" of 1898. Until the late nineties the people of the United States were little aware of happenings abroad, of the inner significance of the rise of new nations like Germany and Japan, of the technologically

19. Evarts to Noyes (Aug. 24, 1880), Noyes to Evarts (Aug. 28, 1880), New York *Herald* (Aug. 23, 1880): cited in Tansill, pp. 181–82.
20. Perkins, pp. 34–39.

shrinking globe, of intensified economic rivalries and new imperialism, of the shifting rivalries of Europe. Intent on developing the vast resources of their sprawling continental domain, shut up behind high tariff walls, with a small navy and virtually no army, Americans seemed unaware of a greater destiny beyond their borders.

If any one man could be singled out who aroused Americans to an awareness of that destiny, it would be Alfred Thayer Mahan, the foremost military theorist the United States has produced. An Annapolis graduate who saw his first active service during the Civil War and who toiled upward through the ranks during the years when the United States Navy was at the nadir of its strength, Mahan's travels and studies gave global dimensions to his thought such as few Americans of his day possessed. In 1890 he published *The Influence of Sea Power upon History, 1660– 1783,* which had an immediate and profound impact on national policies both in the United States and abroad.

Three fundamental concepts underlay the whole of Mahan's theory of sea power. The first of these was that international rivalry is essentially a struggle for power, the second that an expanding foreign trade is vital to national power and prosperity, and the third that since the oceans are the main avenues of trade, sea power (commercial and military control of the sea) is of paramount importance. The naval strategist, following Jomini, preached to his countrymen that war is the ultimate resource of diplomacy, that military considerations must always be uppermost in the deliberations of the statesman, and that since command of the sea lanes is the decisive element of war, sea power— measured in terms of position, human and material resources, production, markets, merchant vessels, warships, and overseas bases—is the most important element in national greatness. All of this Mahan derived from his analysis of the factors that had made Britain the first nation of the world, and as a publicist and propagandist he tirelessly urged these lessons upon his countrymen as directives for American policy.

Mahan exercised great influence on naval and foreign policy through his friends and disciples Theodore Roosevelt and Henry Cabot Lodge. Roosevelt, then Civil Service Commissioner in Washington, reviewed Mahan's first work on sea power most favorably in the *Atlantic Monthly* and wrote the author privately that he considered it "very much the clearest and most instructive work of its kind with which I am acquainted," adding "I am greatly in error if it does not become a classic."[21] Mahan's opinions made a deep impression on both Roosevelt and Lodge, who did everything in their power—which was considerable—to translate them into action.

This was nowhere more true than in the Caribbean area. Mahan recorded in his memoirs that before 1885 he had been an anti-imperialist, but that his historical studies had converted him to expansionism.[22] The policy he outlined for the United States in the Caribbean was one of "predominance," and certainly involved the acquisition of overseas territories, but the purpose of these acquisitions in every instance was the security of the Isthmian canal. Predominance, for Mahan, was primarily a military rather than an economic or political concept. No nation had as vital an interest in the isthmian transit or its approaches as did the United States; therefore the "paralyzing" Clayton-Bulwer treaty must be scrapped; the nation must construct a fleet large enough to meet any force likely to be sent against it and must acquire naval bases to secure the canal approaches,

21. *The Works of Theodore Roosevelt,* Memorial Edition (24 vols. New York, 1923–26), *14,* 306. C. C. Taylor, *The Life of Admiral Mahan* (New York, 1920), p. 45.

22. Alfred T. Mahan, *From Sail to Steam: Recollections of a Naval Life* (New York, 1909), p. 274.

east and west. Mahan applauded the Harrison administration's attempts to get bases on Haiti and Santo Domingo and to annex Hawaii. Cleveland's refusal to take Hawaii he considered strategic folly. Without these prior precautions to ensure American predominance, he wrote, construction of the canal would be an "unmitigated disaster, and the Monroe Doctrine empty rhetoric."[23]

Anti-expansionist sentiment and plain indifference had proved an impenetrable barrier to the grandiose Caribbean schemes of Seward and Grant and had delayed any real progress toward the construction of an isthmian canal up to this time. The acquisition of naval bases at Pago-Pago and Pearl Harbor had caused scarcely a ripple on the placid surface of public apathy toward foreign affairs. But changes were brewing in this country as in Europe. The problems of the industrial revolution were full-blown: depressions, such as the one starting in 1893, seemed to be increasing in amplitude as well as frequency; the closing of the frontier and the pressures of a tidal wave of immigration in a period of unemployment resulted in alarming evidence of social unrest and bred in both capital and labor a psychology of scarcity which led to a restless search for new outlets, both emotional and commercial. A heightened nationalistic spirit became apparent after the centennial celebrations of 1876, signalized by the formation or revival of patriotic societies extolling the military virtues. The stage was being prepared for the new Manifest Destiny.

Public interest in foreign affairs was kindled by the crisis with Germany over Samoa in 1888, and to a greater extent by the continuing question of Hawaiian annexation and the Venezuela boundary controversy. Public opinion and

23. Mahan, "The United States Looking Outward," *Atlantic Monthly* (Dec. 1890), "The Isthmus and Sea Power," *Atlantic Monthly* (Sept. 1893): reprinted in *The Interest of America in Sea Power, Present and Future,* Boston, 1898.

congressional pressure moved Cleveland and Olney to take a strong stand for the Monroe Doctrine—so strong, indeed, that Olney claimed that "today the United States is practically sovereign upon this continent, and its fiat is law upon the subjects to which it confines its interposition."[24] When in 1895 the Cuban revolution broke out afresh, Cleveland had to ignore resolutions by Congress calling for a recognition of Cuban belligerency.

Chief among those who sought to replace the "small policy" with a program of territorial aggrandizement, naval building, and firm support of the Monroe Doctrine were Lodge and Roosevelt. More than any other individual, in all probability, Senator Lodge was responsible for the strongly nationalistic and expansionist tone of the foreign policy plank in the Republican party platform of 1896, which not only pledged support of the Monroe Doctrine "in its fullest extent" but looked "forward to the eventual withdrawal of the European powers from this hemisphere."[25] He supported a concurrent resolution reported out by the Senate Foreign Relations Committee on January 20, 1896, which reaffirmed strict enforcement of the Monroe Doctrine against "any attempt by any European power to take or acquire any new or additional territory on the American continents . . . through force, purchase, cession, occupation, pledge, colonization, protectorate, or any control of the easement in any canal or any other means of transit across the American Isthmus."[26] This general statement was not enough for Lodge, who was concerned about a German threat to purchase the Danish West Indies, so that the Massachusetts Senator introduced a separate resolution directing the Committee on Foreign Relations to inquire

24. Olney to Thomas Bayard (July 20, 1895), House Executive Document 3368, 54th Cong., 1st Sess., No. 1, Pt. I, pp. 545–62.

25. Tansill, p. 208.

26. Ibid., p. 201.

whether the islands could still be bought by the United States, "and whether if these islands are not purchased by the United States it is probable that they will be sold to some other power."[27] Lodge introduced a bill to purchase the islands early in 1898, but it was lost in the excitement of the war with Spain.[28]

Shortly after his friend Lodge introduced his Danish West Indies resolution, Theodore Roosevelt wrote an article on the Monroe Doctrine in which he firmly connected the No-Transfer idea with Monroe's principles. He expressed opinions on the applicability of the Doctrine which are interesting coming from the author of the famous Corollary of 1905, which asserted that if the United States denied the right of intervention in this hemisphere to non-American powers, it bore a responsibility to see that Latin American states behaved responsibly in their international relations. The opinions Roosevelt expressed also illuminate his later actions in the Venezuelan debt controversy:

> The Monroe Doctrine may be briefly defined as forbidding European encroachment on American soil. It is not desirable to define it so rigidly as to prevent our taking into account the varying degrees of national interest in varying cases. The United States has not the slightest wish to establish a universal protectorate over other American states, or to become responsible for their misdeeds. If one of them becomes involved in an ordinary quarrel with a European power, such quarrel must be settled between them by any one of the usual methods. But no European state is to be allowed to aggrandize itself on American soil at the expense of an American State. Furthermore, no transfer of an Amer-

27. Ibid.
28. Ibid., p. 213.

ican colony from one European state to another is to be permitted, if, in the judgment of the United States, such transfer would be hostile to its own interests.[29]

Alluding to the Louisiana crisis in Jefferson's day, Roosevelt recalled that "our statesmen at once announced that they would regard as hostile to America the transfer of territory in question from a weak to a strong European power. . . . The principle which our statesmen announced was in kind precisely the same as that upon which we should now act if Germany sought to acquire Cuba from Spain, or St. Thomas from the Danes. In either of these events it is hardly conceivable that the United States would hesitate to interfere, if necessary, by force of arms; and in so doing the national authorities would undoubtedly be supported by the immense majority of the American people."

Roosevelt, like Mahan and Lodge, instinctively understood power politics. The distinction he made of a transfer from "a weak to a strong power" is of course the key to every declaration of the No-Transfer principle in our history, and the flexibility in application Roosevelt urged would cover common-sense decisions not to invoke the principle in the unlikely circumstances of a transfer which improved the American power position, or were too remote or trivial to command notice. Clearly, in his mind, any threat of transfer of Cuba or the Virgin Islands would not fall in this latter category, and as he wrote to Mahan, the United States should take out insurance at once against such a contingency.[30] He must have felt that these sentiments would not yet be popular if made public, for he cautioned Mahan that his view "must be strictly private, I speak to you with the greatest freedom, for I sympathize

29. Roosevelt, *Works, 15,* 224–39.

30. Roosevelt to Mahan (May 3, 1897), Elting Morison, ed., *The Letters of Theodore Roosevelt* (6 vols. Cambridge, 1951–52), *1,* 607–8.

with your views. . . . But to no one else excepting Lodge do I talk like this.''

A year later Roosevelt need hardly have worried about the reception such ideas would receive, for the people of the United States—horrified by the extravagant reports of Spanish inhumanity in Cuba printed in the yellow press, driven by the frustrations of the reform movement at home to crusade against injustice abroad, and exhilarated by the prospect of martial adventure—had embarked on a war to liberate Cuba. The wave of enthusiasm that carried the nation to arms obscured the fact that the war was in fact unnecessary; Spain had agreed to the American demand for an armistice and for measures leading to independence for Cuba before McKinley sent his war message to Congress. As far as Cuba was concerned, the American blockade and military campaign could only prolong the privations and destruction of life and property they were supposedly intended to end.

The war, to the astonishment of a great many Americans, turned out to involve much more than Cuba. In the grip of an irresistible expansionist urge and in the exuberance of victory, the United States took Puerto Rico, annexed the Hawaiian Islands, and acquired an unexpected Pacific empire in the Philippine archipelago which revolutionized the entire strategic situation of the nation. With heavy responsibilities in both the Atlantic and Pacific oceans, and with only a modest fleet, the country found that the importance of an isthmian canal and its approaches was enhanced a thousandfold.

THE PLATT AMENDMENT AND THE
NO-TRANSFER PRINCIPLE

An independent Cuba was a reality at last, and it would seem that the long history of the No-Transfer principle in connection with that island was at an end. But there was a final chapter still to be written, one that underlines again the primarily strategic emphasis of American Caribbean diplomacy.

To the Joint Resolution of Congress of April 20, 1898, authorizing the President to use armed force to expel Spain from Cuba, Senator Teller of Colorado as spokesman for the anti-imperialists had added his celebrated amendment disclaiming any intention on the part of the United States to exercise sovereignty or control over the island except during the period of pacification, after which the Cubans were to enjoy independence and self-government. This self-denying ordinance did honor to the integrity of American motives in entering the war, but it also presented a problem in securing American strategic interests afterward.

In November 1900, under the auspices of the United States occupation authorities, a Constitutional Convention convened in Cuba under instructions from General Leonard Wood, the Military Governor, to draw up a constitution "adequate to secure a stable, orderly, and free government" and to "formulate what in your opinion ought to be the relations between Cuba and the United States."[31] The Convention in time framed a satisfactory constitution, but it rapidly became apparent to the American government that the liberals and radicals whom the Cuban electorate had chosen to represent them had no interest in defining their future relations with their liberators. The United States thereupon imposed upon Cuba a virtual protectorate in the form of the Platt Amendment, an arrangement specifically designed to provide a constitutional and conventional equivalent for the no longer applicable No-Transfer principle.

Evidence of this relation of the Platt Amendment to the No-Transfer principle is to be found in a letter from Elihu

31. Dana G. Munro, *The United States and the Caribbean Area* (Boston, 1934), pp. 8–9.

Root, the Secretary of War and principal author of the Platt Amendment, to his proconsul in Havana, forwarding the provisions he wished adopted by the Convention.[32] Having freed Cuba from Spanish rule, Root declared, "it would be a most lame and impotent conclusion if . . . we should through the constitution of the new government, by inadvertence or otherwise, be placed in a worse condition in regard to our own vital interests than we were while Spain was in possession, and the people of Cuba should be deprived of that protection and aid from the United States which is necessary to the maintenance of their independence." The heart of the matter was the prevention of conditions which would invite a foreign occupation of Cuba, to which the No-Transfer principle had traditionally stood opposed:

> It seems to me that no one familiar with the traditional and established policy of this country in respect to Cuba can find cause for doubt as to our remaining duty. It would be hard to find any single statement of public policy which has been so often officially declared by so great an array of distinguished Americans authorized to speak for the Government of the United States, as the proposition stated, in varying but always uncompromising and unmistakable terms, that the United States would not under any circumstances permit any foreign power other than Spain to acquire possession of the island of Cuba.
>
> Jefferson and Monroe and John Quincy Adams and Jackson and Van Buren and Grant and Clay and Webster and Buchanan and Everett have all agreed in regarding this as essential to the interests and the protection of the United States. The United States has, and

32. Root to Wood (Feb. 9, 1901), *Annual Report of the Secretary of War for 1901.*

always will have, the most vital interest in the preservation of the independence which she has secured for Cuba, and in preserving the people of that island from the domination and control of any foreign power whatsoever.

Root therefore recommended incorporation into the Cuban constitution of a series of provisions which were substantially the same as those of the later Platt Amendment, the most important of which were Articles I and II. Article I of the Platt Amendment provided that the government of Cuba "shall never enter into any treaty or compact with any foreign power or powers which will impair or tend to impair the independence of Cuba, nor in any manner authorize or permit any foreign power or powers to obtain by colonization or for military or naval purposes or otherwise, lodgment or control over any portion of said island." Article III, which Root later described to the Cuban Convention as "the Monroe Doctrine, but with international force," gave the United States the "right to intervene for the preservation of Cuban independence, the maintenance of a government adequate for the protection of life, property, and individual liberty, and for discharging the obligations with respect to Cuba imposed by the treaty of Paris on the United States, now to be undertaken and assumed by the Government of Cuba."[33] Understandably, the Cuban Convention balked at accepting these limitations on its sovereign independence, being less impressed with the vital interests of the United States than with its newly gained freedom. It was then that the Root provisions, in modified form, were appended by Senator Platt to an Army appropriations bill for the fiscal year 1902, and Cuba was given to understand that

33. Philip Jessup, *Elihu Root* (2 vols. New York, 1938), *1*, 318–19.

American occupation forces would not be withdrawn until the Platt Amendment was not only added to the Cuban constitution but embodied in a formal treaty arrangement as well. The Cubans capitulated, and the United States had a functional equivalent of the No-Transfer principle, which would be used, Root assured Havana, "only to prevent foreign attacks against the independence of the Cuban Republic or when a veritable state of anarchy exists within the Republic."[34]

THE "GERMAN MENACE" IN THE DANISH WEST INDIES

During the next fifteen years the United States arranged for or imposed temporary protectorates in a good many other independent states near the canal site—Panama, Santo Domingo, Nicaragua, and Haiti. In retrospect this policy seems tragically ill-advised and unnecessary, knowing as we do the legacy of bitter resentfulness on the part of Latin America that it left in its wake, and realizing that the danger was in fact not so great as to call for such high-handed indifference to the sovereign pride of neighboring states. But the danger seemed real enough to statesmen of the Progressive era; and who in the mid-twentieth century can say for certain that in our own day we are not overreacting to threats which history will show to have been illusory, or at least less formidable than they now appear? Those charged with making decisions must act on the knowledge they possess; they are the prisoners of contemporary attitudes; they must prepare for the extreme contingency. The fact that men so dissimilar in personality and principles as Theodore Roosevelt, William Howard Taft, and Woodrow Wilson all followed virtually identical courses in the Caribbean suggests more strongly than anything else that there

34. Munro, p. 14.

appeared to be no acceptable alternatives to the protectorate policy in those years.

The Roosevelt Corollary was rooted in a concern for canal security and in a sense of justice. The United States could not now, any more than in the past, suffer a rash of European punitive expeditions like the Anglo–German blockade of Castro's Venezuela in 1902, which might lead to occupations nominally temporary but in fact as "temporary" as that of Britain in Egypt. Ought the Monroe Doctrine to be used, on the other hand, to shield from financial responsibility those contemptible Caribbean dictators who succeeded each other in kaleidoscopic profusion and who looked upon public office as a species of authorized brigandage? Americans, whose business ethic was founded on the sanctity of contract, were repelled by the thought, and undertook while keeping Europe out to enforce on the Caribbean governments a minimum standard of international responsibility.

The only European colonies to occupy American attention in the years between the war with Spain and the first World War were the Danish West Indies, and there the chief threat of transfer was felt to be from Germany. The German menace was very real to Americans long before Sarajevo; Allied propagandists had only to embellish an image already there, to darken the visage and daub the hands with blood. Much of the original bogey was constructed of insubstantial materials, and many of those were received second hand, but it served.

The shadow of Germany had fallen over the Danish islands as early as Seward's day, because of the North Schleswig question, and Americans remained convinced that the Kaiser might effect an exchange of territories that would plant him squarely athwart one of the main avenues of approach to the Isthmus. After 1890, the image of Germany was the image Americans had of William II—aggres-

sive, militaristically minded, shifty, selfish, a braggart who
had publicly expressed his contempt for the Monroe Doctrine. There had been incidents (the unpleasantness over
Samoa, German meddling in the Brazilian revolution of
1893) which seemed the more ominous because of the flood
of German emigration to Brazil. There was the episode at
Manila Bay when Admiral von Diederichs disposed his
squadron as if to prevent the Americans from landing—all
fancy as it turned out, but significant for the readiness
with which Americans were willing to accept it as fact.
There was the interest shown by Germany in taking the
Philippines if McKinley had decided not to keep them, and
German proximity to American Pacific interests after their
purchase of the Marshall and Caroline groups from
Spain. Then came Venezuela, and a sharper trade rivalry
everywhere.

Part of this anxiety was undoubtedly a vicarious participation in the very genuine concern over German policies
felt in Britain. When William II dismissed Bismarck in
1890, he also abandoned the Iron Chancellor's cautious
avoidance of any move that would range Britain against
Germany. With reckless abandon the Kaiser challenged
Britain in Africa, threatened the Suez lifeline with the
Drang nach Osten, and moved aggressively into China; and
this was coupled with the already intense economic rivalry
between the powers. But worst of all William II, who then
possessed the most powerful army in the world, embarked
on an extensive naval building program designed to make
German sea power second only to Britain's. For Germany,
as Winston Churchill once remarked and Bismarck knew,
a fleet was a luxury, while for Britain it was an absolute
necessity.

These challenges to her vital interests drove Britain
gradually to abandon her policy of splendid isolation, to
compose her differences in North Africa with France in

1904, and with Russia in the Straits and Central Asia in 1907—agreements leading to the formation of the Triple Entente which stood explosively opposed to the Triple Alliance in 1914. To be able to concentrate on Europe and to reduce her responsibilities in peripheral areas, Britain concluded an alliance with Japan in 1902, and agreed the same year to the United States' demand for exclusive control of the isthmian canal in the Hay-Pauncefote treaty. In both instances Britain tacitly turned over the protection of her interests to the local power, withdrawing fleet units from both the Western Pacific and the Caribbean for concentration in home waters against the German threat. Although the fact was not generally realized in the United States, the Atlantic approaches were secure after 1902, for Britain stood between Germany and the New World.

Defense of the Hemisphere and the Monroe Doctrine remained, of course, primarily an American responsibility, and the extensive naval building program launched by Theodore Roosevelt was paced by German, not British, naval expansion. As Roosevelt wrote to John Hay, both the Danish and Dutch possessions in the Caribbean area were "constant temptations to Germany, unless or until we take them," and the best way to deliver the Reich from the temptation, in the President's opinion, was to "keep the navy up."[35] The Navy itself was anxious about the German threat and anxious also to acquire coaling stations in the Caribbean while any were to be had. In 1898 Admiral Bradford wrote privately to Secretary of State Hay, urging purchase of the Danish West Indies for a naval station "in order to prevent them from falling into the hands of Germany." Since "in accordance with the principles of the Monroe Doctrine this country would be forced to object

35. Roosevelt to Hay (April 22, 1903), Morison, ed., *Letters of Theodore Roosevelt, 3,* 465.

to their acquisition by Germany," the admiral argued that it appeared "to be a good business proposition to buy rather than risk a war on their account."[36]

Although private individuals in Germany were working to secure German control over the Danish islands, both the Berlin and Copenhagen governments were too well aware of the American attitude to entertain the proposition seriously.[37] The No-Transfer principle may not have been approved in Germany, but given the evident power of the United States, it was respected. There was no way of knowing this in Washington, however, and in late 1901 a fresh attempt to purchase the islands was launched. In response to a request from the Secretary of the Navy, the General Board under Admiral Dewey submitted a memorandum on the strategic value of the islands, which concluded that "both St. Thomas and St. John would be valuable possessions, while their occupation by any foreign power would be a decided menace to us. Their acquisition (Santa Cruz being regarded as unimportant) is therefore strongly recommended by the Board."[38] Impelled in part by a desire to keep Germany out of the Caribbean, the United States Senate in February 1902 gave its advice and consent to the ratification of the new purchase treaty, but this time the Danish Rigsdag withheld its approval. Most Republican leaders in Washington blamed the defeat of the treaty on pressure from Berlin, although Professor Tansill, after a search of both the Danish and German archives, has failed to find any evidence to support this suspicion. Actually Germany was indirectly responsible, for the treaty was blocked by Danish conservatives who could not face losing

36. Bradford to Hay (Sept. 28, 1898), cited in Tansill, pp. 390–91.
37. Ibid., pp. 401, 412.
38. Admiral Dewey, President of the General Board, to the Secretary of the Navy (Nov. 12, 1901), ibid., pp. 426–28.

what they considered to be their best chance for recovering the lost province of North Schleswig.[39]

Discouraged by this setback, which deepened their impression of the Kaiser's cunning malevolence, the American government maintained its vigilance in the Caribbean and awaited its opportunity in the Danish West Indies. That opportunity failed to arise until 1915, and then it was arbitrarily created by Secretary of State Robert Lansing. Shocked by the brutality of unlimited submarine warfare and aware of the value of the Danish West Indies to Germany as a naval base, Lansing seems to have become convinced that Berlin would go to any lengths to get them. Accordingly, he called in the Danish Minister to renew the American purchase proposal, making the somewhat startling assertion that since the Germans coveted the islands they might absorb Denmark to get them, and that therefore continued possession by Denmark had become a threat to Danish independence. The Secretary of State felt it necessary to tell Mr. Brun that "in any event of an evident intention on the part of Germany to take possession of his country or to compel Denmark to cede the islands to her, the United States would be under the necessity of seizing and annexing them . . . as we could never permit the group to become German."[40]

This extraordinary *démarche* so shook the Copenhagen government that they directed Brun to ask whether, if Denmark did not agree to sell the islands, the United States would feel it necessary to take possession of them. Lansing replied that he could conceive of two circumstances which might require such action on the part of the United States:

39. Ibid., pp. 433–53.

40. Robert Lansing, "Drama of the Virgin Islands Purchase," *New York Times Magazine* (July 19, 1931), p. 4, cited in Tansill, pp. 476–78.

[1] The possible absorption of Denmark by a great power [which] would create a situation which it would be difficult to meet other than by occupation of the islands. . . . [2] If Denmark voluntarily, or under coercion, transferred title to the Danish West Indies to another European power, which would seek to convert them into a naval base.[41]

Under the pressure of this threat of preclusive occupation, Denmark saw no alternative to reopening negotiations for sale of the islands. President Wilson approved Lansing's tactics, which were supported once again by a memorandum from the General Board of the Navy pointing out that Denmark could neither defend the islands against an attempt by another European nation at seizing them forcibly nor perhaps even resist pressure by such a power for peaceful cession, and that the Monroe Doctrine would compel the United States in such an instance to oppose the transfer.[42] The treaty of purchase was signed on August 4, 1916, the Senate's consent was given on September 7, and final ratifications were exchanged on January 17, 1917. Another avenue of approach to the isthmian canal, opened in 1914, was thus expeditiously secured against the danger of occupation by a major naval power.

Regardless of the scare tactics employed by Secretary Lansing, the first World War brought no such threat to the security of the Hemisphere through transfers of European colonies as did the second World War. The question of the European islands in both the Caribbean and the Pacific did come up for general and more or less academic

41. Memo of conversation between Lansing and Brun (Nov. 15, 1915), *Foreign Relations of the United States, The Lansing Papers, 1914–1920* (2 vols. Washington, 1939–40), 2, 501–2.
42. Admiral Dewey to the Secretary of the Navy (Dec. 10, 1915), Tansill, pp. 481–83.

consideration by the General Board of the Navy in January 1918.[43] The Board laid down as a "general rule" that the United States ought not to acquire possessions simply to keep them out of the hands of a potential enemy, unless these possessions had intrinsic strategic value. Thus they considered British Jamaica, the Bahamas, and Bermuda valuable enough to acquire, and to defend against transfer. Interestingly, the Board advanced at this early date the notion of purchasing these islands for the war debts then being contracted by Britain, a plan that found much favor later. Bases on the British islands were of course obtained in 1940 under the destroyer-bases agreement, but in 1918 the Board also assigned great importance to French Martinique and Guadeloupe, as well as the Dutch island of Curaçao, all of which figure importantly in applications of the No-Transfer principle during the second World War. On the Pacific side, only the Galapagos Islands, belonging to Ecuador, were considered to be of sufficient value to oppose the establishment there of a non-American power.

The defeat of Germany on the one hand, and the Washington naval limitation treaty, which promised to confine Japanese naval operations to the Western Pacific, on the other, combined with the great power and prestige of the United States to usher in a brief period of more complete military security than the nation had ever enjoyed. American predominance not only in the Caribbean but in the entire Western Hemisphere was an established fact. Under these circumstances the United States found it possible, and certainly expedient, to liquidate its Caribbean protectorates and adopt a Latin American policy guided by principles of peaceful cooperation, respect for the sovereign

43. Admiral Badger (for the General Board) to the Secretary of the Navy (Jan. 24, 1918), Naval Records, Area Files D, Navy Department (1911–27), Box 226.

independence of the American Republics, and absolute nonintervention. Theodore Roosevelt's Corollary was repudiated, to be replaced by Franklin Roosevelt's Good Neighbor policy, and the vital interest of the United States in the security of the canal approaches was eventually entrusted to a system of hemispheric collective security. As the war clouds gathered over Europe and Asia, the American states drew together and pledged themselves to mutual help; in this crisis the United States took an unprecedented step by converting the Monroe Doctrine, including the No-Transfer principle, into a partnership of all the republics of the New World for defense of the Hemisphere.

CHAPTER 10

Prelude to War

For well over a century the fundamental foreign policy of the United States had been continental isolation, the political separation of the Old World and the New. While there was no slackening of the conscious determination of Americans to remain aloof from entanglements outside the Hemisphere after 1900, the emergence of the United States as a great power with world-wide economic interests, the technological revolution that brought Europe and Asia closer than ever before, and the pressure of events all combined to produce strains that made the maintenance of this policy increasingly difficult and artificial.

It seemed that the acquisition of the Philippines might have spelled the end of hemispheric isolationism; and while it may be argued that in view of the protection the United States owed the Filipinos it should have, in fact it did not. America saw the danger involved in this venture into the Asian political sphere, almost instantly regretted its actions, and in effect withdrew. The United States never had any serious intention of defending the Philippines, and had already taken steps to unload an unwelcome responsibility when catastrophe overwhelmed the islands in 1941. Nor did the Open Door notes and Hay's suggestion that the powers respect the territorial and administrative integrity of China represent an American decision to intervene for the maintenance of a balance of power in Asia. The people of the United States were never willing to fight for the Hay policies, and after the rise of Japan only an avowed willingness to use force could have prevented a partition of China.

Americans were even less venturesome in regard to Europe. A few individuals like Theodore Roosevelt or Mahan foresaw a larger world role for the United States, particularly in combination with Anglo-Saxon Europe against the Yellow Peril in Asia. But the country at large was if anything more determined than ever to keep away from what George Washington had called the ordinary combinations and collisions of trans-Atlantic politics. Yet the United States did intervene in the first World War, and that intervention was decisive in the struggle between the Allies and the Central Powers. American money and manpower tipped the scales after the collapse of Russia had given Germany the advantage which might have meant victory, and American political warfare in the form of Wilson's Fourteen Points contributed to the break-up of the Austro–Hungarian empire that redrew the political map of Europe and precipitated a revolution in Germany. British and French statesmen fully understood the contribution America had made, and sought insurance against the withdrawal of the United States from a responsibility for maintaining the peace just won. In the League of Nations and the Treaties of Guarantee they thought they had such insurance, but the United States Senate rejected the League and never considered the treaties. America retreated into political isolation and, with the towering tariff walls and Johnson Act of the interwar years, economic isolation as well.

No one can say with assurance that there would have been no second World War if the United States had been actively committed to the maintenance of a European balance of power, for that commitment in itself would have required a considerable education in the realities of international politics. In the century of relative peace between Waterloo and Sarajevo, Americans lost sight of a truth that had been self-evident to the Founding Fathers, schooled in the fierce international competition of the eighteenth century: the possibility of a policy of continental insularity depended on a stable power structure in Europe. As long as the major European states so counterbalanced each other that none could become predominant and none could spare a substantial part of its military forces for penetration into the New World, America was secure. No superiority in their institutions or particular moral pre-eminence, as Americans fondly imagined, accounted for their liberation from the armaments, the alliances, and other paraphernalia of the struggle for power which characterized European affairs, but a unique and, as it proved, transitory constellation of political forces across the Atlantic. Whenever that balance should be shattered, the conditions of American security were bound to be radically changed.

Americans were both right and wrong in regarding Britain as the chief enemy during the nineteenth century. They were right in the sense that as overlord of the seas Britain was the only power capable of undertaking independent action in the Americas. But while Britain was a potential menace, she was also an actual protector, since quite accidentally and without design her interests more often than not coincided with the desire of the United States to keep this hemisphere free of the contentious rivalries of European politics. If the British had lost command of the sea to an aggressive, predominant continental power such as Napoleon's France or Hitler's Germany, a truly isolated United States would have stood naked to its enemies.

Americans can scarcely be blamed for a failure to appreciate their interest in a European balance of power when the British, despite all the teachings of past experience,

could not see as late as 1938 that their frontier was on the
Rhine. Whatever the practical results of American intervention in the first World War, that intervention did not
present itself to the nation or to Woodrow Wilson in terms
of preventing a collapse of the European state system, but
in terms of an idealistic crusade to "make the world safe for
democracy" and a legalistic crusade on behalf of the maritime rights of neutrals. Lacking a realistic blueprint of the
kind of European order that was a necessary condition of
American security, and guided chiefly by resounding slo-
gans uncritically accepted, the United States delegation at
the Peace Conference contributed to a settlement bristling
with unsatisfactory compromises that would require patient
adjustment later if peace were to be maintained. This done,
the country retired to its policy of hemispheric aloofness,
abdicating responsibility for helping Europe to find a way
through problems which it had helped create and in the
solution of which it had a vital if unsuspected stake.

In 1937 the shaky world order erected at Paris and
shored up afterward by ramshackle alliances, disarmament
pacts, and treaties of guarantee which characterized the
diplomacy of the interwar period began palpably to disin-
tegrate. To those sincerely devoted to the cause of world
peace the dedication that year of the magnificent permanent home of the League of Nations at Geneva stood as an
ironic symbol of shattered hopes, for by this time it was
clear that the Palace of Nations was destined to be a sepul-
cher. Italy had excused herself from the society of law-
abiding nations to complete the rape of Ethiopia, while
Hitler's Germany took advantage of the confusion to over-
turn Versailles and Locarno by marching troops into the
demilitarized Rhinelands. Japan, the first defector from the
League, fabricated an incident and launched its long-
contemplated assault on China. Meanwhile the Fascist and
Soviet dictatorships engaged in full-dress field tests of tac-

tics and equipment by intervening in the civil war that ravaged the barren Spanish land.

These multiplying signs of impending disaster did not go unnoticed in the United States. Indeed, foreign affairs now began to emerge for the first time during the Roosevelt administration as a matter of primary concern for both the government and the public at large. But opinions of the executive branch of the federal government and of Congress and the majority of Americans on how best to deal with these threats to peace tended to diverge; and this divergence conditioned the nation's foreign policy up to Pearl Harbor and fed the Great Debate that raged after that national catastrophe.

Broadly speaking, the choice of security policies that the United States faced was between traditional hemispheric isolationism and a limited adherence to the principle of collective security. For most of the people and their representatives in Congress the rising specter of war in Europe and Asia only confirmed a determination that America could and must remain aloof, and strengthened the underlying assumptions of Monroeism: that virtuous America was separated from an essentially degenerate outside world by still impassable ocean barriers and could best serve the cause of civilization by cultivating its garden and offering precept by example. Toward the new aggressor nations the United States adopted an attitude that can be described as moral indignation with limited liability.

It was in this spirit that Congress enacted the neutrality legislation of 1935–37. Disillusioned by the failure of the complexities of European politics to dissolve before the trumpet-blast of Wilsonian idealism, by the cavalier treatment of the war debts question by the Allies, by the startling revelation of revisionist historiography that Germany had been perhaps not wholly responsible for the first World War, and by the Nye Committee's apparent documentation of the Progressive thesis that special economic interests had duped the United States into a needless war, the nation resolved that it should not happen again. The arms embargo, control of manufacture and sale of munitions, prohibition of private loans to belligerents, the prohibition of travel by United States citizens on belligerent merchantmen, and other provisions of the New Neutrality represented a repudiation of Wilson's choice of neutral policy and an abandonment of the historic defense of Freedom of the Seas. Against fresh threats of incursion by the barbarian hordes, the United States built a legislative Chinese Wall, determined to shun involvement at any cost.

President Roosevelt and his closest advisers doubted isolationist premises and resisted their conclusions. Unable to prevent enactment of neutrality legislation which was overwhelmingly endorsed by public sentiment, they conducted a partially successful campaign to preserve a measure of executive discretion in its application. In the gathering world crisis, the President and an increasing number of Americans felt that the Neutrality Acts were at best amoral, since the arms embargo favored the better-prepared aggressor over his victim. But in a larger sense they felt that a Fortress America policy actually enhanced the danger of war by announcing in advance that the immense industrial and military potential of the United States would not be a factor in any international struggle. The administration intuitively recognized what the Founding Fathers knew, that American security depended on a stable power situation throughout the world, that it had been British sea power which had guarded the Atlantic frontier, and that a technological revolution was destroying the validity of the geopolitical assumptions upon which American isolationism had traditionally rested.

It was some of these home truths, as he saw them, that President Roosevelt tried to impart in his "Quarantine"

speech delivered at Chicago on October 5, 1937. Warning
that mounting international lawlessness might place civilization itself in jeopardy, he cautioned against imagining
that "there is an escape through mere isolation or neutrality." "Let no one imagine," he admonished, "that America
will escape . . . that this Western Hemisphere will not be
attacked, and that it will continue tranquilly and peacefully to carry on the ethics and the arts of civilization."[1]
Then, addressing himself to the irresolute statesmen of
Britain and France, he issued a call to peace-loving states
to join in "quarantining" the aggressors to avoid the contagion of war.

The stormy reaction that greeted this speech demonstrated that Mr. Roosevelt had made one of his rare miscal-
culations of public opinion. At his press conference the
next day, the President denied that "quarantine" implied
any involvement in sanctions or conferences, taking refuge
in vague assurances that it meant an expansion not an abandonment of neutrality.[2]

Whether or not, as Cordell Hull later declared in his
memoirs, the President's quarantine slogan set back the
campaign for collective action by more than six months, it
is certain that the administration henceforward moved with
great circumspection.[3] Hamstrung by isolationist resistance
to any positive diplomatic intervention, administration
moves to bolster opposition by the democracies to the aggressors degenerated by degrees from "parallel action" to
pious declarations in favor of peaceful negotiation, and
finally to what Henry L. Stimson described as "amoral
drift."

If the popular temper necessitated caution in regard to

1. Samuel I. Rosenman, ed., *The Public Papers and Addresses of Franklin D. Roosevelt* (13 vols. New York, 1938–50), *6*, 406–13.
2. Ibid., pp. 422–24.
3. Cordell Hull, *Memoirs* (2 vols. New York, 1948), *1*, 545.

events in Europe, the President could and did find support for increasingly vigorous preparations for national and hemispheric defense. Both before and after the outbreak of war in September 1939, while the United States remained neutral, the No-Transfer principle emerged once again as the keystone of defense planning, military as well as political. Just as had been the case during the Napoleonic Wars, the Holy Alliance threat, and the first World War, national security demanded that a potential enemy be prevented from acquiring European possessions in the Western Hemisphere to use as bases of operation against positions vital to the United States. In this latest application in a period of overwhelming danger, the No-Transfer principle underwent extensive changes; it was vastly expanded geographically because of the global magnitude of the threat and the technological revolution in warfare, and, as had been the case with the other dicta of the Monroe Doctrine, the No-Transfer principle became a cooperative declaration of the twenty-one American republics, in consonance with the spirit and practice of the Good Neighbor policy.

DIPLOMATIC PREPAREDNESS

The first No-Transfer statement applied, not surprisingly, to Canada rather than to the traditional Caribbean area of American concern. Speaking in Kingston, Ontario, during those fateful weeks when the Czechoslovakian crisis cast deepening shadows over Europe, President Roosevelt took the occasion to affirm Canadian–American solidarity of interest. "The Dominion of Canada is part of the sisterhood of the British Empire. I give you assurance that the people of the United States will not stand idly by if domination of Canadian soil is threatened by another empire."[4]

---

4. Rosenman, 7, 493.

Not since 1778, when General Washington expressed his concern lest Canada be transferred to France, had there been reason to fear a change of sovereignty that might transform that most pacific neighbor into one which constituted a threat to the military security of the United States. But in the war scare that accompanied Hitler's brazen demand for supremacy in Central Europe it was not difficult to imagine a chain reaction of catastrophe which would suddenly place a triumphant aggressor in a position to attack Canada. After the disastrous Allied defeats of 1940, when the Germans overran all of Western Europe and only the beleaguered island bastion of Britain still offered resistance, President Roosevelt implemented his pledge to the Canadian people with the creation of the Permanent Joint Board of Defense, pooling the resources of the great North American republics for continental security.

In a sense, of course, it need hardly be said that the United States would not idly observe an assault on Canada. In diplomacy, however, there are few if any axioms of policy so self-evident that there is nothing to be gained by an explicit statement or restatement of them. In this instance a pronouncement of the No-Transfer principle regarding Canada provided the governments and peoples of the United States, Canada, and any potential aggressor with a valuable education in the nature of their respective national interests.

The administration was considerably less agitated in 1938 about Canada, where the danger was at worst contingent and remote, than about Latin America, whose military weakness, susceptibility to Axis political and economic penetration, and strategic importance called for prompt attention to prevent its becoming an Achilles' heel. Germany and to a lesser extent Italy were making a concerted effort to swing Latin America away from its hemispheric orientation into the orbit of the European dictatorships. Axis embassy staffs multiplied with the addition of military missions, economic experts, and information sections which conducted an unremitting propaganda against the "Colossus of the North," while they tirelessly engaged in organizing their large immigrant minorities into fascist parties ominously reminiscent of those in Austria and the Sudetenland. When, less than two months after Hitler's bloodless victory at Munich, the Eighth International Congress of American States assembled at Lima, Peru, on December 9, 1938, the United States delegation, led by Secretary Hull himself, came prepared with a program designed to meet the Axis challenge. The unanimous adoption of Hull's proposals by the Conference, with only minor emendations, and even more strikingly the support the United States later received from the American republics during the war, represented triumphant justifications of the Good Neighbor policy, of the liquidation of the Caribbean protectorates, and the adherence in Washington to the doctrine of absolute nonintervention promulgated at Buenos Aires in 1936. Nazi efforts to resurrect the bugbear of "Yankee Imperialism" failed signally at Lima.

The most important fruits of the Conference were embodied in the Declaration of Lima, in which the American Republics reaffirmed their "continental solidarity" and their intention to defend themselves against "all foreign intervention or activity" that might threaten "the peace, security or territorial integrity" of any of them. Furthermore, they provided for consultation by the Ministers of Foreign Affairs which could be called for at the initiative of any one of the member states.[5] Clearly a threatened transfer of European colonies in the Western Hemisphere

5. Bemis, *Latin American Policy,* pp. 359–60.

would imperil the security of the Americas, and the first Consultative Meeting of Foreign Ministers held at Panama in September–October 1939 was occupied in part by this problem, while the second meeting at Havana in July 1940 was almost wholly devoted to preventing such a transfer of sovereignty to Germany.

When the anticipated war in Europe came, the American Republics acted with remarkable swiftness to seal off the Hemisphere from the holocaust. The armies of the Third Reich crossed the Polish border on September 1, 1939; Britain and France declared war on September 3; and on September 5, after hurried communication among the major American states, the Secretary of Foreign Affairs of Panama issued an invitation for a meeting of foreign ministers to convene on September 23 at Panama City. From the outset an extraordinary atmosphere of unanimity pervaded the proceedings, unmarred for once even by the customary jealous obstructionism of Argentina. No one doubted that war must be kept away from the New World, or that the power and wealth of the United States entitled it to the position of leadership that accompanied a primary responsibility for hemispheric security. It is not surprising, therefore, that to a great extent the various Resolutions adopted at the Panama meeting constitute a "pan-americanization" of United States neutrality policy, together with well-considered moves designed to cushion the economic dislocations arising out of the loss of European markets.

Of greatest interest here, however, is Resolution XVI, dealing with "Transfer of Sovereignty of Geographic Regions of the Americas Held by Non-American States," which stated "that in case any geographic region of America subject to the jurisdiction of any non-American state should be obliged to change its sovereignty and there should result therefrom a danger to the security of the American

Continent, a consultative meeting such as the one now being held will be convoked with the urgency that the case may require."[6]

Resolution XVI marks the beginning of the end of the sole proprietorship of the United States over the No-Transfer principle—fully shared at Havana ten months later. Although no one doubted that the United States alone possessed the military strength to enforce it, still the No-Transfer principle would be henceforth the common policy of all the American republics, and its application would be the expression of a common determination and responsibility for preserving the balance of power in the New World. Weakly implemented though it was at this time— there was only the agreement to consult about an impending territorial transfer—the inter-American No-Transfer resolution of 1939 constituted impressive evidence of the extent to which the United States had abandoned the condescending paternalism of Theodore Roosevelt's Corollary in favor of a firm commitment of even its most vital concerns to a new basis of cooperative equalitarianism. The admission that American security was now the business of all the American states acting in concert was a long step from the nationalism of Monroe and Adams and a long step toward the collective security of the postwar system of alliances.

But Resolution XVI was at most a tentative move in new directions. Inconspicuously buried among dozens of other resolutions, it enjoyed neither the prominence nor the precision of the No-Transfer statement embodied in the Act of Havana during the crisis of July 1940. What action would be taken in case of a threat? There was only the provision that a consultative meeting would "be convoked

6. S. S. Jones and Denys P. Myers, eds., *Documents on American Foreign Relations, July, 1939 to June, 1940* (2 vols. Boston, 1940), 2, 108.

with the urgency the case might require." More important, what area did the declaration cover? Who could exactly define the limits of "any geographic region of America?" If we assume, without particular justification for doing so, that the "Neutrality Zone" proclaimed at Panama, in which all belligerent activity was prohibited, delimited the region of America, then Greenland and Iceland were excluded from the application of the No-Transfer principle, as well as the Azores, Cape Verde, and Canary Islands—all of them areas of acute concern within a year. In the Pacific the only possession of a non-American power included in the zone was France's tiny Clipperton Island, lying a thousand miles west of Nicaragua.

Actually there were good reasons for leaving these matters comparatively vague. No immediate transfer threat had crystallized, and the Panama Resolution left open the possibility of graded responses to a variety of possible challenges. Past applications of the No-Transfer principle had made it obvious to the European colonial powers that cession of their American possessions to Germany or Japan would be considered by the United States an unfriendly act on the part of the old owners and a hostile act on the part of the new. As far as Washington was concerned, there could be no innocent reason for the aggressor nations acquiring territory adjacent to the American continents.

Finally, it is clear that decisions relating to the scope of the No-Transfer principle and the sanctions to apply to violations of it were conditioned by both military capabilities and strategic doctrine. What was the position of the United States armed forces on these questions?

STRATEGIC MILITARY PLANNING

Shortly after Munich, the Joint Board of the Army and Navy directed the Joint Planning Committee, made up of the heads of the War Plans Divisions of the respective services and their chief assistants, to study "the various practicable courses of action open to the military and naval forces of the United States in the event of (a) violation of the Monroe Doctrine by one or more Fascist powers, and (b) a simultaneous attempt to expand Japanese influence in the Philippines."[7] The planners' report, submitted in April 1939, read against the ominous rumble of aggressor forces on the move in Czechoslovakia and China, led the Joint Board to decide to formulate an entirely new set of war plans to replace the old "color" plans which contemplated war against a single nation (e.g. "Orange," for war with Japan). The five new "Rainbow" plans, sketched out by the end of June 1939 and approved by the President the following October, were based on the probability that the United States would be engaged simultaneously with more than one enemy in more than one theater.

Rainbow I and Rainbow IV, which interest us most here, dealt with defense of the Western Hemisphere, defined for planning purposes as bounded by the International Date Line on the west and 30 degrees west longitude on the east. In the Pacific, therefore, the only important non-American possessions would be the French Marquesas and Society Islands, while in the Atlantic, Greenland was included but not Iceland, or the Cape Verde, Azores, or Canary Islands.[8] Both Rainbow I and IV shared the basic premise that the United States would be fighting alone against the Axis nations and Japan—the democracies, particularly British sea power, being either neutral or neutralized. This was a situation that came perilously near being realized in the desperate months of 1940 and 1941. Rainbow I was really

7. M. Matloff and E. M. Snell, *The War Department: Strategic Planning for Coalition Warfare, 1941–1942* (Washington, 1953), p. 5.

8. Ibid., pp. 6–8.

a plan for partial hemispheric defense, for it contemplated sending forces no further than 10 degrees south latitude, just below the Brazilian and Peruvian bulges, while Rainbow IV called for defense of the entire hemisphere, and possibly operations in the eastern Atlantic. Priority in both plans went to continental security and defense of the Panama Canal and its approaches. Considering the military unpreparedness of the United States in 1939, Rainbow I probably represented the maximum capability of the nation for some time to come.

Planning for hemispheric defense naturally raised the question of bases, in terms of what the nation required for its own use and which positions must be denied to a potential enemy. After reading reports of discussions on these subjects, it becomes clear, as one historian of the Army has remarked, that for American prewar planners the No-Transfer principle constituted practically the entire definition of the Monroe Doctrine.[9] On the whole the Army was less interested than the Navy in acquiring foreign territories for defense purposes, so that the modest suggestions in the Rainbow plans represent a compromise. These called for bases in Trinidad, in Brazil (Natal), in Colombia and Venezuela, at Guayaquil in Ecuador, and on Costa Rica's Cocos Island and Ecuador's Galapagos Islands, as well as the long-desired naval base at Samaná Bay in the Dominican Republic. Clearly these positions would strengthen the air and naval defensive perimeter of the Canal Zone only if no hostile forces established themselves in the area, so that the military's recommendations rested on the explicit assumption that no transfers of territory would be permitted there.[10]

9. Stetson Conn and Byron Fairchild, *The Framework of Hemisphere Defense* (Washington, 1958), p. 12.
10. Ibid., pp. 10–13.

The extent to which the No-Transfer principle underlay strategic thinking is illustrated in two Army studies made in 1936 and 1940 on the question of what, if any, territories belonging to nations owing debts to the United States might be militarily valuable acquisitions. The notion that this country might recoup something on defaulted intergovernmental debts by accepting British and French colonial possessions in the Hemisphere as part payment enjoyed a considerable vogue among disgruntled Americans in the thirties. Insofar as strategic arguments in favor of the scheme were concerned, its advocates received little comfort from military professionals. After an exhaustive survey, the 1936 Army memorandum recommended acquiring only Britain's tiny Fanning, Washington, and Christmas Islands, all in the Pacific, for advanced air bases.[11] The authors make clear, however, the conditions understood in these memoranda:

> The conclusions reached in this study, especially those with reference to the extent to which our security may be threatened because of ownership of colonies in the West Indies by Great Britain and France, were based on the assumption that ownership would not be transferred in the future to some other non-American nation. The transfer of such ownership would be clearly a violation of the Monroe Doctrine, since it would extend the sovereignty and political systems of other European nations to the Western Hemisphere and endanger our peace and security. That France and Britain would commit this unfriendly act is unlikely.

The 1940 memorandum was prepared in response to a series of resolutions in Congress looking toward the acquisi-

11. Memo of Deputy Chief of Staff for Army Chiefs of Staff (Dec. 1, 1936), War Plans Division 3977.

tion of British and French possessions in payment for war debts.[12] It is interesting to observe how events of the intervening four years had shifted attention from the Pacific to the Atlantic, foreshadowing the major strategic decision of the second World War, that the defeat of Hitler should take priority over offensive operations against Japan. The Army now believed that our military situation would be materially strengthened by establishing bases in Trinidad, Newfoundland, or St. Pierre and Miquelon, Bermuda, the British Virgin Islands, and Clipperton Island. This report once more emphasized the proviso that any transfer of sovereignty of foreign possessions in the Hemisphere would menace American security, and concluded with a statement more remarkable for its vigor than for its sensitivity to the constitutional locus of the war-making power: "In the event that the owners concerned should be forced, as a result of military reverses, to consider the transfer of sovereignty of any colonial possession in the Western Hemisphere, the War Department will immediately take such steps as may be indicated at the moment to prevent such transfer to a non-American nation."[13]

A few months after this memorandum was written Congress gave blanket authority to the President to act to prevent transfers of territory in the Hemisphere, but in the meantime it is difficult to imagine what sort of effective action the War Department could have taken without invading legislative prerogatives.

Any decision to implement the No-Transfer principle was necessarily conditioned by the availability of troops to

12. House Concurrent Resolution 49 (Feb. 28, 1940), House Joint Resolution 482, Senate Joint Resolution 482, and Senate Joint Resolution 221 (March 4, 1940). See *Congressional Record*, 76th Cong., 3d Sess., Vol. 86, Pt. II, pp. 2122–24, 2284–88.

13. Memo from the Asst. Chief of Staff for the Chief of Staff (March 29, 1940), War Plans Division 3977/2.

be sent to an endangered area, and even as late as the summer of 1941 the Army doubted its capacity to send defense forces simultaneously to Iceland and the Azores without seriously jeopardizing the security of the continental United States and its outlying possessions. The Army's conservative position on bases in the 1936 and 1940 reports is a partial reflection of the physical and psychological effects of the budgetary starvation visited upon the armed forces by Congress in the decade before Pearl Harbor. In May 1940, when Hitler was sweeping over the Low Countries, Chief of Staff Marshall was still asking Congress only for permission to enlarge the Army to the 280,000 men authorized by the National Defense Act of 1920, not because he felt this figure represented what was necessary for national defense but because he thought this was the most Congress would allow.[14] In addition to the traditional American democratic aversion to a large standing army as a possible instrument of internal oppression and of external entanglement, the pacifism of the thirties brought further restrictions on military appropriations for personnel and equipment, so that the outbreak of the second World War found the United States military establishment virtually "closed for alterations." Deceived as to the realities of twentieth-century power politics by their unique historical experience of almost complete security from attack, Americans assumed they would always have a safe margin of time to prepare, or that at the bugle note a million men could spring to arms overnight. What arms they could spring to was not so clear, given the technical complexity of modern weaponry, for as General Malin Craig warned in 1939, appropriations for equipment could not "be fully transformed into military power for two years."[15]

14. Mark S. Watson, *Chief of Staff: Prewar Plans and Preparations* (Washington, 1950), pp. 37, 168–69.
15. Ibid., p. 85. *Annual Report of Chief of Staff* (June 30, 1939).

Another element governing the military's attitudes toward the possessions of non-American states in this Hemisphere was the traditional American belief that armed forces are to be maintained for defensive purposes only. During the interwar years doctrinal thinking had hardened around a policy of narrow, passive, continental defense, and it was only after the nation was thoroughly alerted to its peril by the Allied *débâcle* in Europe that American military planning began to reflect a swing to dynamic concepts involving positive action to secure the strategic outposts of a vastly expanded hemispheric defense perimeter. The air age had made Iceland, the Azores, and Dakar as important to American security as Cuba had always been. As the crisis deepened abroad, the strategic limits of the Hemisphere were enlarged, and the No-Transfer principle of the Monroe Doctrine stretched to cover areas never before thought of as important to the safety of the New World.

CHAPTER 11

Insulating the Americas

During the deceptive winter quiet of the "Phony War" of 1939–40, the first flush of anxiety about the security of the Americas subsided, giving way to an almost leisurely sense of spaciousness in planning for defense. The chief task appeared to be to insulate the Hemisphere against belligerent activity in a war that might go on indefinitely and indecisively, and which might end after all in an accommodation that would not seriously affect the balance of power in Europe or in the world. The Far Eastern situation commanded much of the attention of official Washington, as Japanese militarists advocated taking advantage of the turbulence in Europe to press their vast imperialistic design to fulfillment. While anxiously observing developments in Asia, it was comforting to think that the French army and British fleet stood watch against fresh incursions by the Nazi aggressor.

Then, in a few shattering weeks, while the American people listened incredulously to the torrent of radio reports and stared aghast at screaming headlines, the *Wehrmacht* swallowed up Denmark and Norway, rolled over the Low Countries, drove the British armies in confusion from the continent, and brought France to her knees in surrender. In seventy days Hitler had completely redrawn the political map of Western Europe, made himself the master of the coastline from the North Cape to the Channel ports of France, and revolutionized the distribution of power in the world.

Under this deluge of disasters American complacency gave way to a frantic effort to mobilize the defenses of the continent against the danger of isolation in a hostile world. In this crisis, as had so often been the case in the past, the No-Transfer principle emerged as a major security policy of the United States. Each German victory brought with it new threats of territorial transfers in the New World— Greenland and Iceland, the Dutch West Indies and the French islands in the Caribbean—all of which the Washington government now felt it necessary for imperious strategic and economic reasons to keep out of belligerent hands. This meant not only a determination that they should not fall under German control, but also, in this transition period when the major directions of United States policy were insensibly shifting from complete isolationism to a kind of tacit nonbelligerency favoring Britain, an uneasy resistance to British, Canadian, and French moves to occupy these areas protectively.

Because American public opinion was so divided, because policy objectives were themselves in such a state of flux, because events in Europe and Asia overwhelmed decisions as they were being made, and because of the unprecedented magnitude and urgency of the situation, applications of the No-Transfer principle in these months are filled with contradictions and indecision. No one doubted Germany must be kept out, but about the Allies there was more difficulty. Even after these questions should be resolved, there would be the further problem of how the No-Transfer principle ought to be applied. Congress and isolationists in general tended to favor the "purchase" of European possessions in exchange for a cancellation of war debts—a final, punitive action which could masquerade as a national defense measure. The military advised unilateral, preclusive occupation of strategic European possessions, while the Department of State insisted—with ultimate success—upon preserving the principle of cooperative, inter-American action sketched out at the Panama consultative meeting the year before.

For purposes of clarity, it will be necessary in this and following chapters to treat each transfer crisis as a separate entity, but it should be kept in mind that they overlapped one another and compounded the severity and urgency of the problem. Furthermore they were only a part of the gargantuan issues involved in attempting to forestall Japanese aggression in the Far East, bolster the Allies in Europe, and secure the Hemisphere against the impending danger of a two-ocean war—all against the hot brakes of isolationist aversion to an involvement which the administration was no longer certain it could or should avoid.

GREENLAND

Before the Nazi absorption of Denmark on April 9, 1940, raised the question of the status of Greenland in an acute form, the United States government had been little concerned with the last of Denmark's colonies. Twenty years earlier, however, Washington had had occasion to assert an interest in any possible transfer of the island. In 1920 the Danish government asked Great Britain to recognize its right to extend its political and economic interests in the whole of Greenland—a claim to sovereignty already acknowledged by the United States as a condition of the cession of the Danish West Indies fours years before. The British government replied that it would agree to this proposition only if granted the right of pre-emptive purchase in case Denmark should consider disposing of Greenland. When word of the British demand reached Washington, Secretary of State Colby hastened to serve notice that

the United States was "not disposed to recognize the existence in a third government of a right of presumption to
acquire this territory," and "accordingly reserves for future
consideration what position it may take in the event of a
specific proposal for such a transfer."[1] In the face of this
caveat, Britain softened her conditions, her concern for
Canadian security yielding before this firm statement of
American interest.

Even on the eve of war in Europe in 1939, Greenland's
importance to American security did not seem great enough
to the Roosevelt administration to warrant negotiations to
purchase it. The Department of State advised against such
action when asked for an opinion in connection with Senator Lundeen's proposed Joint Resolution authorizing the
purchase of Greenland. Secretary of War Woodring deemed
it too far from any "practicable sea or air routes of approach
to the United States" for there to be any strategic value in
acquiring it.[2] A few months later this last statement would
have struck most informed persons as remarkably naive, for
by that time the world had received a graphic lesson from
Hitler in the range and deadly tactical effectiveness of a
modern air force.

The full dimensions of the threat became clear with
Hitler's bloodless occupation of Denmark. The Germans
might demand outright cession of Greenland to the Reich,
or simply administer it for the captive Copenhagen govern-

1. Telegram from Colby to Ambassador Davis in London (June
5, 1920), *Foreign Relations of the United States* (1922), 2, 1–2. See
also *1*, 200, and Tansill, *Purchase of the Danish West Indies*, pp. 493–
96.

2. *Congressional Record*, 76th Cong., 1st Sess., Vol. 84, Pt. VII,
pp. 7211–19. Department of State to Chairman of Senate Foreign
Relations Committee (April 19, 1939), and Secretary of War to
Director of Bureau of the Budget (May 16, 1939), Department of
State Files 859B.014/17, 21.

ment. In either case they would command the great circle
air and shipping routes, be able to attack the North American continent directly, gain important meteorological stations and the world's only commercially workable source of
cryolite, a mineral important in the manufacture of aluminum. The German threat never materialized, but the
United States was equally anxious to prevent a British or
Canadian occupation of Greenland, while resisting suggestions from those powers as well as the Greenland authorities
that it undertake the defense of the island itself. This hands-
off policy grew largely out of a desire to deny Japan a pretext for a "protective" occupation of the Dutch East Indies,
should Hitler make his expected assault on Holland. The
United States eventually dispatched troops to protect
Greenland, but only after having kept the question in
suspense for a year.

United States policy rested on the proposition that
Greenland lay within the Western Hemisphere and was
therefore subject to the No-Transfer principle of the Monroe Doctrine. Because the inclusion of Greenland in the
area of primary American concern represented a notable
departure from traditional practice, there was considerable
soul-searching in Washington to decide whether the Doctrine could indeed be applied. On the day the Germans
raced into Denmark, the Under Secretary of State, Mr.
Welles, received an interesting memorandum on this question prepared by an officer of the Department, which included a fairly accurate and detailed sketch of the development of the No-Transfer principle from the "Madison
Doctrine" of 1811 to the Lansing *démarche* of 1915. Here
is a rare instance when an application of the principle has
been urged in a context of precedent, tradition, and continuity. The author concluded that Greenland is certainly
within the Western Hemisphere as geographers conven-
tionally define it, but significantly added that the question

The Neutrality Zone of the Panama
Conference 1939 ··········

F.D.R.'s extended patrol zone
of May 1941

Line of Welles' draft message
May 20, 1941 ·—·—·—

German blockade zone ———

was essentially not one of geography but one of policy.[3] Security considerations have always been the key to applications of the No-Transfer principle, where the national interest overrules any sensitivity to fine technicalities. The "hemisphere" has characteristically been less a legal or geographical than a political concept.

There remained the question of what specific action to take in regard to Greenland. Curiously enough, no direct statement was made to Germany at this time. The day following Hitler's invasion of Denmark, President Roosevelt conferred with the Danish Minister, Henrik de Kauffmann, who remarked to newspapermen on leaving that he and the President had agreed that "Greenland belongs to the American continent." Mr. Roosevelt confirmed this in a press conference the next day, but became evasive when asked about the application of the Monroe Doctrine to Greenland.[4] He could be certain that the cautious warning in his agreement with de Kauffmann would be transmitted to Berlin, and he was not ready to hurl down the gauntlet before Hitler until American public opinion had crystallized in favor of firm action, and until the United States had the military forces to support it.

The main difficulty lay in convincing the British and Canadian governments that Greenland was primarily an American problem to be dealt with by the United States. Secretary Hull accordingly called in the British Ambassador on April 12 to canvass the Greenland situation. Hull reminded Lord Lothian of the United States note to Britain

3. Memo entitled "Applicability of the Monroe Doctrine if Germany should lay claim to the possessions of Denmark in the Western Hemisphere as a result of the absorption of Denmark" (April 9, 1940), File 859A.01/43. See also memo from the Legal Adviser to the Secretary of State (April 12, 1940), File 859B.01/150.

4. W. L. Langer and S. E. Gleason, *The Challenge to Isolation* (New York, 1952), p. 430.

of 1920, saying in a friendly way that "without assuming that the Government of Great Britain has any thought of interfering with the present status of Greenland . . . it is deemed appropriate to call attention to the communication of 1920 and to say that the position of the Government of the United States remains unchanged." He referred to the note as an "express application of the Monroe Doctrine by the United States," adding that "there appears to be no serious question about Greenland forming part of this hemisphere."[5] Lothian replied with the utmost cordiality that he could see no difficulties in adjusting this matter, and was reported later to have stated publicly that neither Britain nor Canada would move into Greenland until there was an immediate threat of German action.[6]

The Canadian government proved not to share the genial complacency of the British Ambassador, and displayed some irritation that he should presume to speak, even unofficially, on their behalf.[7] Lord Lothian, of course, acted in full awareness that anti-British sentiment was strong among certain groups in America, and perhaps he felt he could count on Canada to carry the ball in a problem that involved Canadian security even more than it did that of the United States. If so, he was right, for the Canadian government proved to be most concerned about Greenland, and while giving assurances that it would take no action until it had learned the views of the United States and discussed possible alternatives, it deeply unsettled Washington by announcing that it was considering sending a small defensive force to prevent German landings, protect the cryolite

5. Aide-mémoire to Lord Lothian (April 13, 1940), File 859B.-01/138a. Hull, *Memoirs,* p. 755.

6. Langer and Gleason, *The Challenge,* pp. 430–31.

7. Memo of conversation between Mr. Reid of the Canadian Legation and Mr. Hickerson of the State Department (April 17, 1940), File 859B.01/147.

mine, and aid the local population.[8] The Department of State strongly urged that Canada join in our policy of inaction, emphasizing that we must not provide "other large countries" with an excuse for seizing the colonies of occupied European nations. Only two days previously Mr. Hull had had a disturbing conversation with the Japanese ambassador, who compared Japan's interest in the Netherlands East Indies with the concern voiced by the United States over Iceland and Greenland in the name of the Monroe Doctrine.[9] The Canadian Minister acknowledged the force of Hull's point but made it clear that Canada could leave the matter in American hands only if it were certain that the United States would undertake full responsibility for defending Greenland. This, of course, was precisely the commitment Washington was not yet prepared to make.

Canadian doubts about American determination to counter a German move in Greenland with force, if required, were hardly dispelled by President Roosevelt's remarks during his meeting with Prime Minister Mackenzie King at Warm Springs the last week in April. When Mr. King raised the question of Greenland, Mr. Roosevelt, despite the fact that he had been thoroughly briefed by Hull on Canadian touchiness and our own cautious policy, left King with the impression that he relied on the British navy to take care of any Nazi attack. Alarmed, the Canadians again pressed for assurances that if they stepped aside, the United States would guarantee the safety of Greenland.

Meanwhile, pressures for action were building up in other quarters. Representative Hamilton Fish of New York introduced a new bill for the purchase of Greenland, ac-

8. Unless otherwise indicated, this account of our discussions with Canada about Greenland rests on Langer and Gleason, *Challenge to Isolation,* pp. 431–35, and Hull, *Memoirs,* pp. 755–58.

9. Herbert Feis, *The Road to Pearl Harbor* (Princeton, 1950), pp. 52–53.

companied by the recommendation that it should "be the
policy of the United States to oppose the transfer or further
acquisition of any islands or possessions within the American sphere of influence by any European or Asiatic
power."[10] The Department of State also at this time found
it necessary to sidestep an unwelcome request from the
Governors of Greenland for a United States protectorate.

Clearly some positive acts were necessary to appease
critics of the policy of inaction. Arrangements were made
to send relief supplies to the Greenlanders through the
American Red Cross, and on May 10 the Coast Guard cutter
Comanche sailed on the first of several visits to Greenland.
The apprehensions of the Greenland authorities were also
somewhat assuaged by the establishment of an American
Consulate at Godthaab on May 25, which gave them a more
direct line of communication with Washington. Finally,
some appeasement was offered the Canadians by acting on
their suggestion that a light gun be sent to the Greenlanders
for the defense of the cryolite mine at Ivigtut.

The Department of State was evidently aware that these
feeble gestures might not long dissuade the British and
Canadians from landing troops in Greenland. In late May
consternation greeted reports from Greenland that the
Canadian vessel *Nascopie* with soldiers and Royal Canadian
Mounted Police aboard, and the British ship *Julius Thom-
sen*, carrying a number of naval officers, had appeared in
Greenland waters. In view of the recent landing of British

10. *Congressional Record*, 76th Cong., 3d Sess., Vol. 86, Pt. V, p.
4714. See also the letter from the Congresswoman from Massachusetts
to the Secretary of State (April 26, 1940), urging action to forestall the
occupation of Greenland by a third power: File 859B.01/153. The
chief object of Mrs. Rogers' concern, judging from her remarks in
the House, was England: *Congressional Record*, 76th Cong., 3d Sess.,
Vol. 86, Pt. IV, pp. 4641–42.

troops in Iceland, the Greenland authorities were nervous, and Washington hardly less so. After dispatching *Comanche* as a chaperone, the State Department asked for explanations from Britain and Canada, which to their relief were quickly forthcoming and revealed no basis for anxiety.[11]

A continuous source of friction and a kind of counterpoint to Canadian–American discussions of Greenland were the acrimonious private negotiations between the Pennsylvania Salt Company and the Aluminium Company of Canada about the allocation of Greenland cryolite production. The American concern had formerly supplied the North American market with refined cryolite, while Danish refineries supplied the rest of the world. Now that no shipments were going to Denmark, the Greenland authorities wished Pennsalt to expand production, but the Aluminium Company of Canada aggressively insisted on entering into refining for itself, and succeeded in forcing an agreement assuring it the Canadian, British, and French markets.[12] Although neither the Canadian Ministry of External Affairs nor the American Department of State took part officially in these talks, they had representatives present as observers,

11. Memo of conversation on reported dispatch of British Naval Officers and Canadian Police to Greenland (June 3, 1940), Messrs. Berle and Cumming of State Dept., Mahoney and Reid of Canadian Legation, File 859B.01/210. Memo of conversation on same subject (June 3, 1940), Mr. Berle of State Dept., Mr. Millar of British Embassy, File 859B.01/211. Memo of conversation on same subject (June 5, 1940), Messrs. Berle and Cumming of State Dept. and Mahoney and Reid of Canadian Legation, File 859B.01/212.

12. Letter from the American Consul-General at Godthaab to the Division of European Affairs of the State Dept. (May 9, 1940), File 859B.637/1. Memo of conversation on the allocation of cryolite production from the Ivigtut mines (May 21, 1940), File 859B.01/206. Memo on final agreement on cryolite distribution (June 11, 1940), File 859B.637/18.

and the Americans came away with the distinct impression that pressures from private economic interests accounted at least in part for the strong position on Greenland assumed rather against their will by the Canadian government.[13]

Whatever the force of this hypothesis, security considerations alone are enough to explain Canadian anxieties after Hitler had emerged victorious in the Low Countries and France, leaving Britain in mortal danger. In the face of the realities of the situation, the United States slightly relaxed its jealous quarantine in the Greenland area, but not to the extent of abandoning its opposition to any permanent lodgment there by Britain or Canada. Early in September, Canada notified Washington that a German-controlled Norwegian vessel, the *Furenak,* was proceeding to Eastern Greenland with the evident intention of setting up a meteorological station and landing field.[14] Assistant Secretary of State Berle telephoned the President to ask what position to adopt if Britain acted to intercept the *Furenak.* Mr. Roosevelt replied that Canadian security was obviously involved, and that since the United States Navy was not patrolling these waters, we could not very well object to defensive action taken by Britain. He suggested that a note be sent to the British and Canadians reminding them that the United States considered Greenland a part of the Western Hemisphere and therefore could not acquiesce in any operations which constituted a permanent occupation or change in the status of territory.[15] The familiar No-Transfer formula was accordingly repeated verbally and, after the

---

13. Personal letter from Hugh Cumming of the Division of European Affairs to James K. Penfield, American Consul-General at Godthaab (Dec. 5, 1940), File 859B.637/24.

14. Memo, secret (Sept. 5, 1940), File 859B.01/292.

15. Memo of telephone conversation between Mr. Berle and the President (Sept. 7, 1940), File 859B.01/291.

capture of the *Furenak,* in notes to British, Canadian, and Norwegian representatives in Washington.[16]

The passive policy of preserving the *status quo ante* in Greenland had nearly run its course, however. The more the Battle of the Atlantic mounted in fury, and the more firmly America became established as the arsenal of democracy, the more obvious it was that the corollary of any hands-off for third powers must be the active defense of Greenland by United States forces. In November, when the Nazi-controlled press in Denmark charged that the Americans were building air bases in the Danish colony, the Department of State was able to issue a categorical denial, but within three months negotiations were under way on an airbase agreement that would permit the dispatch of troops to Greenland.[17]

ICELAND

In general, the United States government desired that Iceland, like Greenland, should undergo no change in status during the war, but differing circumstances made the problem less complicated than in the case of Greenland. Iceland was not a colony, but bore a relationship to Denmark almost identical with that of the British Dominions to the United Kingdom, so that as soon as the Germans invaded the mother country the Icelandic Parliament exercised its constitutional right to assume executive functions

16. Memo of conversation of Mr. Cumming of the State Dept., Mr. Butler of the British Embassy, and Mr. Reid of the Canadian Legation (Sept. 11, 1940), File 859B.01/292. Notes of Sept. 23, 1940, File 859B.01/293.

17. Telegram from the American chargé in Copenhagen to State Dept. (Nov. 13, 1940), File 859B.01/320. Telegram from the Acting Secretary of State to the American chargé in Copenhagen (Nov. 14, 1940), File 859B.01/321.

formerly vested in the King. The United States at once recognized the temporary independence of Iceland by receiving an Icelandic diplomatic mission and establishing an American consulate at Reykjavik.

None of this had much to do with defending Iceland against a Nazi invasion. The American government suffered from no shortage of authorities who would certify that Iceland was partly, if not wholly, within the Western Hemisphere as cartographers customarily defined it—that is, between 20 degrees west longitude and 160 east longitude.[18] But as in the case of Greenland, the decision to apply the No-Transfer principle of the Monroe Doctrine was based on immediate political considerations rather than on scientific authority. The fact that Greenland could not successfully be defended against hostile air power based on Iceland argued in favor of including the latter in the scope of the Doctrine. On the other hand, Iceland was closer to Europe than to America, her economic ties were European, and there were still the familiar deterrents— anxiety over setting a precedent for Japanese occupation of the Dutch East Indies, and sensitivity to isolationist charges of interventionism—not to mention the fact that no United States troops were available for the defense of Iceland.

Under these circumstances, Washington received without visible irritation the news of a surprise occupation of

18. See memo from the Geographer of the State Dept. (S. W. Boggs) to the Division of Research and Publication (May 20, 1940), File 859B.014/36. Also a letter from Mr. Boggs to Congresswoman Rogers (June 8, 1940), Jones and Myers, eds., _Documents on American Foreign Relations_, p. 95. Mr. Boggs has also contributed a learned and graceful article on the whole subject of the concept of "This Hemisphere," in the _Department of State Bulletin, 12_ (May 6, 1945), 845–50. See further the extension of the remarks of Congressman Shanley of Connecticut, who cites the cartographical authority of Col. Martin of the Library of Congress, _Congressional Record,_ 76th Cong. 3d Sess., Vol. 86, Pt. XIV, pp. 2186–88.

Iceland on May 10 by British and Canadian ground forces, accompanied by air and naval units. Any ruffled feathers were at once smoothed when Britain volunteered assurances that there would be no interference with the existing administration of the island and that their forces would be withdrawn at the conclusion of hostilities.[19] In the light of our present knowledge that the Nazis were in fact perfecting plans for a descent upon Iceland, both the secrecy and speed of the British operations now appear to have been absolutely necessary to secure the northern approaches to the United Kingdom.[20] The United States let the Iceland situation ride until a year later, when a replacement of British troops with American forces began. By that time the American policy of all-out aid to Britain short of war required Washington to assume responsibility for defending the Icelandic way station on the great circle route.

ARUBA AND CURAÇAO

In many respects the situation confronting the United States in the Dutch islands of Aruba and Curaçao paralleled that in Iceland, and the temporary disposition of the issues raised was much the same, although the initial reaction in Washington was quite different. On May 10, as the Nazi armies began their massive thrust into the Low Countries, Britain not only landed forces in Iceland but also secretly sent a smaller detachment to assist the Dutch in protecting the highly important oil refineries in Curaçao. A handful of French troops simultaneously landed on Aruba for the same purpose. The chief danger they apprehended was that German nationals employed there and on the mainland might

19. Telegram from the American Ambassador in London to the Secretary of State (May 10, 1940), File 859A.01/44.

20. *Fuehrer Conferences on Matters Dealing with the German Navy, 1940* (Washington, Office of Naval Intelligence, 1947), *1*, 60–66.

sabotage the indispensable flow of Venezuelan oil through the refineries to the Allied war machine.

The American government had no quarrel with the importance of British objectives here, but it took instant and violent exception to the way the action was carried out. It was one thing not to consult ahead of time with the United States about the landing in remote Iceland, but the Dutch West Indies were another matter, lying as they do along the southern approaches to the Panama Canal, in the heart of the region traditionally guarded by the Monroe Doctrine and more recently by the Declaration of Panama, from any European intervention or change of sovereignty. Britain had not so rudely challenged the interests and prestige of the United States in the Americas since President Cleveland's day.

Secretary Hull immediately summoned the British Ambassador for an explanation. He made certain that Lothian understood the gravity of the situation by remarking with icy politeness that the United States assumed Britain had no intention of violating the Monroe Doctrine.[21] He went on to observe that the American Republics were bound to be alarmed about the possible transfer of the Dutch islands, since Britain had not seen fit to give prior assurances to the contrary, and alluded significantly to the acute concern felt by the United States over the possibility that Japan might construe the Allied action as a direct precedent for landing troops in the Netherlands East Indies.

Lord Lothian's first reaction was to inquire with blunt irritability whether the United States was prepared to guarantee the oil resources on Curaçao against sabotage. Hull sidestepped this awkward question by insisting that he was discussing the appropriateness of Britain's arbitrary mode of operation and not the purpose of the landings. At length

21. Memo of conversation, Secretary of State and the British Ambassador (May 10, 1940), File 856B.01/20. Hull, *Memoirs*, p. 815.

Lothian conceded the point, and promised to take the matter up with London at once. Two days later the British government vouchsafed an entirely satisfactory statement, in which they explained that (1) they were acting at the request of and under the authority of the Netherlands government, (2) they would stay only until adequate Dutch forces were available, and that in any case they would withdraw their forces at the end of hostilities, and (3) they had no intention of altering the status of the islands. Thus ended this challenge to the No-Transfer principle.[22]

One or two things remain to be said about the episode which underline the points made by Hull in his conversation with Lothian. The first of these concerns the malignant shadow of Japan, which had already clouded the Greenland question but which now took on added substance with the imminent fall of Holland. Britain, the Netherlands, and the United States were equally anxious to avoid providing Japan with any pretext for seizing the oil, bauxite, and rubber of the Dutch East Indies, so that Hull's warnings about the danger of the landings in Aruba and Curaçao were not slow in making an impression in London and The Hague. The Dutch government hastened to make it clear that the Allies were acting on their invitation, and even persuaded the Department of State to request that corrections be made by certain press and radio commentators in the United States—particularly those on the West Coast whose reports reached Japan—who had referred to the "occupation" of the Dutch West Indies.[23]

22. Hull, *Memoirs,* pp. 815–16. Also memo of conversation, the Assistant Secretary of State and the British Ambassador (May 11, 1940), File 856B.01/18.

23. Memo of conversation, Counselor of the Netherlands Legation and the Political Adviser of the Department of State (May 11, 1940), File 856B.01/27. Telegram from the Assistant Secretary of State to a San Francisco radio station (May 12, 1940), File 856B.01/11a.

At Hull's suggestion, the British government at once publicly confirmed the fact that they had no intention of intervening in the Dutch East Indies, but it is interesting to observe that Washington at this time (May 15) declined British and Australian requests for the dispatch of United States naval forces to Singapore and for an extension of the No-Transfer principle to cover the Dutch East Indies.[24] Such a commitment was too provocative, too far beyond the military capabilities of the nation to consider seriously, no matter how keenly the administration felt that Japan must be prevented from accomplishing this particular piece of aggression.

The threat was by no means illusory, but it was not in exactly the form Hull pictured it. He was led astray by a particularly nerve-wracking conversation with the Japanese ambassador on May 16, the day following Holland's surrender, concerning the Allied move in Aruba and Curaçao. The Secretary of State found himself on the defensive, faced witht the familiar Japanese attempt to draw an analogy between the Monroe Doctrine and Japan's interests in Manchuria, China, and the East Indies. Hull suspected that Horinouchi's probing questions about the Allied landings in the West Indies were aimed at developing a justification for Japanese intervention in the Dutch East Indies, and his austere patriotism aroused, he carefully reviewed the conditions under which Britain and France had acted, and once again forcefully demonstrated the contrast between America's openly defensive policies in the Caribbean and Japan's exclusionist imperialism in Asia. It is now clear from Japanese records that the Yonai cabinet genuinely sought assurances at this time out of a fear either that Germany or Britain would arrange a surprise transfer of the Dutch East Indies, or that the Japanese military would take

24. Feis, *Road to Pearl Harbor,* p. 57.

matters into their own hands, against the wishes of the civilian government.[25]

Besides the shadow of Japan, Hull also invoked in quite another context the shadow of the other American republics in his remarks to Lothian, pointing out the serious consequences that might follow any misapprehension among them that Britain intended to seize the Dutch West Indies permanently. The British government was made aware of the obligation contracted by the United States at the Panama Conference to consult with its neighbors about any threatened transfer of European colonial possessions in the Hemisphere, but Washington had no desire to take any such formal steps in connection with the British action, and London's prompt disavowals in fact made them unnecessary.

Of the Latin American states, only Venezuela exhibited any real interest in a consultative meeting on this question. There was a good deal of sentiment there in favor of annexing the nearby Dutch islands, which were assuredly an integral part of the Venezuelan oil industry.[26] The Department of State successfully quieted Venezuela's agitation, however, first by forwarding Britain's assurances, and later by holding forth the prospect of the full-dress meeting on the danger of transfers of territory scheduled to be held soon at Havana.[27]

During the early stages of the war, then, in Greenland, Iceland, and the Dutch West Indies, challenges to the No-

25. Hull, *Memoirs*, pp. 891–93. Feis, pp. 57–58.

26. Report of conversation between American chargé in Caracas and the Foreign Minister of Venezuela (May 8, 1940), File 856B.01/8.

27. Dispatch from the United States Embassy in Caracas to State Dept. (May 10, 1940) and instructions from State to Embassy in Caracas (May 11, 1940), File 856B.01/4. Also note from the Venezuelan Ambassador to the Secretary of State (July 3, 1940), Department of State Files, 710.Consultation (2)/337.

Transfer principle of inter-American diplomacy came from the hasty defensive maneuvers of the Allies, not from the Nazi Reich. The United States government, though not without understanding of and even sympathy for the desperate situation in which the Atlantic powers found themselves, could scarcely be expected to ignore actions which threatened to bring war closer to the Americas, to breach the defensive barrier declared at Panama, and perhaps to foreshadow permanent changes of status in territories within the area covered by the Monroe Doctrine. In Greenland the proposed landings were prevented by steady diplomatic pressure and evasive tactics; in Iceland and the Dutch islands Washington registered its complaints against *faits accomplis* but let them stand after receiving assurances that the action was temporary, because American forces were simply not available to perform an admittedly vital defensive mission.

Certainly there was no feeling in Washington that American security was directly endangered by these Allied moves, as there would have been had Germany made them, but at the most a sense of irritation at evidences of an aggressive inconsiderateness which embarrassed the United States in its relations with Latin America and which could have had grave consequences in Asia.

CHAPTER 12

The Choice of Means

The accumulating disasters suffered by the Western democracies in May and June 1940 produced a profound effect in the United States. In stunning succession the Nazi armies swept over the "impassable" water barriers of Holland, crashed through the forest of the Ardennes to flank the supposedly impregnable Maginot Line. With Panzer units raging almost at will through the French and Flemish countryside they drove the King of Belgium to surrender, enveloped the French and British armies, and swiftly forced France herself to sue for an armistice. Britain alone remained in the field, staunchly resolute but in deadly peril of invasion, her navy terribly vulnerable from the air in the narrow seas and her merchant fleet open to submarine attacks. Her armies were weakened by the loss of equipment that lay abandoned in flight on the roads and beaches of Belgium and France, and her air power was locked in dubious battle with the numerically superior Luftwaffe for control of the skies above the Channel.

Something like a wave of panic gripped the American people as these tumultuous events unfolded. Gone was the complete assurance of eventual Allied victory, and gone with it was last-ditch isolationism. There were few now who would suggest that the European struggle bore little relation to American security. If politics did not yet stop at the water's edge, isolationism was at least no longer a strong partisan issue. When the Republican National Convention met to choose a candidate to oppose Mr. Roosevelt, they nominated Wendell Willkie, a dark-horse former Democrat whose views on foreign policy were, if anything, more fervently internationalist than the President's.

Spurred by an aroused public opinion, Congress abruptly abandoned its niggardly attitude toward military appropriations and actually authorized expenditures in excess of the amounts requested by the War and Navy Departments. Funds were voted for a vast air armada, a greatly expanded navy, and the largest peacetime army in the nation's history. Selective Service legislation was framed and enacted in a few weeks' time, though not without difficulties from a hard-core opposition.

Much of the impetus for this heightened tempo of military preparation came from a general conviction that the Hemisphere was in imminent danger of Axis penetration. The American public as well as official circles felt that Britain might well go down to defeat and that the military, political, and economic vulnerability of the republics of Latin America was a weak spot that Hitler would surely exploit at his earliest opportunity. A Roper poll taken in June revealed that 78 per cent of those questioned believed Hitler would attempt to extend his influence to Latin America, while 63 per cent thought he would try to seize territory in the New World.[1]

Clearly the logical place for Germany to begin an extension of power to the Hemisphere would have been the American colonies of defeated European nations. The United States government naturally bent every effort to prevent such transfers, and it is no exaggeration to say that in mid-1940 the No-Transfer principle was the nation's most important single security policy. And what is most remarkable about this period is not the unanimous support

1. *Fortune,* 22 (1940), folded insert.

of the goals of the principle but the rich diversity of means for achieving them that were suggested or tried in the emergency created by the fall of France—a showcase of alternative methods for preserving the colonial status quo in the Americas, all within the range of practical policy.

There were, for example, numerous schemes involving the purchase of European possessions in the Hemisphere in return for various considerations, and others for the long-term lease of bases by the United States. Military planners tended to urge direct, preclusive occupation, with or without prior negotiation with the owners, while the Department of State argued for some form of inter-American trusteeship of the sort finally embodied in the Act of Havana. There were also direct negotiations wth the local authorities in the French West Indies, ending in an agreement to neutralize their territories. Many of these approaches are relatively novel in the history of the No-Transfer principle, but resort was also had to the traditional caveat directed to Germany, Italy, and France, supported in this instance by a Joint Resolution of Congress, which marks the noteworthy revival of a technique not used since 1811.

A brief examination of each of the alternatives—their genesis, how and why they were accepted, rejected, modified, or combined—is worth while not only in connection with the development of the No-Transfer principle but also as a study in the intricacies of gauging the national interest and in the selection of means appropriate to immediate ends and long-term policy objectives.

PURCHASE

There is no particular novelty in the suggestion that the United States should purchase strategically located European possessions in the Western Hemisphere in order to eliminate the danger of transfer to another power. The first of several proposals to purchase Cuba was made by President Polk, and the immediate decision to buy the Danish West Indies in 1917 can be traced to rumors of German interest in the islands.

The popularity enjoyed by the purchase idea during the late thirties rested on considerations that went beyond the perfectly valid military objectives of denying use of these territories to a potential aggressor and completing an outlying screen of defenses for the continental United States and the Panama Canal. For a number of years before the outbreak of war in Europe several nationalistic organizations and certain newspapers with strongly isolationist and neutralist editorial policies had been urging acquisition of British and French colonial possessions in this Hemisphere as part settlement of war and reconstruction debt payments then in default. This proved a captivating scheme to a public undergoing the rigors of the Great Depression, whose innocence of international economics kept their responses on the war debts question at the general level of President Coolidge's "they hired the money, didn't they?" It found favor also with politicians whose Anglophobe constituencies loved to see the Lion's tail twisted periodically, and with those many Americans for whom anticolonialism was a traditional, if vague, article of faith.

The deepening European war crisis early in 1939 evoked the first of a series of purchase proposals in Congress. Shortly after General Arnold of the Army Air Forces told a Senate committee that the chief danger to the United States of attack by the Luftwaffe lay in the possibility that Hitler might seize Caribbean bases, Senators McNary and Lodge introduced a resolution to accept strategic raw materials and title to or lease of bases in European possessions in lieu of war debts payments.[2] The following month the

2. Langer and Gleason, *Challenge to Isolation*, p. 623. See also *Christian Science Monitor* (March 1, 1939), p. 1.

chairman of the Senate Foreign Relations Committee sent to the Department of State for comment two proposed resolutions to authorize the purchase of Greenland and of Curaçao and Dutch Guiana. In both cases the State Department replied that they considered it inadvisable to open such negotiations at the moment.[3]

The Administration was no more receptive to similar projects a year later. On February 28, 1940, Representative Case of South Dakota introduced a resolution authorizing the purchase of Caribbean bases to be paid for partly in gold to be withdrawn from the Treasury's stabilization fund and partly in credits on war debt account, and a few days later Senator Reynolds sponsored a like measure applying only to British West Indian possessions and British Honduras.[4]

More will be said later about the attitude of the President and the Department of State toward these matters, but briefly stated, their objection to the purchase proposals rested on a conviction that there were better ways of guarding the national security than by abandoning an established policy of seeking no further territorial expansion, and by entering on a course that would certainly cause needless friction with both the colonial powers and Latin America.

If domestic political considerations had been the principal yardstick applied to the question, undoubtedly the solution by purchase for war debts would have been most satisfactory, for it was widely popular with the groups most bitterly opposed to administration foreign policies in general. Variations on this scheme also won approval. A poll taken in June 1940 on the question of whether to accept

3. Proposed Senate Joint Resolution 119 for the purchase of Greenland, and Proposed Senate Joint Resolution 120 for the purchase of Curaçao and Surinam (April 19, 1939), File 859B.014/17, 20.

4. House Concurrent Resolution 49 (Feb. 28, 1940), and Senate Joint Resolution 221 (March 4, 1940): *Congressional Record,* 76th Cong., 3d Sess., Vol. 86, Pt. II, pp. 2122–24, 2284–88.

bases in British and French possessions in return for credits to be extended for purchases of war materials found 61 per cent of those questioned responding favorably.[5] There seems little reason to doubt that the lengthy education on the strategic value of European possessions received through discussion of various purchase plans had something to do with making the destroyer-bases deal with Britain more palatable to the American public than it might otherwise have been.

PRECLUSIVE OCCUPATION

The smashing German victories of May 1940 had an electric effect not only on Congress and the public at large but on American military leaders. Almost overnight an entire defensive deployment based on the unstated assumption that the British and French fleets would continue to secure the Atlantic approaches to the Hemisphere had to be hastily recast to take account of the distinct possibility that the United States would have to go it alone. The skeleton blueprint for last-ditch hemispheric defense, Rainbow IV, now became the basis for detailed planning, with the question of denying Hitler the use of European possessions near our shores a matter of immediate and major concern.

As the steel pincers of the Wehrmacht's armored columns were closing about the Allied forces in northern France, the Army Chief of Staff in Washington received a memorandum on May 21, presumably from the Secretary of the General Staff, which advised that "in view of the present world conditions, it is believed that this country should take immediate steps to acquire British and French possessions in the Atlantic. . . . If Germany is victorious over France and

5. Elmo Roper, public opinion survey in *Fortune,* 22 (1940), folded insert.

England in the very near future . . . establishment of German air bases on certain key islands in the Atlantic before the year is over is not a fantastic dream."[6]

It was too early to take decisive action on the question of European possessions, but it was apparent that it must have a high priority among strategic objectives. This fact was emphasized in an important memorandum submitted to the Army Chief of Staff the next day by the War Plans Division, which reviewed the critical military position the United States might occupy in the event of a complete German victory, and urged a major decision on the missions of the armed services in the contemplated emergency.[7] Since it was necessary to prepare for the extreme contingency, the memorandum presented a somber picture of the nation beleaguered on every side—a possible Japanese attack from Asia, a British defeat in Europe, and Nazi-inspired revolts in Latin America, particularly in Brazil and Mexico, followed by an actual German thrust into the Hemisphere. Given the military weakness of the United States at the moment, any attempt to deal with all these threats at once would have resulted in a suicidal dispersal of forces; the planners suggested that some decision be made on which areas would receive priority. Their own conclusion was that the United States would have to confine its efforts to "conduct of offensive-defensive operations in South America in defense of the Western Hemisphere and of our own vital interests; such limited offensive operations in Mexico as the situation may require; possible protective occupation of European possessions in the Western Hemisphere; and the

6. Memo (unsigned) for Chief of Staff, Office of the Chief of Staff, Emergency Measures, 39–40, Binder 2. See also Watson, *Prewar Plans,* pp. 105, 477.

7. Memo fom War Plans Division to Chief of Staff (May 22, 1940), Watson, *Prewar Plans,* pp. 105–6, 477. Conn and Fairchild, *Framework of Hemisphere Defense,* p. 47.

defense of the Continental United States and its overseas possessions east of the 180th meridian."

General Marshall was in complete accord with these views, and immediately showed the memorandum to the President, Admiral Stark, and Under Secretary of State Welles, all of whom agreed that there must be no involvement with Japan in the Western Pacific and that the South American situation took precedence over others.[8] This basic strategic decision led to the revival of Rainbow IV, the war plan which most nearly corresponded to prevailing conditions, and work began at once on elaborating its skeleton provisions.

The next few days witnessed feverish discussion in Washington of the problem of European possessions. The day following his meeting with Marshall, Admiral Stark directed the Navy War Plans Division to draw up a plan "for occupying Allied and Dutch West Indies and American possessions, to prevent such from falling into the hands of Germany by surrender or cession."[9] The next day, May 25, having received reports from British intelligence that the Germans were contemplating an early attack on the Guianas with a force of six thousand men, President Roosevelt directed the naval and military chiefs to prepare plans for supporting the Brazilian government against Axis-bred revolts.[10] Meanwhile, Army War Plans Division submitted a memorandum to General Marshall which stressed particularly the importance of British possessions in the Hemisphere to American defense, and suggested that the Department of State be approached as to the advisability of early diplomatic overtures to Great Britain and perhaps Canada, to get permission for United States occupation of

8. Watson, *Prewar Plans*, p. 106. Langer and Gleason, *Challenge to Isolation*, p. 475.

9. Watson, *Prewar Plans*, p. 106.

10. Langer and Gleason, p. 626. Watson, p. 106.

several positions stretching from Newfoundland to Trinidad, "in the event of so complete a German victory in Europe that these territories might fall into German hands by surrender or cession."[11] Here is a graphic indication of how desperate Britain's plight appeared to Washington military circles. The destroyer bases deal the following September relieved the Army's anxiety about British possessions, but by that time the danger of an immediate invasion of Britain was fading.

The Army memorandum on British possessions envisaged prior negotiations with the European owner for permission to land troops, but the Navy report covering all European possessions, prepared in response to Admiral Stark's directive of May 24, significantly omitted any such provision.[12] In fact the Navy planners, laboring during those chaotic days when the British Expeditionary Force was being delivered from the beaches at Dunkirk, went to the radical length of advising that in case Germany demanded any American possessions in its peace terms to the defeated nations, the United States in the interests of national defense ought to assert sovereignty over such territories, acting without prior negotiation or publicity. While the plan contemplated eventual return of the colonies to their former owners, they were to be ruled as United States territory in the interim.

One is tempted to observe that this plan illustrates the truth of the old saying that war is too important to be left to the generals, but considering the swiftness with which Allied resistance was collapsing when the report was submitted, it is not difficult to understand how such drastic action might have seemed necessary. At any rate, the Joint

11. Memo of Assistant Chief of Staff, War Plans Division for Chief of Staff (May 27, 1940), War Department Files, War Plans Division, 4175–79.

12. Watson, p. 106. Conn and Fairchild, p. 48.

Planning Committee itself altered these provisions to permit an attempt to secure approval of the European governments before occupying their possessions when they submitted their plan to the Joint Board on May 30.[13]

In roughly this form the plan was incorporated into Joint Army-Navy War Plan 4 (Rainbow IV), of which Joint Task Number 1 of Section 5 is entitled, "Establish United States Sovereignty in British, French, Dutch and Danish Possessions in the Western Hemisphere."[14] Because of the urgency of the situation, completion of Rainbow IV proceeded with extraordinary speed. On June 7 the Joint Board adopted it, and six days later it received the approval of the Secretaries of War and Navy.

It now remained to submit these arrangements to the President as Commander-in-Chief. On June 22 General Marshall and Admiral Stark presented to Mr. Roosevelt for discussion the draft of a *Basis for Immediate Decisions Concerning the National Defense,* which contained the fundamental strategic premises on which military planning would proceed in the next few months.[15] This important conference took place against the background of the fall of France—it was on this day that the Bordeaux government accepted Germany's armistice terms—and the deliberations at the White House were marked by a somber awareness

13. Conn and Fairchild, p. 48.

14. War Department Files, JB325/642–44. The scope of the No-Transfer principle for the military is indicated by the territories named in the plan. In the Atlantic: Greenland, Newfoundland, Bermuda, Bahamas, Jamaica, Leewards, Windwards, Barbados, Trinidad, Tobago, British Guiana, British Honduras, St. Pierre and Miquelon, Guadeloupe, Martinique, French Guiana, Curaçao, Aruba, and Surinam. In the Pacific: Gilbert and Ellice Islands Colony, including the Line Islands, Western Samoa, Pitcairn Island Group, Tuamotu Group.

15. Watson, pp. 110–13.

that an hour of deadly peril for the United States might be close at hand.

At the meeting the President agreed with the Chiefs of Staff that if the French Fleet passed into German hands, major units of the United States Navy would have to be moved from Hawaii to the Atlantic, though he wished to defer final decision on such a move. He argued for more generous allotments of war material to Britain than the Chiefs thought prudent, but concurred in their view that little or no military aid for Latin America was immediately possible and that for the present no action by the United States forces should be undertaken south of Venezuela. With a view to increasing the nation's capabilities, the Chiefs recommended increased arms production, industrial mobilization, and a military draft, but found the President unresponsive to any measures that seemed to endanger the precarious economic gains of the New Deal, or that might prove unpopular in an election year.

If a narrow preoccupation with preserving the integrity of his domestic program threatened to run counter to the best interests of the national security, the President's devotion to the spirit of his Good Neighbor policy introduced some useful modifications into the military's arrangements in the matter of European possessions in the Hemisphere. General Marshall's notes of the conference indicate that while Mr. Roosevelt took no issue with the necessity for protective occupation by American forces of any territories in danger of passing under German control, he specified that occupation should take place only "after consultation with, and if possible in agreement with the other American Republics." In the final draft of this document, rewritten to conform to the President's suggestions and submitted on June 27, the phrase "and British dominions concerned" was also added.

Thus without seriously hampering the effectiveness of

the military's program of direct action, plans for dealing with the threatened transfer of European possessions were meshed with the diplomacy of continental cooperation in defense which the administration had begun to develop at Lima and Panama and Kingston, and which would presently be further perfected in the historic meetings of Foreign Ministers at Havana and of Mr. Roosevelt and Prime Minister King of Canada at Ogdensburg, New York. While the Chiefs of Staff were quite justified in discounting the military contributions Latin America could make to hemispheric defense, it would have been a serious political mistake to underestimate the detrimental effect to American security that would have been produced by any unilateral action which neighbor republics could interpret as a slight to their prestige, an indifference to their interests, or a hazard to their safety, thus driving them into alignment with the Axis. As it was approved by the President on August 14, Rainbow IV had been purged of most of the distinctive contributions of the military planners to the implementation of the No-Transfer principle—action would not necessarily be taken alone, but perhaps in concert with other nations, and at least not until after consultation with both the European owners and the other republics in the Hemisphere to the north and south. The disturbing suggestion of an assertion of United States sovereignty remained; but as we shall presently see, that was rendered a dead letter by the Act of Havana.

THE PITTMAN-BLOOM RESOLUTION AND THE NOTES TO GERMANY AND ITALY

While the inner councils of the Roosevelt administration were feeling their way toward a general policy for implementing the No-Transfer principle, steps were taken to advertise the principle itself to the belligerents in hopes that the crisis could be averted altogether by a timely warning. The Department of State accordingly drafted a joint resolution which was sent on June 3 with the President's approval to Senator Key Pittman and Representative Sol Bloom, chairmen respectively of the Senate Committee on Foreign Relations and the House Committee on Foreign Affairs. The substantive clauses of the resolution declared:

> That the United States would not recognize any transfer, and would not acquiesce in any attempt to transfer, any geographic region of this hemisphere from one non-American power to another non-American power; and
>
> That if such transfer or attempt to transfer should appear likely, the United States shall, in addition to other measures, immediately consult with the other American republics to determine upon the steps which should be taken to safeguard their common interests.[16]

In a letter to Mr. Bloom urging adoption of the resolution, Secretary Hull referred to the "traditional policy" of the government that European possessions "shall not become the subject of barter or conquest between rival European powers or be made the scene of settlement of European difficulties."[17] "The first part of the resolution," he remarked, "is in effect a restatement of the position which the Government has taken for more than a hundred years," while "the second part of it is a reaffirmation of the policy adopted in recent years of cooperation with the other American republics in matters of common interest." The State Department, then, favored a "pan-americanization" of the No-Transfer principle, and in contrast to the views of the

16. *Documents on American Foreign Relations, 1939–1940*, 2, 90.
17. Hull to Bloom (June 4, 1940), ibid., pp. 88–89.

military based its proposal "squarely upon the idea of full respect for established sovereignties."

Congress acted swiftly on the resolution. Reported out of committee almost immediately in both houses, it was given a high priority on the calendar, and was approved unanimously in the Senate on the day France requested an armistice, and by a vote of 380–8 in the House the following day, June 18.

The overwhelming congressional support given the Pittman-Bloom Resolution, as well as the widespread popular approval which greeted its passage, strengthened the administration's hand in dealing with the impending crisis. For the first time since 1811 a President had received prior instructions from Congress to act to prevent territorial transfers inimical to national security, and while the use of force was not specifically authorized as it had been in Madison's time, neither was action limited to particular contingencies, and it was generally understood in Congress that the "other measures" mentioned in the resolution included fighting if necessary.[18] In effect Mr. Roosevelt had sent a blank check to the legislative branch which they had signed and returned, to be filled in as the President saw fit in applying a policy universally regarded as the cornerstone of American defense in mid-1940.

June 17, 1940, was an important day in the history of the No-Transfer principle. The fall of France simultaneously triggered the Pittman-Bloom Resolution, the notes to Germany and Italy, and the dispatch of invitations to the consultative meeting of American foreign ministers at Havana. The notes to Berlin and Rome came curtly to the point, stating simply that it was understood that the government of France had requested armistice terms and— in language practically identical with the first paragraph

18. Langer and Gleason, pp. 626–27.

of the congressional resolution—reminding the belligerents of the traditional American attitude toward transfers of European possessions in the Western Hemisphere.[19] Copies of this communication were also forwarded to the British, French, and Netherlands governments for their "information."

Ribbentrop responded on July 1, in mixed tones of offended innocence and hooded menace.[20] He protested that the Nazi government had asked for no possessions in the Western Hemisphere, nor given any reason to assume that it intended to acquire them, and he insinuated that the American note implied an interpretation of the Monroe Doctrine which conferred on some nations and not others a right to hold territory in the New World. The German Foreign Minister pointedly reminded the United States government that the Reich considered it a corollary of the Nonintervention principle of the Doctrine that America in turn not interfere in the affairs of Europe.

Secretary Hull issued a public reply four days later, in which he observed tartly that the Monroe Doctrine was "solely a policy of self-defense," carrying with it no suggestion of hegemony on the part of the United States, unlike Germany's New Order in Europe or Japan's Greater East Asia Co-Prosperity Sphere.[21] Hull dismissed the allegation of favoritism toward certain colonial powers, pointing out that the Doctrine is exclusive only in the sense that it stands opposed to fresh incursions by non-American powers, while not undertaking to interfere with existing holdings. The Secretary declared the No-Transfer principle to be a fundamental part of the Doctrine and, lest Ribbentrop should

19. *Documents on American Foreign Relations*, 2, 90.

20. Ibid., pp. 91–93. Hull, *Memoirs*, *1*, 817. Langer and Gleason, p. 628.

21. Statement by the Secretary of State (July 5, 1940), *Documents On American Foreign Relations*, 2, 91–93.

have missed the point of the June 17 note, repeated that "the Government of the United States will neither recognize nor acquiesce in the transfer to a non-American power of geographical regions in this hemisphere now possessed by some other non-American power."

What immediate effect, if any, the Pittman-Bloom resolution and the notes to Germany and Italy had on Axis policy it is impossible to judge from materials at present available. Beyond the campaign of economic penetration and political subversion already on foot in Latin America, it seems unlikely that Hitler had immediate plans for aggression in this hemisphere, although had circumstances permitted, it would doubtless ultimately have come. This vigorous restatement of long-standing American policy surely had something to do with the fact that he did not demand any French or Dutch possessions, but in practical terms these territories could not have been occupied by him any more than Napoleon could have occupied Louisiana, until the obstacle of British sea power had been removed. It certainly did no harm in the darkest days of 1940 to indicate forcefully that American power had also to be reckoned with, at least in the Americas.

The congressional resolution and the diplomatic caveats were only emergency stop-gaps—reaffirmations of an interest in maintaining the colonial status quo without any elaboration of measures to be taken to ensure it. The final choice of means had still to be made, and this was done at the Havana consultative meeting of foreign ministers, where the twenty-one American republics united in support of the No-Transfer principle and agreed on procedures to implement it.

COLLECTIVE TRUSTEESHIP

The provision for a collective, inter-American trusteeship for European colonial possessions in danger of being transferred to Germany, which was the most distinctive feature of the Act of Havana and the convention that accompanied it, originated in the mind of Franklin Roosevelt. Early in 1939 Under Secretary of State Sumner Welles informed the President of reports from Ambassador Armour that the government of Chile was thinking about selling Easter Island, apparently not having considered "that the sale of this island to a non-American power would violate any hemispherical doctrine of non-transfer of territory or prejudice the defense of the continent."[22] Welles suggested offering to purchase or lease the island, and inquired about price. Roosevelt pointed out the possible importance of Easter Island as an air base, and agreed that "it should, therefore, under no circumstances be transferred to any non-American nation," but he opposed the thought of further territorial expansion in the Hemisphere by the United States.[23] Instead he advocated some form of "joint trusteeship of the American Republics" over not only Easter but also the Galapagos and perhaps Cocos Island, to preserve them for colonization and for natural science and to keep them out of the hands of non-American powers. The cost of administration would be borne by the trustees in proportion to their national wealth. This idea remained in the President's mind, and we find him writing to Welles a few months later in connection with Admiral Byrd's Antarctic expedition that "we should give some study to a new form of sovereignty, i.e. a claim to sovereignty of the whole sector lying south of the Americas in behalf of, and in trust for, the American Republics as a whole."[24]

22. Letter from Welles to Roosevelt (March 14, 1939), Franklin D. Roosevelt Library, President's Secretary's File, Sumner Welles.

23. Roosevelt to Welles (March 25, 1939), ibid.

24. Roosevelt to Welles (Aug. 5, 1939), Elliott Roosevelt and Joseph Lash, eds., *FDR, His Personal Letters, 1928–1945* (4 vols. New York, 1947–50) 2, 909.

All of this was in harmony with the cooperative policies of the Good Neighbor and the declarations of mutual interest in defense at Lima and Panama; so that before the crisis of 1940 had fully developed, the Department of State was already emphasizing that "any proposed transfer of sovereignty to a non-American power of existing European colonies in the New World would be of immediate concern to all the American Republics."[25] During the period when purchase proposals were flourishing in Congress and military planners were thinking in terms of preclusive assertions of United States sovereignty in threatened colonial territories, the President was developing his trusteeship idea for use in the emergency. In a note to Mrs. Roosevelt, who had forwarded to him the plan of a private citizen for taking over the British, Dutch, and French Guianas, he said that "it is very doubtful if the United States should undertake sovereignty or sole charge of development. I am, confidentially, considering the broad thought of creating a form of Pan American trusteeship for situations of this kind. . . . It is worth studying—especially if there is a remote possibility that the American Republics may be forced to do something about European possessions in this hemisphere."[26] Welles, when he saw this memorandum, emphatically agreed that any such acquisition of territory by the United States would be disastrous for relations with Latin America and that if steps had to be taken to prevent European possessions from passing into other European hands "the Pan American trusteeship idea would be the only solution."[27]

25. Memo by the Division of American Republics (Feb. 23, 1940), cited in Langer and Gleason, p. 624.

26. Memo of President Roosevelt for Mrs. Roosevelt (May 4, 1940), ibid., p. 625.

27. Letter from Welles to Roosevelt (May 6, 1940), ibid.

At the Havana conference, held July 21–30, 1940, the United States government accordingly built its entire project for the "pan-americanization" of the No-Transfer policy and of the means for enforcing it around the principle of collective action. On July 11 the Department of State sent out to the other American nations a draft convention and resolution embodying their proposals for dealing with the problem of European possessions, the main points of which may be summarized as follows:

a. The American Republics reaffirm their policy of non-recognition of and non-acquiescence in the acquisition of territory in this hemisphere by force.

b. They would regard any transfer, or attempted transfer of the sovereignty, jurisdiction, possession or any interest in or control over any such region to another non-American state as inimical to their peace, safety and political independence.

c. No such transfer or attempt to transfer, direct or indirect, will be recognized or acquiesced in by the American Republics or any one of them.

d. The American Republics reserve the right to judge whether any change in the political relations of the European holders of American territories has impaired their political independence or freedom of action, even though no formal transfer or change of status has occurred.

e. Because these are matters of common concern to all the American Republics, they pledge that they will act only after prior consultation, and take no independent action except as provided in this instrument, or in connection with territorial disputes already pending between them and non-American nations.

f. In the event action on European possessions in the hemisphere becomes necessary, the American Republics renounce any thought of territorial aggrandizement for themselves, and declare their intention either to restore the possessions to their original sovereigns when security considerations permit, or recognize their independence if they are deemed capable of self-government.

If it becomes necessary for the American Republics to assume a measure of control over European possessions in the hemisphere, they shall be governed under a collective trusteeship participated in by all the states which ratify this convention. A trusteeship committee shall be formed of one member from each ratifying state, action to be taken by vote of two-thirds of those present, two-thirds of the membership constituting a quorum.[28]

The draft resolution, which in modified form was later adopted as the Act of Havana, was nearly identical in purpose and provisions with the draft convention. It was designed solely as an emergency measure, to provide machinery in the form of a committee for dealing immediately with a threat of transfer while the convention was going through what might be a perilously long process of ratification by the various American republics.

It became evident before the Havana conference convened that the United States program would not enjoy entirely smooth sailing there. True, there were heartening assurances of complete support from influential Brazil and Mexico as well as from Cuba, whose Foreign Minister had advanced a mandate plan for European possessions at a

28. Langer and Gleason, pp. 692–93.

meeting in Ciudad Trujillo a few weeks earlier.[29] The Peruvian government, however, revealed a cautious hesitancy, based on suspicions of the motives of some of its neighbors.[30] Those Pan-American nations with a particular interest in certain European colonies preferred other solutions to the one offered by Washington. Guatemala suggested it be allowed to take over Belize on the condition that whenever the situation warranted, the dispute with Britain was to be submitted to arbitration, while Venezuela, with Aruba, Curaçao, and Bonaire in mind, favored plebiscites to determine if the people of European dependencies desired annexation to the "nearest American Republic."[31] Finally, the Argentine Foreign Minister, Cantilo, gave a foretaste of the massive obstructionism his delegation would display at Havana by complaining that the Pittman-Bloom Resolution and the unilateral United States action in sending notes to Berlin and Rome removed any possible purpose in discussing the problem of territorial transfers at Havana, and by attempting to reserve the Falkland Islands from discussion or collective action under any agreements entered into at the conference.[32]

29. Telegram from U.S. Embassy in Mexico to State Dept. (July 12, 1940), State Dept. Files, 710.Consultation 627/280. Memo by State Dept. summarizing Latin American attitudes (July 17, 1940), 710. Consultation (2)/695 1/2.

30. Telegram from U.S. Embassy in Lima to State Dept. (July 9, 1940), 710.Consultation (2)/232.

31. Telegram from U.S. Embassy in Guatemala to State Dept. (June 26, 1940), 710.Consultation (2)/119. Guatemala was mollified by the adoption at Havana of Resolution XIX, expressing the desire of the American Republics for a just, peaceful, and prompt solution of the Belize question. See *Report of the Secretary of State, Second Meeting of the Ministers of Foreign Affairs of the American Republics* (Washington, 1941), p. 75. Telegram from U.S. Embassy in Caracas to State Dept. (July 13, 1940), 710.Consultation (2)/291.

32. Telegram from U.S. Embassy in Buenos Aires to State Dept. (June 21, 1940), File 710.Consultation (2)/98.

These centrifugal tendencies were hopefully observed by the Nazis, who were anxious to reduce the inter-American solidarity nurtured by the United States to the confused disarray they had so successfully exploited in Europe. Particularly in the smaller Latin countries, Germany brought to bear strong diplomatic pressure against joining in agreements at Havana aimed directly or indirectly at the Reich, and used her prospective control of European markets to reinforce these warnings with threats of economic retaliation. The Axis propaganda machine shrieked vilifications of "Yankee imperialists," the Monroe Doctrine, and decadent democracies, while less than a fortnight before the conference at Havana opened, Nazi plots to overthrow the governments of Chile and Argentina were uncovered.[33]

This was a fight Washington was determined to win, and Roosevelt and Hull swiftly marshaled their resources. A tentative agenda for the Havana meeting prepared at the Department of State announced that in addition to the question of territorial transfers the conference would discuss united action against political subversion and measures to relieve the severe economic dislocations resulting from the war in Europe. Meanwhile Hull gave vigorous diplomatic support to nations Germany was attempting to intimidate, and the President moved dramatically to counteract Nazi economic threats by asking Congress to authorize increased lending by the Import-Export Bank to the amount of 500 million dollars to aid "our neighbors south of the Rio Grande" in the marketing of their surpluses.[34]

In his opening address to the conference on July 22, the Secretary of State stressed the common danger to the Americas of transfers of European colonies to other non-Amer-

33. Hull, *Memoirs, 1,* 820–21. Langer and Gleason, p. 689.
34. Hull, *1,* 821–22. Langer and Gleason, p. 695.

ican powers, and urged adoption of the collective trusteeship proposal, emphasizing at the same time, and perhaps more pointedly, the problem of political subversion and particularly the measures for economic relief which were to Latin America the most attractive part of the United States program.[35] Unquestionably for the United States the panamericanization of the No-Transfer principle was the salient objective at Havana, a fact that was signalized when Mr. Hull assumed the chairmanship of the committee on transfer of territories.

From the moment the No-Transfer convention and resolution were introduced on July 23, it became clear that the principal opposition would come from Argentina, as had been the case in so many previous inter-American conferences, and that the success or failure of Washington's policies depended on overcoming Argentine objections. A proud people, the Argentinians had long been jealous of the pre-eminence of the United States in American affairs, and wary of seeming to be a rubber stamp for Yankee policy. Although they had suffered less than most Latin American nations from the proprietary abuses of the Monroe Doctrine, they were unwilling to underwrite it at Havana, especially to prevent transfers of territory along the Caribbean approaches to the Panama Canal, a region remote from their interests. The chief of the Argentine delegation, Dr. Leopoldo Melo, declared that his country was willing to join in a simple No-Transfer declaration, but opposed collective trusteeship. It was premature, he argued, because the British fleet remained intact, and it was impolitic, especially for a nation whose ties to Europe were as strong as Argentina's, to skirt the edges of unneutral behavior by assuming joint sovereignty over European possessions. In case Latin American nations got into trouble by doing so,

35. *Report of the Secretary of State*, pp. 46–55.

could the United States defend them? Dr. Melo and a good many other delegates seriously doubted it.[36]

With dogged patience Secretary Hull argued with Dr. Melo that there was every necessity for unanimity on this matter, and that there was no disagreement on ends, only on means. Reviewing recent European history, he reminded the Argentine delegates of the ruthless disregard Hitler had repeatedly shown for neutrality, and for words that were not backed by an obvious intent to act. The emergency might develop overnight, and there must be machinery ready at hand to deal with it. Dr. Melo was personally most cooperative, but obviously bound by rigid instructions to oppose collective trusteeship. Finally Hull was forced to resort to an expedient which had proved successful under similar circumstances at the Lima Conference. He personally appealed for new instructions over the heads not only of Dr. Melo and Foreign Minister Cantilo, but of the Acting President of the Argentine Republic as well, to the ailing President Ortiz. The old friendship held, the instructions arrived, and Argentine objections dissolved. Argentina not only supported the No-Transfer policy at the Conference but, uncharacteristically, actually ratified the Convention of Havana later on.

The two instruments produced by Hull's committee— the Convention of Havana and a resolution, the Act of Havana—varied only in detail from the original Department of State drafts, and practically duplicated each other in language.[37] The resolution was designed as a temporary by-pass of the constitutional treaty-making authority in the various American republics, to go into immediate and con-

36. This discussion of the Havana Conference is based largely on Hull, *1*, 823–27; Langer and Gleason, pp. 695–99; and Bemis, *Latin American Policy of the United States,* pp. 367–73.

37. For the full texts see *Report of the Secretary of State,* pp. 75–77, 84–89.

tinuing effect while the convention was in process of ratification. Actually it served throughout this critical period, for ratification by two-thirds of the signatories, which was required to put the convention into effect, took place only in January 1942, after the United States had entered the war.

As it happened, the Act of Havana has never been specifically applied, not because it was lost in the jungle of neglect that has claimed so much of the elaborately contrived machinery of inter-American cooperation but because no actual transfer threat materialized. As we shall see, it was referred to in some United States actions later, but the trusteeship committee never administered a European dependency. It is nevertheless important, both as an immediate act of policy and as a milestone in the development of the No-Transfer principle of the Monroe Doctrine.

In the first place, the proceedings at Havana were an impressive demonstration to the totalitarian nations of American intercontinental unity at a time when such a stand constituted the most useful deterrent to aggression against the Hemisphere. At the same time the Act of Havana quieted Washington's fears that a Latin American state might accept an offer from Germany of European colonial possessions in return for a form of political or economic vassalage that would shatter the solidarity of the American front. There was always the remote chance, too, that unless it were pledged to collective action, some American nation might move into a European colony, giving Germany or Japan a pretext for similar action elsewhere in the world. It would have been acutely embarrassing for the United States at this time to have had to assert the strictures against transfers to an American state that it had narrowly avoided having to direct to Mexico and Colombia in 1825.

On the other hand, Washington's renunciation of territorial expansion and the willingness of the United States to collectivize the Monroe Doctrine lulled lingering suspicions of the Colossus of the North and made Latin America less susceptible to Axis blandishments. The No-Transfer principle was now wholly continentalized; the Panama Conference had achieved multilateral agreement on the principle itself; and the Havana Conference a similar agreement on the mechanism of enforcement.

All this had been accomplished without seriously hampering United States freedom of action or the instant effectiveness of the No-Transfer principle. For the Act of Havana contained an "escape clause" for use in sudden crisis:

> Should the need for emergency action be so urgent that action by the committee cannot be awaited, any of the American republics, individually or jointly with others, shall have the right to act in the manner which its own defense or that of the continent requires. Should this situation arise, the American republic taking action shall place the matter before the committee immediately, in order that it may consider the action taken and adopt appropriate measures.[38]

In effect, therefore, the Act of Havana constituted a collective mandate for the United States to act to prevent territorial transfers in accordance with its time-honored security policy. Here is a superbly skillful diplomatic achievement —to have neutralized the possible harmful effects of unilateral applications of a defense policy by collectivizing it, but yet not sacrificing the essential flexibility of sole proprietorship; to be able to act without fear of jealousy on the part of neighboring states, while at the same time affording the Axis or Japan no justification for occupying the possessions of colonial powers.

38. Ibid., pp. 76–77.

NEUTRALIZATION

Before the Havana Conference finished its work, an emergency developed in connection with the French West Indies which was eventually dealt with not by an application of the trusteeship formula but by the expedient of a neutralization agreement negotiated with the local authorities. The situation was not unlike that in Aruba and Curaçao a few weeks before, with the important difference that while the Dutch government in exile continued to fight the Axis from London, the Vichy regime, which the United States chose for various reasons to recognize as the government of France, not only capitulated and asked for peace terms but moved steadily toward collaboration with the Reich. Thus Washington was confronted with a double danger: the Nazis might demand the outright cession of the French islands and French Guiana, or they might through their influence over Vichy exercise effective control over these strategic positions without any formal transfer of sovereignty.

The No-Transfer note of June 17 to Germany was designed to counter the first danger, and as we have observed, a copy was sent to the French government at that time. In the chaotic circumstances attending the collapse of French military resistance and the dissolution of the Reynaud ministry, the American note failed to reach Ambassador Bullitt until July 5. Bullitt, whose entire public career was marked by a regrettable penchant for grandiose gestures, had elected not to retreat southward with the French government but to remain in Paris, and was therefore out of touch with the situation. He doubted the wisdom of delivering the caveat at so late a date, but after consultation in Washington, Hull and Welles decided to do so, in order to go on record against a possible French decision to transfer the colonies.[39]

As had been the case with the Dutch possessions, the immediate problem arose out of British actions rather than any material threat from Germany. The focus of British interest in Martinique was the presence there of several French warships, including the cruiser *Emile Bertin,* and the aircraft carrier *Béarn* laden with 106 American planes recently purchased by France, as well as nearly a quarter-billion dollars in French gold, shipped from Canada in the crisis. In late June the British governor of Trinidad made a vain effort to persuade the French High Commissioner for the Antilles and Guiana, Admiral Robert, to declare for the Free French movement of General de Gaulle, and to turn ships, planes, and gold over to Britain, or at least permit British surveillance of the islands to prevent German use of these resources.[40] In the face of Robert's stubborn loyalty to Vichy, the British on July 4 established a naval blockade of Martinique.

Despite the recent friction over Curaçao and Aruba, London neglected to consult beforehand with the United States about this move, with the result that the British once again had an opportunity of experiencing Washington's sensitivity to forcible action by a non-American state in the Caribbean area. On July 1 Under Secretary Welles had warned Lord Lothian against any assumption of authority by Britain in the French Antilles, and after the destruction of the French squadron at Mers-el-Kebir by the Royal Navy on July 3, Secretary Hull informed the British Ambassador that any move to seize the French vessels or oc-

39. Telegram from Bullitt to Hull (July 5, 1940), memo of Welles to Hull (July 11, 1940), telegram from Hull to Biddle at Vichy (July 12, 1940), File 710.Consultation (2)/205.

40. Langer and Gleason, p. 690.

cupy Martinique would lead to "real trouble" between the United States and Britain.[41] Hull then undertook to work out a suitable arrangement between the British and French governments, while Roosevelt underscored the warning to Lothian by dispatching a cruiser and six destroyers to Martinique to chaperone the British squadron.

Having reasserted its primacy of interest in the Caribbean, the United States at first found it virtually impossible to accommodate the British and French positions. Suggestions that the French ships be interned in American ports or that the planes be resold to the manufacturers were rejected by the French ambassador, whose government was under heavy pressure from the German armistice commission to prevent the aircraft from taking part in the Battle of Britain.[42] The Chief of Naval Operations sent Admiral John W. Greenslade to Martinique to confer directly with Admiral Robert about ships, planes, gold, and the denial of French Antilles harbors to German submarines. No agreement could be reached.

Matters remained at this impasse until late September 1940, when the United States adopted a more forceful attitude toward Vichy, partly as a result of British urging and partly because of the mounting concern felt in Washington over an increasing French tendency toward collaboration with Hitler. With the destroyer-bases agreement of September 2, the nation had burst the bonds of technical neutrality and tacitly acknowledged its stake in British survival. As the Nazi air armada poured destruction over English airfields and cities in preparation for invasion, Prime Minister Churchill enlisted American diplomatic support to prevent the French from throwing in their lot with Hitler. Mr. Roosevelt responded at once with a warning to the French

41. Conversation of July 5, 1940, Hull, p. 819.
42. Langer and Gleason, p. 691.

Ambassador that a declaration of war by France on Britain
might require the establishment of an inter-American
trusteeship over French colonies in the New World.[43]

A week later, having received reports that the French
were planning the construction of new military installations
on Martinique, the President bluntly informed Ambassador Henry-Haye of United States opposition to any
change in the status quo there, and demanded a public
declaration that French possessions in the Western Hemisphere would be neutralized. After hasty consultation with
Vichy, Henry-Haye gave assurances to Mr. Welles on
October 8 that the French government would "under no
conditions . . . agree to any of their possessions in the
Western Hemisphere becoming directly or indirectly, the
source of disquiet or of danger to the United States."[44] He
went on to state that his government would accept American observers in any of its New World dependencies, and
to suggest that another mission to Admiral Robert would
this time produce results.

Washington took no action until the Hitler-Pétain conference of October 24 at Montoire produced a fresh scare.
Secretary Knox urged the landing of five thousand troops
on Martinique within seventy-two hours, but was overruled
by cooler heads. Welles issued another warning against "indirect alien control to be exercised in Martinique or in any
other French colonies in the Western Hemisphere," and
Admiral Greenslade was dispatched again, this time armed
with threats of naval action to prevent sorties by the French
warships from Fort-de-France. In due course he was able to

43. Memo of conversation between Welles and Ambassador Henry-
Haye (Sept. 24, 1940). Unless otherwise indicated, this account is taken
from W. L. Langer and S. E. Gleason, *The Undeclared War* (New
York, 1953), pp. 71–75, 90–91.

44. Memo of conversation (Oct. 8, 1940), Roosevelt Library, President's Secretary's File, Welles.

conclude a satisfactory arrangement with the High Commissioners for neutralizing French possessions.

Vichy's retreat from obduracy owed a great deal to an expressed concern over any action the United States might be contemplating under the terms of the Act of Havana.[45] Anxious to prevent the substitution of Pan American trusteeship for French sovereign control, and reasonably certain that Hitler had no immediate demands in mind for the Antilles, the Pétain government hastened to freeze the status quo by giving adequate guarantees to the United States against an indirect transfer of these territories to Germany. The Act of Havana had borne its first fruits without being invoked.

45. See, e.g., the note from Ambassador Saint-Quentin to Acting Secretary Welles (Aug. 14, 1940), 710.Consultation (2)/666a.

CHAPTER 13

The Expanding Hemisphere

The passage of the Lend-Lease Act on March 11, 1941, was perhaps the most important milestone along the road to American entry into the second World War, for it represented, as events proved, an irrevocable commitment not merely to the survival of Britain but actually to eventual British victory. Having pledged the resources necessary to keep Britain fighting, the Washington government at once found itself faced with the problem of ensuring their delivery, which led step by step to more active participation in the Battle of the Atlantic, an extension of the Neutrality Patrol, the shift of fleet units from the Pacific to the Atlantic, the establishment of new outlying bases, and finally actual escort of convoy by the American Navy. Many weeks before Pearl Harbor the United States was engaged in an undeclared shooting war with Germany at sea.

With what the activists inside and outside his official family regarded as suicidal hesitancy, Mr. Roosevelt cautiously moved in the direction his concern for the national security dictated, content it seemed to follow public opinion rather than guide it, and perhaps underestimating the extent to which a candid declaration of his private views might have helped consolidate support for more forthright action. Certainly he wished to avoid war; just as certainly the logic of all-out aid to Britain and later to the Soviet

Union, coupled with increasing tension vis-à-vis Japan, pointed more and more inevitably to American involvement.

In 1941, as the nation prepared itself in spirit and strength for full partnership in the struggle against totalitarianism, a marked change was perceptible in concepts of hemispheric defense. The main emphasis was no longer a negative impulse to insulate the Americas against the contagion of war, no longer a passive continentalism, but an active extension of the area of American vital interests to the far-flung Atlantic outposts of Greenland, Iceland, the Azores, Cape Verde, and Canary islands and even to Dakar in French West Africa. In the course of the year all these positions were brought within the enlarged purview of the No-Transfer principle, to deny them to the Axis and keep the war at arm's length. This also meant retaining positions from which eventually the fight could be carried to the enemy by land and by sea.

Few of the decisions were taken with calm deliberation. They were hectic months when crisis succeeded crisis, when the agonizing uncertainty of what moves Germany or Japan would next make caused a bewildering confusion of plans which had to be abandoned, of orders given and countermanded, of policies hastily conceived and clumsily executed. Part of the trouble rested with the President's reluctance to take the nation into his confidence, despite the fact that the election was safely past, so that a "business as usual" psychology prevailed which produced the incredible spectacle of a Selective Service extension bill which passed by a single vote at a moment when Hitler ruled half the Eurasian world and Japan stood poised to conquer the rest. Having failed to make clear the urgent necessity for an extensive mobilization of national manpower and industrial resources, the Roosevelt administration found itself hamstrung for want of troops to perform important defensive missions in support of the No-Transfer policy, and to relieve British forces for duty elsewhere.

As the United States committed itself more deeply to British fortunes and moved toward more active participation in the war, it was London rather than the Latin American capitals that Washington consulted in connection with problems of transfer of European possessions. Recent irritation over British defensive maneuvers in the Dutch islands and the French Antilles was forgotten, and applications of the No-Transfer principle came increasingly in response to threats to the security of the Atlantic lifeline. While the Act of Havana did not become entirely a dead letter, it was frequently paid merely lip service even in the Caribbean area. The first instance of neglect of the cooperative prin- iple in favor of unilateral action by the United States ppeared in the Defense of Greenland Agreement.

GREENLAND

Early in 1941 the United States was forced by a combination of Canadian pressure and German activity to abandon its policy of masterly inaction in Greenland. Since the summer of 1940 Canada, urged on by Britain, had been pressing the American government to establish an airfield there for ferrying planes across the Atlantic, or to give them permission to do so. The United States had been considering construction of a field, and had sent an Air Corps Officer on a fruitless reconnaissance flight for sites in August, but had lapsed into inactivity with the winter closing of navigation. Then in January 1941 the Canadian government reopened the question with the strong intimation that if the United States failed to take action, they would do so themselves.[1]

1. Report from Assistant Secretary of State Berle to the Secretary of State on the History of the Greenland Negotiation (April 30, 1941), State Dept. Files, 859B.7962/120.

For nearly a year United States policy toward Greenland had rested on a series of propositions which still controlled State Department thinking: (1) Greenland was in the Western Hemisphere and therefore within the scope of the Monroe Doctrine and more recently the Act of Havana, (2) the transfer of Greenland or any change in its status was intolerable, (3) every effort should be made to keep the subcontinent outside the sphere of belligerent activity, while if possible avoiding American occupation.[2] In line with this, the first impulse following receipt of the Canadian note was to let the Greenlanders build an airfield for the use of American states, with United States financial and technical assistance but without the dispatch of American forces.[3] It rapidly became apparent that the day for the old antiseptic approach had passed, when in rapid succession came news of Hitler's extension of the war zone to include the coast of Eastern Greenland, a German air raid on Iceland, and reports of flights of Nazi aircraft over Scoresby Sound in Greenland. Immediately afterward Mr. Berle informed Danish Minister de Kauffmann that Washington had determined on defense facilities constructed and protected by the United States alone. The increased fury of the Battle of the Atlantic, the effectiveness of German attacks in the sea lanes by U-boat wolf packs, surface raiders, and aircraft which were taking a fearful toll of British tonnage, forced the United States to take the plunge to prevent Greenland from becoming "a point of attack by a non-American power."[4]

Events now moved swiftly. An Army survey party was

2. Hull, *Memoirs*, 2, 935–36.

3. Memo from Assistant Secretary Berle to the Secretary of State, identical copy to the President (Feb. 7, 1941), File 859B.7962/18.

4. Telegram from State to American Consul at Godthaab, Greenland (April 4, 1941), File 859B.01/348a.

ordered, organized, and dispatched, all within the space of ten days, while the Department of State discussed the terms of agreement with de Kauffmann. On April 5 the President allocated five million dollars for the project from his Emergency Fund. On April 9, the anniversary of Hitler's attack on Denmark, Secretary Hull and Minister de Kauffmann signed the Defense of Greenland Agreement.[5]

This agreement is worth examining in some detail, partly because it served as a prototype for similar arrangements in the other European possessions in the Western Hemisphere, partly because of the special problems it presented. It took the form of an executive agreement rather than a treaty, not, as has so often been the case with such instruments, to preserve secrecy (it was publicly anounced the following day), or to bypass the treaty-making power of the Senate, but because there could be no hope of ratification by the parliament of German-occupied Denmark. There is little doubt that the United States Senate would have given over-whelming consent to the Greenland Agreement, and in fact the enactment by the Senate on April 10 of Public Law 32, which gave final legislative affirmation and approval to the Pittman-Bloom No-Transfer Resolution of the previous June, can be taken as evidence of the temper of Congress at this moment.[6]

The substantive sections of the Greenland Agreement gave the United States the right to construct, maintain, and operate such landing fields, seaplane facilities, and radio and meteorological installations as were necessary to protect Danish sovereignty and to prevent the strategic lodgment of a non-American aggressor in Greenland, under the terms of

5. Watson, *Prewar Plans*, p. 485. Letter from Hull to de Kauffmann (April 7, 1941), File 859B.7962/53c. Letter from President to Secretary of War Stimson (April 5, 1941), File 859B.7962/43.

6. *Documents on American Foreign Relations, 1940–41, 3,* 94–95.

the Act of Havana.[7] Since the Act of Havana is specifically referred to both in the Preamble and in Article I of the agreement, it is surprising that there was no prior consultation with any of the American republics about Greenland, although in Article IV it was stipulated that all facilities there would be made available to the aircraft and ships of all the American nations for purposes of hemispheric defense. What had become of the pan-americanization of the No-Transfer principle? To be sure, there was no immediate peril that would invoke the emergency clauses of the Act of Havana. It may be argued that Greenland was geographically remote from Latin America, that Canada was the nation most intimately involved, and that since there was to be no interference with sovereign control by Greenland authorities, no question of collective trusteeship would arise. Still it is difficult to escape the impression that Washington in this initial test regarded the Act of Havana more as a convenience than as a primary obligation. That impression is heightened by the circular instructions sent by the Department of State to all Chiefs of Mission in the American Republics, which directed them to inform the foreign ministers at their respective posts of the Greenland Agreement, but "in doing so . . . [to] avoid making any statement as to the interpretation of the agreement and especially its reference to the Act of Havana until you receive subsequent instructions."[8]

Latin America received news of the Greenland Agreement complacently enough, which proved that the United States had not risked hemispheric solidarity by acting independently. Anguished outcries issuing from the Axis cap-

7. *Defense of Greenland: Agreement between the United States of America and Denmark,* Executive Agreement Series, 204 (Washington, 1941), pp. 1–3.

8. State Dept. to Chiefs of Mission in the American Republics (April 10, 1941), File 859B.7962/45a.

itals, on the other hand, indicated a palpable hit on the aggressors. Rome newspapers fulminated against the"fraudulent agreement" as a "further blow to the Monroe Doctrine," while the Nazi press unblushingly spoke of "United States imperialism against a small nation."[9] In Greenland itself, Governors Svane and Brun displayed some petulance at not having been consulted or even notified in advance of the agreement, but expressed substantial satisfaction with its terms.[10]

The reaction in Copenhagen was necessarily more complicated. Although the American chargé reported that most Danes learned of this blow to their oppressors with pleasure, the government, under heavy Nazi pressure, felt it necessary to repudiate the agreement and to recall de Kauffmann, who had courageously exceeded his authority in undertaking the negotiation.[11] In a series of communications culminating in a telegram from President Roosevelt to King Christian X, the United States informed the Danish authorities that since it considered them to be acting under duress and therefore could not accept their protests as reflections of their true position, it would continue to recognize Henrik de Kauffmann as the official representative of Denmark, and to consider the Greenland Agreement as in legal force. As Washington well knew, this reply could not help being privately gratifying to the old king, who stood as a magnificent symbol of Danish fortitude and dignity before his people in their years of captivity.

9. Telegram from Embassy in Rome to State Dept. (April 11, 1941), File 859B.7962/49. Telegram from Embassy in Berlin to State Dept. (April 30, 1941), File 859B.7962/101.

10. Telegram from Consulate in Godthaab to State Dept. (April 12, 1941), File 859B.7962/50.

11. On the de Kauffmann episode in general see Hull, *Memoirs*, 2, 937–39; *Documents on American Foreign Relations, 1940–41, 3*, 236–39; and Langer and Gleason, *The Undeclared War*, p. 430.

At it turned out, there was little danger to Greenland from the Nazis, and the American garrison there was reduced drastically after the United States entered the War.[12] This relative security owed a great deal to the decision taken at an all-day White House conference on April 10, 1941, to extend the patrol activities of the United States Navy as far as 25 degrees west longitude, which included most of the east coast of Greenland, and to report to the British all German air and sea forces seen there. The move to defend Greenland was in part an element of the larger decision to take definite steps to ensure the arrival of supplies to Britain. The later importance of Greenland to the war effort was chiefly as a way station in the air ferry route to Europe and for its meteorological stations, which supplied weather information used by General Eisenhower to set the date for the invasion of the continent in 1944.

THE ATLANTIC ISLANDS AND DAKAR

The dispatch of defense forces to Greenland did no special violence to reasonable definitions of the Western Hemisphere, but the projection of the No-Transfer principle to cover the Portuguese Azores and Cape Verde Islands and the Spanish Canary Islands—not to speak of French West Africa—threatened to expose the increasing fictitiousness of American neutrality once and for all. In this the No-Transfer principle resembled the closely related problem of naval patrol and convoy, and is bound up with identical concerns about the security of shipping lanes.

In the autumn of 1940 Hitler began pressuring Spain and France for concessions which would have given him Gibraltar and North African bases for control of the western

12. Watson, *Prewar Plans*, p. 486.

Mediterranean. The next spring his lightning Balkan campaign and landing on Crete and General Rommel's spectacular successes against the British in North Africa placed Hitler in a position to close the Suez end of the Mediterranean and threatened to leave the Cape route as Britain's only communication with the east. Under these circumstances it was imperative to prevent a German occupation of island air and naval bases along that route, or to let Hitler establish himself at Dakar. Whatever the fate of the Mediterranean, the Azores, lying a thousand miles due west of Lisbon, constituted an ideal base of operations against the easterly shipping routes from America to Europe, and for that reason alone could not be allowed to fall into German hands.

During the winter of 1940–41 and during most of the following months before Pearl Harbor, Washington also viewed the problem as one of hemispheric defense, of interdicting to Hitler locations from which he might launch attacks on, say, the Brazilian bulge near Natal, less than two thousand miles away. Even before the Japanese attack, as it became clear that the Soviet Union would survive for a time and that Britain might be spared invasion, there was a growing tendency in the United States to consider these positions in terms of their eventual usefulness as jumping-off places for offensive operations against the Axis. Passive doctrines had begun to give way to more active conceptions of hemispheric defense.

In line with these strategic objectives, United States policy toward France, Spain, and Portugal was in varying degrees conditioned by a desire to prevent an extension of military privileges to Germany in these critical areas. The special economic arrangements for supplying French North and West Africa and the close liaison maintained through Robert Murphy with General Weygand served this purpose, as did the economic leverage Washington used to keep needy Spain from closer collaboration with the Axis.[13] In May and June 1941 relations with Lisbon were completely dominated by the question of the Azores, and the near-panic that gripped Washington at the time resulted in a clumsy mishandling of the whole business that seriously strained the bonds of Portuguese–American friendship and required the intercession of Britain and Brazil to ease the tension by setting Dr. Salazar's fears at rest.

The danger of German moves against the outlying islands was never as great as British and American strategists imagined, partly because of the basic flaws in Hitler's strategic insight which ultimately cost him his chance for victory. For Hitler never fully appreciated the absolute necessity for the defeat of Britain and therefore failed to recognize the importance of command of the sea in accomplishing that end. Basically a continentalist like Napoleon before him, he first wasted his air power in futile assaults on England and then turned to the disastrous campaign against the Soviet Union, lured on to destruction in the vastness of Russian space by his geopolitical misconceptions.

Thus the Fuehrer failed to make the closing of the eastern end of the Mediterranean a prime objective during the favorable interval immediately after the fall of France, and when in the autumn he belatedly turned to this "flank attack" on British supply lines, he allowed the crafty counterdemands of Pétain and Franco to give him pause in pressing home his Gibraltar project. His heart was never wholly in it, nor was it the following April when he drove to Crete, only to abandon Syria to a British counterattack, in order to concentrate on Russia. The Mediterranean lifeline remained open, most precariously to be sure, but still usable.

13. For full accounts of these policies see W. L. Langer, *Our Vichy Gamble*, New York, 1947; and Herbert Feis, *The Spanish Story*, New York, 1948. See also Langer and Gleason, *The Undeclared War*.

Because he thought primarily in terms of land power, Hitler's attitude toward the Atlantic islands was essentially defensive. His conferences with Grand Admiral Raeder reveal a conviction that if Germany acquired any of the islands (he had the Canaries particularly in mind), the United States or Britain would at once seize the others. Raeder wanted Dakar as a base for German naval operations, and before the destroyer-base agreement he thought the Canaries might be held for Germany, but he was inclined to write off the Azores and Cape Verdes as impossible adventures, militarily speaking.[14] At their mid-September conference in Berlin, Ribbentrop asked Serrano Suñer for the cession of one of the Canaries to Germany, and was rebuffed.[15] After this, Hitler largely confined himself to aiding the Spanish to strengthen their forces there, influenced by his naval chief's waning confidence in Germany's ability to maintain bases in the Atlantic. What the Fuehrer could and did do was to threaten occupation of Spain and Portugal if they allowed the democracies to enter their possessions. For the time being, Germany's interest in maintaining the status quo in the islands matched that of Britain and the United States.

None of this was known in London or Washington, of course, and the Roosevelt and Churchill governments formulated policy on the basis of what Hitler might do to hurt them most. Af first the United States found itself comparatively helpless. As Cordell Hull wrote to the President in reply to a suggestion that support be given an independent Azorean government if Hitler occupied Portugal: "for practical reasons I do not see that there is anything this country can do, as much as we might like to."[16] The Department of

14. See *Fuehrer Conferences, 1940, 2*, 19–20, 31, 33–34, 40–41, 53–57.
15. Feis, *Spanish Story*, p. 80.
16. Memo from Hull to FDR (June 18, 1940), Roosevelt Library, President's Secretary's File, State Dept.

State did notify Madrid and Lisbon of its concern about the future status of the islands, and received gratifying replies, but without American forces adequate even to the defense of the Caribbean area, the situation continued to be discomfiting.[17] Three months later the President still had to write regretfully to Samuel Eliot Morison that he could not include the Azores within the Western Hemisphere, though the difficulty was not, as he artfully suggested, a cartographical one but a matter of strategical impossibility. By mid-1941 Mr. Roosevelt was finding the limits of the hemisphere more elastic, but this was after America's military strength had grown greater and her moral and material commitment to Britain's cause deeper.[18]

That commitment, signalized at the outset by the destroyer-bases agreement and intensified by the Tripartite Pact of September 27, 1940, which joined Japan to the European Axis, was formalized in the Lend-Lease Act enacted by Congress after lengthy and acrimonious debate on March 11. While HR 1776 was under consideration on Capitol Hill, American and British military and naval staff officers were meeting in profound secrecy a few blocks away to discuss strategic objectives and assignments in the event the United States should enter the war. Their conclusions, reported on March 27 as the now-famous ABC-1, in no sense represented a binding military commitment, nor were they tantamount to a covert "alliance," as isolationist critics have since charged. There can be no doubt, however, that these discussions conditioned American strategic planning henceforth, and indeed ABC-1 formed the basis for the new Joint Army-Navy War Plan (Rainbow V) which was submitted to the President early in June.[19]

17. Langer and Gleason, *Challenge to Isolation,* pp. 737–38.
18. Ibid., pp. 64 n.
19. On the staff conversations see Watson, *Prewar Plans,* pp. 367–82; and Langer and Gleason, *The Undeclared War,* pp. 285–89.

Army and Navy tasks as defined in Rainbow V included preparation for protective occupation of the Azores and Cape Verdes, as well as the immediate relief of British garrisons in Iceland and Aruba and Curaçao as soon as the United States should declare war.[20] Even though for prudential reasons the President withheld formal approval of ABC-1 and Rainbow V until the country actually engaged in hostilities, these plans guided the actions of his administration as far as it was possible to carry them out. The dispatch of American marines to Iceland preceded Pearl Harbor by five months, and during the crisis of May 1941 a task force was actually prepared to take over defense of the Azores.

The abortive plan for an expedition to the Azores was a desperate decision reluctantly taken during the panicky confusion of the April-May crisis in Europe. The first preference of Roosevelt and Hull, as in the case of Greenland and the Caribbean islands, was to freeze the status quo, to undertake no action themselves, and to discourage any impulsive British occupation. But Hitler's massive spring offensives blew apart whatever basis there had been for a policy of reserve, and galvanized Washington into frantic if somewhat undirected activity. In a matter of days Nazi armies slashed through Yugoslavia, scattered the Greeks and British forces sent from Africa to help them, and captured Crete in a gigantic airborne operation, while Rommel's *Afrika Korps* rumbled victoriously toward Egypt. Suez appeared doomed to Nazi domination, and it could be assumed Gibraltar would be next, for after such a display of irresistible power Franco it seemed must surely yield to Hitler's demands. And if Spain joined the Axis, Britain's traditional ally Portugal would be overrun. This

20. Rainbow V is printed in *Hearings before the Joint Committee on the Investigation of the Pearl Harbor Attack,* 79th Cong., 2d Sess., pp. 2877–2941.

is the way the British viewed the situation in their extremity of peril, and after an interval Washington also had to admit the danger.

Anxious for some token of American interest to stiffen Salazar and Franco, Mr. Churchill asked for an American naval visit to the Azores and Lisbon. The President was receptive to the idea, but discovered that the Portuguese government opposed any such display on the grounds that it might provoke the German occupation it was designed to discourage. The Franco government at the same time forestalled a visit to the Canaries by pleading a lack of oil for refuelling *U.S.S. Milwaukee* there.[21] Caught between British insistence and Portuguese nervousness, the Secretary of State fell back on verbal reaffirmations of confidence in British victory, which competed feebly with the thunder of Nazi arms for the ears of the Portuguese and Spanish dictators. A week later he found it necessary to reassure the Portuguese Minister that rumors of an intended American occupation of the Azores were unfounded.[22]

Unaware of Portuguese resistance to the idea, Churchill on April 23 again strongly urged his naval visit scheme, at the same time notifying Roosevelt that Britain had an expedition in readiness to sail to the Azores if Hitler entered Spain or Portugal. This moved the President to explain Lisbon's position to the Prime Minister and to add an unwelcome cautionary warning in the form of a modified No-Transfer declaration. He wished the British to move into the Azores only in case of direct German attack on Portugal or the islands, and also that it be made clear to the American people that no change of sovereignty was envisioned. In Churchill's view, any such delay would amount

21. Langer and Gleason, *The Undeclared War,* p. 367; memo from the State Dept. to Miss LeHand (April 19, 1941), Roosevelt Library, President's Secretary's File, State Dept.

22. Hull, *Memoirs,* 2, 940.

to handing over the islands to Hitler.[23] The British leader's promptings were not in vain, however, for in the next few weeks Roosevelt proved himself thoroughly alerted to the need for decisive action and prepared to go to extraordinary lengths to secure these strategic Atlantic outposts from German occupation.

On May 6, 1941, Senator Claude Pepper of Florida delivered a speech from the Senate floor in which he advocated occupying the "points of vantage from which [the] monsters are preparing to attack us. In that category I include Greenland, Iceland, the Azores, the Cape Verde Islands, the Canary Islands, Dakar, and with the British, Singapore."[24] The senator was willing to do this in the name of national security even without an "easement from the owners of the land." This speech drew immediate, alarmed inquiries from Madrid, and threw the Portuguese government into a state of agitation that persisted for two months, despite efforts by the Department of State to disavow any official sanction from the executive branch of the government for Pepper's suggestions.[25]

All such disavowals notwithstanding, the President's actions in the next three weeks tended strongly in the direction of Senator Pepper's proposals. On May 14 the President ordered the long-debated transfer of fleet units from the Pacific to the Atlantic. Mr. Hull's objections, based on the importance of the ships as deterrents to Japan, at last gave way before the arguments of Secretaries Stimson and Knox

23. Telegram from Roosevelt to Churchill (May 1, 1941). Langer and Gleason, *The Undeclared War*, pp. 367–68.

24. *Congressional Record*, 77th Cong., 1st Sess., p. 3617.

25. Note from the Spanish Ambassador to the Secretary of State (May 7, 1941), File 853B.014/16. Telegram from American Legation in Lisbon to State Dept. (May 9, 1941), File 853B.014/13. Telegram from State Dept. to American Legation in Lisbon (May 9, 1941), File 853B.01/14.

that the Atlantic patrol must be reinforced. The addition of a carrier, three battleships, and appropriate auxiliary vessels significantly strengthened the Atlantic Fleet and—after Admiral King's Operation Order Number 3 had extended patrol operations to include the Azores area—underlined the determination forming in Washington to prevent German penetrations in the Atlantic islands.[26] Two days later Roosevelt asked Hull to sound out the British on the idea of approaching Dr. Salazar on a protective occupation of the Azores, if the Portuguese government were forced to move there to escape the invading Germans. The British, as Portugal's allies, agreed to make the first approaches, though they had refrained from doing so previously for fear of alarming the sensitive Lisbon government.[27]

Before an answer to these queries could be had, the President embarked on a pair of abortive ventures which emphasized how serious a view he took of the situation. The first of these was the Welles draft message of May 20, and the other the order of May 22 for the preparation of an expedition for the Azores. Sumner Welles was deeply disturbed over the danger to the Atlantic islands, Britain's deteriorating military position in the Mediterranean, and indications that the French were on the point of making major concessions to the Reich. Word had leaked out of Vichy that Admiral Darlan, Pétain's violently Anglophobe aide, in his conversations with Nazi representatives in Paris was giving special privileges to Germany in Syria and North and West Africa. As it turned out, this was true, but pressure from American Ambassador Leahy and General Weygand caused Pétain early in June to reject the portions

26. Langer and Gleason, *The Undeclared War*, pp. 388–89, 444–51. Watson, *Prewar Plans*, p. 390.

27. Conn and Fairchild, *Framework of Hemisphere Defense*, pp. 116–17, and memo of conversation between Welles and Lord Halifax (May 17, 1941), Roosevelt Library, President's Secretary's File.

of the agreement dealing with Africa, particularly German use of Dakar.[28] Meanwhile the Under Secretary of State persuaded Roosevelt that drastic action was required, and received instructions to draft a message to Congress along the lines he considered necessary. The result was an extraordinary document which declared against the transfer, direct or indirect, of control to Axis governments "of the islands of the Atlantic which lie south of the 40th degree, north latitude, or of ports or territories in West Africa south of that parallel of latitude and north of the Equator, now under the sovereignty of the British, French, Spanish, Portuguese or Liberian Governments. Any passage of these islands, ports or territories into the hands of the Axis powers would be regarded as constituting a direct threat to the security of the eastern coast of South America and, consequently, as a direct threat to the security of the United States."[29]

Had this message been sent to Congress, it would certainly have represented the high-water mark of the No-Transfer principle of the Monroe Doctrine. But the Secretary of State persuaded the President against sending it. Always jealous of the prerogatives of his office, and resentful of Welles' easy access to Roosevelt as a personal friend, Hull felt his subordinate's actions in this instance were incautious in the extreme, and argued against the draft message on the grounds that it might provoke a German move in Africa and that it would arouse an unfortunate isolationist reaction at home.[30]

As he so frequently did when confronted with conflicting views among officials in his administration, Roosevelt

28. Hull, *Memoirs*, 2, 958–64. Langer and Gleason, *The Undeclared War*, pp. 504–9.

29. Draft Message to Congress (May 20, 1941), Roosevelt Library, President's Secretary's File, Welles.

30. Hull, *Memoirs*, 2, 959–60.

abandoned a policy he had seemed to approve, leaving everyone somewhat disgruntled and the ship of state temporarily rudderless. This was a most difficult period for the President. Torn by the radical demands of isolationists and interventionists, acutely aware of the desperate situation abroad, uncertain of Hitler's next move, and conscious of the necessity for a major decision about the direction of American policy, Roosevelt in an unseasonable May hot spell took to his bed pleading a persistent cold, but suffering most of all, according to Missy LeHand, from "a case of sheer exasperation."[31]

As if to cap the confusion, the *Bismarck* broke free to sink the British cruiser *Hood,* and Rudolph Hess parachuted inexplicably onto the estate of the Duke of Hamilton in Scotland. It was in the indecision of these turbulent days that the President directed Admiral Stark to prepare an expeditionary force of 25,000 men to be ready to sail in thirty days for the Azores, only to rescind the order a fortnight later in favor of the Iceland expedition.[32]

In truth Roosevelt didn't know what to do. He had been scheduled to deliver a major address, his first since the third term inaugural five months before, on Pan-American Day, but had postponed it for ten days hoping in vain that events might liberate him from his dilemma. When on May 27 he finally broadcast his speech, it was remarkable only for the declaration of an unlimited national emergency, an essentially meaningless gesture designed to give an impression of decisiveness.[33] While the President dwelt at considerable length on the danger to the security of the country that

31. Robert E. Sherwood, *Roosevelt and Hopkins* (2 vols. New York, 1950), *1,* 358.

32. Matloff and Snell, *Strategic Planning for Coalition Warfare,* pp. 49–50.

33. *Documents on American Foreign Relations, 1940–41, 3,* 51. Sherwood, *Roosevelt and Hopkins, 1,* 357–66.

would result from a German lodgment in the Atlantic Islands or Dakar, he failed to announce any plans for dealing with a situation that would bring the war "to the brink of the Western Hemisphere itself."

However innocuous these remarks may have appeared to American listeners, they produced a terrified outburst from Lisbon, where it was felt that if they did not foreshadow a move by the United States forces to occupy the Azores, they were at the very least a reckless provocation for increased Axis pressure on Portugal and her possessions. In a note to Washington the Salazar government stressed its neutrality and its determination to defend itself against every threat to Portuguese sovereignty, and demanded written assurances that the enlarged definition of the vital area of American self-defense contained in the President's fireside chat represented no such threat from the United States.[34]

Washington was somewhat surprised at the intensity of the Portuguese reaction and at the evident misinterpretation of the President's remarks that it revealed, but the Department of State, instead of hastening to set these fears at rest, intensified them by delaying their reply for more than a week. When it arrived, Lisbon found the American note "vague and generic" and lacking the categorical denial of intent to send forces to the Azores which they sought.[35] Indeed, the Roosevelt administration found it difficult to give any such assurance in good faith at a moment when an expedition for the Azores was in fact being prepared, when

34. Note from the Portuguese government (May 30, 1941), File 853B.014/36. See also Langer and Gleason, *The Undeclared War,* pp. 516–17.

35. Telegram from American Legation in Lisbon to State Dept. (June 7, 1941), File 853B.014/22. Note to Portuguese government (June 10, 1941), 853B.014/36. Memo of conversation, the Portuguese Minister and the Under Secretary of State (June 13, 1941), File 853B.014/23a.

instructions had been sent to sound out Brazil on participation in the expedition, and while conversations were in progress with British representatives on the question of securing Portuguese consent to a joint British-American defense of the islands in case a German threat materialized.[36] Though the United States government could and did stress their adherence to principles of respect for established sovereignties, and clearly hoped to be able to act on Portuguese invitation if the Azores were endangered, there was no evading the possibility that overriding considerations of self-defense might make arbitrary protective action necessary in an emergency.

This crisis of confidence that clouded Portuguese-American relations was dissipated largely through the good offices of friendly foreign governments. The Foreign Minister of Brazil, Senhor Aranha, did yeoman service in persuading the Portuguese government that the President's words could not be interpreted as a threat to Portuguese sovereignty or possession of the islands, and the British government quietly conveyed the same impression to their ally during discussions of defense arrangements for the Azores.[37]

Hitler's attack on the Soviet Union in late June of 1941 relieved some of the tension in Washington about the Atlantic islands and Dakar, although such relief was thought to be only temporary, given the generally gloomy predictions about Russia's chances for survival. Troops

36. Memo from President to Secretary of State (May 31, 1941), File 853B.014/34 1/2. Memo of conversation, British Minister of Embassy and the Under Secretary of State, File 853B.014/23.

37. Telegram from United States Embassy in Brazil to State Dept., and reply (June 2, 1941), File 853B.014/34. Telegrams from Embassy in Brazil (June 13–14, 1941), File 853B.014/24. Memo of conversations, British Minister of Embassy and the Under Secretary of State (June 4, 18, 1941), File 853B.014/23, 30.

which might have been used to defend the Azores were dispatched instead to Iceland, where they released British forces and help guard the northern approaches to the British Isles. News of American landings in Iceland produced a fresh spasm of anxiety in Portugal, which was finally allayed by a personal letter from Roosevelt to Salazar.[38] Writing in his most warmly cordial tone, the President expressed his regret at the misunderstanding that had arisen between the two governments, and emphasized in a way calculated to set Salazar's fears at rest the firm desire of the United States that Portugal remain in sovereign control of her possessions. Any American action in the Azores would consist of emergency assistance to the Portuguese in their defense and at their request, possibly in association with Brazil, whose participation could be counted on to soothe Lisbon's alarm. Roosevelt had written President Vargas a few days earlier, and though the Brazilian government decided that it could make no military contribution to the defense of the Azores for the time being, it gave its hearty approval to the objectives of the United States.[39] All this had the desired effect on the Portuguese dictator, and greatly facilitated the successful conclusion of the British negotiations for defense of the Azores in case Hitler should attack Portugal.[40]

The Atlantic islands and West Africa were an important subject of discussion at the Atlantic Conference of Roosevelt and Churchill in August. The Prime Minister agreed that Salazar's reply to the President's letter constituted a "green light" to American action (only permissible if the

38. Dispatch from United States Embassy in Lisbon to State Dept. (July 12, 1941), File 859A.20/63. Roosevelt to Salazar (July 14, 1941), Roosevelt Library, President's Secretary's File.

39. Langer and Gleason, *The Undeclared War*, pp. 387–88.

40. Memo of conversation, British Ambassador and the Under Secretary of State (July 30, 1941), File 853B.014/58.

British could not undertake it). Thus at the Conference a tentative division of responsibility assigned the preventive occupation of the Azores to the United States, after Britain had arranged it with Lisbon, while British forces would take over protection of the Canary and Cape Verde groups. By September 15 Churchill had an organized force in readiness to occupy the Canaries, and shortly before Pearl Harbor he felt it might be necessary to move into these islands whether or not the Axis attacked Spain, in order to combat the appalling losses from Nazi submarine operations in the South Atlantic. Actually, it was not until mid-1943 that United States forces finally set up bases in the Azores, and then by friendly arrangement with the Lisbon government.[41]

These discussions about the Atlantic islands illustrate some important changes in the American administration of the No-Transfer principle that were taking place in 1941. Britain was now clearly admitted as a partner, and if the policy could be said to have been pan-americanized at Havana the year before, its proprietorship now extended to include the free Atlantic community. The No-Transfer principle served as part of the nucleus of the developing coalition policy Washington was formulating in the interests of American security—interests which in the air age extended far beyond traditional hemispheric delineations, and which demanded departures from static concepts of continental defense.

The main impediment to a resolute pursuit of these goals remained the lack of sufficient military power. Conscious of the restrictions placed on them by shortages of trained personnel, by the statutory limitation on service by draftees and National Guard units outside the Hemi-

41. Conn and Fairchild, *Framework of Hemisphere Defense,* p. 170. Sherwood, *Roosevelt and Hopkins, 1,* 431, 495 ff., *2,* 343, 363. Langer and Gleason, *The Undeclared War,* pp. 664–70, 763.

sphere, and by the critical shipping problem, military chiefs were less enthusiastic about far-flung preventive occupations than were the politicians. The Army staff agreed that the Azores occupation was of primary importance and might barely be practicable, but Secretary Stimson, with the islands and Dakar in mind, uttered a warning in October about getting bogged down in "side shows" to the detriment of the vital problems of the northwest approaches to Britain.[42] The result was that no working military plan for forestalling a German move into Dakar or Casablanca was formulated before Pearl Harbor, the defense of that indispensable area being entrusted to the diplomats, armed with No-Transfer declarations and threats of economic coercion.[43] Happily these proved sufficient, given Russia's survival.

ICELAND

The announced reason for the landing of United States Marines in Iceland on July 7, 1941, was the prevention of a German occupation there, but that threat was actually negligible. Other considerations were more immediately operative in the decision. Like the development of American policy toward the Atlantic islands and West Africa, the Iceland episode reflects not only the geographical extension of the No-Transfer principle but also the shift it was undergoing from a largely negative strategy of defense, designed to insulate the Hemisphere from war, to an armory of active measures in support of Britain's war effort.

It will be remembered that British troops had arrived to defend Iceland with the full acquiescence of the Reyk-

42. Conn and Fairchild, *Framework,* p. 169. Langer and Gleason, p. 778. Matloff and Snell, *Strategic Planning,* pp. 102–4.

43. Langer and Gleason, pp. 584, 785. Langer, *Our Vichy Gamble,* p. 187. Hull, *Memoirs,* 2, 1040–44.

javik government in May 1940. During the darkest hours of Britain's peril the following December, Iceland put out feelers to discover how the United States would receive a request for protection if the British position deteriorated further. Secretary Hull found it necessary to turn aside these overtures, expressing sympathy but also an unwilling-ness to undertake any commitments at the moment.[44] This attitude of detachment began to change, however, with the Lend-Lease program for supplying the British war effort and with Berlin's extension of the war zone and in-tensification of naval and air activity around Iceland in March. Churchill urged the dispatch of American forces to Iceland to relieve the British garrison there for duty elsewhere and, perhaps more important, to reduce the bur-den borne by the Royal Navy.[45] In April negotiations to this end began in earnest, conducted with utmost secrecy on behalf of the President by Harry Hopkins.

The main diplomatic problem proved to be how to wangle an invitation from the Icelandic government. No longer so anxious about Britain's ability to defend the is-land, Prime Minister Jónasson did worry about the Ger-man reaction to a formal request for United States protec-tion, and tried to avoid making it. The British considered the issue relatively unimportant, but the Department of State, mindful of the watchful malevolence of Japan, of recent experience with Portugal over the Azores, and of Latin–American sensibilities, was insistent. Churchill ap-plied pressure on Reykjavik, the American expedition ac-tually delayed sailing for two days awaiting an invitation, and finally Jónasson acquiesced, though he adroitly avoided using the word "invite." Unfortunately his note arrived after the convoy had put to sea, so that for security reasons

44. Hull, 2, 946.
45. Langer and Gleason, pp. 452–53, 522–23.

the Icelandic proposal, the American acceptance, and the landing of the 1st United States Marine Brigade all had to be announced simultaneously on July 7.[46]

Though the President in his message to Congress listed the dangers to hemispheric security that would follow a Nazi occupation of Iceland, it seems evident that the immediate impulse behind his dispatch of forces was not fear of a transfer to Germany but a desire to make some decisive gesture to give heart to the British people and some relief from their military overextension.[47] Certainly this was the safest gesture he could make, for while the Iceland project was planned before Hitler invaded the Soviet Union, it was put into execution after the German forces were fully engaged in the East. The Azores expedition would have been more important for the defense of the Hemisphere, but the attitude of Portugal made it unfeasible for the moment. It may be noted parenthetically that neither the Army nor the Navy chiefs were especially enthusiastic about the reduction of combat effectiveness that would result from an adequate garrisoning of Iceland, but they were after all committed under ABC-1 and Rainbow V to relieving British troops there at some unspecified future date.[48]

While the Iceland expedition was extremely gratifying to American interventionists, the President had no intention of using it as a direct challenge to isolationist opinion.

---

46. Samuel Eliot Morison, *History of United States Naval Operations in World War II* (13 vols. to date, Boston, 1947–59), Vol. 1, *The Battle of the Atlantic*, pp. 74–79. Memos of conversations, the British Ambassador and the Under Secretary of State (June 22, 26, 1941), File 859A.20/20 1/2, 3/12. Langer and Gleason, pp. 524–75 ff. Exchange of notes with Iceland (July 1, 1941), *Documents on American Foreign Relations, 1940–41, 4*, 454–57.

47. Message to Congress (July 7, 1941), *Documents . . . 1940–41*, pp. 457–58.

48. Matloff and Snell, *Strategic Planning*, pp. 46, 49.

In his message to Congress he was careful not to assert that Iceland lay within the Western Hemisphere, and his use of volunteer troops avoided the danger that the issue might be raised in connection with the statutory prohibition on the use of draftees outside the limits of the Hemisphere. When he was questioned at his press conference the next day about the inclusion of Iceland in the Western Hemisphere, he was jocularly evasive, saying that it was all a matter of which geographer one had talked to last, inferring at the same time that definitions of the Hemisphere depended on the defense requirements of the nation.[49] The previous April, Roosevelt had set the limits of the neutrality patrol at 25 degrees west longitude, which left Iceland outside the Hemisphere, but a few days after the Iceland landings he drew a revised map for Harry Hopkins which "bent" the line of demarcation to include the island. Admiral King at once translated this definition into standing operating orders for the Atlantic Fleet.[50]

The unexpectedly favorable public and congressional reaction to the Iceland expedition emboldened the President to take steps toward a more dynamic support of Britain in the Battle of the Atlantic which Churchill had been delicately but urgently suggesting for some time. On July 19 the Commander in Chief of the Atlantic Fleet issued Operation Plan No. 6, which directed the Navy to supply escort protection to convoys of American and Icelandic vessels and to the "shipping of any nationality which may join such convoys." At the last moment, however, the President drew back, and suspended for the time being the provision for convoying British vessels as far as Iceland. The United States Navy now swept the sea lanes of hostile craft two-

49. New York *Times* (July 9, 1941).
50. Sherwood, *Roosevelt and Hopkins, 1,* 356–57, 376–79. Morison, *Battle of the Atlantic,* p. 74.

thirds of the way to Britain, and that was a great advance over the mere reporting of enemy warships that prevailed before the American landing in Iceland.[51]

However cautiously, the United States was proceeding nearer the brink of war through this application of the No-Transfer principle. Churchill called it an "event of first-rate political and strategic importance," and Grand Admiral Raeder inquired of the Fuehrer whether Germany should not treat it as a declaration of war. Hitler wanted no provocation of the United States until the Russian situation was under control, but his Navy chief waited apprehensively for an American move against the Atlantic islands or Dakar.[52] The Iceland expedition clearly had produced the effects Mr. Roosevelt had hoped for.

ARUBA, CURAÇAO, AND SURINAM

The Act of Havana was never mentioned in connection with Iceland, but it could hardly be avoided when negotiations got under way for the relief of British forces by American units in Aruba and Curaçao, which had also been provided for in the ABC-1 staff agreements. Although the reason for the dispatch of United States troops was not in this case any alleged threat of transfer to Germany but simply the protection of the oil refineries on the islands and of the bauxite mines in Surinam (Netherlands Guiana), the proximity of these areas to interested Latin American nations made some gesture in the direction of a cooperative policy necessary. In the case of Aruba and Curaçao this necessity infinitely complicated the process of arranging with the Dutch government for the protective occupation.

51. Langer and Gleason, *The Undeclared War,* p. 579. Morison, pp. 78–79.

52. Langer and Gleason, p. 579. *Fuehrer Conferences, 1941, 1,* 29; 2, 3.

At the time the Iceland expedition was being prepared the British government approached Washington about taking over the defense of Aruba and Curaçao, but the Department of State stalled, taking refuge behind the need for prior consultation and agreement with the other American Republics under the Act of Havana.[53] This project did not actually reach the negotiation stage until November 1941. Meanwhile, under the urgent prodding of General Marshall, who was greatly concerned about protecting the indispensable supply of bauxite for the American aluminum industry, talks were initiated between the Netherlands government in exile in London and the United States about sending American forces to Surinam to bolster the inadequate Dutch defenses there.[54]

At American insistence, Brazil was invited by the Netherlands to participate in the defense of Surinam, though the Dutch sought to limit such participation to increased vigilance along the common frontier and a Brazilian military mission to be stationed in Paramaribo. Brazil was satisfied with these arrangements, and by the middle of October the road to agreement seemed open. Then the Netherlands government balked, presenting objections about questions of command and other details that consumed over a month of precious time, and that President Roosevelt later characterized as "perfectly childish."[55] Finally, on November 24 the joint announcement of the agreement was released,

53. Memo of conversation, Under Secretary of State and the British Minister of Embassy (June 4, 1941), memo of conversation, Under Secretary and the British Ambassador (June 16, 1941): File 856B.-014/16, 18.

54. Unless otherwise indicated, this discussion of the Surinam negotiations rests on the excellent, compact account in Langer and Gleason, *The Undeclared War*, pp. 603–4.

55. Memo of the President to the Assistant Secretary of State (Jan. 29, 1942), File 856B.20/77.

and United States troops began disembarking in Surinam the following day.

While these discussions were in their final stages, the British ambassador renewed his request that the United States consider assuming protection of Aruba and Curaçao, which Britain was finding increasingly burdensome. This time the Department of State was in a more receptive mood, and entrusted the early negotiations with the Netherlands to Britain. Things moved smoothly enough toward a request for United States protection, but the Dutch proved stubbornly resistant to Washington's desire for Venezuelan participation along the lines of Brazil's in Surinam. The British failed to appreciate fully the importance attached to the inclusion of Venezuela by the Department of State, and somewhat irritably suggested that Washington take the question up directly with the Netherlands government.[56]

This was done by an exchange of personal messages between President Roosevelt and Queen Wilhelmina. Despite the fact that American entry into the war had now increased a thousandfold the urgency of protecting the oil refineries and ensuring the solidarity of the Americas—and despite the fact that Washington was still chafing over the Surinam negotiations—the tone of the American notes was cordially patient. The President urged the inclusion of Venezuela in the defense forces for Aruba and Curaçao on the grounds of inter-American agreements (the Act of Havana), the stimulating effect it might have on Venezuelan measures against Axis propaganda and sabotage, and hemispheric solidarity (Venezuela had broken off diplomatic relations with the Axis). The Dutch remained adamantly opposed, however, partly because of suspicions of Venezuela's motives arising out of old disputes about claims to

56. Memos of conversations, Under Secretary of State and the British Ambassador (Nov. 12, 28, Dec. 29, 1941), Files 856B.20/14, 16, 30.

the islands, partly out of pique at the appointment of General Wavell as Supreme Commander in the Far East, with no Dutch officer even included on his staff. This latter grievance arose not simply from wounded vanity but from a concern for the future of the Netherlands East Indies and the possible results of this omission on the effectiveness of Dutch control over the somewhat difficult authorities at Batavia.[57]

In view of the Netherlands' attitude and of the mounting need for action, the United States found itself forced to consider sending its troops without waiting for agreement about the Venezuelan token mission. The President was prodded toward this reluctant conclusion by his military chiefs, who were smoldering with exasperation at the delay in protecting the vital flow of oil to the United Nations war machine, and who had never appreciated the State Department's emphasis on inter-American cooperation in defense to begin with. The Dutch had already given their assent to the dispatch of United States military aircraft to the islands, so that the President decided to move alone, meanwhile going on record at Caracas and with the Dutch authorities at London as placing the utmost emphasis on the importance of Venezuelan participation.[58]

The Venezuelan reaction to this decision was immediate and violent. President Medina warned that Venezuela might find it necessary to withdraw its delegate to the

57. Telegrams from the President to the Queen of the Netherlands (Dec. 30, 1941, Jan. 2, 1942), Files 856B.20/17, 859B.20/18. Telegram from American Minister to the Netherlands (in London) to State Dept. (Jan 5, 1942), File 856B.20/20.

58. Telegram, State Dept. to American Minister to the Netherlands (Jan. 24, 1942), File 856B.20/32. Letter from Secretary of War Stimson to the President (Jan. 29, 1942), Watson, *Prewar Plans,* pp. 491–92. Memo from President to Assistant Secretary of State (Jan. 29, 1942), File 856B.20/77. American Minister to the Netherlands to State Dept. (Jan. 20, 1942), File 856B.20/31.

trusteeship commission set up under the Act of Havana, which had never met. The Department of State tried desperately to forestall any such lesion to the policy of cooperative hemispheric defense by stressing that since no question of transfer of territory was involved in the Dutch islands, there was some doubt as to whether the Act of Havana applied.[59] This was quite a different argument from the one employed in earlier conversations with the Dutch, but neither position is really uncandid, for it would be accurate to say that the United States government wished to proceed in the spirit of the Havana agreements and the general framework of inter-Americanism even though not required to do so in this particular instance by the letter of the law.[60]

Fortunately everything worked out well at the last moment. Sumner Welles closeted himself with the Netherlands Foreign Minister, who was in Washington in early February, and together with Venezuelan Ambassador Escalante they worked out an agreement on Venezuela which was substantially the same as the arrangement for Brazil, except that the military mission would not reside in the islands but would travel back and forth. On February 7 Washington announced the Netherlands invitation and the landing of troops in the islands. That the danger was not illusory was demonstrated a week later, when German submarines shelled the mammoth refineries at Aruba and sank five tankers in neighboring waters.[61]

59. Telegram from State Dept. to American Embassy in Caracas, (Feb. 1, 1942), File 856B.20/40.
60. Memo from the Division of American Republics to the Under Secretary of State on the problem of including Venezuela in the defense of Aruba and Curaçao (Feb. 3, 1941), File 856B.20/46.
61. Telegram from State Dept. to the American Minister to the Netherlands (Feb. 6, 1942), File 856B.20/37; State Dept. release on the defense of Aruba and Curaçao (Feb. 7, 1942), *Documents on American Foreign Relations, 4,* 468. Watson, *Prewar Plans,* p. 492.

ST. PIERRE AND MIQUELON

The only actual instance of a transfer of control of European possessions in the Hemisphere during the second World War period was the forcible occupation of the French Islands of St. Pierre and Miquelon by Free French Forces on Christmas Eve 1941. This was an *opéra bouffe* affair in many ways, a teapot tempest as Roosevelt said, but it had important effects on our relations with Canada and Britain, it might have aroused difficulties with Latin America, and it certainly complicated the already difficult Vichy policy of the United States. Cordell Hull called it a footnote that threatened to become a whole chapter in history, and in fact devoted a chapter in his *Memoirs* to recording the anguish he suffered over the episode.[62]

These tiny fishing islands lie off the coast of Newfoundland in the mouth of the Gulf of St. Lawrence. The sole remnants of France's once great North American empire, they had little strategic significance in 1941, except that they had a powerful radio transmitter that could have been used to guide enemy submarines or aircraft against shipping entering the North Atlantic sea lanes. The Canadian government was under considerable pressure from Newfoundland and its own armed services to occupy the islands in order to prevent such use of the radio, but was deterred by opposition from Washington. St. Pierre and Miquelon were under the jurisdiction of Admiral Robert at Martinique, with whom, as we have seen, the United States after lengthy negotiation had concluded an agreement to neutralize French possessions in the Western Hemisphere. Robert was living up to his side of the bargain, and the

62. The best accounts of the St. Pierre–Miquelon affair are in Hull, *Memoirs*, 2, 1127–38; Sherwood, *Roosevelt and Hopkins*, 2, 48–60; and Langer, *Our Vichy Gamble*, pp. 212–26. Unless otherwise indicated, this narrative is based on them.

State Department felt that any abrupt political or military move on the part of Canada would disturb these arrangements and throw open the entire question of French possessions once again. Maintenance of the colonial status quo remained a primary object of United States policy, and this was the crux of the problem when Admiral Muselier and his little band of Free French upset the applecart.[63]

The St. Pierre–Miquelon affair is a microcosmic study of the vicissitudes of coalition warfare, with its frictions over primary objectives, its frustrations, its little "treacheries," and conflicts of personalities—with the added difficulty in a democracy of necessary reliance on public opinion. The British government had broken diplomatic relations with France at the advent of the Pétain regime, and had meanwhile adopted General Charles de Gaulle's Free French movement, which it supported with money, arms, and publicity. The United States maintained an embassy at Vichy with the object of keeping the French Fleet and colonial possessions in North Africa and the Western Hemisphere out of German hands, a policy which had the enthusiastic private support of Churchill's government but to which he was unwilling to give the public stamp of approval that the Department of State wanted for its unpopular course of action. Just how unpopular the Vichy policy had become was made abundantly and painfully clear to Hull during the crisis over the French islands.

The Canadians found themselves uncomfortably in the middle of an affair that after all had more to do with them directly than it did with Britain or the United States. In early December the British suggested to Ottawa that the Free French be allowed to occupy the islands, this solution

63. Memo of conversation, member of the Division of European Affairs and the Counselor of the Canadian Legation (June 5, 1941), File 851A.014/9. Dispatch from the American Minister in Ottawa to State Dept. (July 16, 1941), File 851A.014/8.

being politically less complicated than the direct negotiations with Vichy authorities for control of the wireless by Canadian forces which Washington now favored. Canada consulted Washington and met the familiar objections to this plan. Meanwhile de Gaulle sent his Minister of Marine, Admiral Muselier, to Canada to inspect Free French corvettes operating there and to rally the islanders to his cause. Muselier approached the American minister in Ottawa about his project, while the British made advances directly to Washington on behalf of a Free French occupation. Mr. Roosevelt, coached by Hull, flatly opposed any such action. By December 17 the British were convinced that there was no hope of budging Washington in this matter and sent word that they had received assurances from de Gaulle that he had abandoned any plans for occupying the islands. On December 22 the Canadian government informed the State Department that in view of Britain's disinclination to favor the plan for Canadian control of the radio station, they were dropping that negotiation. So at the time of Churchill's arrival at the White House matters stood at total stalemate but with Washington's hemispheric policy intact.

This logjam was suddenly shattered by de Gaulle's secret orders to seize the islands, in arrogant violation of his pledges in London. Admiral Muselier reluctantly obeyed his Chief, whose action he later characterized as "that of a dictator," and "not democratic enough to fit his ideal of France."[64] Ottawa was "shocked" at the Free French coup, which would inevitably "embarrass" their future relations with de Gaulle, and stood ready to accept any solution agreed on by Britain and the United States. The British were also taken by complete surprise, but at first adamantly refused to consider any move to expel the Free French

64. Sherwood, 2, 50.

Forces, and only later under heavy pressure from Washington did Churchill and Eden bend at all. Even so, they insisted that de Gaulle agree to any final solution, and since the French leader stubbornly refused to compromise, no agreement was ever reached.

Cordell Hull was driven to admit the final impasse only after a tenacious struggle to salvage his Latin American and Vichy policies. De Gaulle's *fait accompli* was acutely annoying to State Department officials, who had renewed their commitments to Admiral Robert to maintain the colonial status quo only a few days before and who had to endure the fretting and threats of the Vichy ambassador. Henry-Haye hinted darkly at German demands in North Africa and a possible reopening of the question of French Caribbean possessions.[65] To make matters worse, there was the Havana accord with Latin America, which unquestionably applied in this unhappy incident and which might be wholly disrupted by a failure to restore Vichy to authority in St. Pierre and Miquelon.

Under these circumstances Hull could see no alternative to withdrawal by the Gaullist invaders. On Christmas Day he issued a public statement in which he said that "the action taken by three so-called Free French ships at St. Pierre–Miquelon was an arbitrary action contrary to the agreement of all parties concerned and certainly without the prior knowledge or consent in any sense of the United States Government."[66] His suggestion that the Free French be expelled was greeted with furious indignation by the American public, many of whom indicated their resentment at

65. Telegrams from American Embassy in Vichy (Dec. 26, 1941), File 851A.01/19. Memo of conversation, Secretary of State and Ambassador Henry-Haye (Dec. 26, 1941), File 851A.00/47.

66. Statement of State Dept. (Dec. 25, 1941), *Documents on American Foreign Relations, 1940–41, 4,* 466.

what they considered a slur on the Free French by addressing themselves to the "so-called State Department" and the "so-called Secretary of State."[67] The Gaullist cause was growing more popular in the United States, and the daring descent on St. Pierre and Miquelon was one bright spot in the otherwise depressing war news. It seemed nothing short of criminal to restore the collaborationist Vichy regime. For the first time in his career as Secretary of State, Cordell Hull found himself the object of widespread, bitter criticism, and it hurt the old Tennessean sorely. He turned to the President for support, but Roosevelt, perhaps amused at Hull's vulnerability to the kind of attacks he and the rest of the Cabinet had endured for years and certainly preoccupied with far more important and urgent problems, failed at first to back him up strongly.

The Secretary of State could not erase a growing conviction that the British had stabbed him in the back. In the first few days after the seizure of the islands, Hull had some "blunt" conversations with Churchill and Lord Halifax, and got the impression that they appreciated the force of his position. Then on December 30 the Prime Minister journeyed to Ottawa to deliver what Hull bitterly described as a "violent diatribe against Vichy along with fulsome praise of de Gaulle."[68] Churchill, of course, had the French Canadians, among others, in mind when he made these remarks, but the Department of State was less interested in problems of Commonwealth unity or the French Resistance movement than in the impression left by the Prime Minister's speech that Britain and the United States were at odds over our Vichy policy. For reasons of state Churchill was still an ardent supporter of de Gaulle; it was not until many troubled months later that disillusion set in and he

67. Sherwood, *Roosevelt and Hopkins*, 2, 53. Hull, *Memoirs*, 2, 1130–31.

68. Hull, 2, 1133.

would remark sourly that the heaviest cross he had to bear during the war was the Cross of Lorraine.

When Churchill refused to issue a restatement or clarification of the views implied in his Ottawa speech, Hull's exasperation reached such a peak that he considered resigning his office.[69] In the face of this serious development, the President's attitude of amused indifference evaporated, and by the middle of January he was actually threatening to send a naval force to expel the Free French from St. Pierre and Miquelon.[70] The British Prime Minister relented to the extent of accepting Hull's face-saving formula for what amounted to a joint British–Canadian–American condominium for control of the radio station, but still only on the condition that de Gaulle's consent could be obtained.[71] This proved impossible, but as tempers cooled the whole incident receded to proper proportions amid the gigantic war effort against the Axis, and this one transfer of control remained a fact. As the incident proved, the Havana agreements and the Vichy policy rested on large considerations of national interest on both sides, and if legal technicalities could upset them, any pretext would suffice. The old, rigid policies of hemisphere defense were being outdated by the war, and while the State Department was rightly concerned about the solidarity of the Americas and the security of North Africa from German control, there were other interests which must also command high priorities now, and paramount among these must be the maintenance of confidence and morale in relations with our allies.

69. Ibid., p. 1137.
70. Sherwood, 2, 60.
71. Memo of conversations, American Minister to Canada and representatives of the Canadian Office of External Affairs (Jan. 14–19, 1942), File 851A.01/1–1842.

The United States had entered the war, but it had done so in a way that tended to obscure rather than to illuminate the real issues, in a way that concealed from Americans the enduring conditions of United States security upon which both wartime decisions and planning for the postwar world must proceed. The United States did not enter the war altogether because of the catastrophic attack at Pearl Harbor, as most Americans believed; that attack came because the nation was already deeply involved in the global war to prevent an upset in the world balance of power that would place the United States in mortal danger. Roosevelt's interventionist advisers ceaselessly urged him to take the country into his confidence, to make clear the strategic reasoning upon which his decisions were based. At the time of the Iceland expedition, Secretary Stimson pleaded with the President to state frankly that his hopes for avoiding the use of force were growing dim, and that the nation must mobilize in support of the free nations who were fighting our battle as much as their own.[72] A year before, at the time his appointment was up for confirmation by Congress, Stimson had boldly declared his own conviction that passive doctrines of hemisphere defense had been outmoded by circumstances, and that in effect the Monroe Doctrine could be upheld only by abandoning it, by extending our line of defense "far out into the Atlantic Ocean."[73]

The President, however, fearful of isolationist opinion, equivocated and evaded the hard truth in his public utterances, not only on the subject of Iceland but on naval patrolling, Lend-Lease, and the Atlantic Islands, preferring to the end to present these measures solely as instruments of traditional hemispheric defense. To the extent that he

72. Henry L. Stimson and McGeorge Bundy, *On Active Service in Peace and War* (New York, 1947), pp. 372–73.

73. Ibid., pp. 325–26.

was uncandid Roosevelt did public understanding a disservice and failed to provide a sound basis for public opinion on matters of policy. Surely in a democracy this is a necessary function of a chief executive—not to utter, Cassandra-like, prophecies of doom but not to act as a tranquilizer either. The President occupies a unique position and enjoys a unique opportunity for informing the nation of its needs and interests. It is certainly better to "do good by stealth," as Roosevelt did, than to do nothing at all, but it is always a mistake to underestimate the capacity of the public for understanding and accepting unpalatable truths, especially when the leader can control the way in which such information is presented.

The United States became involved in the second World War without a clear notion of the kind of world order that was necessary to its security, and this fact contributed to a good many unfortunate decisions during the war, as well as to a real danger that in the aftermath there would be another ostrich-like retreat into isolationism and false doctrines of defense. Some of these dangers did actually materialize after 1945, to the confusion of American policy, and if the great disturber had not been a Communist power, it is not clear that the United States would have responded in time to the challenge. As it was, the response was less realistic than it might have been had the nation been fully aware of the stake it had always had in stable power structures in Europe and, more recently, in Asia.

CHAPTER 14

Epilogue: The Exploded Hemisphere

The history of the No-Transfer policy has a beginning and in a sense an end. Of course it would still be set in operation to prevent an unwelcome transfer of colonial possessions in the New World if the occasion arose: the Treaty of Havana remains in force, and the No-Transfer principle has been embodied by inference at least in the inter-American security structure set up at Rio de Janeiro in 1947. But in a fundamental sense it has passed into history with the passing of American hemispheric isolationism; it has burst the bonds that confined it to the Americas and merged insensibly and, it seems, finally into the global policy of containment.

The beginnings of the No-Transfer principle, like most foreign policies, were extremely casual. The Founding Fathers, who were political realists through experience and conviction, instinctively developed the idea to implement the basic objective of their foreign policy, the political separation of the New World from the broils of Europe in the interest of peace and prosperity. In the early years when the United States was surrounded by European possessions, the principle evolved as the basic instrument for promoting the grand designs of American security policy—isolation, the preservation of a balance of power among our neighbors, access to the Mississippi outlet, and continental expansion. It was not for a long time stated or conceived of as a generalized principle, but devised ad hoc for each occasion of danger and declared without reference to precedent by George Washington in regard to Canada, Alexander Hamilton and Thomas Jefferson in Louisiana, James Madison in the Floridas, and John Quincy Adams in Cuba. Only in the mid-nineteenth century did a sense of tradition and continuity cluster about it, and not until Grant and Fish was it stated as applicable to any and all transfers of European possessions in the Hemisphere, rather than being specifically applied to a single colony.

A great deal has been written in recent years about the tendency of Americans to conceive of foreign policy in moralistic and legalistic rather than in power-political terms, and their tendency to lose sight of the fact that force is the ultimate sanction underlying every political system, national or international. The unquestionably nonpolitical cast of American thought and action in foreign affairs had its origin in the unusual experience of the United States in having developed to great power rank between the Napoleonic wars and the first World War, a period unique in European history for political stability and the absence of a general war. Geographically isolated from the centers of power by the ocean, guarded fortuitously and unconsciously by the British navy, lulled into forgetfulness that the silent working of the European balance of power kept the peace, and totally free from a military threat on their own borders, the people of the United States fondly imagined that through some superiority of morals and institutions they had engineered an escape from the realm of power politics which was the blight of the Old World into a purer region where ethics and law ruled human behavior. Certainly they were spared the burden of expenditures for armaments, and permitted to enjoy the matchless abundance of the land in a state of military security unparalleled by any great nation of modern times.

Nevertheless, even during these golden years of relative security the United States continuously practiced power politics, though of a peculiarly negative sort, designed to banish the European brand of balance of power from the Americas. The No-Transfer principle and the doctrines of Monroe which were evolved out of it to meet the changed circumstances after the independence of Latin America were policies realistically based on strategic considerations and frequently backed by threats of force. Americans never wholly lost touch with the fact of power in their practice, however their precepts ran, for the No-Transfer principle has been the most consistently applied, the most unanimously approved, and the most frequently declared foreign policy of the United States. It was rudimentary political common sense to oppose transfers of territory to stronger colonial powers in our neighborhood, just as it has always been for Britain to oppose the occupation of the Low Countries by a major continental power. The primary objective of the No-Transfer policy has been to prevent an upset in the local constellation of power by keeping American colonies in the hands of weak nations, by preventing the introduction of new colonial proprietors in the Hemisphere, and by working toward the eventual elimination of these alien influences from the political life of the Americas. As soon as the nation was strong enough, it turned the Caribbean into an American lake and asserted its predominance throughout this hemisphere in order to establish a *Pax Americana*, to achieve the most desirable of power positions—unrivaled supremacy.

All of this was genuinely defensive, genuinely pacific, aimed not at the exercise of dominion but at the exclusion of a political system that was thought to lead to inevitable wars. The heyday of American isolation from Europe in the 1930's was also the honeymoon period of Pan-Americanism. The United States abandoned its patronizing attitude toward the American republics and assiduously cultivated a sense of solidarity among equal sovereignties in an attempt to erect an impregnable hemispheric bastion against the winds of doctrine and tides of power from across the oceans. That this effort had been brilliantly successful was demonstrated at Panama in 1939 and Havana in 1940, where the nations of the New World acted with remarkable swiftness and unanimity to insulate the American continents from the wars abroad, partly through the agency of a multilateralized No-Transfer principle.

Notwithstanding these impressive evidences of vitality, the Western Hemisphere concept was actually entering a fatal decline.[1] For the second World War, which produced an extraordinary flowering of hemispheric unity, also set in motion currents of thought in the United States which have undermined the traditional assumptions upon which hemispheric isolationism had rested, and led to its virtual abandonment as a functional element in political planning at Washington.

The revolt against the Western Hemisphere complex was led by the interventionists, public officials like Stimson who candidly declared that defense policies confined to the conventional limits of the Hemisphere were dangerously ill-suited to the facts of a world made smaller by the technological revolution in warfare, and organizations like William Allen White's Committee for Defending America by Aiding the Allies, which ceaselessly urged the importance to American security of keeping Britain and later Russia in the field against the rampant aggressiveness of Hitler's Germany. These arguments were reinforced in

---

1. Arthur P. Whitaker has written a brilliant essay on the demise of this concept in *The Western Hemisphere Idea: Its Rise and Decline,* Ithaca, New York, 1954. Cf. J. Fred Rippy, *Globe and Hemisphere,* Chicago, 1958.

depth by the heralds of the "new political science," followers of the geopolitical school of power analysis developed by
Admiral Mahan, Sir Halford Mackinder, and Karl Haus-
hofer, which captured the citadels of American university
lecture halls and filtered down gradually to mold popular
attitudes toward foreign affairs.[2] These critics of isolationism not only suggested the impossibility of pursuing a policy of aloofness during the current emergency but went
far beyond to attack the notion that there had ever been
any validity in the concepts of the two spheres, of the di-
chotomy between the European and American systems, or
of a common bond uniting the nations of the New World.
With relentless and persuasive logic they attacked the very
foundations of the Monroe Doctrine.

They demonstrated again what the Founding Fathers
had known from direct experience but what subsequent
generations in their unique security had forgotten, that the
safety of the United States had always depended on a European and more latterly on an Asian balance of power, and
that Americans had been spared the burden of armaments
and the inconvenience of alliances partly because of geographical circumstances which no longer offered protection,
and partly because of a configuration of political forces
which was unhappily at an end, leaving the nation in dire
peril of confronting on two sides agglomerations of expan-
sive power which could be warded off only by turning the
country into an armed camp. The true policy of America
in these circumstances was not to huddle back in hemispheric isolation but to seek and support serviceable allies
among strong powers fighting on other continents, to keep

2. On the writings of Eugene Staley, Archibald C. Coolidge, Walter
Lippmann, and Nicholas Spykman, see Whitaker, pp. 160–66. See also
Edward M. Earle, "National Security and Foreign Policy," *Yale Re-
view*, 29 (1940), 444–60; and Alfred Vagts, "The United States and the
Balance of Power," *Journal of Politics*, 3 (1941), 401–49.

the war at arm's length, and eventually to fight ourselves, if necessary, on other ground than our own.

Any true appraisal of the strategic situation, interventionists argued, proved Latin America to be a broken reed, more a liability than an asset—weak in military force, limited in manpower, negligible in industrial output, and remote in geographical terms from the center of conflict. What basis after all, Americans wondered, had there been for the notion of solidarity among the American republics, or at least between the great republic of North America and the Latin nations to the South? Culturally they were distinct, not only in language but in their total orientation; both had closer cultural ties to Europe than to each other, but they were linked to different Europes. The United States looked to Britain and northern Europe, while Latin America was Mediterranean. Politically and socially the two Americas could not have been more dissimilar, for despite superficial likenesses of constitutional forms, Latin America had never really practiced democracy and class structures there were much more rigid and sharply differentiated than north of the Rio Grande. John Quincy Adams, before he was partially converted to Henry Clay's vision of hemispheric unity, had remarked that if there was an American system, the United States had the whole of it, and in the mid-twentieth century Americans who critically re-examined the idea of hemispheric solidarity of interests found it wanting, and tended to conclude that beyond the remote historical fact of a common escape from colonial status there was little cohesiveness in the Americas. London was closer in air miles to New York than Rio de Janeiro, not to speak of Buenos Aires, and in the World War and to a greater extent in the Cold War, London was infinitely more important.

The policy of Pan-Americanism has never been officially repudiated in the post-war era, but its inner vitality has been sapped, and it is clearly moribund. It enjoys more favor among Latin American intellectuals today than ever before, but in the United States support for it has died with the demise of hemispheric isolationism. The principles of the Monroe Doctrine, and with them the No-Transfer policy, have historically been instruments of an insular, hemisphere defense, and while they still would operate as measures of local protection, their overriding importance as front-rank security policies has been overshadowed by the global containment of Communism in recent years.

This new direction of American policy was not immediately apparent in its full dimensions after V-J day, of course, and the prewar momentum of Pan-Americanism carried it forward for a time into the new world order created by the second World War. The first regional security treaty entered into by the United States under the provisions for individual and collective self-defense of the United Nations Charter was the Pact of Rio de Janiero of 1947. In this instrument the American republics reaffirmed the principle that an attack on one of them was an attack on all, and pledged mutual defense against aggression. The No-Transfer principle was at least implicitly included in the provision in Article 6 for action against not only armed attack but "any other fact or situation that might endanger the peace of America."[3] With the rising threat of Soviet power and the formation of the North Atlantic Treaty Organization, as well as the massive economic effort in the Marshall Plan designed to buttress Europe against Communism, United States security policies moved beyond the Hemisphere into global concerns which seem likely to mark the permanent end of continentalism.

3. *Inter-American Conference for the Maintenance of Continental Peace and Security, Report of the Delegation of the United States of America* (Washington, 1948), p. 61.

Since the establishment of NATO, the United States has moved steadily away from its traditional policies of aloofness and nonentanglement to become the leader of a vast coalition of nations the world over, grouped in regional or bilateral alliances for defense against Soviet expansion. Latin American nations, retaining a parochial attitude, have resented the neglect of inter-American affairs in Washington, and especially what they consider to be a failure on the part of the United States to rain on them in fair proportion the bounty in foreign economic aid enjoyed by more recent and less firm friends.

The novel responsibilities of managing a global policy have created a good many difficulties for the United States in its relations with the American republics, one of which is illustrated by the question of European colonies, which has arisen at two inter-American conferences in recent years and which throws light on the current status of the No-Transfer policy. At Bogotá in 1948 Argentina and Guatemala sponsored Resolution XXXIII, which put the American States on record as favoring the end of colonialism and of the occupation of American territories by noncontinental powers in the Americas, and setting up a "Committee on Dependent Territories" to study the problem.[4] The sponsoring nations indicated their interest in the measure by strongly advancing their long-standing claims to the Falkland Islands and British Honduras, respectively. The United States delegation abstained from voting on the resolution, and Secretary of State George Marshall explained this stand by reaffirming his government's devotion to the principle that peoples of dependent territories should be helped toward an increasing measure of self-government, while he took issue with the suggestion that an inter-Ameri-

4. *Ninth International Conference of American States, Report of the Delegation of the United States of America* (Washington, 1948), pp. 85, 268.

can committee, which would not hear the colonial powers' side of the case, was the proper forum for the discussion of these matters. In the course of his remarks Marshall reasserted the principles of Monroeism as American policy:

> The policy of the United States of America in regard to European colonies in the Western Hemisphere has been one of opposition to the extension of such colonies or of European political influence in this Hemisphere. This policy has been strongly asserted on several notable, I might say, historical occasions.[5]

The No-Transfer principle remained in force, and with it, in a general way, the ultimate aim of freeing the Hemisphere from European influence. But these were matters of relative indifference to the United States as a leader of a world-wide resistance to Soviet aggrandizement, unless the danger of transfer involved international Communism. The strong reassertion of the Monroe Doctrine by President Eisenhower in the summer of 1960 against Soviet penetration in Fidel Castro's Cuba, as well as the hastily improvised special economic aid program for Latin America announced shortly afterward, graphically illustrate this fact. The No-Transfer principle had never been truly anticolonial in spirit or application, it must be remembered. It guarded—and accepted—the colonial status quo in the Americas, subject to the vaguest ultimate expectations that eventually all European influence would be eliminated from the New World. Now as the ally of the British, French, and Dutch, Washington found it neither expedient nor particularly in the national interest to press for the withdrawal of these nations from their possessions in the Americas. To the extent that anticolonialism was a popular cause among the newly liberated nations of Asia and Africa, the United

5. Ibid., p. 86.

States could boast a good record on this question dating
from its own struggle for independence and including its
voluntary relinquishment of the Philippines and the Caribbean protectorates. Washington applauded the granting of
independence to the former dependent territories wherever
it occurred, as well as movements toward greater autonomy
such as the formation of the West Indian Confederation by
Great Britain, but it was loath to offend its allies by taking
too inflexible a stand on these matters.

At the Tenth Inter-American Conference held at Caracas, Venezuela, in 1954, Secretary of State John Foster Dulles had as his primary objective the adoption of a resolution
to include within the category of threats to the peace subject
to collective action under the Rio Pact the domination or
control of an American State by a communist government.
This provision, as worded, would not have applied to dependent territories, but the swift action of Great Britain
the year before in suspending the constitution and establishing martial law in British Guiana to oust the communist
ministry that was formed under Dr. Jagan gave some indication of the sort of cooperation the United States could
now expect from its allies.[6] Less impressed than the United
States with the threat of communism in the Americas, and
without obligations to the European colonial powers, the
American republics after considerable dissension voted for
Mr. Dulles' proposal, but also repeated the anticolonial
resolution of 1948 over Dulles' objections.[7]

The No-Transfer principle and its sister hemispheric
defense policies have been preserved, but one might almost
say preserved as fossilized relics of an earlier era of Ameri-

6. *Documents on American Foreign Relations, 1953* (New York,
1954), pp. 399–402.

7. *Tenth Inter-American Conference, Report of the Delegation of
the United States of America* (Washington, 1955), pp. 10–11, 63–64,
159–61.

can foreign policy. Under the tensions of the Cold War and in the day of nuclear weapons, with its emphasis on massive retaliation as a deterrent to aggression, the Western Hemisphere has lost its traditional significance in United States defense planning. If any hemisphere is of outstanding strategic importance in a struggle that involves the entire planet, it is the Northern: Strategic Air Command maps look at the world from a polar projection which emphasizes the adjacency of North America to the Eurasian land mass across the North Pole rather than the old Mercator projection of the seafarers, which emphasized the contiguity of North and South America and their separation from the rest of the world by ocean barriers.

It may even be wondered whether, after intercontinental ballistic missiles have been perfected and are operational, territory and position themselves may not lose entirely the importance they have occupied in strategic planning from the beginning of human society. The No-Transfer concept and its modern counterpart, the containment policy, are fundamentally policies of geographical position, based on military considerations which, if no workable agreement on disarmament is reached, may soon be wholly outmoded by technological changes in warfare. With this eventuality now clearly in sight, international competition between the rival power blocs can already be seen shifting to new grounds, to rivalry in the area of foreign aid and for the minds of men in their allegiance to one or the other social, economic, and political philosophies. To the extent, however, that it remains improbable that the world will choose self-destruction through a resort to all-out nuclear attack, and to the extent, therefore, that conventional modes of warfare will continue as the ultimate arbiter in international affairs, territory will remain important, and with it security policies based on traditional strategic considerations, such as the No-Transfer principle.

References

This study is based in large part on the conventional materials of American diplomatic history. They include the various series of printed diplomatic correspondence, both of the United States and of other nations, the files of the Department of State, records of debates in Congress, and the memoirs, public addresses, and collected personal correspondence of men who influenced decisions about foreign policy here and abroad. There has seemed no point in enumerating the titles, which are liberally cited in the footnotes, and which in any case can be easily located through bibliographical aids. The best of these aids, for the period up to 1921, is Samuel Flagg Bemis and Grace Gardner Griffin, *Guide to the Diplomatic History of the United States: 1775–1921*, Washington, G.P.O., 1935. For more recent publications we now have Oscar Handlin, Arthur M. Schlesinger, Samuel E. Morison, Arthur M. Schlesinger, Jr., and Paul H. Buck, *Harvard Guide to American History*, Cambridge, 1954; and, indispensable for the 1920's, William L. Langer and Hamilton Fish Armstrong, *Foreign Affairs Bibliography: 1919–32*, New York, 1933.

Below are listed the principal monographs used in preparing this book, to emphasize again their pertinence to a study of the No-Transfer principle and to supplement the full citations and short titles used in footnotes.

Adams, Henry, *History of the United States of America during the Administrations of Thomas Jefferson and James Madison,* 9 vols. New York, 1889–91.

Aimes, H. H. S., *A History of Slavery in Cuba,* New York and London, 1907.

Bemis, Samuel Flagg, ed., *American Secretaries of State and their Diplomacy,* 10 vols. New York, 1927–29.

——— *The Diplomacy of the American Revolution,* New York, 1935.

——— *Jay's Treaty: A Study in Commerce and Diplomacy,* New York, 1924.

——— *John Quincy Adams and the Foundations of American Foreign Policy,* New York, 1949.

——— *The Latin American Policy of the United States,* New York, 1943.

——— *Pinckney's Treaty: A Study of America's Advantage from Europe's Distress,* Baltimore, 1926; New Haven, 1960.

Brooks, Philip C., *Diplomacy of the Borderlands: The Adams-Onís Treaty of 1819,* Berkeley, 1939.

Burt, A. L., *The Old Province of Quebec,* Minneapolis, 1933.

——— *The United States, Great Britain, and British North America from the Revolution to the Establishment of Peace after the War of 1812,* New Haven, 1940.

Callahan, James M., *Cuba in International Relations,* Baltimore, 1899.

Caughey, John W., *McGillivray of the Creeks,* Norman, Okla., 1938.

Conn, Stetson, and Fairchild, Byron, *The Framework of Hemisphere Defense,* Washington, G.P.O., 1958.

Corwin, Edward S., *French Policy and the American Alliance of 1778,* Princeton, 1916.

Cox, Isaac J., *The West Florida Controversy, 1798–1813,* Baltimore, 1918.

Darling, Arthur B., *Our Rising Empire,* New Haven, 1940.

Doniol, Henri, *Histoire de la participation de la France à l'établissement des Etats-Unis d'Amérique,* 5 vols. and supplement to vol. 5, Paris, 1886–92.

Feis, Herbert, *The Spanish Story,* New York, 1948.

—— *The Road to Pearl Harbor,* Princeton, 1950.

Ford, Worthington C., *The United States and Spain in 1790,* Brooklyn, 1890.

Gayarré, Charles, *History of Louisiana,* 4 vols. New Orleans, 1903.

Goebel, Julius L., *The Struggle for the Falkland Islands,* New Haven, 1927.

Griffin, Charles C., *The United States and the Disruption of the Spanish Empire, 1810–1822,* New York, 1937.

Jessup, Philip, *Elihu Root,* 2 vols. New York, 1938.

Kaufmann, William W., *British Policy and the Independence of Latin America, 1804–1828,* New Haven, 1951.

Knollenberg, Bernhard, *Washington and the Revolution: A Reappraisal,* New York, 1940.

Langer, William L., *Our Vichy Gamble,* New York, 1947.

Langer, William L., and Gleason, S. Everett, *The Challenge to Isolation,* New York, 1952.

—— *The Undeclared War,* New York, 1953.

Lockey, Joseph B., *Pan-Americanism: Its Beginnings,* New York, 1926.

Lyon, E. Wilson, *Louisiana in French Diplomacy, 1759–1804,* Norman, Okla., 1934.

Manning, William R., *Early Diplomatic Relations between the United States and Mexico,* Baltimore, 1916.

——"The Nootka Sound Controversy," in *Annual Report of the American Historical Association 1904,* Washington, G.P.O., 1905.

Matloff, M., and Snell, E. M., *The War Department: Strategic Planning for Coalition Warfare, 1941–1942,* Washington, G.P.O., 1953.

Morison, Samuel Eliot, *History of the United States Naval Operations in World War II*, 14 vols. Boston, 1947–60.

Munro, Dana G., *The United States and the Caribbean Area*, Boston, 1934.

Nevins, Allan, *Ordeal of the Union*, 2 vols. New York, 1947.

Patrick, Rembert W., *Florida Fiasco*, Athens, Ga., 1954.

Perkins, Bradford, *The First Rapprochement*, Philadelphia, 1955.

Perkins, Dexter, *The Monroe Doctrine, 1823–1826*, Cambridge, 1932.

———*The Monroe Doctrine, 1826–1867*, Baltimore, 1933.

———*The Monroe Doctrine, 1867–1907*, Baltimore, 1937.

Portell-Vilá, Herminio, *Historia de Cuba en sus relaciones con los Estados Unidos y España*, 4 vols. Havana, 1938–41.

Pratt, Julius W., *Expansionists of 1812*, New York, 1925.

Rauch, Basil, *American Interest in Cuba, 1848–1855*, New York, 1948.

Rippy, J. Fred, *Rivalry of the United States and Great Britain over Latin America, 1808–1830*, Baltimore, 1929.

——— *Globe and Hemisphere*, Chicago, 1958.

Robertson, William S., *The Life of Miranda*, Chapel Hill, N.C., 1929.

Sherwood, Robert E., *Roosevelt and Hopkins*, 2 vols. New York, 1950.

Smith, Justin H., *Our Struggle for the Fourteenth Colony*, 2 vols., New York, 1907.

Tansill, Charles C., *The Purchase of the Danish West Indies*, Baltimore, 1932.

——— *The United States and Santo Domingo, 1798–1873*, Baltimore, 1938.

Tatum, Edward H., Jr., *The United States and Europe, 1815–1823: A Study in the Background of the Monroe Doctrine*, Berkeley, 1936.

Watson, Mark S., *Chief of Staff: Prewar Plans and Preparations*, Washington, G.P.O., 1950.

Whitaker, Arthur P., *The Spanish–American Frontier*, Boston, 1927.

——— *The Mississippi Question, 1795–1803*, New York, 1934.

——— *The United States and the Independence of Latin America, 1800–1830*, Baltimore, 1941.

——— *The Western Hemisphere Idea; Its Rise and Decline*, New York, 1954.

Index

Subentries are arranged roughly in chronological order of the events they index.